*Foundations
of History
Library*

Pierre Vilar

London: NLB

Atlantic Highlands: Humanities Press

A History of Gold and Money 1450–1920

Translated by Judith White

First published as *Oro y Moneda en la Historia (1450–1920)*
by Ediciones Ariel, Barcelona, 1969

© Pierre Vilar, Paris 1969

This edition first published 1976
© NLB, 1976

NLB, 7 Carlisle Street, London W 1
Filmset in Monophoto Garamond by
Servis Filmsetting Ltd, Manchester
and printed by Lowe and Brydone

Designed by Ruth Prentice

ISBN 902 308 181

Contents

Preface

This book has not been written either by a monetary expert or by an economist, but by a historian. I am not therefore trying to make suggestions to the International Monetary Fund, nor to advise the reader on how to trade in gold or dollars. This book began as a course of university lectures, and it simply attempts to provide some clarification of the problems which historically money has raised.

The reader might think that this means it is irrelevant to the problems of today. In his recently published *La monnaie et ses mécanismes*, Pierre Berger confidently writes that: '. . . historical data often make it more difficult to understand monetary phenomena. With no disrespect to history, one is obliged to believe that an excessive concentration on research into the past can be a source of confusion in analysing the present, at least as far as money and credit are concerned.'[1]

This was not Marx's view. His analyses of money are, characteristically, a model of theoretical elaboration, but based on the most thorough historical research. A more recent example, from the opposite ideological position, is Milton Friedmann. His theoretical and practical economic writings constantly remind us of the fact that he also wrote *The Monetary History of the United States, 1867–1960*.

There is, of course, no more dangerous illusion than that of novelty, which often reflects nothing more than an ignorance of history. While history does not aim to prove that 'nothing is new', it should indicate that not everything is as new as contemporary opinion believes. If the economists of the 1920s failed to understand monetary instability, which in their eyes was something 'new', it was because they only looked at recent history. Had they gone back to the 14th or 17th centuries, they would have seen what devaluation really was. Many economists are

[1] Pierre Berger, *La monnaie et ses mécanismes*, Paris 1966, p. 8.

convinced that credit and the World Bank are something 'new', because they have never heard of the fairs at Piacenza or the Burgos *Consulado*. Similarly, Alexandre Chabert has advanced the hypothesis that the quantitative theory of money was valid in the age of metal coinage but is no longer so today. In so doing he ignores, or tries to forget, the vast pyramid of nominal money that was built on the basis of the precious metals arriving from America in the 16th century. Milton Friedmann, on the other hand, although immersed in the complex mechanisms of today's monetary system, has called for the 'rehabilitation' of the quantitative theory.[2] Are we, then, closer to the 16th century than might at first sight appear? Or does the extent to which the quantitative theory equates the two epochs merely depend on how ingeniously the comparison is made?

Earl J. Hamilton, in writing of the 16th and 18th centuries, says that Europe was transformed by the arrival of gold and silver. The 20th century now believes that everything will be different if only we can increase or decrease the money supply or can expand and contract credit. It is dangerous to make this kind of simplified analysis, either in interpreting history or in monetary matters. The real problem is the extent of man's freedom vis-à-vis what he has created. Great discoveries and the opening of the California mines are as much the creations of man as the Scottish banks and the imprint on bills of credit.

It is illusory to think that the concrete object – gold or silver – affected men without them reacting to it, and that token money was simply imposed on them. The old debate between *realism* and *nominalism* is too charged with philosophical prejudices for the controversy about money not to be influenced by them, and Marx, at the beginning of his theoretical observations on money, observes ironically: 'In a parliamentary debate on Sir Robert Peel's Bank Act of 1844 and 1845, Gladstone remarked that not even love has made so many fools of men as the pondering over the nature of money. He spoke of Britons to Britons. The Dutch, on the contrary, who, from times of yore, have had, Petty's doubts notwithstanding, "angelic wits" for money speculation have never lost their wits in speculations about money.'[3] The Spanish are the most unfortunate of all peoples, given what happened to their original fortune; but while they may have expended large quantities of blood and sweat to bring silver from the Indies in the form of *treasure*, they also

---

[2] Alexandre Chabert, *Structure économique et théorie monétaire*, Paris 1956, pp. 33–8; Milton Friedmann, *Dollars and Deficits*, New Jersey 1968, part 1.

[3] Karl Marx, *A Contribution to the Critique of Political Economy*, Chicago 1904, p. 73.

used up gallons of ink writing about silver as *money*.[4] There are more 'memoranda' about money in 17th century Spanish archives than there are in the hands of the International Monetary Fund today. In one picaresque novel, *El Diablo Cojuelo* (*The Lame Devil*) by Velez de Guevara (1641) there is an 'expert' who is so excited by his fight against rising inflation that he sticks a pen into his eye and goes on writing without noticing what he has done.

'Experts' in this field have a tough life. With every recurrence of monetary fever a hail of articles and open letters signed by the most learned professors and perceptive amateurs pours down on the press. As recently as 1963 one of the big Paris publishers, which specialises in economics, published a book with the following introduction (the author has also published a *Practical Manual for use in Car Accidents*): 'It occurred to me that now that everyone has money it would be useful to provide the layman with an account of the legal and economic problems raised by money today. . . . Like justice, money is something everyone needs; it must inspire trust in all; and it has the same value in a poor man's pocket as in the hands of a rich man, the only difference being the amount they have.'[5]

Only the amount. . . . As Tomás de Mercado, a remote precursor of marginal economics, put it, 'the difference in quantity occasions the difference in esteem', so that 100 'old' or 'new' francs, for example, do *not* have the same 'value', the same subjective 'esteem', in a beggar's pocket as in the pocket of a millionaire. This so-called egalitarian quality is one of money's main enigmas. It is as deceptive, in fact, as the illusion of 'universal suffrage'.

This naive book while aiming to make money comprehensible to the man in the street has to invoke learned authority when emphasising money's political importance. It even quotes from an article by Charles Rist, written in the early 1950s, as follows: 'I remain convinced that the problem of money is the basic problem, to be solved before all others. I remain convinced that today the conditions for solving it exist. The statesmen who have the courage to seize this opportunity will ensure the prosperity and security of the international community better than they could in any other way, and will at the same time reserve for themselves a place of honour in the history of our age.'[6]

Robert Triffin's dedication of his *Gold and Dollar Crisis* is also

---

4 cf. Chapter 17 below, pp. 157 ff.
5 A. Toulemon, *Situation paradoxale de l'or dans le monde*, Paris 1963.
6 Charles Rist, *Monnaie d'hier et de demain*, Paris 1952.

relevant here. With the hint of humour which is obligatory for an Anglo-Saxon, he writes: 'To my children: Nicky, Kerry, Eric – who undoubtedly will, some years from now, feel inordinately proud or amused, when discovering this intrepid attempt of their father to prophesy history and deflect its course.'[7] In the same way, between 1630–1680, Guillen Barbón, Gerardo Basso and Somoza y Quiroga sincerely hoped to pass into history on the basis of their monetary orthodoxy. They are now known only to specialists in the field.

Is such scholarship pointless? The answer is no, because in studying the monetary theories of the past, the persistence of certain questions underlines the fundamental problems, while the differing interpretations reveal the truly new facts that have determined a given conjuncture. Economists, like historians, exist within history, and see money differently depending on whether they are writing in 1570 or 1780, in 1923 or in 1968. In the 19th century, in the epoch of stable currency, the unchallenged gold standard and the convertible bank note, the economist believed that products were simply exchanged for other products and that money was neutral. A government which altered the legal relationship between gold and its own currency was guilty of fraud. Historical experiences survived only as anecdotes: Philippe le Bel was nothing but a vulgar 'falsifier', and Dante apparently shares this view, as this was what he called him in the *Inferno*. Of course, governments which depreciate currencies have never been popular with intellectuals, who tend to live on fixed incomes. They have never been popular with theoreticians either, since such people are often clerics, moralists or mathematicians all at once, who are engaged in investigating the related notions of justice and measurement, equilibrium and stability. Irony aside it must also be said that some of the greatest minds of all times have concerned themselves with the mystery of money: in the 14th century, there was Nicholas Oresme, a wise bishop and a great mathematician; around 1520, Nicholas Copernicus, and around 1700, after Berkeley and Locke and before Hume, one of His Britannic Majesty's 'Masters of the Mint' by the name of Isaac Newton.

Money as a unit of value poses a difficult logical problem. A measure must be fixed, like any unit of length or the hours on a clock. But when the theologian Tomás de Mercado first pointed this out it was in 1568, in the very midst of the 'price revolution'; and having lived in Seville and Mexico City, he had noticed that the price of a silver ingot

---

[7] Robert Triffin, *Gold and the Dollar Crisis*, Yale 1961, p. v.

changed 'for the same reasons as cloth did', and that the same quantity of silver had a different 'value', a different 'buying power', in the Indies and in Seville, in Italy and in France. From this he derived a theory of exchange based on the differences in buying power, a theory which was to be re-discovered by Gustav Cassel only in 1920. Money, which itself changes in value, is therefore a strange measure of value. This is so however money is defined: money concretely defined in terms of an object, such as gold, has like any 'commodity' a production price and a market price. As Mercado observed these change in the case of gold as they do for cloth. If, however, we define money in the modern and abstract manner as 'all the buying power in the possession of an economic agent', we know that this buying power in turn varies, that prices can both rise and fall simultaneously, that there can be a 'flight' from a currency or a demand for it, and that it may or may not be preferred to other commodities. But why is it then that money is *not* a commodity?

The very formation of capitalism requires this. Perhaps it is not clear what an unshakeably stable monetary system would mean for capitalism. If it existed the heirs of a man who had invested a penny at compound interest 2,000 years ago, would long since have given up all productive activity to live off this one investment. All progress reduces the value of the objects produced, and if a single stable monetary system existed, a perpetual fall in prices would have continually discouraged producers and sellers, for whom the prospect of increases is the best stimulus. If then – within a capitalist framework – rentiers and wage-earners automatically fear depreciation of the currency, it is understandable that debtors, entrepreneurs and salesmen welcome it, if in a confused way. This is, of course, as long as it does not reach catastrophic proportions, even though some catastrophes, like that of 1923 in Germany, have facilitated the liquidation of excessive debts.

In the end, it has been left to the 20th century to proclaim the positive, or rather, necessary aspects of currency depreciation (in cases where it has been possible to determine the optimal rate). The 'dynamic debtor' is favoured as against the 'passive rentier' – and more indirectly, against the wage-earner. It is a rather curious fact that the arguments for this have been sought far back in history, and in particular, in the history of precious metals. Simiand believed that Mexican silver and Californian gold contained the secret of the positive phases of modern development. Keynes sung the praises of the 'stimulating' effects of the great plunderings of ancient, mediaeval and modern times, as well as of the mining discoveries. On the eve of a period of monetary thinking in which little attention was paid to gold, the myth of precious metals was revived.

In 1930 Keynes proposed to historians that Sumerian civilisation could be explained by the gold of Arabia, the greatness of Athens by the silver of Laurium, that of Rome by the dispersal of Persian treasures at the hand of Alexander, and the stagnation of Western Europe in the Middle Ages by the scarcity of precious metal coin.[8] In 1946, Fernand Braudel wrote in a famous article: 'To sum up. In the early 16th century, Sudanese gold, which the Portuguese had already diverted from its usual channels towards the Mediterranean, was launched along new paths, towards the Indian Ocean. As if by coincidence, the early Italian Renaissance was fading, vacillating, growing weaker. . . . Thirty years later the metals of America were pouring into Europe through Seville. Again, it appeared by coincidence, the power of Spain waxed strong. . . . The great route by which the manna was distributed was the ocean. From Laredo to Antwerp, it was as if arid Spain and fertile Flanders were blessed by a new Concordat. This lasted until this route was cut and Antwerp therefore began to decline, and Medina del Campo to languish: Leon was no longer the triumphant city of the fairs, and Spain was isolated from Flanders even by sea. But at the same time the sea route from Barcelona to Genoa was becoming more important, and Spanish gold was conquering the whole Mediterranean; it was thereby prolonging its prosperity until the mid-17th century, when the white metal, perhaps attracted to Manila, or absorbed on the spot by the progress of the Americas, ceased to flow into the Mediterranean, and from there through into Europe. The resulting decline and decadence were remedied only on the eve of the 18th century by a new influx of wealth in the shape of money, an influx of gold: gold from the Brazilian mines, from Minas Gerais. The chapters of world history thus follow the rhythms imposed by the legendary metals.'[9]

It is worth recalling this magnificent panorama at the beginning of a book like this, which is devoted to the subject of gold, money and history. The dramatic synthesis given here is further supported by Keynes's considerations of ancient civilisations. Hamilton and Chaunu writing on Spanish silver, Magalhães Godinho on Portuguese gold, Frédéric Mauro on Brazilian gold, Fernand Braudel himself on the Mediterranean circuit, and Frank Spooner on the monetary circulation of pre-revolutionary France have all provided not only suggestions but

---

[8] John Maynard Keynes, *A Treatise on Money*, London 1930, vol. II, p. 150.

[9] Fernand Braudel, 'Monnaies et civilisations. De l'or du Soudan à l'argent d'Amerique', *Annales* 1946, p. 22.

serious studies and masses of data on the relationship of money and history. But these facts still do not always exorcise the genie entranced in the dance of the precious metal. Frank Spooner writes: 'This silver, wrested from America, not prized enough in Spain, roams the world. The sovereigns of the Mediterranean world are here in Marseilles, Leghorn, Venice. . . . They are carried in sealed barrels to the Isles of the Levant . . . and lo, they are at the gates of Alexandria, they reach Tripoli and Syria, then straight to the cities of the interior: Aleppo, Damascus, Cairo and Baghdad. . . . A moment's distraction, and already we find them in the Indies and China. . . .'[10] I am particularly fond of the 'moment's distraction'. It symbolises the transitory, volatile nature of money. Everything depends on it, and it is dependent on nothing: in any case it is a strange quality for money which is an object, a metal.

But perhaps in the 16th century the metal exercised an attraction over men which was not economic, but based on the mentality, and the psychoanalytic structure of the period. The historian would hesitate to say so; but the philosopher goes further: '. . . the signs of exchange, because they satisfy desire, are sustained by the dark, dangerous, and accursed glitter of metal. An equivocal glitter, for it reproduces in the depths of the earth that other glitter that sings at the far end of the night: it resides there like an inverted promise of happiness, and, because metal resembles the stars, the knowledge of all these perilous treasures is at the same time knowledge of the world.'[11] The trouble is that the author claims the authority of a passage from Davanzati, written in Florence in 1586. But Davanzati only said that if from a given moment all the gold in the world had by social convention to measure everything desirable, someone looking down from heaven or some other high place, would say: '. . . there is on Earth just so much Gold, so many things, so many Men, so many Desires. As many of those Desires as any thing can satisfy, so much it is worth of another thing, so much Gold it is worth.'[12]

Davanzati's speculation was not the result of the dangerous, dark, accursed shining of gold. His was an embryonic theory of money, however elementary, since the author attempted to take into consideration the number of men, the relationship of things and the idea of need. Davanzati was groping for Fischer's equation; he wanted to be a planner on a world scale, knowing enough of the terms of the equation to determine the level of prices or the mass of money. Many have dreamed

[10] Frank Spooner, *L'économie mondiale et les frappes monétaires en France*, Paris 1956, p. 25.
[11] Michel Foucault, *The Order of Things*, London 1970, p. 173.
[12] Bernardo Davanzati, *A discourse upon coins*, London 1696, pp. 15–16.

of doing the same. Still, in the 16th century as today, it was well known that merchants – and planners – only achieve a 'just price' in a rough way. Whatever Foucault thinks, *divinatio* has nothing to do with it. Davanzati expresses the quantitative theory of money in the words of a peasant woman: '. . . as money was brought down from twelve to one, so the Prices of things were raised from one to twelve. The old Country-woman that used to sell her dozen Eggs for an Assis of twelve Ounces, seeing it look now so deform'd, and reduc'd to one Ounce, would have said, Gentlemen, either give me an Assis of twelve Ounces, or twelve of these paultry ones that weigh but one Ounce; or I'll give you an Egg apiece for your Assis.'[13]

Davanzati knew that money was gold, but he also knew it by name: a *pound* (of money) is the name given to a fraction of an ounce of gold, though the ounce as a measure of weight, is only a fraction of a *pound* (by weight). A large part of monetary history can be encompassed in this remark.

But was the peasant woman wrong to take part in the game – was her attachment to the weight of the metal not an out-dated fetish? One thing Marx showed very clearly was this contradiction of 'commodity production': if everything is a commodity, how can we measure exchange value with something which is not a commodity? 'A price therefore implies both that a commodity is exchangeable for money, and also that it must be so exchanged. On the other hand, gold serves as an ideal measure of value, only because it has already, in the process of exchange, established itself as the money-commodity. Under the ideal measure of values there lurks the hard cash.'[14]

Still, '. . . in this process which continually makes money pass from hand to hand, the mere symbolic existence of money suffices. Its functional existence absorbs, so to say, its material existence. Being a transient and objective reflex of the prices of commodities, it serves only as a symbol of itself, and is therefore capable of being replaced by a token. One thing is, however, requisite; this token must have an objective social validity of its own, and this the paper symbol acquires by its forced currency. This compulsory action of the State can take effect only within that inner sphere of circulation which is co-terminous with the territories of the community, but it is also only within that sphere that money completely responds to its function of being the

---

[13] ibid, p. 23.
[14] Karl Marx, *Capital*, vol. 1, Moscow 1961, p. 103.

circulating medium, or becomes coin.'[15] This distinction between 'circulating money', the internal level of which depends on the state, and internationally valid currency, which is exchanged between big businesses and between states themselves, is a problem of our own times, as much as it was the problem of the past. There may be some value in studying its history, and this is my aim.

Pierre Berger might object that the money and credit arrangements of today have little in common with those of the past. But there is scarcely a modern phenomenon without its theoretical (I would not say institutional) equivalent in the experience of the past as a whole. Every country has given up distinguishing between its internal money (*moneda corrent*, as the Catalans used to call it) and the currency or precious metal necessary for foreign exchange (*moneda corrible*). A single currency has now been imposed on most of the world: but is it any more a universal phenomenon than the Spanish piastre was, or more recently, the pound sterling? The fact is that until the world does away with all currencies, they will be devalued and revalued against each other, and all of them together against commodities, whichever of them is chosen as the standard for measuring and payment in international exchanges.

It is a fact that money has never been less substantial, more nominal, and more built on paper promises. (Whose promises, we might ask?) But it has never had to express such an enormous quantity of accumulated products, even if the dollar value of a Pakistani's income makes a mockery of this. Further, 'deflation' is necessary, even in the short term, to deal with the volumes involved. The American worker keeps his savings in a bank account, not in a woollen stocking, and this is more in keeping with the Fuggers than with his peasant forebears. But the growth of his needs, which is replacing the driving force of want, may re-open a road which was thought to be closed, that of loans for consumption, or usury: which will make the American workers more akin to Charles V of France than to the Fuggers. In a period in which the domination of productive investment is unchallenged, this would be one odd effect of the dialectic of capitalism. It should be added, however, that capitalism is no longer alone in the world, and this of course does not make things any simpler. In fact things never have been simple, but this has sometimes been forgotten.

Paris, 7 June 1971

[15] ibid. p. 129.

I

Introduction: Gold In World History

Provided enough basic information is available, a history of gold should begin by comprehending its antecedents.[1] This provides the basis for analysing the relations between:

(1) the very fact of money, economic history and history in general;
(2) problems of gold and the broader questions of money;
(3) the main stages of economic history.

(1) Money, economic history and general history

'Of all the barometers capable of revealing to the historian the deeper movements of an economy, monetary phenomena are without doubt the most sensitive.'[2]

The novice in economic history may well ask whether monetary history is just a specialised and secondary branch of knowledge (i.e. numismatics), or whether, as has been suggested, it contains the whole secret of how economies and even societies evolve. Bloch's answer is that monetary questions are primarily informative indications of deeper, more complex, problems.

For example: from the 11th to the 13th centuries Christian Western Europe did not mint gold coin, while even within Europe solid gold coin from Byzantium and the Moslem world – the bezant and the mancus – enjoyed a wide circulation. The map of the circulation of

[1] Such a synthesis has fortunately been provided by Marc Bloch, in 'The problem of gold in the middle ages', reprinted in *Land and Work in Mediaeval Europe*, London 1967, and in 'Esquisse d'une histoire monétaire de l'Europe', a course of lectures given in 1941 and published in 1954 in *Cahiers des Annales* no. 9. These two analyses deal with the relationship linking gold to monetary mechanisms, and to history in general. Although they are particularly concerned with the Middle Ages, their definitions and concepts make them basic tools for all work in this field.
[2] Marc Bloch, 'The problem of gold in the middle ages', p. 186.

money corresponds to deeper contrasts in demography, society and commerce; it is the clearest indication of them. If money is not the only line of investigation, it is often the first to be of use. To take another example; facts about money also bring out contrasts over time. The 19th century experienced monetary stability, and all the economically advanced countries clung faithfully to the gold standard; in the 20th century they have gone off gold one after the other, and their respective national currencies have undergone 'inflation', 'deflation', 'stabilisation', and 'falling exchange rates'. This monetary drama did not create the crisis. It highlights it, and enables it to be located and dated. It is a useful way to study it.

To make use of such an instrument in studying the past, some knowledge of numismatics[3] is necessary, and some idea of present-day monetary systems is essential for the contemporary period.[4] A certain level of theoretical clarification is also required. But given the disagreements in this field, the historian must tread carefully. We are not interested in money as such, but only insofar as it is a factor in history.

If money records certain movements in the economy it is because it itself is affected by these movements. But every result in its turn becomes a cause. Marc Bloch says that monetary phenomena are 'like a seismograph that not only registers earth tremors, but sometimes brings them about.'[5] This reciprocal relationship has not always been freely admitted. The economists of the 19th century, an era of monetary stability, thought of money as 'neutral'. The monetary crises of 1923, 1925 and 1932, on the other hand, led economists not only to observe movements in the economy through monetary movements, but to explain the one by the other. 'Monetarism' is expressed, for example (though in very different ways) in, for example, the works of both the sociologist François Simiand, and the economist John Maynard Keynes. Marc Bloch does not fall into the trap of 'panmonetarism'. He simply says that 'at times' the seismograph produced the tremor, and what he is thinking of is Germany in 1923, Law's system, and the *assignats* of the French revolution, all of which are cases of the irresponsible issuing of currency.

Does this mean, though, that a *general, widespread, long-term movement* can be produced by monetary factors? Some writers have accepted this

---

[3] The classic work, *Manuel de numismatique française* is by J.-Adrien Blanchet and Adolphe Dieudonné. The most accurate monetary history is by L. von Ebengreuth, *Allgemeine Münzkunde und Geldgeschichte*, Munich and Berlin 1925.

[4] The most recent basic text is J. Marchal's *Monnaie et credit*, Paris 1964.

[5] Marc Bloch, op. cit. p. 186.

and have even attempted to justify it theoretically. Take the following rather exaggerated passage from Carlo Maria Cipolla: 'In the early Middle Ages, the European economy suffered very large currency deflation. . . . As Keynes has said, it was not by pure chance that this exceptional deflation took place in a period which also experienced an exceptional depression in consumption and investment: the two phenomena are closely united, and the one is the cause of the other.'[6] If this means that a scarcity of currency (deflation) and a declining economic activity (depression) have an effect on each other, I am in complete agreement. But Cipolla (like Keynes) suggests *unilateral* causation by the monetary factor. In the early Middle Ages, according to him, there was a low level of production and exchange because of the shortage of money. He offers as proof the most simplified form of the equation attributed to Irving Fischer: $P=(MV)/T$, or $PT=MV$, P being the level of prices, T the quantity of goods exchanged, M the mass or volume of money in circulation and V the velocity of circulation. Every equation is, however, both a statement and a relationship. The statement says that the quantity of goods exchanged (T) multiplied by their price (P), is equal to the volume of money employed (M) multiplied by the number of times this money has changed hands (V). The relationship is such that if the movement of money (volume and velocity) varies, the total price of goods exchanged varies in the same direction. Conversely, if the exchange value increases, the circulation of money must also increase. This is no way proves that the monetary factor 'came first'. Only history can verify that. The equation can be used to calculate one factor if the other three are known. If none is known, as in the case for Carolingian Europe, it is of no help to us whatsoever.

The relationship of the two types of phenomenon can be verified and dated only by history. During the Middle Ages, history shows that for centuries (though the start of the period is in dispute) there was no division of labour, and the rudimentary means of production were destroyed more often than they were renewed. Communications were difficult, and labour was not paid in money, but was rather a personal service. Was this state of affairs a result of the lack of money in circulation, or was it simply that there was no demand for such circulation? Whatever the case may be the two phenomena undoubtedly affected each other. A society with little activity does not attract money, and the lack of money in turn discourages exchange. The two factors reinforce each

[6] Carlo Maria Cipolla, 'Encore Mahomet et Charlemagne: l'économie politique au secours de l'histoire, *Annales*, *E.S.C.*, January–February 1949, pp. 4–9.

other until such time as local or marginal revivals spread out in successive waves.

The historian should not then give money some special significance, but should observe it closely, and this requires research. Within the scope of Marc Bloch's essays and of my own book it has not been possible to start new researches of this kind, and only already established facts are used. Theories such as Cipolla's can be of help in posing the problems, but should not anticipate the results.

(2) Gold and money

My theme is gold and gold is quite different from money. Gold is a mineral substance. It has its own technology, its own geography and its own economics as an artistic and industrial substance. There already exists a full bibliography on all this, which saves me from having to start by defining nuggets and veins of gold, or the difference between natural, mineral and refined gold.[7] Because this is a history, and at each stage of technology man encounters new problems, it is best to relate them as and when they occur. It is always useful to have a basic level of information about these technical problems.

Let me give some idea of the quantities involved. In 1905 the statistician De Foville was astonished to discover that all the gold in the world taken from the earth by that date could be confined within a 10-metre cube (1,000 cubic metres). Yet a similar block made of all the gold available in Europe in 1500, the date at which my investigation begins, would have measured only 2 metres each way (8 cubic metres). This means that at the beginning of our period, very small discoveries or transfers could disrupt the market in gold. It also means that the question of gold is never to be confused with that of money: the quantity of gold could never have equalled the total money circulation.

Money is made up of no particular substance. It is more complicated and abstract. For a long time economists have defined it not according to what it is, but according to its uses: (a) as the intermediary of exchange, or *means of payment*; (b) as an index of comparison between goods to be exchanged, or *measure of value*; (c) eventually, when it is saved, as a *store of value*.

More recently, this kind of definition has come under attack. Money

7 cf. Henri Hauser, *L'or*, Paris 1901; L. de Launay, *L'or dans le monde*, Paris 1907; V. Forbin, *L'or dans le monde*, Paris 1941; J. Lepidi, *L'or*, Paris 1958. The latter book is useful on the technical and geographic aspects, but superficial on economics and history.

can be a means of payment without universally fulfilling the other two functions; an economist of the status of Robertson has recently proposed that the term money should be applied to anything which is widely accepted as a *means of payment*. On the other hand, money has other qualities: Keynes emphasised its 'liquidity' function (to have liquid money at one's disposal is a service which is paid for). In a recent book of his, Jean Marchal has unhesitatingly defined money as follows: as *buying power* accorded to economic agents; and as an *instrument of government policy*. Orthodox 19th-century economists would have shuddered at such a definition; but the historian can find money performing all these functions in the past, especially the function of being an instrument of those in power. To understand this it has to be made clear that the term 'money' has been applied to three quite different things:

(i) *Money as an object or commodity*, an object whose substance and weight give it a realisable trading value throughout the world market. For a long time it was taken for granted that this was the only real money, as its position in determining and forming reserves of value made it a universal standard in commerce. Nowadays the idea of money as a commodity is regarded as somewhat out of date. It is redolent of the famous historical portraits of Italian or Flemish money-traders weighing their ducats, where the money-traders' scales were the supreme arbiters of money. Any precious commodity which could be preserved unchanged or divided into equal parts could function as commodity money. Even pepper is known to have been used, but it has been gold which has performed this role *par excellence*.

(ii) *Token or 'fiduciary' money*, a token accepted as of a certain value although it is known that it itself could never be sold at the same value. This is of course the case with modern paper money, which has no 'intrinsic value', but is accepted for what it represents. Paper money is not the only example of this. Modern copper coin and even, before 1914, divided coins, have been acquired at values above their value as commodities. This is all 'fiduciary' money, because its use as payment is due to the decision of an institution, and continues as long as the public has confidence either in the ability of the issuing authority to cash it (as with a currency 'convertible' into gold), or in the stability of the buying power it represents (if it is not convertible into gold). If its buying power declines, but the money cannot officially be refused, attempts are made to get more of it for all commodities. Prices then rise, and the vicious circle of inflation has begun.

These observations are valid for modern every-day money, and they also apply to most of what used to be called 'common coin'. The latter's metallic value remained unsettled until economic movements had established a large difference between its buying power and the buying power of 'strong' or commodity money, which was internationally acceptable. The numbers of coins in circulation (as many as 80 types in 17th century France) and the ignorance of the users, meant that 'common coin' had no more 'intrinsic value' than modern copper coin, or even modern banknotes. The fact that the 14th and 17th centuries experienced 'inflation' similar to the inflation of modern paper money, is to be explained by the fiduciary aspect of circulation in former times (although many textbooks persist in describing it as 'metallic', implying that money was clearly defined in commodity terms). Minting casts were at times as dangerously abundant as today's banknote plates.

(iii) *Nominal money* (or accounting money), an indication of value representing no specific currency. It has only one of the three classical functions, that of 'measuring value'. It is the result of practices which survive when a monetary system disappears (as when today the French still count in old francs). A 'pound' was originally a pound's weight of silver. This was abandoned because it came to be too large a unit; but a unit of price was still called a 'pound'. This accounts for the paradox that an ounce of silver is worth several 'pounds', though there are 16 ounces in a pound weight, and this epitomises the separation between *money as a measure* and *money as an object*.

For centuries France and other places too priced all goods by the pound (*livre*), though with rare exceptions no actual unit of currency had the same value. In each transaction both the goods being sold and the possibly quite different currencies in which payment was made, were calculated in pounds and subdivisions of the pound. Governments were therefore able to 'manipulate' currency much more easily than they can now. They only had to decide from one day to the next to change the legally determined relationship between the accounting money which measured all prices, and the actual coin in circulation. Then as now, monetary problems were produced by the interaction of three kinds of money: *nominal money* (for measurement), *token money* (the current means of payment) and *commodity money* (an object which can be exchanged internationally). The question of money is not therefore the same as the question of gold. The two were confused only in the 19th century (1815–1914) and even then there were exceptions (as in the notorious inflation of the American Civil War, and the devaluation of the *peseta* in 1898). The universal gold standard did not exclude 'bimetallist' systems (with an official silver standard) and these only disappeared when the relative value of silver plummeted at the end of the 19th century. Nonetheless gold and money have always been linked, since gold has always been the easiest commodity money to handle in limited quantities. It has therefore acted as the universal medium of international payment, and the means for balancing one country's balance of trade deficit with another. Movements of gold are indications of the economic conditions of any country and in any epoch. Is this still so? Some say it is not. But it is the historian's task, and the very function of the historical sense, to illuminate the present through the long history that has preceded it.

2

Primitive Times and the Ancient World

This is not intended to be a comprehensive history of gold and money. It is designed rather to record certain facts and to make some observations relevant to the rest of the analysis. Nor shall I refer, as authors traditionally have done ever since Aristotle, to what the theologians and economist of the ancient world called 'the birth' or 'the appearance' of money; such preambles normally consist of a logical account of the supposed reasons for money appearing useful. What I am concerned with is its real, historical appearance, because this unveils a complex and highly instructive sociological process.

(1) Money and primitive societies

In 1934, the historian François Simiand published an article entitled 'Money, a Social Reality', which was followed by a discussion on money by various economists and sociologists.[1] Simiand gave more thought to the history of prices and money than any other member of his generation, and his conclusions should therefore be taken into account. They are that money is a social rather than an economic phenomenon, a kind of myth or belief universally held in society; it is not just another commodity, although as in gold coins it can take the form of an object.

Marcel Mauss supported Simiand's theory by reference to fetish-money, the money given divine attributes by certain Indian and Polynesian peoples. According to Mauss, money expressed a universal relationship between the individual and society, and his confidence in that society.

These observations are correct in saying, first that the transition from barter to a money economy is not the result of a straightforward econo-

[1] François Simiand, 'La monnaie, réalité sociale', *Annales Sociologiques*, 1934.

mic calculation of its convenience, but derives from a much more complex sociological phenomenon; and secondly that when two societies of quite different levels of development come into contact, they do not have the same conception of money or of value (hence the astonishment of the Spanish explorers when the Indians gave them gold in exchange for trinkets). These remarks do not, however, lead to the conclusion that money is a purely psychological phenomenon, independent of the laws of economics. This operates for a certain time in the relations between two different societies. But when there is continuous exchange, money in the end comes to reflect value relationships. Within a national economy, public confidence in money is a psychological fact, but the relationship between the buying power of money and the international price system does not depend on psychology alone.

(2) The coexistence of developed monetary economies and economies where money plays little or no part

For money proper to be used, there must already exist generalised, multilateral exchange between products, giving them a recognised exchange value – what classical economists would call their 'natural' price – which can be expressed in a single medium. In other words, there must be a *market*. While it is doubtful whether there ever existed economies 'without exchange' – the concepts of 'natural economy' and 'closed economy' being highly debatable – there have been economies 'without a market' (in the economic sense of constant free interchange between goods). Pre-Columbian and especially Inca societies, for example, had no money as such, but possessed a complicated accounting system for individual production, personal labour services, and the accumulation and distribution of products by the state. There was no market and no money, but there were vast quantities of precious metals. The existence of these metals did not automatically mean that money was used. One of the first questions we shall look at is the result of the contact between these societies without money, and the Spanish conquistadores, for whom mintable gold was the very symbol of wealth. At the same time some societies have evidently reached a high degree of complexity without an abundance of gold to generate commercial activity. Ancient Egypt is a case in point, or at least a close approximation.

To take another example: while the Roman Empire had an almost modern monetary system, contemporary Germanic society carried on not entirely without money but without minting any money (that is, without according metal coin any official position as a medium of payment and a measure of value). Gallic and Iberian societies, on the other hand, were more closely influenced by the Greeks and Phoenicians, and minted money themselves. In Germanic society the word 'Vieh' meant both 'cattle' and 'wealth', in the same way as 'pecunia' (money) derives from 'pecus' (cattle). This was because the standard of value (the point of reference for other products) was for a long time the head of cattle (cows, oxen, etc.). Some primitive coins are stamped with an ox's head, to denote this role. In some other places the coins are cast in the shape of the objects (as in China). Any commodity could serve as the unit of value, as is illustrated by a twelfth century account of the inhabitants of Kügen Island, in the Baltic: 'They have no money, nor are they accustomed to employ coins for purchase. If they wish to acquire a thing in the market, they pay the price of it in linen cloth. The gold and silver they obtain by plunder or as ransom for prisoners or by what means soever, is fashioned into jewels for their women, or stored in the coffers of their temples.' Bloch, who quotes this, stresses that this is an archaic phenomenon; it is clearly so by the 12th century. But it is another example of how, despite the existence of a local market and of contact with the outside world, precious metal does not acquire a monetary role simply by being there.

The evolution towards classical monetary forms was slow and uneven, and the volume, use and circulation of money depended both on economic conditions and on the social structure. To take a final example from modern Europe. I have found instances as late as 1760 where highly localised economies in the Catalan area of the Pyrenees used money so little that the villagers took sacks of grain to market in order to pay for their purchases. In any period of history similar pockets of resistance to the circulation of money are found. It must be pointed out that this may signify conscious resistance in the case of those who are in advantageous positions within social systems that may be completely undermined by the circulation of money. One of the main features of what is schematically referred to as the 'transition from feudalism to capitalism' is the transition from a system of social relations where monetary arrangements are secondary and subordinate, to one in which money (in the broadest sense) plays a major role. In discussing the influence of gold and precious metals, it should be remembered that it is no simple matter for these metals to penetrate all sectors of exchange within a social system. It is always necessary to specify the limits which the state of a society's evolution puts on the circulation of coinage.

(3) The stages of evolution towards metal coinage

Gold has been known and used since prehistoric times, but it was not the earliest material to be used for coins. Silver and copper were more abundant but more difficult to extract and shape, and they at first had a higher value relative to gold than they now do. They were used as coin before gold, and on a wider scale. When gold was discovered in its pure condition it was fine, shining and malleable and it was used first and foremost for ornamentation.

What served as money in the Eastern empires, in the ancient societies of the Mediterranean, and even in the 3rd millenium in China? In Mesopotamia, for instance, barley was as much the standard of value as gold and silver. But in the palaces and temples there were legalised, standardised scales of weight and measure in order to compare value. Variations in value between the different standards were measured here. For example, a bad harvest could in the short term halve the amount of barley corresponding to a given weight of silver. (This meant that the silver price of barley had increased by 100%, and would be in line with the violent fluctuations in agricultural prices known to have taken place in ancient times.) In the long run there were variations in what economists call the 'bimetallic ratio', that is, the ratio of the values of gold and silver: around 2700 BC it was 9 to 1, around 1800, under Hammurabi, it was 6 to 1, and in the 6th century BC 12 to 1. In this very ancient civilisation, there was then a system of variable exchange values. But did money really circulate? Stamped ingots were used as a means of payment, but only for exceptional expenditure. They were not in daily or domestic use. In particular, we find that though silver may have been used for internal payments, small quantities of the rarer substance, gold, were kept for external payments (what today would be called 'international' payments). Hammurabi's empire, with silver ingots in the palace treasury, and gold kept in reserve for international payments, therefore in some respects prefigured the state banks of today. The difference is that while today there are large quantities of money in circulation, the state systems in Egypt, Assyria and China used hardly any coin internally, as did the Inca empires.

The new stage began in the Mediterranean area where Troy, Crete, and then (around 1500) Mycenae, began to use stamped metal discs, more like modern coin, instead of ingots. But the decisive stage came when a portrait, representing the guarantee of the sovereign or other authority, was 'minted' on the metal coin. This allowed it to circulate at a given value without needing to be weighed or have its 'legal measure' taken (that is the measure of the proportion of pure metal to alloy). This had always been necessary with ingots. The appearance of real money dates only from the end of the 7th century or the beginning of the 6th century BC, first in the Greek cities of Asia Minor, then in Greece (where silver was coined), and in Lydia, where first electrum (the alloy of silver and gold) then gold was minted in the reign of Croesus. The names of Croesus, Giges and the river Pactolus evoke the legendary effect of these innovations.

To sum up, we can say that money proper appeared late in the day, and it did so on the periphery of the trading system of the ancient world and not within the great empires. Trade created money rather than money trade.

(4) Precious metals as objects of prestige and treasure

Metals used for prestige or hoarding increase their value in men's eyes, but circulation is restricted and this for a long time reduces the possibilities of their being used economically. This is not specific to ancient times: even in modern times, in the East and Far East, products were exchanged for gold and silver which were then saved in the form of luxury objects or deposited in hiding-places.

From ancient and mediaeval times onwards, such phenomena were accompanied by sharp changes in circulation of the metals which were concentrated in this way. In Egypt, at the end of the first millenium, something of the sort happened as a result of the first wave of pillage of the pyramids and of other treasure sites; and after Egypt was conquered by the Arabs, there was a second wave of pillage, and even cases of systematic excavation. When Tutankhamun's tomb was opened in 1922, it contained twice as much gold as was held by the Egyptian Royal Bank at that time. In ancient times, a single find of this order could upset the whole gold market. The dispersal of treasure often resulted from wars. Alexander the Great's conquest of Persia affected gold circulation as much as did the Spanish conquest of America. Later, the Roman conquest of the Hellenic kingdoms occasioned a further redistribution, this time towards the west of Europe. It must be borne in mind that with gold so scarce (NB the 8m³ of 1500) and hoarding so extensive, non-economic developments (this does not mean chance developments) are as important in its history as the conditions of actual production (the mines and seams).

(5) Concluding remarks

The great economist Keynes, in his *Treatise on Money*, wrote with what the historian must regard as a measure of rashness: 'It would be a fascinating task to re-write Economic History, in the light of these ideas, from its remote beginnings; to conjecture whether the civilisations of Sumeria and Egypt drew their stimulus from the gold of Arabia and the copper of Africa, which, being monetary metals, left a trail of profit behind them in the course of their distribution through the lands between the Mediterranean and the Persian Gulf, and, probably, farther afield; in what degree the greatness of Athens depended on the silver mines of Laurium – not because the monetary metals are more truly wealth than other things, but because by their effect on prices they supply the spur of profit; how far the dispersal by Alexander of the bank reserves of Persia, which represented the accumulated withdrawals into the treasure of successive empires during many preceding centuries, was responsible for the outburst of economic progress in the Mediterranean basin, of which Carthage attempted and Rome ultimately succeeded to reap the fruits; whether it was a coincidence that the decline and fall of Rome was contemporaneous with the most prolonged and drastic deflation yet recorded; if the long stagnation of the Middle Ages may not have been more surely and inevitably caused by Europe's meagre supply of the monetary metals than by monasticism or Gothic frenzy.'[2]

Here gold is first described as a stimulus, and subsequently appears as an element on which the greatness of Athens 'depended', then as 'responsible' for the splendours of Rome, and lastly, by its absence, as 'causing' the economic depression of the Middle Ages. Now there is a great difference between a 'stimulus' and a 'cause'. If the movement of gold was a stimulus, in what way did the scarcity of gold (the 'meagre supply') bring about the mediaeval depression? Was the 'meagre supply of the monetary metals' cause or effect? Lastly, to make any distinction between 'income inflation' (clearly the case with the Alexandrian and Roman generals) and 'profit inflation' (supposedly created at the time by 'entrepreneurs' introducing price increases), we would surely need to know everything about the economic life of the times, including prices,

[2] John Maynard Keynes, *A Treatise on Money*, London 1930, vol. II, p. 150.

wages, the economically active population, hours of work, and the level of savings.

Keynes' call to 're-write' economic history from the point of view of the precious metals also came a little late: this had already been done by the Spanish (Saravia de la Calle) in the 16th century, and the British (Hume and his disciples) in the 18th century. Marx criticised their attempts in 1859 in his *Contribution to the Critique of Political Economy*: 'The favorite references of Hume's followers to the rise of prices in ancient Rome in consequence of the conquests of Macedonia, Egypt and Asia Minor, are quite irrelevant. The characteristic method of antiquity of suddenly transferring hoarded treasures from one country to another, which was accomplished by violence and thus brought about a temporary reduction of the cost of production of precious metals in a certain country by the simple process of plunder, affects just as little the intrinsic laws of money circulation, as the gratuitous distribution of Egyptian and Sicilian grain in Rome affected the universal law governing the price of grain. Hume, as well as all other writers of the 18th century, was not in possession of the material necessary for the detailed observation of the circulation of money.'[3]

This is the most important methodological point for us to learn. Before discussing the 'effects' of the movement of gold on the world, it is necessary to learn to observe such movements and relate them to other economic phenomena. Facile 'monetarism', and catching formulations about the 'legendary metal', are to be avoided at all costs. Everything I have said in this chapter shows that gold need not necessarily play the role of money. This does not mean that gold cannot be an important economic factor. But its use depends on the social complex within which the gold supply is located.

[3] Karl Marx, *A Contribution to the Critique of Political Economy*, Chicago 1904, pp. 221–222.

3

Some Observations on the Middle Ages

(1) The early mediaeval period: depression in the Christian west and the gold of Islam

We must first rapidly sketch the main outlines of the monetary history of the period. In the 4th century under Constantine, after the re-organisation of the Roman Empire, the situation with regard to money became clear, almost modern. The unit of money was the 'solid gold' (that is, high carat) crown coin, the *aureus solidus nummus*, or *solidus*, the 'golden sovereign'.[1] It contained 4.48 grams of fine gold and was subdivided into half sovereigns and thirds of sovereigns (*triens*). There were also silver and copper coins bearing a legal relation to the sovereign. This monetary system was similar to the best of the 19th century.

The small barbarian kingdoms that came later all claimed to be the heirs of the Empire and coined their own gold sovereigns. But before long they were coining less each time; coining more thirds of sovereigns than sovereigns; and adding more and more base metal. This meant that the need for large coins was constantly declining; and that gold was becoming scarce and dear. In effect, the 'triens', which contained 1.51 grams of gold under Constantine, had only 0.39 grams under Charlemagne. Charlemagne carried out a monetary reform and after that no more gold was coined.

The barbarian kings did not have enough authority to circulate 'token' copper coinage. As labour was in general a personal service, there was little need for small coin. Silver money was sufficient for intermediate transactions, and became the main form of coinage. In theory, the silver penny was worth one twelfth of the gold sovereign, which was in turn worth a twentieth of a pound's weight of silver. This was the origin of the system whereby 1 pound equalled 20 shillings, and

---

[1] The name *solidus* survives in the Italian word *soldo*, payment or money, and the French *solde*.

1 shilling equalled 12 pence. Yet as time went by, the silver penny itself contained less and less silver: under Philip Augustus it contained only 27% of what it had contained under Charlemagne. Throughout this period, no gold was coined in Western Europe (with some exceptions, which we shall look at). There was little internal commerce, and what there was tended to be carried out by payment in kind, without money being used.

Even at the height of the Roman Empire, Western gold had been flowing eastwards as payment for precious goods (silk and spices). The treasures of the Lagids and Seleucids, which Rome had seized, thus made their way back to their countries of origin through trade. Byzantium too lost in this way to Sassanid Persia, where gold was kept as treasure and silver was the circulating currency. Nevertheless, the gold accumulated by the Eastern cities and the mines of Nubia (in Upper Egypt), made it possible, as long as Byzantium controlled Asia Minor and Egypt, to maintain the 'gold sovereign' at its original level (72 sovereigns to a pound's weight of gold). The *solidus*, known in Greek as the *nomisma*, remained the dominant coin.

From 640 the Muslims invasion swept in turn over Persia, Syria, Egypt and Mesopotamia, then over North Africa, Spain and Southern Italy.[2] In 694, the caliph Abd al-Malik had gold coins engraved following the pattern of the *solidus*, but with Muslim inscriptions, which were phrases from the Koran. From then on the Muslim *dinar* (and its silver subdivision, the *dirham*) competed with the bezant (the Western name for the Byzantine 'sovereign'). In the West the dinar was often called the 'mancus': the origin of the word is unknown, but it seems to come from the Arabic *manqusha* (literally 'engraved'), a piece of money coined or engraved with fine lettering. The fineness of the Muslim inscriptions seems to have reinforced the prestige of the coin. When there were several caliphates gold was coined in Cordoba and Cairo, as well as in Baghdad. Where did this Muslim gold come from? There was one non-economic source: pillage – of the Persian treasury, the churches of Syria and the tombs of Egypt. Secondly there was the production of the mines of Nubia. And lastly there was 'caravan gold', the gold nuggets from the rivers of Ghana and the Sudan which reached Egypt and the rest of North Africa via the Sahara. The gold from the caravans was, in particular, the source of the money used by the Almoravids when they

[2] For an understanding of this phenomenon as a whole, see the article by the all too little known Maurice Lombard, 'L'or musulman du VI au XI siècle' *Annales E.S.C.*, 1947, pp. 143–160.

invaded Spain: their 'morabati' became the 'maravedi', which in turn came to be used in Spain as the money for accounting.

For a long time gold could circulate easily around the Mediterranean, as the Muslims occupied the coasts of Spain, the Balearic Islands, Sicily, and Southern Italy. The old-established system of exchange between East and West of the Mediterranean, whereby gold was exchanged for the precious goods of the Orient, continued to operate. Even the barbarian parts of the West were affected by this monetary and commercial system: the Muslims bought tin, arms, skins, and above all slaves. But the Muslim gold used to pay for these purchases rapidly returned, via Byzantium, to the East, to pay for the precious goods purchased by the Western upper classes (the Church and the great lords). There were two routes for this traffic: one through Italy (which made the fortune of Amalfi in the south and Venice in the north) and one through the steppes, running from Scandinavia down to the Black Sea. The gold moved around Western Europe, not into it.

The following factors contributed to the scarcity of gold in feudal Europe. (a) As luxury expenditure continued, gold was exported to pay for precious goods. (b) It was looted, especially by the Normans. The wealth of gold objects in Scandinavian museums is proof of this. (c) It was kept as treasure, especially in the churches (where it served as a store of value, to be sold or requisitioned in emergencies). (d) There was the simple fact that Europe itself produced little or no gold. According to Marc Bloch, these factors 'condemned' Europe to go far afield in search of gold and to conquer other lands (in the 16th century). But such arguments should not be taken too far. Keynes used to say that where there is gold, there is wealth and civilisation. If we add that where there is none, expansion takes place in pursuit of it, we shall never get beyond useless generalities.

It must not be forgotten that there was a reciprocal relationship between money and the economy in general. The scarcity of money restricted economic activity in the West, but the low density of population, unpaid feudal labour services and bad communications, also help to explain this scarcity. One proof of this is the large number of mints which existed for so little money. The circulation of money became a *local* phenomenon, although, as has been said, gold continued to be the dominant means of general trade (to say 'international' trade would be anachronistic). This means that from the 11th to the 13th centuries gold was used in general trade, but it flowed out of the West rather than flowing into it. If the West had sold more commodities than it bought, it would have retained or attracted gold instead of losing it. The 'balance of trade' was unfavourable. It is even possible that lack of demand rather than lack of capacity was the reason that gold production in Europe ceased, although it did start again after 1200 in the Alps and in Silesia.

The explanation of the scarcity lies in the economic, demographic and social condition of West European Christendom. When and how did this change? In noting where and when gold came back to Western Europe, we shall perhaps also discover how and why. First, did mediaeval Europe really do without gold until 1250? References to bezants and mancusi do not necessarily prove that gold was available: what they do show is that there was a need to refer to the main international money. Just as today serious pledges are made in dollars in countries where the currency has depreciated, so in the 9th and 10th centuries debts were expressed in terms of mancusi: that is, as the equivalent of a given number of mancusi, with the words *in rem valentem*, or similar expression, being added, meaning that the value could be paid in kind. Although the means of payment was sometimes specified, as being corn, dried fish or horses, the actual sum was expressed in gold. It had therefore clearly not been forgotten.

The basis of comparison was arrived at in the countries that had direct contact with Islam, i.e. Spain and Southern Italy. Spanish mediaevalists, such as Sanchez Albornoz and Valdeavellano, have noted that around the year 1000 precious cloth was being bought for gold in markets such as Leon, which were especially busy because of their proximity to Muslim wealth.

This raises the question of when formal reference to the mancus gave way to payment in real gold. By classifying the passages on gold in the 9th and 10th century archives of Catalonia chronologically, it has been possible to discover when the expression *in rem valentem* began to be replaced by expressions which indicate clearly that payment was being made in actual gold, in commodity-money: *'mancusos de oro cocto'*, *'auri puri et legitimi'*, *'pensatos ad pensum legitimum'*.[3] They appear at the end of the 10th century and become prevalent between 1033 and 1048. This gold came from a number of sources: from Christian plunder which replaced Muslim plunder; from the tribute (*paria*) exacted from the Muslims; and from the particularly lucrative sale of slaves to the Muslims.

---

[3] 'Mancusi of processed gold', 'Pure and genuine gold', 'Weighed to the legitimate weight'.

This change marks the beginning of a new phase. The Muslim princes were still rich: they were able to pay tribute and buy slaves. But they had no political or military *power*. The triumph of Christendom (which was of course interrupted by temporary Muslim successes, such as the invasions of Spain by the Almoravids and the Almohads) began, like the triumph of Islam, with non-economic transfers of gold, such as that celebrated in the epic of *El Cid* after the fall of Valencia (1094):

'Grandes son los gozos – que van por es logar
quando mio Çid gañó a Valencia – e entro en la ciudad.
Los que foron de pie – cavalleros se fazan;
e los otros averes – ¿quien los podrie contar?
Todos eran ricos – quantos que allí ha.
Mio Çid don Rodrigo – -la quinta mandó tomar,
en el aver monedado – treynta mill marcos le caen,
e los otros averes – ¿quién los podrié contar?'.[4]

This is poetic exaggeration. But Muslim gold did become a tangible reality to Christians. From the 11th century onwards the Spanish kings carried out the following series of measures. First they put Muslim gold coin into circulation. They then minted money from uncoined gold, covertly imitating Muslim coins which were generally accepted. Next they produced such coins openly (these were known as 'Barcelona mancus'), but retained the same form, including the phrases from the Koran. Later still it was considered better to replace the quotation from the Koran with Christian inscriptions, though these were still written in Arabic letters (which shows the importance of external form in the acceptance of coin). And finally in 1175, learning that the Muslim mint in Murcia had closed, Alfonso VI of Castille decided to mint gold coin under his own name. With this we come to the end of the 12th century.

It is conventionally said that the minting of gold in Europe began again around 1250. This is true in so far as the Spanish minting and Frederick II's minting in Sicily were marginal; they prolonged the Muslim period rather than inaugurated the period of Christendom's economic triumph. If an influx of gold is to have a profound economic meaning, there must be a profound economic reason for it: it must correspond to an upsurge in exchange and in production, and cannot

---

[4] 'Great was the rejoicing hereabouts / When El Cid took Valencia and entered the city / All who had walked rode on horseback / And the rest of the wealth to be had was beyond measure / Whosoever was there was made rich / El Cid don Rodrigo ordered a levy of a fifth / Thirty thousand marks in coin were his / And the rest of the wealth to be had was beyond measure'.

result simply from enrichment through war. In other words, Europe's return to gold was the culmination of a long process of internal evolution.

This raises the question of where gold was being regularly and successfully minted around 1250. Marseilles claimed the right to do so in 1227, but was unsuccessful. Florence and Genoa both took the decisive step in 1252. Gold was being minted in Perugia in 1259, in Lucca in 1273, in Venice in 1284, and in Milan by the end of the century. Interestingly, the great kingdoms of France and England tried after 1257 to follow the example of Florence, but were unable to mint gold until the 14th century. Apart from Spain and Sicily, which were special cases, the real economic impetus towards gold appeared in the prosperous economic centres of the Mediterranean. A new epoch had begun.

(2) The zenith of the Christian middle ages

The minting of gold by Florence and Genoa was the consummation rather than the beginning of a process, the culmination of the recovery of Europe which had been taking place since the 11th century (the year 1000 was not when it began, but was a convenient date, and contemporaries were by then already aware of a surprising degree of recovery). It has to be remembered that between the 6th and the 14th centuries, the population of Christian Europe increased by perhaps 2.7 or even 3.7 times. Estimates vary, but 3 is a reasonable figure. This corresponds to the development of agricultural technique and rotation; the feudal system was being perfected and must at this time have produced its maximum yields. Markets were formed and cities grew, and the Christian world as a whole was not contracting but expanding (into Spain and the Teutonic areas of the North East, and through the Crusades). All this could not have been based on any influx of gold. The extremities which experienced such an influx – the Russian steppes, and Spain, once it was regained – were not the areas producing the impetus towards development. Gold came back to Europe, in fact, when there was a trade surplus to attract it, or more simply, when Europe began selling more than it bought. It was the 'import-export' cities which reaped the fruits of this European trade: exchanging European products for Eastern products (Venice and Genoa), and sometimes producing quality commodities themselves in considerable quantities – as with Florentine textiles.

Although whole regions were isolated and fell outside the sphere of its activity, commerce had developed in a considerable scale, and therefore required a strong coinage. Initially large silver coins were minted, and on the basis of the silver standard some cities developed production and exchange and built up considerable economies. Barcelona was one example. But the triumph of the commercial cities, especially those around the Mediterranean, was formalised in the adoption of internationally-accepted gold coin: the Florentine florin, minted with the fleur de lys, and the Venetian ducat, depicting the Doge and St. Mark's, became, between 1250 and 1300, the 'dollars of the Middle Ages' (the expression is Roberto Lopez's). Till then only bezants and dinars had played this role. The minting of gold was therefore a consequence of Western economic development and not a cause (even though there is always some inter-action). Once the prestige of the florin and the ducat were established, everyone in Europe wanted to imitate them: especially France, England and the kingdom of Aragon. As has been pointed out, these great states did not achieve this until the 14th century: and it is curious that the whole of Europe went over to minting gold at the very moment when a generalised crisis (for which there is plenty of evidence, but little explanation) struck every economy and every population in the continent.

(3) The 14th and 15th centuries: the monetary side of the European crisis

In the period from the famine of 1315–1320 to the 1348 plague, catastrophe fell upon Europe. While the causes are still in dispute, and they can scarcely have been monetary, famine, epidemics, wars and the abandonment of lands did have their influence on money. With fewer buyers and less trade, prices in general and gold prices in particular tended to fall; but as there were fewer workers (and from then on they were often wage-labourers), wages rose. The spontaneous reaction of great and small states alike was to increase the supply of small common coin, debase good coin, and modify the relation between token money and real money. These manipulations of the currency (parallel to modern 'inflation' followed by 'devaluation') made it possible to pay labour less, while appearing to pay more, to reduce the burden of debts and to compete for a time with foreigners, by exporting at very low prices. While such advantages were always temporary, the increase in low value common coin became dangerously excessive. This is not the place to study these 'manipulations',[5] except to say that the general economic

---

[5] The different forms these took are outlined by Marc Bloch in his 'Esquisse'.

crisis produced internal monetary crises with extremely interesting social manifestations – urban revolts – and theoretical expressions: monetary theory began with Nicholas Oresme, adviser to Charles V of France. Those, however, have little to do with the problem of gold.

After 1450, the problem of gold did become important, when an increase in population, production and cultivation brought about a fall in all prices relative to gold. This made the search for gold extremely profitable. The starting point for this book's analysis may be taken as 1450, when what is called the 'price revolution' of the 16th century was already in preparation, and when the Portuguese were sailing off in search of African gold. I shall therefore divide the subsequent account chronologically into the following periods.

From 1450–1475 to 1500–1525, Western Europe experienced a recovery in population and in the economy, with crop rotation and technical inventions, and a tendency, between 1450 and 1500, for prices to fall, especially relative to gold. The upward valuation of precious metals and such products made them much sought after. The Portuguese seized African gold and discovered the route to the Indies via the Cape; the Spanish discovered the West Indies, and they too found gold. The tendency of prices to fall was then reversed, especially in Portugal and Spain.

From 1500–1525 to 1598–1630, there occurred the period of European expansion and the 'price revolution'. It is important to understand the relation between on the one hand the extension of the world market (to the Far East and America); the circulation of gold and of silver (which was plentiful enough for it to circulate in a pure form); and of credit; and, on the other hand, the appearance of expanding national economies (mercantilism). It is significant that the indirect influx of precious metals into continental Europe and England was a stimulus to production, while the massive direct influx into Spain ruined its economy, although it at first appeared to benefit from it.

From 1598–1630 to 1680–1725, there was a relative decline. Less silver was reaching Europe, and it was dearer: gold was dearer still. As with mediaeval periods of economic depression, we must try to see what relation if any exists between the decline in economic activity, the relative fall in prices and the 'deflation' (that is, the greater scarcity of money). The picture has to be modified to take in regional variations and variations over time (crises and temporary recoveries).

Between 1680–1725 and 1812–1817 it is well known that Europe underwent an '18th century boom'. This coincided with a growing exploitation of Brazilian gold and then of Mexican silver. From 1726 most European currencies were stabilised, and prices expressed in gold and silver rose. The results are well known:[6] but the causes and in particular the relation between price movements and colonial exploitation need further study.

The period from 1812–1817 to 1914–1920 is that of the triumph of industrial capitalism in Europe and, in monetary terms, of fidelity to the gold standard (first with gold–silver 'bimetallism' and then without). It lasted roughly a century, but was divided into periods of rising and of stagnant prices, and these may be related to the opening of new mines (in California, Australia and South Africa).

The period from 1914–1920 to 1945–1965 was one of world crisis (the wars of 1914–18 and 1939–45, the economic slump of 1929), and this was reflected in monetary affairs. Gold now appears to be giving way in the face of new conceptions of money, though some think that this abandonment of the yardstick of commodity-money is itself one of the causes of crisis and uncertainty.

[6] Ernest Labrousse, *Esquisse du mouvement des prix et des revenus en France au XVIIIe siècle*, 2 vols., Paris 1933.

4

The Conjuncture and Price Movements, 1450–1500

The alternation in Western Europe between long periods of economic growth and equally long periods of recession (at least by comparison with other economies such as those of the Far East and Africa) forces us to give some thought to the concept of the *conjuncture*. Between 1920 and 1940 economists were extremely interested in the concept. Those of today are less so, since they believe that we have moved into a 'conjunctureless' 'self-sustained' world, from which there can be no turning back. Not everyone can agree. The historian, moreover, must investigate the past, when growth was never sustained, and was always in jeopardy. Our observation of the conjuncture involves investigating the unevenness of the rhythm of development, and the alternation of boom and recession, growth and stagnation, looking for where these occur, and how they are spread out over time. We must ask how useful this concept is, what the difficulties in it are, and what bearing it has on the problem we are investigating.

(1) How useful is the concept of the historical conjuncture?

Broadly speaking, the conjuncture means 'the totality of all the conditions' in which a problem or an event is located. The historian, like the man of action, must constantly define this 'general conjuncture', since even the apparently most remote facts may influence the understanding of a given moment. For example, the weakness of Louis XVI's character obviously affected the development of the French Revolution. But in the favourable economic conjuncture of 1726–1774, it would not have taken on the tragic meaning it acquired in the difficult conditions of 1778–1787 and the extreme crisis of 1788–1789.

It is one of Ernest Labrousse's most important achievements to have shown that even in its narrowest economic sense (of good times or bad) the concept of conjuncture can be historically explanatory.[1] It compels us to go beyond the bounds of the area under study. We tend always to look for local, internal, immediate explanations. If we know that some success or problem has a parallel far beyond the boundaries of the century under discussion, our system of explanation is broadened. As Simiand used to say, 'Do not forecast the weather from your back garden'.

Secondly, the concept of conjuncture precludes naively political, voluntaristic interpretations. Man has always tried to master economic conditions; but he has been unable, even today (with 'planning' still so unreliable) to *master* the economy. We should therefore be wary of crediting any man or any government with achievements that are not uniquely theirs. In a recent study of Russia in 1900, I came across the following sentence: 'Nicholas II decided to industrialise Russia'. This creates a false picture: not because the Tsar and his court were irrelevant, but because in a phase of generalised development (such was the 'conjuncture') capital was attracted to new countries and this gave an incentive to the industrialisation of Russia well before Nicholas II.

It is, then, worthwhile not only in economic but also in 'general' history to inquire into the overall, spontaneous economic tendencies which bring complex factors into play: while the decisions of individuals and legislative initiatives have their part to play, their significance and especially their effectiveness, depend on the 'conjuncture' in which they are located.

(2) Dangers and difficulties in the concept of conjuncture

The concept should be used with care (especially by those using it for the first time). It should, above all, not be used for effect. To say 'this can be explained by the conjuncture' is like saying 'the storm can be explained by meteorology', i.e. it is a purely verbal explanation. It is often better not to use the term while showing some understanding of the concept, and locating a problem in its broadest context.

The concept of the 'conjunctural cycle' can be usefully employed, but it is difficult to do so. It should be emphasised that very long-term tendencies ('secular' trends) do occur throughout fairly heterogeneous areas: Europe went through stagnation in the 14th century, growth in the 16th, stagnation in the 17th, and growth again in the 18th. It is

---

[1] Ernest Labrousse, op. cit.

necessary to know what these trends are, and to be familiar with the discussions about how far they extend geographically, as well as over time. Within these secular trends, at least since the end of the 18th century, there have also been what are called 'Kondratieff' cycles, lasting roughly 50 years; they are divided into 25 years of growth (Simiand's phase 'A', when there are general price rises) and 25 years of price stagnation, and therefore less trading (Simiand's phase 'B'). This should not be taken literally – the phases last only *roughly* 25 years.[2]

Within these 'long-term' cycles there occur the better known kind of oscillations, referred to as 'short cycles' ('Juglar' cycles[3]) or 'interdecanal' cycles (Simiand's term). These last about 10 years. In the 19th century, they involved a rise in industrial prices for four or five years while trade boomed, and then a 'crisis' followed by recession when trading became harder. Before the 19th century, in some countries during it, and even today in the non-industrialised countries, prices also under-went a 'short cycle'. In this case, it involved agricultural prices. Instead of a crisis of industrial over-production leading to a slump in prices, this crisis was one of agricultural under-production leading to a rise in food prices such as terrified the poor. A cycle of this kind is deter-mined by the probability of the recurrence of bad harvests. It is quite distinct from the 'industrial cycle', but nonetheless lasts roughly as long. There are also still shorter cycles, the simplest being the quite consider-able seasonal one. In ancient economies the 'gap' between two harvests brought a high point in food prices which could have fatal consequences. The multiplicity of cycles is what makes analysis of the conjuncture so difficult. A 'good' or 'bad' period must be further defined according to whether it is on a very long, long, short or very short cycle, and whether the crisis is of the 'old style', or an industrial, capitalist crisis.

Any study of conjuncture must nonetheless answer the following questions: whether there is an upswing or a downswing (growth or recession); whether it is phase 'A' or 'B', i.e. whether times are good or bad, and for whom; at what stage of the short-term cycle we are; what is happening to production; what is happening to prices; who is gaining most: the worker, the owner, the retailer, or the consumer; whether there is growth, crisis or stagnation, and who is affected by it. For a

---

[2] François Simiand, *Les fluctuations économiques à longue periode et la crise mondiale*, Paris 1932, pp. 35–50.
[3] Clément Juglar, *Des crises commerciales et de leur retour périodique en France, en Angleterre, et au Etats-Unis*, Paris 1889; partly translated as *A Brief History of Panics and Their Periodical Occurrence in the United States*, New York 1916.

precise event, it may also be necessary to know the season. In history it is always important to establish precise chronology.

Mechanical generalisations are not to be trusted. Although the importance of a conjunctural situation lies in its generality, this does not mean that in a period of prosperity all countries are equally prosperous, or that all social classes benefit equally. In every general conjuncture, different countries react in different ways: this produces the unevenness of development which in the end is what makes history. Every prosperous conjuncture in which there are rising prices impoverishes the wage-earner through wage-lag, since the overall development only takes effect in the long run. On the other hand, it may happen that a short-term general depression can grant relief, or at least a breathing space, to the mass of consumers, because prices fall and this can have positive demographic effects. The expressions 'period of prosperity' and 'period of depression' should not therefore be used loosely. Their meaning must be specified.

There is one final difficulty, which brings us back to the problem of gold. While historians have carefully studied the consequences of conjunctures, the economists have as yet given no coherent explanation of them, at least in-so-far as long-term conjunctures are concerned. We should here distinguish between two concepts of the 'conjuncture'. One concentrates on the most visible signs: price movements. Prices rise and bring prosperity to some and poverty to others. Whatever happens, trade and industry grow. When prices fall the reverse happens. The other concept of conjuncture involves the whole economy: the population, production, exchange, competition, war. This raises the question of whether price movements result from this general movement, or whether the general movement is the consequence of price movements. The *reciprocal* relationship between them is indeed what we must examine. But first, what is a price?

(3) 'Price', 'the general movement of prices', and gold

The concept of price is itself complex and involves distinguishing between long and short-term prices, and local, national and international ones. The market price is the immediate price of a product in a given place: it depends on supply and demand at that place and time. The *average price* over a number of years gives the level around which the market price varies, and this average price is itself variable in the long run. This 'price trend' may depend on the specific conditions of the given product, as for example the conditions of its production: an advance in technique will lower the price and this is why such falls are known as 'technological' ones. Here the factors affecting price are intrinsic to the product in question. This underlines the concept of a 'natural price', held by the classical economists, and defines the concept of 'value'.

A movement which simultaneously alters the prices of all products is not however deducible from the specific conditions of each. It may result from a variation in the overall demand for all products at once (such as results from population movements). It may result essentially from what is common to all prices, namely, the fact that they are expressed in money. A fairly general, homogeneous movement of all prices tends to reflect a variation in the value of money. If there is a change in one country's prices, the peculiarities of the country's currency must be examined; if there is a change in world prices we must look at what is common to all these national currencies, namely, the commodity money by which they are evaluated on the international market. This is where fluctuation in the value of the monetary metals, gold and silver, comes in.

The question of gold is the question of the change in the relation of the value of gold to the value of commodities as a whole. The 'conjuncture', in so far as it is expressed in price changes, is tied to the problem of the abundance or scarcity, circulation, discovery, and conditions of production, of gold. It should, however, be borne in mind that silver is sometimes more important for monetary purposes than gold: the two are certainly comparable, locally or on a world scale, in given quantities and given market conditions. The essential points to establish are therefore: the conditions under which the monetary metal is produced and distributed; the conditions of the production and sale of commodities within a given medium of exchange; and the points of contact and the circulation channels through which the metal and commodities are exchanged.

(4) The period 1450–1500

The example of this period brings out the relationship between the general level of economic activity, price changes, the search for gold and the great discoveries. The classical theory is that the gold, silver and precious goods provided by the discoveries, launched the great expansion of the 16th century.

While this is not untrue, I would add that there was a different kind of movement which launched men into exploration and discovery, from 1450–1500 onwards. To find out how this occurred we should begin by examining general price movements. Although much that we should like to know is unavailable and though there was considerable variation among products, there is general agreement that between 1450 and 1500 prices fell throughout Europe. The American historian and economist, Earl J. Hamilton, who as we shall frequently be reminded, has made a major study of the 16th century price revolution, also tried to check price movements in 15th century Spain, where they were very closely interconnected with the discoveries. He found adequate data for Valencia and Aragon,[4] and after collecting the greatest possible number of prices, he calculated the average in order to obtain the general movement. He established indices (taking 1421–1430 as 100) for nominal prices (i.e. those expressed in local money), silver prices (using detailed reconstructions of monetary standards to calculate the silver content of local coin), and gold prices (reached by calculating the gold content in the same way).

The following are the five-yearly indices for the 15th century.

In Valencia, on the basis of 1421–1430 = 100:		
	Nominal prices	*Silver equivalent*	*Gold equivalent*
1396–1400	104.6	110.1	112.7
1446–1450	102.5	102.5	95.6
1466–1470	94.5	91.5	85.1
1496–1500	89.2	86.7	67.0

[4] Earl J. Hamilton, *Money, Prices and Wages in Valencia, Aragon and Navarra* (1351–1500), Cambridge (Mass.) 1936.

A parallel movement took place in Aragon, though it was more sharply expressed in gold prices.

	Nominal prices	Silver equivalent	Gold equivalent
1401–1405	104.7	—	105.9
1446–1450	79.7	—	77.8
1466–1470	96.2	—	70.4
1496–1500	78.5	—	50.3

In other words, throughout the 15th century, those who had gold were able to buy more and more commodities. It was therefore only natural that people should go out and look for gold. Nor was this situation peculiar to the Iberian peninsula. Research on Germany, the Low Countries, England and Italy, shows it to have been a universal phenomenon. But the Iberian peninsula was on the route to the gold of Africa. Portugal first and then Spain went off to look for gold (and spices); they thereby plunged into the great discoveries.

5

African Gold and Genoese-Iberian Discoveries

We shall begin from the fact that in the second half of the 15th century Europe experienced a fall in prices, especially as expressed in gold, and this indicates that the value of gold was increasing relative to that of commodities. There was therefore good reason to go in search of it.

(1) Where was the gold?

For the men of the 15th century, as for those of mediaeval times, gold came from Africa, and Africa was remote and unknown, the only contact being through Egypt or North Africa. There are two maps we can compare to illustrate this: the 'Catalan Atlas' of 1375–1380 (in the *Bibliothèque Nationale* in Paris) and the map known as the 'Christopher Columbus' map. The former gives an excellent picture of the whole of Northern Africa, but the arc of the Niger and Guinea are entirely occupied by a single symbolic figure, a black king, who is the master of gold. In the centre, south of the Atlas mountains, is a man on a camel, sketched by a single continuous line, and bearing the following legend: 'All this part is inhabited by men who wear veils, so that only their eyes can be seen; they dwell in tents, and move about in camel cavalcades.' There were, then, three distinct worlds: the familiar area of North Africa, the desert with its caravans ('the Mediterranean Sahara') and the mysterious black world, the source of gold.

The map known as the 'Christopher Columbus's map' (drawn around 1488–1492) is much more precise about this source. To the east of Chad, a name, 'Isle of Tibir', indicates the area where gold dust (Tibir gold) came from. Although the interior of Africa was scarcely known at all, the whole coast, from Morocco to south of the Gulf of Guinea, is depicted with an impressive wealth of detail.

A comparison of these two maps shows the progress made in one century. It was a progress made by sea: the gold-bearing sands and primitive mines (whose ruins can still be found, from Senegal to Sudan) remained inside the black world: they enriched the empires of Ghana and Mali and then ensured the prosperity of Ualata and Timbuktu.[1] For a long time this gold was taken northwards only by caravan. There were famous markets and fairs where they met the European goods coming in through North Africa: Mesa, in the south, Tarudant, and above all, Sijilmesa, in the Tafilelt area, 'the gateway to the Sahara', as one Arab trader called it, 'to the land of the negroes and the source of gold. One of the greatest cities of North Africa and the most famous of the whole universe . . . whither traders take goods of no value and return with their camels laden with coarse gold. . . .'[2] Sijilmesa was in fact the place where all the caravans met, whether from the west of the Sahara (Mauritania) or from Tuat in the centre of North Africa: the merchants came from Marrakesh, Fez, Tlemcen and the Figuig oases. Despite the passage just quoted, there is no reason to think that the traders of Sijilmesa were not shrewd. Fortunes of 100,000 dinars (between 375 and 400 kilos of pure gold) were apparently made, credits of 40,000 (150–180 kilos) were given, and a tax imposed on traffic yielded some 400,000 per year (1,500–1,800 kilos of gold) around 1450. The merchants most closely connected with North Africa naturally wanted to reach the 'Tibir' gold themselves. These men were mostly Genoese, Spanish and Portuguese, though there were some from other parts of the Mediterranean. The Venetians, for example, who had other traditions, concentrated on trade 'in kind' with the East, exchanging European goods for precious commodities, without using money at all.

(2) The gold-seekers

The Genoese
For the Genoese the search was a commercial operation, although that did not prevent it from bearing some of the features of a competition or a military expedition. Gold for them had a trading value. It was when gold was particularly high in value – 13 or 14 times more expensive than silver – that the Vivaldi brothers of Genoa tried to circumnavigate Africa in the late 13th century, two centuries before Vasco da Gama. They lost their way, but the sailors sent to look for them by the capitalist

[1] See map on p. 54.
[2] V. Magalhães Godinho, *L'économie de l'empire portugais aux XVe et XVIe siècles*, Paris 1969.

who had financed them, Tedisio d'Oria, re-discovered the 'Happy Isles' of antiquity, the Canaries. Today, one of them still bears the name of the Genoese Lanzarote. After 1350 these attempts ceased because the ratio of gold to silver returned to a more normal level, and economic activity in Europe decreased; when around 1450 it picked up again and gold increased in value, the Oceanic and African expeditions began again. Genoa needed gold not only for trade but for her industry: she produced gold cloth, precious thread and jewels for Rome, Tunis, and the Genoese aristocrats themselves, and for the latter such luxuries were a way of saving, as highly-priced gold was also a reserve of value. This gold was obtained through eastern North Africa, from Tunis and Tripoli which are nearer Genoa: but it was cheaper and more plentiful in the west, in Oran, Honein, and the Moroccan cities. On the Berber coast all values were expressed in terms of 'Tibir' gold (in the form of dust, ingots, Sudanese or Sijilmesa coin). Gold was a commodity, and another commodity money was Tabasco pepper (*mereghera*, *manegata*). Payment was sometimes denominated 'in gold and Tabasco'. The 'Christopher Columbus' map bears the inscription '*hic manegata*' ('here there is Tabasco'). Spain – the Muslim Spain of Granada as well as Christian Spain – was often an entrepot for this traffic: silk was bought there, while North African wheat was sold.

Efforts were also being made to reach the African gold markets directly: the best-known example is that of Malfante in 1447; he was a Genoese who had learned the trading practices and geography of Africa from his stays in Majorca, Malaga and then Honein, and had even gone beyond Sijilmesa, to the Tuat caravan station. He was received by the brother of the greatest merchant of Timbuktu. While it seems that the venture was not a commercial success, and it is an exaggeration to call Malfante 'the first explorer of the Sahara', it was an important pioneering voyage. More important was the effort of the Genoese made to trade with the Canaries and to move all the way down the west coast of Africa: it is recorded that in 1455–1456 Antonio di Nol, better known as Antonio Usodimare, sailed beyond Cape Verde and visited Gambia, which was possibly the outlet for Tibir gold. In 1470, Benedetto Dei claimed to have reached Timbuktu. This all required the Genoese to associate with the Portuguese, who for their part needed the experience of Genoa over a long period, especially in trade.

The Genoese were nonetheless quick to react when it became clear that Portugal was turning into a great maritime and trading power. In 1415 the Portuguese captured Ceuta, one of the great gold centres (coin had been made there since the 10th century), and thereby dealt a severe blow to the Genoese trading agency established there. Later on, in other parts of Morocco as in Arcila in 1470, the Genoese had no compunction about entering into military alliances with the Muslims against the Portuguese, in at least private expeditions. They maintained their trading strength in Lisbon and throughout western Morocco, especially in Safi. Christopher Columbus's own early activities were also in Portuguese trade with the Azores and Africa. The refusal by the Portuguese to accept his plans for sailing westwards in a sense marked the transition from collaboration to rivalry in Portuguese–Genoan relations. At this time the Portuguese rejected Columbus because they thought that they were well ahead in the race for the Indies and for gold. We shall now see why this was so.

The Portuguese
Portugal is a small country of 35,000 square miles. Around 1400 it had a population of one million, and around 1520–1530, 1.4 million, less than Spain, France or Morocco. (Godinho estimates that at this time Morocco had a population of some 6 millions.) It was a country which acquired undreamt-of world importance, owing to its position at the crossroads of the Mediterranean, Africa, the Atlantic and the Northern European countries, and also owing to its poverty, since as the population rose there was growing emigration.

Godinho states that the following are the main causes of Portugal's expansion:[3] (a) the thirst for gold; (b) the political disturbances and depreciation of the late 14th century, which ruined the gentry and impelled them to seek their fortune through foreign ventures; (c) the shortage of corn, which drove them to seek new sources; (d) the dynamics of the sugar economy created in Portugal and the islands of the Atlantic; (e) the need of such an economy for slaves; (f) the need for gum-lac (for dyes and processing); (g) the need for skins and hides; (h) the extension of Portuguese fishing grounds. Factors (a), (b), (c) and (d) led to the seizure of Tangiers, Ceuta, Ksar al-Kabir and Arcila, in Morocco; others led to the colonisation of Madeira and the Azores, and some took the Portuguese southward along the coast of Africa.

The general question of the discoveries lies outside the scope of this discussion, but some controversial points should be mentioned. The role of Prince Henry the Navigator, and his motives, are in considerable

[3] Godinho, op. cit.

dispute. The latter have been variously described as economic, scientific or mystical. Within the overall situation a single individual was of slight importance: only a third of the Portuguese voyages were initiated by him, the remaining two-thirds being undertaken privately by merchants or knights, or by the Regent Peter. One man could not have been responsible for all this activity. Another dispute concerns technical developments, but the greatest progress had already taken place in the Mediterranean, without provoking any revolutionary change – the inventions of the rudder, the sea-compass, cartography and related phenomenon. The perfection of the three-masted caravel, in 1439, was the only important original development associated with the discoveries. It had previously been impossible to make the return journey from Africa via the coastal route, and not every ship had been able to take the trade winds across the open sea.

Bearing in mind that the whole process was much more complex, we can outline the stages of the Portuguese discoveries which relate to the problem of gold.

(1) The conquest of Ceuta in 1415, which began the process, was not caused by gold alone, but it nevertheless affected one of the traditional markets for African gold; prevailing forms of Mediterranean trade were changed, and Portugal developed the capacity to mint gold – reproductions of Ceuta coin – thereby initiating the first phase of the European processing of African gold. It marked the beginning of a systematic policy of aggression against Moroccan cities (of which the attack on Tangiers in 1437 was a part) and affected all the Mediterranean trading cities. This led to Malfante's journey to Tuat, and to the 'Berber Galley' expeditions by Venice in 1440 and by Florence in 1458.

(2) Portuguese operations were next concentrated on the west coast of Morocco: from 1447 there was constant traffic with Mesa and the Sus fairs for gold, slaves, sugar and indigo. At the same time, gold reached the Portuguese-held towns of Safi and Azemmur: in the nine years from 1491–1500, 41,520 gold 'doubloons'[4] a year reached Safi in the royal coffers alone; in the 15 years 1486–1500, 6,200 'doubloons' per year reached Azemmur. Gold was cheap here, and silver relatively dear, and they were profitably exchanged.

(3) Then there was the Arguin factory:[5] the dreaded Cape Bojador, for long the frontier of the known world, was rounded in about 1436. On the deserted beaches were the tracks of men and of camels. These

[4] The 'doubloon', Spanish dobla, contains 4.4 grams of pure gold.
[5] 'Factory' is here used in its original sense of a trading establishment.

explorers discovered the mouth of a river, the 'Rio de Ouro' (Gold River), which was in fact already known to the Spanish, though they confused it with the Senegal. This was the point where gold was brought down to the coast. In 1442 the first 'barter' took place: gold was exchanged for prisoners, and in 1444 gold was exchanged for cloth. ('Barter' is used here to mean a non-commercial exchange of goods, in which the products do not have a value agreed by both parties, and the transaction is often accompanied by threats or violence.)

By this time the caravels had already rounded Cape Blanco and discovered the Arguin archipelago. Caravans came there, frequently laden with salt; but the Portuguese were, above all, in pursuit of men. In 1448 Arguin was farmed out to 'rendeiros' (leasees), perhaps from Madeira. None came from Italy (Ca' da Mosto records that there were no Italians). A castle was built in 1455, though there were no stone walls until 1460–1461. The factory came before the fortress. At Arguin slaves were at the rate of 800–1,000 a year, the main item exchanged for horses, wheat, cloth, canvas, silver and Granada silk; the trade described by Münzer and by João Fernandes around 1492 included little in the way of gold – some 20–25 kilos a year were traded until 1524. But Arguin was always a place of 'barter' and a useful base (as is clear from the 'Columbus' map).

(4) Senegal, Gambia and Guinea were explored up as far as Cape Rojo once Cape Verde was passed in 1444. For the first time, the explorers encountered people, some of them converts of Islam, who had organised their own defence with poisoned arrows. The climax was fierce and their earliest experiences were disastrous. Later, prisoners were taught to be interpreters (a practice Columbus was to follow) and by 1455 the Venetian, Ca' da Mosto, was able to carry on conversations with the natives. The expedition sent up the Senegal thought it was on the point of discovering gold. When the Felu waterfalls proved an obstacle, a plan was even devised for blowing up the rocks! But in fact it transpired that the Senegal was only useful for supplying slaves.

Gambia however represented a decisive step in the discovery of gold. Diego Gomes got as far as the great market known as 'Cantor' (Kantora). The fortresses of Futa Jalon really seemed to be the home of the 'Tibir Isle' gold dust. There were river-banks where men waded looking for gold-bearing sand, which the women then washed – and there were also mining shafts 20 metres across, with galleries. The negroes who produced the gold carried it to Diego Gomes's men, although the country itself remained closed to them. Here a tradition of 'silent trade' (of gold for salt) prevailed: the seller put down his wares and disappeared; the buyer took it, if he liked it, and left his remuneration.

The fair at Cantor remained dominant. Cantor, 720 kilometres up-river, could be reached by 50–60 ton caravels; one single ship of this kind returned to Lisbon in 1502 with 4,500 'doubloons' alone; and between 1510 and 1516, the leasees of the monopoly paid the king 454,000 crowns a year, while many private merchants went to the 'barterings' there to make profit for themselves. Even at the end of the 16th century, Botero wrote: 'The Portuguese have a factory known as the "Ransom of Cantor", where they procure the gold of those countries in exchange for diverse commodities.'

(5) Next came Sierra Leone, which brought the explorers into direct contact with the equatorial forests and the gold-producing area. There were other products here as well as gold (iron, horn and marble) but in the 16th century Sierra Leone gold was still considered as 'the finest in the world'. Between 1456 and 1460, the coastline was explored as far as Cape Ledo (now Freetown). In 1469 the area was farmed out to the Lisbon capitalist Fernão Gomes. The price of gold was very low there, and the Portuguese visited all the estuaries on the coast; despite the concession, the country was still dominated by private competition. Its yield was of some 20,000 'doubloons' a year.

(6) São Jorge 'da Mina' comes last. In 1469 Fernão Gomes pledged, that, in return for his monopoly, he would explore 100 leagues further down the coast each year. In 1471 he reached the Cape of Three Points (now between Bassem and Accra). The first gold 'barter' took place on the São João River (today the Pra), and later, six leagues to the East, in the twin villages known as Duas Partes. This was where, after 1480, the castle of 'São Jorge da Mina' was built. Here was the real source of Portuguese gold, and for several years a caravel was meant to, and usually did, ply the route each month to carry gold. Around 1505 the amount involved was roughly 170,000 'doubloons' of fine gold a year. This was the crowning achievement of Portugal's search for gold.

6

Portugal, Spain and the Gold Trade

(1) Portuguese organisation of the gold trade (1469–1530)
Having described the stages of the Portuguese search for gold in Africa,
I shall now turn to the stages of colonisation and organisation of the
trade.

The colonisation of the Gold Coast
This process began with the Sierra Leone concession to Fernão Gomes
and the pledge he made to explore 100 leagues a year. In 1471, the best
captain of the period, Alvaro de Esteves, rounded the Cape of Three
Points, carried out the first 'barter' and chose the site of 'Mina'. After
1471 the results were so brilliant that Fernão Gomes was given a title,
and his coat of arms showed the heads of three negroes wearing collars
and pendants of gold. In 1478 Gomes became a member of the Royal
Council. During the war between Portugal and Castille Spanish ships
captured caravels carrying up to 6,000 gold 'doubloons'. In 1481 nine
caravels and two sloops under the command of Diego de Azambuja
arrived with stone, beams and bricks; Portuguese builders organised
squads of black labourers who were recruited by all possible means, and
in a few weeks a castle was built; 'São Jorge da Mina' grew under its
protection and was accorded the status of a city in 1486. Other forti-
fications were at Axim (on the near side of the Cape of the Three Points),
and at Redes (beyond Mina), which supplied pure 23-carat gold. The
'Mina Company' or 'Guinea Company' was founded in 1509 to administer
this trade, and the writings of João de Barros, its administrator between
1539 and 1549, are evidence that at this date it was still hoped that the
source of the gold would be discovered. In fact the decline had already
begun.

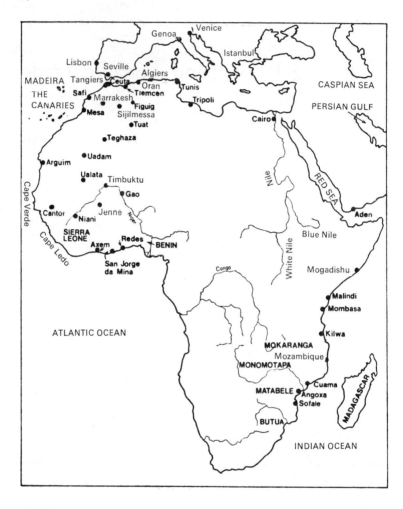

Figure 1. Africa in the 16th century.

The Mina gold trade

This trade was governed by Mina Company regulations, and the Company checked all ships' cargoes. In exchange for gold the natives received clothing (capes and robes), red and blue cloth, canvas, copper and brass goods (chains, pots and pans), coral, glassware, red shells and white wine. There are precise data and inventories of this trade. These show that Portuguese 'Mina' gold did not come from mines, but from trade, and that goods had to be produced in exchange.

Gold was not even produced near the coast. It came from the 'Ashanti' or 'Mossi' country (in the Upper Volta) and sometimes even further, from 'Bor Mali'. It was brought by native traders; they had no horses, and the bearers were men, who were very heavily laden, especially on the return journey. Slaves were needed, and the Portuguese supplied them, buying them in Benin and selling them in Mina itself. John III, who was a pious king, wanted to suppress this traffic, and according to João de Barros, he was rewarded by the discovery of new treasures: but it is doubtful, in any case, whether the measure had much effect.

The king did not receive all the income from the monopoly, although all the gold from Mina had to pass through his hands. Soldiers, officials and commercial agents could buy gold in proportion to their stipends, wages or profits, and these were checked and certified. Nothing could be brought from Lisbon except registered personal effects, and if these were not brought back then only gold up to the same value could be re-imported. Whatever happened, the gold belonging to individuals was deposited in royal coffers aboard the kings' ships. All gold coming into the Tagus estuary was taken first to the Mint, and individual owners were then given theirs back in the form of money. The ships were registered in both Lisbon and Mina. Despite all these restrictions, some Portuguese grew rich, through fraud, or special dispensations, or inside contacts.

The gold arrived, in principle, at the rate of one caravel a month. By 1505, Venetians were warning their government that the king of Portugal was receiving 10,000 ducats from Guinea twelve times a year. In fact the movement was more irregular but was larger; the caravels varied in size and were sometimes accompanied by larger ships. The average annual cargo from Mina has been placed at 170,000 'doubloons', with an additional 10,000–12,000 coming from Cape Redes. The following are figures for gold denominated by weight, although they are not continuous:

Annual average receipts from Mina:

1504–1507	433.368 kg
1511–1513	413.922 kg
1517–1519	443.676 kg
1519–1522	411.864 kg
1543–1545	371.578 kg

These figures are only for the royal gold from Mina. The Mint however, has more continuous records which give a figure of 410 kg a year from 1500 to 1521, with a fall between 1522 and 1530 which brought the average down to about 210 or 215 kg. This was followed by a rise to approximately 300 kg, reaching a maximum of 392 kg in 1540; after 1544 the figure again fell to some 200 kg a year, and around 145 in 1560–1561. There was also the gold from Sierra Leone, Gambia, Senegal, Mauritania and Morocco. In all, the annual receipts must have been roughly 700 kg between 1500 and 1520, the period when they were at their height.

During the sixteenth century private gold trading in West Africa gradually dried up. No gold at all now came from Arguin, for a number of reasons. Individual traders challenged the royal monopoly; the French, English and Dutch were getting gold through trade or piracy; and the Sultan of Morocco's authority was growing – a factor which attracted the gold northwards taken by the caravans. This was retribution for the caravels! We shall return to these points in the section on the late 16th century.

Meanwhile, the first minting of 'escudos' (1436) and of 'cruzados' (1457) had demonstrated the potential for Portuguese coin. The cruzado maintained its weight and gold content for 80 years, at 23.75 carats and 3.58 grass weight (64 to the mark), or 3.54 grams of fine gold. The former commercial powers of the Mediterranean, such as Venice, were slow to admit the primacy of Portuguese currency. On the other hand, Guinea gold was one means of carrying out the trade with the Far East opened up by Vasco da Gama's circumnavigation of Africa. The following is the explorer's own account of an incident in one of the ports of Guinea:

'A caravel arrived from Mina under the command of Fernando de

Montarroyo, carrying 250 gold marks in chains and jewels of the kind the negroes are accustomed to wear. The Admiral had with him Gaspar of India, whom he had brought from Angedive, together with the ambassadors of the Kings of Cannanore and Cochin. He wished to show them this gold, not for the quantity of it, but so that they might see it just as it was, as yet unrefined and unworked, and learn that Dom Manuel was master of the "Mine" of gold, and every year twelve or fifteen barks brought him such a quantity.' The astonished Indian ambassadors confessed that in Lisbon some Venetians had tried to convince them that Portugal was too poor to carry on exchange, and that it was only by the grace of Venice that the Portuguese fleet in the Indies was able to take cargoes on board. The gold of Guinea convinced them to the contrary. From 1505, however, as has been noted, the Venetians did admit that the shipments were regular, and 1519 they were referring to the King of Portugal as 'il Re di l'oro' (the King of Gold).

The decline of Portuguese gold

However, the relative decline of Portuguese gold was then already beginning, and in particular its effects on Europe were diminishing. Through trade with the East Indies and the Far East via the Cape, the King of Portugal was actually becoming as much the 'King of Spices' as the 'King of Gold'. The 'Indies Company' far outstripped the Mina Company. African gold was diverted from Europe and the Mediterranean and sent directly to the East to buy spices.[1] Moreover, the route back from Guinea and Mina still lay not along the coast, but via the open sea. This led to the discovery of the Cape Verde Islands and then of Brazil by Alvarez Cabral in 1500. The islands and Brazil, together with trade with the East, gave the Portuguese resources other than African gold, which now took second place. Meanwhile, the Spanish were now also finding other 'gold routes'.

To sum up. Portuguese gold probably played an important part in the transition from the 15th century, the century of 'gold famine', to the 16th century and the 'price revolution'. But Portuguese gold appeared gradually and was not very plentiful; it was obtained by means of exchange, and was never the only factor in Portugal's economy (pepper and sugar were factors too). Gold's importance declined

[1] Cf. Fernand Braudel, 'Monnaies et civilisation' op. cit, where he attributes the decline of the Italian renaissance to this loss of gold.

markedly after 1520, and especially after 1540. It could scarcely have played a 'revolutionary' role.

Nonetheless it was an episode of major significance in the discoveries as a whole. Gold was diverted from North Africa and the Mediterranean into Portuguese hands and later to the East Indies, and it therefore helped to make Portugal a wealthy, entrepreneurial power, while shifting the main axes of commerce towards the Atlantic. A similar experience, with certain important differences, fell to the lot of that other peninsular country, Spain.

(2) The origins of the Spanish discoveries

The Reconquest bound Spain to the rich Muslim world, which was now in decline; from here she obtained her wealth, and in particular her gold. In the 13th and 14th centuries however there were two Spains, a Mediterranean Spain and an interior or Atlantic Spain. Mediterranean Spain, although known as 'Aragon Spain' because the king bore the title of 'King of Aragon', was dominated by the Catalan-speaking maritime cities, Barcelona, Valencia and Palma de Majorca. These were linked to Italy, Sicily and Sardinia, and had considerable trade with Tunis, Tlemcen and Morocco.[2] The Catalans visited the Canaries and the Gold River, and the traditions of these cities played an important role in the discoveries; this was especially true of Majorcan cartography.

The Spanish interior and Atlantic coast, Castile, appeared in the 14th and 15th centuries to be rent by internal disputes. For a long time it was only of secondary importance in the rivalries of the Genoese, Catalans and Portuguese, and in the south of the peninsula it left untouched the last of the Muslim kingdoms, Granada, which was still prospering from the silk trade.

In the 15th century there was a gradual change. Mediterranean Spain recovered only painfully from the great plagues, its economy declined, and it fell largely into the hands of the Italians. Castile, on the other hand, revived, and began to exploit the very real advantage of facing both onto the North Atlantic and onto the Mediterreanean and the south. From the mid-15th century, Castile laid seige to the rich gold markets of North Africa, competed with Portugal on the West African routes, and brought about the dynastic union with Aragon (thereby uniting Mediterreanean traditions with the new developments of the Atlantic part). It captured Granada, driving Islam from Spain and at

[2] C. E. Dufourcq, *L'Espagne catalane et le Maghreb aux XIIIe et XIVe siècles*, Paris 1965.

once came into direct military contact with North Africa, the refuge of the expelled Muslims; this tempted it to carry the Reconquest into Africa. It was no accident that the fall of Granada occurred in 1492, the same year as the discovery of America. Given the background to the two events, their fates were interrelated.

Africa was being plundered from the 15th century onwards. A document dated 1506 advised the Spanish crown to use the services of the Andalusians in Africa, . . . 'because they have for many years been accustomed to carry out assaults in the African mountains, on the Barbary coast as well as the Levant'. More precisely, the advice is to choose certain people: 'from Jerez de la Frontera and the Port of Santa Maria, Cadiz, San Lucar and the duchy of Medina Sidonia, Gibraltar, Cartagena, Lorca and the sea-coast, for in these places *they are accustomed* to going to Africa, raiding and assaulting, sacking the camps and villages of the Moors and taking their ships. . . . Among the people of these parts, there are chiefs who know everything that is to be known about the area from Bugia to Tetuan, and Ceuta: there is no place, no city, village, encampment or fortress which is safe from their attacks and war-making.'³ This extension of the Reconquest had a strongly feudal and military character. At this time there were no economic concessions of the kind that the King of Portugal made to Fernão Gomes. In 1449, the King of Castile gave the Duke of Medina Sidonia the concession of 'the land and sea' between Cape Aguer and Cape Bojador (south of Morocco) 'in return for conquering them' (i.e. *not* for exploring). In 1494 the Catholic Monarchs gave the courageous Hernan Perez del Pulga 'grace and mercy and the gift of all mills there are and may be throughout the kingdom and the cities of Tlemcen in Africa, from the day when he will happily conquer them. . . .' It was with the same conception of combined economic privilege and military conquest that America was won.

Andalusia, in the South, bristled with fortresses against the danger of piracy. The overlords of these fortresses were known by the Muslim name of 'alcaides', and they too carried out raids. In 1480, the alcaide of Rota captured Azemmur; the nobles of Jerez conquered Ksar al-Kabir; and in 1497 the 'caudillo' Pedro de Estopinan took Melilla. Moroccan towns such as Al Hoceima and Fedala were all attacked. Where a place was occupied, overall control went to the Spanish King, and the overlordship to the Duke of Medina Sidonia, but the immediate profit from the looting went to the victorious soldiers. The fact that the Portuguese

³ Rafael Altamira, *Historia de España*, vol. 2, pp. 394–5.

were removing gold from west Africa did make these raids of the North African cities less and less profitable, but the great lords of Andalusia grew rich on the basis of these expeditions, together with the exploitation of their own lands by semi-colonial labour, that of the 'moriscos', Muslims who had stayed on in Spain. The Duke of Medina Sidonia, the Marquis of Cadiz, the Marquis of Aguilar and the Count of Cabra were all immensely wealthy. When in 1480 Queen Isabella reformed privileges that were being abused, these great lords handed over enormous sums for unpaid taxes and debts, without ruining themselves (Albuquerque paid out 1,400,000 maravedis). Contact with African gold had already led to the accumulation of treasure. The question to be asked is: how did this wealth, military and feudal by origin, relate as it did in Portugal to the calculations of merchants and financiers?

Rivalry with Portugal, which alternated between war and the demarcation of spheres of influence, came into the open in 1474 when Queen Isabella succeeded her brother Henry VI; she thereby displaced the latter's daughter, Bianca, whom the king of Portugal had been promised as a wife. Isabella, who had been married in 1469 to Ferdinand, the heir to the throne of Aragon, was destined to unite the traditions of Mediterranean Spain with the ambitions of Castile. Bianca, on the other hand, would have tied Castile to Portugal, i.e. would have united the two sets of discoveries. But, if that had happened, would America have been discovered?

After plundering Portuguese ships right up to the gates of Mina, the Spanish signed a peace treaty with Portugal in 1479, the year Ferdinand succeeded to the throne of Aragon. This treaty recognised Isabella as the Queen of Castile, and reserved Guinea and the southern Atlantic for the Portuguese. The Canary Isles (which were to be important in the history of the discoveries) remained Spanish, though to a large extent they still had to be conquered. The Portuguese had already obtained from the Pope lands 100 leagues west of the Azores, a vague allotment which would have to be reconsidered after Columbus's expedition.

The union of Castile and Aragon, the fall of Granada, the expulsion of the Jews, the Inquisition against Jewish 'converts' and the forced Christianisation of the Muslims, which all took place around the famous date of 1492, appear to bear no relation to the question of gold. They were in fact very closely related. Ferdinand of Aragon was typical of a milieu steeped in Mediterranean ways of business and political skills, and accustomed to making use of able men wherever they came from.

Ferdinand's thoughts were turned towards Italy and Africa. A Venetian counsellor by the name of Vianello first aroused his interest in the wealth of Africa. Ferdinand's counsellors, secretaries and financial advisers were Catalans, Valentians and in several cases 'converts', Jews who were all the more faithful to the King in that he protected them from the Inquisition recently established in Castile. There is a study by the Spanish historian Giménez Fernandez, of the influence of this 'Aragon faction' at the beginning of the colonisation of America. Whatever the precise situation, the man who organised the financing of Columbus's expedition was the King's Treasurer, Luis de Santagel, a 'convert' from Valencia, together with Coloma, a Catalan living in Valencia, and an Italian called Pinelo. Columbus, who came from Genoa, was presented to the Duke of Medina Sidonia by a Florentine banker. This all happened at the Santa Fé camp during the seige of Granada. Such dealings were inspired by the prospect of profit, gold and spices. But this does not mean that they were in conflict with the mystical, factual, military spirit of Isabel and the Castilians: the two elements seem to have come together quite naturally. Isabella and her confessor, Cisneros, enthused by the fall of Granada, of course hoped for a decisive victory over the forces of Islam. The first objective was once again Africa. After Isabella's death, when he was made Archbishop of Toledo, the richest see in Christendom after Rome, Cisneros personally undertook the conquest of Oran in 1509. The successes in Africa and the plans for a crusade were especially loudly acclaimed by the Cortes of Aragon, Africa and the East having always been the goal of Mediterranean Spain.

The conclusion must be that it was no accident that Christopher Columbus played the part he did. He was from Genoa. He was in touch with the Portuguese and gained experience under their patronage, even though they later rejected him. After some hesitation he was welcomed by the Mediterranean group around Ferdinand and by the monks of La Rabida; they were well informed about the Atlantic voyages, and persuaded Isabel that she could hope to evangelise far-off lands.

Columbus himself apparently had the most contradictory motives: a greed for gold and slaves, the mystique of a Christian mission, and instructions to establish political relations between the Catholic monarchs of Spain and the far-off rulers of the East. In reality, Columbus was to find something quite different from what he was looking for. But the union of Castile and Aragon and the expansion of Spain made it essential to outflank the Portuguese either to the East or to the West. The solution provided by Columbus surpassed all expectations.

7

The Spanish Discovery of Caribbean Gold

The previous chapter has outlined the basic reasons for the Spanish discoveries: the tradition of the African raids, competition with Portugal and the unification of the speculative practices of Ferdinand's Mediterranean circle with the practices of feudal conquest and holy war characteristic of Isabella and the Castilians. All these factors came together at the seige of Granada in 1492, and were intensified by the victory there. It was at this point that Columbus intervened.

(1) Christopher Columbus and the discoverers
Columbus was Genoese, and had been an agent for some well known traders, the Centurioni. He had sailed the whole of the Mediterranean, including the East, where he had encountered the challenge of Turkey. He had participated in Spanish piracy, and drew his inspiration from the Florentine, Toscanelli. Though he was a Mediterranean person, he knew all the routes around Portuguese Africa, and had obtained gold at the factories there. He married the daughter of a Madeira planter, and this, according to Chaunu, united him with a 'pre-slave economy'. His preoccupations were Portuguese: how to obtain native interpreters, as well as labour, gold and the means to build a fortress to guard it. Yet it was natural that his plan for sailing West should have been rejected by the Portuguese. Around 1485, they believed, with some justification, that they already had control of the gold routes and had almost acquired control of the spice routes. They were more advanced than Columbus, while the English and French were too backward to listen to him.

The Spanish, however, were drawn into it. On the one hand, they were persuaded, and after much hesitation, by the Franciscans of the La Rabida monastery; the latter lived facing the coast of Africa, and shared Columbus's sense of 'spiritual imperialism'. On the other hand, they were swayed by the speculative calculations of those surrounding Ferdinand, who were accustomed to voyages that were extremely risky but were equally full of promise. 1,600,000 maravedis or 14–15 kg of gold had to be found. They could only hope that more would come back. The crown of Castile advanced 1,140,000 maravedis and Columbus paid an eighth of the remaining costs. But it was Luis de Santangel, the banker Berardi and the nobility of Andalusia who raised the capital. As for supplies and men, the little port of Palos supplied two caravels, and two local families, the Pinzones and Niños, equipped them. This was no chance occurrence either. The sailors of the 'Niebla' on the Portuguese border had been privateering for gold for a long time, and as a punishment for some crime committed in the course of this activity, Palos had been ordered to provide the king with two caravels. They were the best boats and the best men for the expedition. The *Niña* and the *Pinta*, of 55–60 tons, proved themselves superior to Columbus's 130-ton vessel the Galician ship the *Santa Maria* which was shipwrecked on 24 December 1492 and did not return to Spain.

Columbus's discovery was not, then, some chance 'extra-economic' occurrence. It was the culmination of an internal development in the Western economy, which for very specific conjunctural reasons was reaching out in search of gold and spices. In this search Portugal pioneered the way, while the Spain of 1492 and its Andalusian coastal provinces were destined to carry it a stage further.

(2) Was Columbus looking for gold?

The answer to this question is definitely yes. Between 12 October 1492, when he reached the first island, and 17 January 1493, when he began the return voyage, Columbus's diary mentions gold at least 65 times. It is true that the diary has come to us only indirectly, but it has now been accepted as genuine. Its very naivety is so revealing and there is no doubt that it is dominated and obsessed by hunger for gold.

It is mistaken to ask whether this indicates unadulterated greed. The men of those times did not distinguish between the temporal and the spiritual in the way that we do, just as they did not distinguish between firm scientific observation and fantasy. It would be wrong to say that what Columbus was looking for was the way to the China of the Grand Khan, and not gold or spices. He was looking for both, just as the Portuguese were when they rounded Africa. The first question he asked on discovering the Caribbean islands was whether there was gold.

Secondly, he took note of other products (and sometimes took on cargoes of them): aloes, gum and cotton, the latter being abundant in the West Indies. He occasionally repeated as though trying to remind himself. 'I am still determined to give the letters of your Highness to the Grand Khan'. But he was obsessed by gold. As soon as he saw that the Indians did not value it very highly, and would exchange it for trinkets, he even took the trouble to convince them gold was the only thing he was interested in.

He himself did not distinguish between his evangelising missionary zeal and his other hopes. This is clear from his reasoning: the Indians are good people, and ready to become Christians, so they must be converted; through this it will be possible to earn great riches. Meanwhile, I have acquired useful information about various commercial goods (gum, cotton, aloes) and ports which might be used. If it proves possible to reach the Far East, it would be a good market for these products.

The following passage is typical: 'So your highness should resolve to make them Christians, for I believe that, if you begin, in a little while you will achieve the conversion to our holy faith of a great number of peoples, with the acquisition of great lordships and riches and all their inhabitants for Spain. For without doubt there is in these lands a very great amount of gold'.[1] This mixture of spiritual and material arguments is not peculiar to Christopher Columbus. Around 1450, a group of Barcelona merchants wrote to their king in the following manner: 'Considering how sweet is the name of peace, the fruit of it is sweeter; and it is scarce to be marvelled at, since when the Son of God came down from God the Father and was made incarnate in the virginal womb of the holy Virgin, on the day of his birth Peace was proclaimed; and once his message had been given out, he returned to God the Father and left Peace in the world. And with such peace, most excellent Lord, your subjects and vassals could gain great profits as they could engage in commerce in the lands of the Sultan, and so increase their goods and merchandise.'[2] This dual tradition was also expressed in the projected Crusade. On 26 December 1492, after his flagship had been shipwrecked, Columbus noted that the gold he was to bring had been pledged to the Crusades. The Monarchs had laughed at this promise, because they did

[1] Christopher Columbus, *The Voyages of Christopher Columbus*, London 1930, p. 173.

[2] A. de Campany, *Memorias históricas sobre la marina, comercio y artes de la antigua Ciudad de Barcelona*, Barcelona 1779–1794. vol. 2. Coleccion diplomatica, p. 275, document CLXXXII; quoted in Pierre Vilar, *La Catalogne dans l'Espagne moderne*, Paris 1962, vol. 1, p. 492.

not really believe in Columbus's gold. This may seem surprising: but some twenty years later, in 1510, the Aragonese in the Cortes of Monzon were still prepared to vote £500,000 to King Ferdinand to enable him to annex Jerusalem to the kingdom of Aragon, and to concede a monopoly of the African trade to the Catalans. Such is the complex relation between the spiritual and the material, that it would be anti-historical to separate the one from the other.

As for the material side of all this, gold was in the 15th and 16th centuries, the most lucrative as well as the most symbolic of all commodities. Columbus even accused Martin Alonso Pinzon of once having abandoned the convoy for a time, just in order to look for gold.[3] And when a number of men had to be left in a makeshift fort, as in Africa, Columbus wrote that 'many of them still wanted to know where the mine was from which the gold was taken, as much to serve your Highnesses as to please me'.

(3) Did Columbus find gold?

On his first voyage he in fact came across very little; to begin with, the instructions the Indians gave him were vague and inaccurate, or mis-understood. In Cuba gold seems to have been forgotten amidst the splendours of nature but on the Island of Hispaniola (or Santo Domingo) he found the first quantities. Columbus mentioned a 'keg' of gold and stated that 'he had found what he was looking for'. He had collected enough information, seen enough gold-bearing sands and made enough 'barterings' for a second voyage of very different scope to be decided on immediately. Instead of three small boats and 87 men, the new expedition set out with 17 ships, 14 of them caravels, and 1,500 men. From then on the search for an eastward passage and the idea of a mission can be said to have been displaced by the will to explore and to colonise.

As Pierre Chaunu has written. 'The period from January to the end of April 1494 saw the opening of a new orientation for the conquest: in January, the first expeditions from the north coast of Santo Domingo reached the area of Cibao in the interior, which the first voyage had reported as a possible source of gold. This led almost at once to an outburst of violence and was fatal in that, from the moment preparations began, the attempt to find the route which had failed and which Columbus alone had not abandoned, gave way to the prospect of gold.

[3] Columbus, op. cit. p. 179.

Gold, or rather the promise of gold, together with the certainty of success and the disappearance of danger, explain the difference in the number and choice of men for the two expeditions.'[4]

By the time of Ovando's expedition in 1502 perhaps 2,500 men and 4,000 tons of shipping were involved. It was gold which unleashed the conquest of America and ensured that it was carried out in a rushed, haphazard and dispersed manner. As on other occasions, the myth of 'El Dorado', the land of gold, played an important part.

(4) Santo Domingo, Puerto Rico, Cuba: the 'gold cycle' in the islands

The 'gold cycle' is Pierre Chaunu's term for the fairly short span of time, 1494–1525, in which the gold of the West Indies was exploited. The period began with the draining away of existing gold from the territory of the Indians, who used it not for money but for ornamentation. Chaunu estimates that in two or three years all the gold produced by the Indians of the Caribbean Islands in 1,000 years was siphoned off.[5] Once this 'collection' was over, 'river gold' or alluvial gold began to be produced. The sand had to be washed and then riddled in washing pans known as *bateas*. Forced labour, often female, was subjected to this work from dawn until dusk. It is perhaps not the most exhausting kind of work, but it destroyed the previous equilibrium of agricultural production and prevented the growing of subsistence crops; continuous work was moreover too much for the strength of the work people, who lived on the produce of a very undeveloped economy. The effects on the population were, as is well known, disastrous: the indigenous population was almost wiped out, first in Santo Domingo, then in Puerto Rico and then in Cuba. In each of these islands the 'gold cycle' was very short because it was so destructive, not of raw material, but of the labour force. There is considerable doubt about the size of the population at the time the Spaniards arrived. Modern experts (the 'Berkeley school' and Chaunu) tend to accept the very high figures advanced by Bartolomé de Las Casas, the 'Defender of the Indians': 1,100,000 inhabitants for Santo Domingo in 1492, and 10,000 in 1530; 600,000 inhabitants in Cuba, reduced to 270 households by 1570. Although one hesitates to accept these figures totally there is no doubt that the 'gold cycle' did virtually wipe out the Indian population of these islands.

[4] Pierre Chaunu, *Seville et l'Atlantique*, vol. 8, Paris 1959, p. 104.
[5] ibid. p. 510.

It is true that alluvial gold, which should have been very expensive to produce, was obtained cheaply through this process. But not for long: on the Island of Hispaniola, production began in 1494, reached a peak in 1510, fell from 1511 and ended around 1515; in Puerto Rico, it rose from 1505 to a peak between 1511 and 1515, and afterwards fell off very rapidly because of the shortage of labour and overseers; in Cuba, exploitation began only in 1511 in order to relieve the other islands, but by 1516, the Spaniards had begun to leave again, attracted by the discovery of Mexico. By 1525 there were scarcely any inhabitants left. In Jamaica no gold was discovered until about 1518, by which time the island had been almost totally depopulated by the export of labour to the other islands.

(5) Spanish imports of Caribbean gold, and the beginning of price rises

The volume of Caribbean 'production' is not known (it would be necessary to calculate the amounts acquired from 'barter' and from the production of gold nuggets). But from 1503 there are precise entries for precious metals in the records of the 'House of Commerce' (Casa de la Contratación) in Seville, through which everything was supposed to pass. Earl J. Hamilton has calculated the receipts for the following five-year periods (see graph on page 78):[6]

from 1503 to 1510	4,950 kilos of gold
from 1511 to 1520	9,153 kilos of gold
from 1521 to 1530	4,889 kilos of gold

After 1533–1535, the amount increased, reaching 42,600 kilos of precious metals for the decade 1551–1560; but silver became so important that gold made up only 15% of the value of what was coming in. To sum up: gold came in modest quantities before 1530 but it was all there was, and the greatest quantity of it arrived between 1511 and 1520. Later, silver became dominant.

Was this low-cost gold (derived from plunder, barter, and the forced search for gold nuggets) sufficient in itself to reverse the tendency for prices expressed in gold to fall? This would appear to be the case in Andalusia, where, taking the decade 1521–1530 as 100, the price indices rose from 65 in 1503 to 85 in 1519 and 122 in 1530. Unfortunately these

[6] Earl J. Hamilton, *American Treasure and the Price Revolution in Spain* (1501–1650), Cambridge (Mass.) 1934, p. 42.

price series are not completely reliable, and are often discontinuous. What is more striking is that prices of which we are more certain, in New Castile, Old Castile and Valencia, also rose in similar if not identical proportions. This indicates that a change in the direction of price movements seems to have taken place around the turn of the century, in Spain at least. The question is whether the same is true for Europe – whether the limited quantities of gold reaching Lisbon and Seville were responsible for all this, or whether, if we understand by 'conjuncture' something much more complex than price movements, far broader conditions have to be taken into account. The question is at least worth posing.

8

The Conjuncture of 1450–1530

After 1450, and especially after 1480 and the first exploration of the New World, gold was imported through Lisbon and then Seville, though it never went above 700 kilos a year for Lisbon and 1,000 for Seville. A peak was reached sometime before 1520, and between 1520 and 1530 the volume fell; after 1533–1540 large quantities of gold arrived from Peru, but these were soon swamped by the wave of silver from the mines. The question this poses is whether the influx, until 1530 almost solely of gold, really affected the conjuncture in Europe.

If 'conjuncture' is basically taken to mean 'price movements', it is undeniable that around 1500–1503 the tendency for prices to fall was reversed. But one should not rush to conclusions. The argument of this chapter is (a) that gold was not the main impetus behind the general take-off of the European economy, which had begun in the period when prices were low; (b) that the most marked effect of the influx of gold was to change price trends in the Iberian peninsula with prices in Europe changing much more slowly; and (c) that gold was no more important a factor in the 16th century transformation of trade than other products (e.g. spices), and was certainly less important than silver.

The demographic and economic revival of Europe predated the influx of gold. The great economic changes of the 16th century were not caused by the annual arrival of 1,000 or 1,500 kilos of gold on the western tip of Europe; they were the result of a long evolution in demography, agriculture, technology and industry, of the exploitation of the European silver mines, of communications, of commercial and financial techniques, and of the organisation of national economies by their rulers. These different factors will now be examined in more detail.

Demographic Expansion

There are general signs and some local evidence of a rapid recovery in

population throughout the whole of Europe between 1470 and 1520–
1530. This was obviously not caused by the influx of gold. It may,
however, have been caused by the periods of low prices in the 15th
century: in such periods traders suffer, while the mass of consumers
prosper. Fourastié, in his work on long term real prices, has calculated
on the basis of Strasbourg prices that at the end of the 15th century a
worker had to spend the wages of 60 hours' labour to purchase a
hundred-weight of wheat: after the price revolution of the 16th century
it cost him as much as 200 hours' labour.[1] Phelps Brown and Hopkins, in
their studies of the price revolution, have discovered that the purchasing
power of wages in Spain fell from an index of 126 in 1480–1490 to 80 in
1531–1540.[2] Perhaps after all, as it has long been said, the late 15th
century was indeed a golden age for workers. Much more specific
research would be necessary to prove this. But it is obvious that most
people have a better standard of living and reproduce better when prices
are low. Such periods as this, often characterised as periods of economic
decline, may actually help to prepare a later upturn in the economy by
increasing the population.

In France, population increases prepared the ground for the development of the 16th century: in the Paris area, for example, the population
of the village of Antony rose from 100 to 300 between 1470 and 1503;
in Bures-sur-Yvette, the population was completely wiped out around
1470 by war and plague, but rose to 260 by 1520; the population of
Chevreuse, which had fallen from 1,500 to 200 during the years of disaster, rose to 1,100 between 1450 and 1564; and in the same period the
population of Monthléry and Dampierre trebled, that of Marly doubled,
and at Jouy-en-Josas it increased sixteen times over. According to
Baratier, the total population of Provence trebled between 1470 and
1540.[3] After 1450 Abel notes a similar movement in Germany, and
Postan has done the same for England.[4] In Catalonia there was a rise of
20% between 1497 and 1553, which was relatively small, but the population of Castile was visibly too large from the time of the civil wars of
the late 15th century: in 1480 Isabella expelled 4,000 undesirables from
Seville; and the expulsion of the Jews and Moors, as well as emigration,
were at first welcomed in Castile as giving some relief. These data presage

[1] Jean Fourastié, L'Evolution des prix à long terme, Paris 1969, p. 89.
[2] E. H. Phelps Brown and S. V. Hopkins, 'Builders' wage rates, Prices and Population:
some further evidence', Economica, 1959.
[3] Edouard Baratier, La Demographie provençale du XIIIe au XVIe siècle, Paris 1961.
[4] Wilhelm Abel, Agrarkrisen und Agrarkonjunktur, Hamburg and Berlin, 1966, pp. 92–96.

a century of expansion as much as do the figures for gold imports.

Changes in Agriculture

Coming as it did before the price rises, the population appears initially to have increased less than the production of foodstuffs. This latter development was due to renewed cultivation of good lands which had been abandoned; and an improved organisation of cultivation. There were, in fact, two phases of rent movements. One favoured the peasant tenantry, and lasted as long as there were few of them and plenty of land available. Then came a phase favouring the landowners, now that there were more prospective tenants; only poorer lands were left, and rents rose all the time. The transition between the two phases came around 1525; and this process via the effects of agricultural prices was rather more important for the 'conjuncture' than was the influx of gold.

Industry and Technology

Bertrand Gille has written that 'in the late 15th and early 16th centuries, an astonishing economic expansion, sustained by technology, took place in France. . . .'[5] The 'milling fever' of the Franche-Comté has been well described by Lucien Febvre and that of the Ile-de-France by Yvonne Bézard.[6] The blast furnace was introduced around 1535, in both France and England. The metallurgical and glass-making industries of Lorraine began to grow. The printing press caused a sharp fall in the market value of books. According to one American study there were more inventions in the 15th than in the 18th century.[7] Technological change may have been due to falling prices, since the small profit margin would tend to sharpen mens' wits, and it may itself have contributed further to the fall. As has already been said, this fall acted as a stimulus to the search for gold and silver and the development of new techniques of processing these metals.

Technique for Producing Gold and Silver

While the gold was sought out in distant lands, silver was found in the mines of Europe. In 1451 the Duke of Saxony gave instructions for the use of a lead amalgamation process that separated silver from copper

[5] Bertrand Gille, *Les Origines de la grande industrie métallurgique en France*, Paris 1947, p. 7. See also his *Les ingénieurs de la Renaissance*, Paris 1964.

[6] Lucien Febvre, *Philippe II et la Franche-Comté*, Paris 1912, pp. 103, 193ff; Yvonne Bézard, *La vie rurale dans le sud de la region parisienne de 1450 à 1560*, Paris 1929, pp. 172–178.

[7] For the latest research on the technology of the 15th century, cf. *Historie générale des techniques*, Paris 1965, vol. 2, especially the introduction by Maurice Dumas.

more easily. At this time there was not a mine in Europe which produced more than 10,000 marks of silver per year (1 mark is approximately equal to 230 grammes). Eighty years later, in 1530, eight mines were producing more than 50,000 marks a year. Yet this expansion had begun in the 15th century: Scheenberg, which in 1450 was producing some few hundred marks, produced 31,000 in 1470–1476; Schwats produced 14,000 marks from 1470–1474, and 45,000 in 1485–1489. This was the 'second age' of German mining. Under the direction of German technicians, prospecting was carried out in the Tyrol, Hungary, Bohemia, Silesia, Alsace and Saxony; and between 1510–1520 there appeared the first 'talers' (from *Joachimstalers*, the coins from Joachimstal in Bohemia); this was the origin of the famous Austrian 'taler' from which the word dollar is derived. Minting of coin began in the Tyrol in 1485, in Saxony in 1500, in Bohemia in 1518 and in Austria in 1524. In other words silver was as actively sought after as gold, but in different places and with quite different methods.

The ratio of the prices of silver and gold ('the bi-metallic ratio') obviously changed according to the success of one kind of exploration or the other.[8] To know exactly how the respective cost prices of gold and silver affected the movement of prices in general it would be necessary to establish parallel series of nominal silver and gold prices for all areas of Europe (as E. J. Hamilton has done for Valencia and Aragon). Soetbeer, the first historian of gold and silver to put forward figures for production, thought that silver production for the period 1493–1520 was around 47,000 kilos per year, and gold production around 5,800 kilos; the value of the silver produced was half that of gold.[9] But these estimates are very high, at least for gold. The essential point is that gold was not the only factor in the process. The period of low commodity prices encouraged both the growth of European mining and the Iberian discoveries; and central European silver, after helping to create the Fuggers' fortunes, continued to be good business at least until the mid-16th century.

---

[8] Frank Spooner, op. cit. I disagree with Spooner on the period 1450–1530; it was not a period of abundant gold and of high silver prices, but one in which gold as well as silver was expensive relative to commodities. This is why they were both in demand. The favourable position of the one metal vis-à-vis the other did however vary, depending on the place and time: the Iberian part of the Mediterranean was a gold area; central Europe was a silver one; and Venice was somewhere in between.

[9] Adolf Soetbeer, *Edelmetallproduktion und Wertverhältuis zwischen Gold und Silber seit der Entdeckung Amerikas bis zur Gegenwart*, Gotha 1879.

Financial, Monetary and Commercial Techniques

The 'age of the Fuggers' (the title of Ehrenberg's famous work) was not so much the 16th century as the period 1470 to 1550. Raymond de Roover[10] has shown that the Middle Ages had made great advances, in exchange and credit techniques, which were developed further in the 15th century; the use of bills of exchange as a means of credit, and payment by balancing credits and debts in simple account books, economised on costly transfers of actual money and so served to provide what is nowadays called 'book money'. The documents of the house of Datini in Prato and de Roover's studies of Bruges and the Medici bank in Florence suggest that a great deal of exchange could have taken place with only relatively small movements of actual gold being necessary. By 1450–1470 the geography of the centres of exchange (Italy, Spain and Flanders) was largely the same as that of the 16th century.

The development of the fairs contributed to this. The fairs of the 16th century grew in the previous century; the Lyons fair had been started then by the kings of France; Medina del Campo was established by royal decrees in 1421 and 1439, and reorganised in 1483; it was followed by Villalón and Medina de Rioseco in 1493, and obviously preceded the discovery of America.

Internal and External Trade and the Communications Network

If Spain had such fairs before the discovery of America, it was because her production and internal communications were already developing. The production and sale of merino wool were based on a sheepfarmers' association, the *mesta*, whose flocks migrated seasonally across Spain from north to south and thereby contributed to the links between Cantabria and Andalusia; they supplied wool for luxury cloth made in Segovia, while still more was exported to France (La Rochelle), Flanders (Bruges) and England. Each year fleets were formed in the ports of Cantabria (Laredo) or the Basque country (Bilbao) for the transportation of this wool. Institutions known as *consulados* were established for selling and dealing in wool (in Burgos in 1494, and in Bilbao in 1511); the Spanish dealers had branches in Nantes, Saint-Malo, Bruges, and Hamburg. Payment was made at the fair of Medina del Campo, under the control of agents of the *consulados*. As the system of fleets for the expeditions to the Indies and the House of Trade in Seville were modelled on the wool trade corporations, it may therefore be concluded

---

[10] Raymond de Roover, *L'évolution de la lettre de change*, Paris 1953.

that colonial trade and the import of gold followed already existing practices, and not the other way round. Land communications also developed around 1500: in 1494, a 'Roads Commission' for the difficult routes of Castile was established; and the first royal contract for regular mail services was signed in 1505 between Philip I and the Taxi family of Milan; in 1551 they became postmasters to the Emperor Charles V.

The Emergence of National Economies

These too developed in the 15th century. The Burgundian monarchs, Maximilian and then Philip, adopted 'mercantilist' policies, as did Louis XI of France, Henry VII of England and the Catholic Monarchs of Spain. The latter issued proper 'navigation acts' restricting maritime trade to the Spanish fleet; and the measures issued by Ferdinand in 1511 in Seville included one hundred and eleven articles relating to textiles.

It must be concluded that if there was an 'economic revolution' of some kind in the 16th century, it cannot be put down to gold, which appeared at a very late stage. Nonetheless the importing of African and American gold through Lisbon and later Seville *did* provide a new stimulus; it provoked a trade revival and a rise in prices which then encouraged business. The reason gold is useful and perhaps necessary in international trade is that, even though all transactions may be carried out by book payments, at a certain point there is a balance to be paid, and the country to which it is due will insist on collecting it in internationally valid currency. Kings in particular may resort to accumulating loans at ever higher rates of interest, but when the date of repayment can no longer be delayed they have to pay them off in actual gold or silver.

To take one example, there is the famous 1519 election to the throne of the Holy Roman Empire of Germany. This was contested by both Charles I of Spain and Francis I of France,[11] the issue being purely and simply who could pay the electors. The Hamburg and Augsburg bankers cut off credit to Francis I, who had to pay in gold; but the Fuggers raised bonds redeemable after the election, to the value of 850,000 florins. That is why when Charles I became Emperor he was up to the eyes in debt. The Spanish kings were destined never to escape from it. At this time (1515–1520) they had a good security to offer: the gold of the Americas. But the gold was already be-spoke before it arrived. Though a few years between 1521 and 1525 are missing from Hamilton's figures,[12]

---

[11] cf. the account by Henri Hauser in *Peuples et Civilisations*, vol. 8, pp. 98–9.
[12] Hamilton, *The Price Revolution*, p. 35; see also below pp. 103–104.

this may be because fear of royal greed prevented the 'House of Trade' from keeping proper accounts. The lists of receipts are also defective because of corruption. The amount of gold obtained in America (through plunder, barter and the search for nuggets) differed from the amount reaching Spain and Europe. It is difficult to estimate the exact difference, and equally there is no hope of establishing a statistical, numerical or 'econometric' relationship between the production of American gold, on the one hand (or even the receipts in Seville), and circulating currency and price rises, on the other. They are nonetheless inseparable, and we must therefore give some attention to the relationship between them.

9

The Beginnings of the Price Revolution

The answer given here to the question of whether the discoveries and the influx of gold, imported by the Portuguese and Spanish, were what made the 16th century such a dynamic period in Europe, is that at least in the second half of the 15th century there had already been profound changes in population, agriculture, technology, mining, trade, finance and politics. These changes undoubtedly shaped the future far more than the modest quantities of gold which reached Lisbon and Seville up to the period 1530–1540. Nonetheless, the 'treasure', American and African gold, did cause a fall in the value of gold relative to other commodities, that is, a rise in 'general prices'. This 'price revolution' was undoubtedly a very important development. Yet its meaning has been much disputed. This was true during the 16th century itself, with the debate between Jean Bodin and de Malestroict, and the writings of the Spanish theologians; later, in the 18th century with Montesquieu, Cantillon and Hume; and even down to modern times.

The issues of debate are, or should be: (a) the rate of the 'price revolution' (whether it was fast or slow, strong or weak); (b) its extent (where it occurred first and where later); and (c) its causes: there is no doubt that the influx of gold and silver and the increase in prices were related but the problem is the nature of the relationship – whether it was automatic, proportional, or unilateral. The mechanism of rising prices needs reconstructing.

(1) Handling the Evidence

E. J. Hamilton set himself the task of testing the hypothesis known as the 'quantitative theory of money', the theory that the more money there is the higher prices rise;[1] the more the stock of gold is increased,

[1] Hamilton, op. cit. p. 4.

the greater is inflation. To do this he drew up a graph, that has been reproduced on many occasions.[2] The price curve (which had to be filled in because of gaps in the figures) seems to a surprising degree to correspond to the curve for incoming precious metals. Prices generally rose quickly after increases in gold imports. When, after 1600, such imports fell off, prices sometimes fell and sometimes stabilised, but they did not in any case increase. The conclusion that has been drawn is that: 'There is no doubt about the effect of the import of gold and silver from the New World. The curve for the imports of gold and silver from America and the curve of prices throughout the 16th century coincide so closely that they seem physically bound together. The governing factor was the increase in the stock of gold and silver.'[3]

This may be so, but there is an ambiguity about what is meant by prices and stock. Hamilton gives *Spanish* prices and imports *into Spain*. The price revolution occured in *Europe* as a whole. If all the gold and silver reaching Spain remained there, the correlation between the prices and the stock of precious metals would not hold for the rest of Europe; but if they did not stay there, how can we speak of 'Spanish' stocks? A further objection is that the increase in European prices has never really been measured. Each country reacted in a different way. Moreover, though in many places rising prices stimulated economic activity, the Spanish economy, the one most closely affected by price increases, was in the long run retarded. Hamilton's graph therefore cannot provide a simple answer to the question.

François Simiand has also remarked that it is not imports that should be taken, but the growth of stock, that is to say, the stock at the beginning of a given period, plus imports and minus exports. The problem is that the latter are often unknown. Whatever the situation, the 'quantitative theory of money' should never be expressed in the simplistic way it was employed by Montesquieu, when he said that when the quantity of gold and silver doubled in the 16th century, prices did so too. In fact, the circulation of metal coin in the 16th century increased perhaps eight or ten-fold, while in Seville, the city which experienced the 'price revolution' most intensely, prices only went up four-fold. As well as estimating the mass of metal at any given time it is also necessary to calculate the mass of commodities exchanged, the number of exchanges using metal coin (the velocity of circulation), and the

[2] ibid. p. 301.
[3] Fernand Braudel, *La Méditerranée et le Monde méditerranéen à l'époque de Philippe II*, Paris 1949, p. 400.

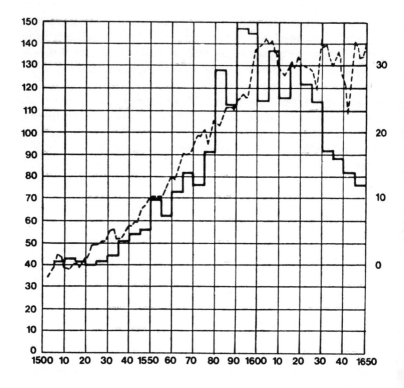

Figure 2. Spanish imports of precious metals and price movements in Spain, (1500–1650) (from Hamilton).

———— Imports of precious metals at Seville, in millions of pesos per five year period (taking gold and silver together, and expressed in pesos of 450 maravedis).

------ Combined index of all kinds of prices for four regions of Spain='general prices' (reduced to silver content). Arithmetical scale expressing absolute values.

existence of monetary practices not dependant on coin (book payments and bills of exchange).

In attacking Hume and the 'quantitative theory of money' Marx stressed two further points.[4] (a) In the 16th century, most of European society lived outside the commercial circuit where capitalist motives were dominant (this is the circuit of 'Money-Commodity-Money' where money is the object and the commodity the means, while in pre-capitalist society, money is only an intermediary and the commodity is the object, the circuit being here 'Commodity-Money-Commodity'). Under such conditions, the relationship between precious metals and prices was confined to the circuit of large-scale trade, which was still not predominant. (b) Since the value of gold (or silver) depended on its production costs, falling costs, not simply the availability of greater quantities, were a basic cause of price rises for other commodities. The first place to examine the phenomenon, therefore, is where commodities encountered the precious metals *as a commodity*, that is, in the West Indies where it was produced; and secondly, in Seville, where European commodities were exchanged for it. Seville, seen as part of the commercial circuit of the Indies, is the best place to study the origins of price rises.

(2) Inflation and price movements in Spain

Tomás de Mercado, the Spanish theologian, priest, and author of a *summa* on the legitimacy and illegitimacy of different kinds of business, wrote: 'I have seen a situation in which velvet is selling in Granada for 28 or 29 reals, and a fool from the *gradas* then comes along and starts to barter and buy so recklessly for the cargo of a caravel that in a fortnight he has sent the price up to 35 or 36 reals. So the merchants and weavers of course keep it at this high price, and sell the velvet at this price to the people of the city. . . .'[5]

This account is a late one (1569), but it applies to the whole period under consideration. The *gradas* were the flights of steps around the cathedral of Seville, near the 'House of Trade', where cargoes for the caravels were purchased. The need to obtain these cargoes quickly, and the certainty that the merchandise could be exchanged in the Indies for large quantities of gold, sent prices up. Mercado writes that when a man left for the Indies 'his heart was so filled with generosity that he would

---

[4] Karl Marx, *A Contribution to the Critique of Political Economy*, Chicago 1904, pp. 219ff.
[5] Tomás de Mercado, *Summa de tratos y contratos*, Seville 1571, folio 90.

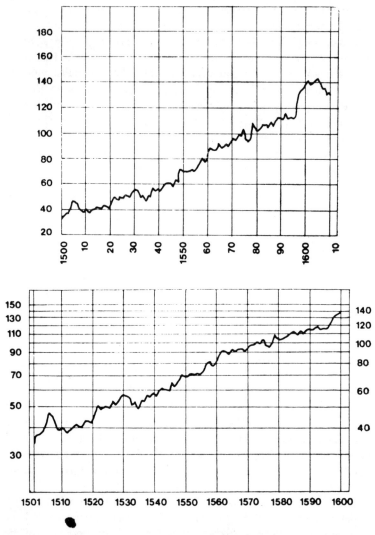

Figure 3. Price movements in Spain. Nominal prices. Index: 1571–1583 = 100. *Above:* arithmetical scale (Hamilton). *Below:* logarithmic series (Nadal).

NB. The second graph shows that the *relative* movement of prices was much stronger at the beginning of the century.

pay as many reals as he would normally give maravedis, i.e., forty-four times as much. No one is a prophet in his own country, Mercado writes; so the gold produced in the Indies was not given its proper value there. What he unwittingly demonstrates is the fact that precious metal cost the Spanish who lived in the Indies so little that they were happy to pay for the European merchandise they needed with large quantities of coin. In the Indies gold was cheap and commodities scarce. In Seville, the volume of commodities rose and yet prices did so too. This occurred right from the start, indeed it was especially so then, because that was when plunder, barter and the search for gold nuggets provided gold at its cheapest, while in the Indies European commodities were still very scarce.

Hamilton called one of his chapters: 'The Price Revolution Begins, 1501–1550' and 'The Price Revolution Culminates, 1551–1600'. This might suggest that prices rose more rapidly after 1550 than before. In fact, the 'price revolution' reached its zenith in 1600 and after that prices tended to fall. But the fastest rise took place before 1550. This at least is clear from the work of Jorge Nadal,[6] who, instead of measuring absolute price increases like Hamilton, advances two ways of measuring the relative increase.

The first, classical way involves replacing the graph of the arithmetical series (like the one on p. 78) with a graph of a logarithmic series, so that instead of showing increases from 1 to 2, 2 to 4, 4 to 8, 40 to 80, or 400 to 800, by respective increases of 1 mm, 2 mm, 4 mm, 40 mm, 80 mm, or 400 mm – the absolute values – all such increases are indicated by the same relative increase, i.e. by a doubling of the amount. The logarithmic method is better for showing price increases, as there is a difference for a shopper in seeing the price of bread rise from 15 pence to 30 pence and seeing it rise from 60 pence to 75 pence (even though in both cases the increase is by 15 pence). It would be the same if the price rose from 60 pence to £1.20. In both cases the price would then have doubled. Drawing up such a graph for prices in Spain (opposite), it becomes apparent that the rises which occurred early in the century, influenced by a slight, but unexpected and cheap, supply of gold, were sharper than the rises later in the century which resulted from an enormous influx of silver. This shows that the gold from the Caribbean had a very strong impact.

The second method confirms this. It involves a mobile scale of com-

---

[6] Jorge Nadal, 'La revolución de los precios españoles en el siglo XVI. Estado actual de la cuestion', in *Hispania*, 1959.

parison showing the percentage increase of one five year period over another. The figures are as follows:

1506–1510	16%	1556–1560	10%
1511–1515	—8%	1561–1565	15%
1516–1520	5%	1566–1570	1%
1521–1525	17%	1571–1575	8%
1526–1530	7%	1576–1580	0%
1531–1535	0%	1581–1585	9%
1536–1540	4%	1586–1590	2%
1541–1545	6%	1591–1595	3%
1546–1550	12%	1596–1600	12%
1551–1555	6%		

The 16th century therefore experienced only one fall, and that was between 1511 and 1515; and two periods of stability (between 1526–1530 and 1531–1535; and 1576–1580 and 1571–1575). The highest increases – 16 and 17% – came between the periods 1501–1505 and 1506–1510 and from 1516–1520 to 1521–1525; and there was a fall in the rate of the increase from 1556. It never again reached 12% until the last years of the century and only then because there was a notoriously bad famine in 1599–1600.

In the 'years of gold', 1501–1530, the increase was strong but irregular. This was because it was still largely a result of bad harvests in Castile: for example, in 1506 and 1507, the price of wheat rose by 96% above the average for the previous 5 years in New Castile; rye rose by over 100%. This occurred again in 1521–1522 and again in 1530. However, it is a surprising fact that while the increase of 1506–1507 was followed by a fall, as was normal after a famine, there was no absolute fall in the years after 1522 and after 1530, and this was due to the scarcity of grain. Prices in general remained high, even after good harvests. The period of long-term increases had begun.

In Andalusia, although there is no continuous information about grain prices we do know that ships' biscuits rose in price by 178% between 1505 and 1507. This record increase was due to two factors: the scarcity of grain was obviously the first, and the other was the urgent demand from American expeditions. According to Chaunu's studies (which are based on the tonnage of ships leaving Seville for America), neither famine nor plague could usually hold back these colonial expeditions, and they were only affected once, in 1509, by the plague. This indicates that in Andalusia the climatic crises characteristic of the old agrarian economies combined with the demand for ships' cargoes to produce price movements that were extremely irregular but which were inexorably in an upward direction.

10

The Price Revolution and the Channels of Trade

To understand the importance of the discovery of the West Indies and of the first shipments of gold, it is necessary to look at the places the gold first came to, where it encountered the commodities for which it was exchanged, and how its value was established. Most of it arrived at the port of Seville, where the caravels were unloaded and their cargoes registered, where incoming gold was processed by the 'House of Trade', and where prices and contracts were negotiated on the steps of the cathedral. There is a very informative account of this by Tomás de Mercado in which he says that Seville, and with it the whole Atlantic coast of Spain, had been transformed from being the most remote part of the world into being its very centre. This was true economically, and even politically, during the whole of the 16th century.[1]

Just as in the previous chapter we looked at the basic way in which prices increased, i.e. at the man in a hurry to buy a cargo to fill a caravel, so it is necessary here to find out how such increases spread. This could only occur through the trading channels and the manner in which they were organised, whether spontaneously or deliberately. This is the next point to be examined.

(1) The Origins of Spanish-American trade

Around 1930, the economic historian André-E. Sayous published some interesting work on the origins of trade with the West Indies.[2] This work is still of interest (pending the publication of the work of the German scholar Otte, at present researching in Seville),[3] because together with Hamilton's and Chaunu's great work in statistics, it offers the possibility of understanding the basic mechanisms of the Seville trade. Such 'microeconomic' research is needed to complete our overall

[1] Tomás de Mercado, *Summa de tratos y contratos*, Seville 1571.
[2] André-E. Sayous has only published articles and these have not been brought together;

knowledge, to show how the expeditions were financed, how the capital was repaid (or how it was meant to be repaid), and who the men were who handled it. These details are to be discovered in legal archives. Unfortunately, the material which Sayous saw in these archives was imperfect. Even so, the documents involved enabled him to evaluate the kind of business they represented. As a specialist in the commercial practices of the Mediterranean in the Middle Ages, he was then able to analyse how these methods were modified for use in the Spanish-American trade.

Business in Seville
Seville's exports were varied and unexceptional, and did not initially show any signs of specialisation. The products mentioned include flour, oil, rye, vinegar, salted pork, biscuits, honey, some spices, silks, serges, velvet, shirts, clothing, sandals, hats, gloves, ironmongery, soap and glassware. Anyone could sell such articles, but the problem was to ship them and be able to wait for payment. This was a very slow and risky process, and was still not done in coin but in ingots, since at the beginning there was no minting in the Indies. A very large number of sellers might benefit from price increases but the trade itself had to be financed by capitalists who could afford to arrange credit and to wait.

The ship owners of the 16th century were brave men and good sailors, but they were not able to finance the expeditions themselves. The capital was frequently provided by a Genoese, while the ship owner was an Andalusian and the 'factor', the merchant who took the risk of going to the Indies, would come from Castile. Sayous mentions dozens of Genoese names including all the great families of Genoa commerce – Centurione, Doria and Spínola. These men took 'shares' in the ships and gave 'maritime loans', which were repayable not in America, but on the return of the ship to Spain itself. The risk of loss justified the very high

the *Bibliothèque Nationale* in Paris has only a partial collection. The main ones are available in photocopy form at the *Institut d'Histoire Economique et Sociale* and discuss the following: the systems of payment between Spain and America; monetary circulation in America; the financing of the expeditions in the form of partnerships (ships being financed through being divided into shares); the role of the Genoese in Seville at the beginning of the 16th century; the exchanges between Spain and America; and the theory of exchange in Tomás de Mercado. The author's main conclusions can be found in 'Les débuts du commerce de l'Espagne avec l'Amerique', *Revue Historique*, II, 1934, pp. 185–215. There also exists an excellent book on various aspects of the peninsula's economy under Charles V, Ramón Carande, *Carlos V y sus banqueros*, 3 vols, Madrid 1943, 1949, 1967.

[3] Heinrich Otte's researches are based on the financial archives and the records of ships' cargoes. No general work of his has yet been published.

rates of interest, but the need for funds among the Spanish navigators also played its part.

It would, however, be wrong to imagine that no Spaniards were involved in this kind of speculation. The historian Giménez Fernandez[4] has described the different contributions made by the 'Aragon party' around Ferdinand, and the evangelising mission of some ecclesiastics (see above). Archbishop Fonseca, the organiser of the colonisation of the Indies, and an opponent of Christopher Columbus, openly favoured such speculation, especially as a means of financing expeditions by companies of *conquistadores*. When there were protests, and ecclesiastical sanctions were threatened because of the enormous interest rates masquerading as 'exchange', these were silenced, with the excuse that 'everyone was doing it', that it was 'of great importance for the Indies trade' and that any sanction could result in 'universal evil'.

This shows the extent of the interest in speculation, which far surpassed the extent of the business itself, and this also explains why the price increases came so early and so quickly.

The Repercussions in Andalusia and Castile

By comparing prices quoted by Hamilton, Carande has shown that between 1511–1531, the increase in prices in Andalusia depended largely on the extent of demand for exports to the Indies; the product most sought after was wine, followed by oil and then flour. Taking 1511 prices as the bases, he obtains the following indices:[5]

	Oil	Wine	Wheat
1511	100	100	100
1513	106.25	100	105
1530	212.50	425	273.30
1539	297.50	350	264.40

It would appear, then, that this increase especially favoured cultivation of vines and olives; it may even have been in this period that the great

---

[4] Manuel Giménez Fernández, *Bartolomé de las Casas, vol. 1: Delegado de Cisneros para la reformacion de las Indias, 1516–1517*, Seville 1953, and vol. 2: *Politica inicial de Carlos I en las Indias*, Seville 1959.

[5] Carande, op. cit. vol. 1, p. 83.

vineyards around Jerez and the great olive groves of Jaén, which resemble colonial plantations, were created. A possible objection to this is that wine was also sold to Flanders and to England; but this is explicable by another, more complex, possibility, namely that English and Flemish merchandise was sold in the Indies at a profit which itself was used to buy wine. This was the period in which price increases had a creative and stimulating effect; and this was true for the Granada silk industry, for the leather and arms industries of Toledo and for the production of soap and gloves in Ocaña. Castile also sold more: its products were drawn to the Indies, and its prices therefore rose, even though in all this it was some way behind Andalusia. An indication is that the network of roads and bridges was improved to facilitate trade.

Effects in the Rest of Spain
Around 1520, there were attempts to involve various Spanish ports (in Cantabria and on the Mediterranean coast) in the American trade. But most of the petitions were refused and those granted quickly withdrawn, both because Seville defended her own monopoly, and because fiscal control over the import of gold and silver made it necessary to have a single port and organised 'fleets'. It is not true however, as has sometimes been suggested, that Castile monopolised trade with the Indies, in so far as many foreigners (such as the Welsers) were granted privileges, and even monopolies, and also because in the legal documents there are 'company' contracts made by non-Castilians (such as Catalans) for sending 'factors' to the Indies to sell the products of a particular manufacturer. Anyone who had commodities to sell could send them to the fair at Medina del Campo, and from there they would be sent on either to Seville and the Spanish Indies, or to Lisbon and the Portuguese Indies.

There are two documents which show that this trade was important for the provinces furthest away from the Atlantic. In 1521, the city of Barcelona refused to join the revolt of the cities of Castile against Charles IV; but they did not imprison emissaries of these cities because they did not want to prejudice their business in Castile. In Valladolid, it was said, 'many natives of this city (Barcelona) customarily reside to receive and to sell cloth and other merchandise', as they also did in Medina del Campo, 'to remit money exchanged here for these fairs, since this is the safest business to be found in these times'.[6]

[6] *Archivo historico de la ciudad de Barcelona* (AHB), sealed letters, 1521–1522, fo 32 ro-vo; quoted in Vilar, op. cit. vol. 1, p. 530, n. 5.

Later, in 1553, it was affirmed that: 'Every year a great quantity of cloth goes to the above-mentioned kingdom of Castile, from the principality of Catalonia and the counties of Roussillon and Cerdagne, and most of it is bought by Portuguese and other persons to be imported into Portugal and the Indies, to your Majesty's Indies as well as the Portuguese Indies, the Canary Isles and other places. The proportion of the above mentioned cloth exported in this way from the kingdom of Castile is so great that of four rolls of cloth taken in this way from our country to that one, three followed this route (to the Indies) and only one remained in Castile.'[7]

The effects of the commercial circuit Indies–Seville/Lisbon–Medino del Campo reached afar to Barcelona and Perpignan. The whole of Spain thereby underwent price rises in the first half of the 16th century. It was because of the high prices that the textiles produced on the shores of the Mediterranean were taken by the difficult routes through Aragon and Castile to the fair of Medina, and it was in this period that fairs developed near Medino del Campo, in Vallalón and Medina de Rioseco, clear indications that the first alone was insufficient.

(2) Gold and silver's role in European price increases

The question to be answered now is whether the arrival of gold and silver in Seville, which as we have just seen contributed to the price increase and the development of trade in Spain itself, also affected Europe – and if so, how and when.

The problem is, for various reasons, a complex one. Factors other than American gold or silver (and German silver before the influx from America), may have increased prices in Europe independently. Secondly, increases were not apparent in all countries, and were, above all, uneven. Finally, as many countries had 'manipulated' their internal currency in the first half of the 16th century (reducing its gold and silver content, minting low carat coin, or increasing the nominal value of existing currency), it is difficult to know whether price increases were caused by manipulation of this kind or by American gold. In England, for example, the falling prices characteristic of the 15th century seem to have been arrested by 1480. By contrast, in Italy, it has been possible to talk of the 'so-called' price revolution, and prices there did not begin to rise before 1552. Lastly, in France there has been a dispute since the 16th century itself, about whether rising prices were due to the fact that coin contained less precious metal (in other words, whether 'silver prices', if defined by

---

[7] AHB, sealed letters, 1553, folios 186–189; quoted in Vilar, op. cit. vol. 1, p. 544.

the actual silver content, actually rose at all).

Around 1566, the theory that prices in terms of silver content had not risen, was put forward by de Malestroict, the king's counsellor and master of the accounts. De Malestroict provided a familiar description of rising prices: 'the extraordinary rise in prices which we see today in everything', so that 'each person, whether he is important or not, should feel the increase in his pocket'.[8] He believed this was because the official currency – the livre – contained less silver in 1566 than in the 15th century and, with more justice, than in the time of King John or King St. Louis. The kings had constantly debased the currency with the result that if more livres were paid for something, the amount of gold and silver contained in the coins was the same as before.

The theory was, on the surface of it, correct, since the coinage had been frequently debased and, in the 16th century alone, the official silver content of the livre tournois fell from 17.96 grammes in 1513 to 14.27 grammes in 1561. Malestroict provided concrete data and made the distinction between prices in years of bad harvests and 'common' prices i.e. averages over several years. He was a perceptive observer, who knew that an increase in nominal prices, though it did not mean an increase in silver value, ruined people on fixed incomes which were expressed in the nominal currency (in this case, the livre tournois).

Malestroict was nonetheless wrong and his short book would undoubtedly have been forgotten were it not that Jean Bodin, one of the best minds of the late 16th century, and author of the *Six Books of the Commonwealth* and major works on historical method, published a *Response to Malestroict* in 1568, to show where the other was wrong about money.[9] Bodin's critique of Malestroict was humanistic, critical and erudite, both on the subject of prices, which he used as an example, and in its propositions about the nature of money. He showed that in France the price of land appeared to have trebled in 50 years, whilst the silver content of the currency had not fallen by the same proportions. He brought in examples from ancient history, and said that if prices had risen it was because there was more gold and silver in circulation. Later, in Chapter 19, I shall show that his analysis was quite complex and sophisticated. What interests us at this stage is how he dated and explained the rise in prices.

[8] Jean Bodin, *The Response of Jean Bodin to the Paradoxes of Malestroit, and the Paradoxes*, Washington 1946, p. 3.

[9] ibid.

Bullion and Portuguese Commerce

The views of Jean Bodin, partly expressed in the 1568 edition of the *Response to Malestroict*, partly added to the 1578 edition, illustrate how the men of the last third of the century understood the origins of the great price rises. This should facilitate our own search for these origins. Bodin knows that high prices are related to the increase in trading activity and he does not argue that they are the result only of an abundance of gold and silver; in fact, he takes the starting point of French prosperity to be the end of the Hundred Years' War ('it is a hundred and twenty years since we drove out the English', he says) and he lays emphasis on the resultant rise in population and the agricultural expansion. This confirms what was said above about the need to look in the 15th century for the early demographic and agricultural origins of 16th century prosperity.

He also observes, however, that this expansion coincided with the Portuguese discoveries: '. . . the Portuguese, sailing the high seas with the compass, has been made master of the Persian Gulf and, in part, of the Red Sea, and by this means has filled his vessels with the wealth of the Indies and of Arabian luxuriance, thereby taking the place of the Venetians and Genoese, who were taking the merchandise from Egypt and Syria, whither it had been brought by the caravans of the Arabs and Persians, to sell it to us retail, and at the weight of gold.'[1]

Bodin, then, considered that the most important component of the Portuguese discoveries was their capture of the Levant trade in the precious products. He attributes more importance to the spice trade than to Mina gold, and he goes on to show the importance of the Spanish discoveries: 'And at the same time the Castilian, having placed under his power the new lands full of gold and silver, has replenished Spain

[1] Bodin, op. cit. p. 28.

with them.'[2]

In the 1578 edition (and in *The Commonwealth*) Bodin gives further details: 'It is unbelievable, but nevertheless true, that since 1533 there has come from Peru, which was conquered by Pizarro and his men, more than a hundred millions of gold, and two times as much of silver. The ransom of King Atahualpa was reported to amount to 1,326,000 bezans of gold.'[3]

These figures appear to be genuine, and it was in Peru itself that high prices began: 'In Peru at that time cloth breeches cost 300 ducats; a cloak, 1,000 ducats; a good horse, four or five thousand; a bottle of wine, 200 ducats.'[4]

These figures, which are taken from contemporary accounts of the Indies, show that the places where gold was produced (or seized) were the very places that the price rises began. The transmission of these rising prices through Spain is then described in the following way: 'Thus it is that Spain, that holds onto life only because of France, being constrained by unavoidable force, to take from here grains, cloths, linens, crayons, tanners' sumach, paper, books, indeed woodwork and all hand-work went to find for us gold, silver and spices at the ends of the earth.'[5]

Although Bodin exaggerates the degree of Spanish dependence on imports from France, the exchange of precious goods for ordinary products is what caused the prices of the latter to rise. A geographical differentiation in prices was thereby created, and French labour was attracted by the high wages paid in Spain. '. . . everything is dearer in Spain and in Italy than in France and higher in Spain than in Italy. Likewise service and handwork is higher, the thing that attracts our Auvergnians and Limousins into Spain, as I have learned from them themselves, because they get triple what they make in France. For Spain is rich, haughty and indolent, sells its labour very dearly, as Clenard indicates, who puts in his letters in the chapter on expenses, in one article only, namely to get saved in Portugal, fifteen ducats per year. . . . It is therefore the abundance of gold and silver that causes, in part, the dearness of things.'[6]

Note that he is cautious and says: 'in part'. But all this together does

[2] loc. cit.
[3] loc. cit.
[4] loc. cit.
[5] ibid. p. 29.
[6] ibid. pp. 31–32.

clarify some important points: (a) there was a hierarchy of high prices with Peru foremost, then Spain, then Italy, the financial centre, and lastly France, the exporter; (b) the flow of trade resulted from this: commodities went from Europe to Spain, and from Spain to America; gold and silver went from America to Spain, and from Spain to France and other parts of Europe, often via Italy; (c) Spanish 'wealth' created both a demographic flow from France to Spain (one of labourers) and a monetary flow from Spain to France (a transfer of wages); (d) the chronology which is indicated is also interesting: the key date for Spanish precious metals is apparently the discovery of the 'treasures' of Peru by Pizarro in 1533; but the reference to Clénard's letters, which were written in 1530, shows that life in Portugal was already considered particularly dear; it cost six times as much to go to the barber's there as in France.

What apparently happened in France in the first third of the century was that after 1500 prices stabilised and rose markedly from 1524; but they did not rise faster than the rate at which the livre was being devalued relative to silver until the middle of the century. The recently published lists of Paris grain prices confirm that it was not until the grain crisis of 1545 that the increases began to affect people (according to the documents of the lawyer Du Moulin).[7] By 1530, however, it was well known that in Spain and Portugal gold and silver were abundant, and that, although life was expensive, good wages could be earned.

What happened after the years 1530–1533 will be dealt with below, but before moving on to the mines and treasures of Peru, we must finish the discussion of Portugal. Portugal, the first country to discover gold, was by 1540 no longer bringing gold into Europe. This book is, however, concerned with gold in the world as a whole, and Portugal continued to be the intermediary between Europe and the old world, i.e. Africa, the Middle East and the Far East, India, Persia and China. These were whole worlds in themselves, larger and sometimes wealthier than the much younger continent of Europe. Without daring to analyse these little-known economies, we should at least examine the information we have about Portuguese trade so as to establish the vast scope of the non-European aspects of the problem.

(1) The decline of Mina gold

As has already been indicated, this decline was in evidence by 1530.

[7] Micheline Baulant and Jean Meuvret, *Prix des céréales extraits de la mercuriale de Paris, 1520–1698*, vol. 1, Paris 1960.

Between 1548 and 1573 contemporaries tell us that the annual expenditure of the Portuguese state was greater than its income; there was a 100,000 cruzados deficit in gold. It was therefore planned to turn Mina into a plantation colony. Moreover, Castile, England and France were becoming more and more competitive, and around 1600 they were to be replaced by the Dutch. Morocco, meanwhile, was again drawing gold away from central Africa, and it even occupied Timbuktu for a time. This all put an end to the flow from São Jorge da Mina to Lisbon and then Hamburg, where African gold was exchanged for the copper and silver of central Europe. All trade consists of taking commodities to where they will obtain the best price, that is, the greatest quantity of products in exchange for them, and this is just as true of gold and silver: when gold became more abundant, its price was less favourable and it was not attracted towards northern Europe as much as before.

(2) Monomotapa gold

Monomotapa was the name of the sovereigns who ruled the Zambezi region. 'Monomotapa gold' is the more general name for that from the African gold producing areas of today: from Butua (the Transvaal), Mokaranga (now Rhodesia), and Matabele (the area between the Zambezi and the Limpopo). In those days there were no mines. Extraction took place seasonally, i.e. only in the period known as the *crimo* between the harvests and the rains. It was carried out by nomadic Kafir families, who dug small shafts the width of a man; these were sometimes interconnected by galleries, and were subject to constant flooding. They distinguished between gold dust, gold chippings, gold crystals and 'common' *matuca* gold which was mingled with rock and needing to be purified by crushing and heating. All this work was dangerous and not very profitable. The Portuguese never tried to get involved in producing it directly, even by using slaves. They preferred to obtain it through exchange. The Kafirs did not value gold very highly and wanted textiles and necklaces instead. But the presence of gold had been attracting merchants there for a long time, and small independent Arab trading centres had been established along the coast of east Africa, at Sofala, Angoxa, Kwama at the mouth of the Zambezi, Mozambique, Kilua, Mombasa, Melinde, and Mogadishu.

Portugal played every card she had: alliances, missionary work, wars, massacres, and campaigns into the interior with or against the small Kafir chiefs, the Arab sultans and the Monomotopa rulers. In trade they had no consistent policy either, but, at different times, they tried the monopoly system, the farming out of trade, and completely free trade. Portuguese trade followed the traditional pattern of Arab trade; they obtained gold and marble, and slaves in exchange for textiles and glass beads brought from the Gujarat area of India.

The export of Monomotopa gold, which was insignificant in the middle of the 16th century, reached 573 kg in 1583, 716 kg in 1610 and around 1,500 kg in 1660. This gold went to India, where it was turned into coin in Goa, the Portuguese trading post. These coins were known as *saotomes* from São Tomé or St. Thomas, who was depicted on the coin, and in their weight and gold content they were modelled on the *pagoda*, a Hindu coin. The profit from this minting process increased five times between 1554 and 1594. After their victory against a Turkish attack around 1580, the Portuguese became the real lords of 'Monomotopa gold' and its east African outlets. This gold was used in trade with the East, and only a very small portion, in the form of private earnings, ever returned to Lisbon.

In the 16th and 17th centuries the two main areas of India, Hindustan and the Deccan, paid very high prices for gold and even more for silver. 'Silver hunger' attracted merchants, and Portuguese *bandeirantes*, or bandits, ransacked the African jungle for deposits of silver, without success. The lesson here is the same: the demand might be far away in India and China, but price differentials were what determined trading routes and prospecting activities. Although trade depends on precious metals, the production of precious metals also depends on trade. Coins are, in the last analysis, commodities.

(3) Malacca gold and the Far East

In 1511, Albuquerque captured Malacca in the Malayan peninsula, and so brought the main focus of naval communication and gold trading in the Far East under Portuguese control. This involved acquiring more than just gold produced nearby, or a single area of production: all the gold of the Far East came to Malacca to be exchanged for Indian merchandise. India was the great producer of cotton cloth, and had no gold or silver mines. She was therefore a focus of attraction for these metals; if India was a cyclone, Malacca was an anti-cyclone (a point of diffusion).

The main areas of production were on the Indonesian islands: Sumatra which in around 1600 produced about 600 kg of gold per year and Java, which exchanged the gold of both islands for cotton cloth from Gujarat in India, at 20% profit. Borneo and the Celebes also had gold, and there was even some in the Philippines. The latter, however, belonged to Spain, and Spanish fiscal policies plus the abundance of American silver prevented Philippine gold from acquiring any importance.

The monetary situation in the Far East can only be treated very schematically here, and I shall simply indicate how varied conditions were. Japan was rather different from other areas.[8] In north east Asia, the main collecting point for gold was the Ryukyu islands, north of Japan. Around the middle of the 16th century, Japan produced and exported little in the way of precious metals. Between 1580–1620, however, a significant increase in the price of precious metals produced a real mining rush in Japan. Japanese production of gold and silver was a reflection both of internal conditions – the desire of the Daimyos for enrichment and military power, rising population and increase in internal trade – and of external conditions – the pull of Chinese demand and the opening of Japan to Portuguese shipping.

China had plenty of silk and gold, but she paid a high price for silver. The ratio of silver to gold was 5 or 6 to 1. In Japan it was 10 or 11 to 1. In Europe, where imports from Potosí were producing a superabundance of silver, the ratio was around 14 to 1. It can, then, be imagined that the export of silver to China became extremely profitable. Mexico took advantage of it and sent silver annually by what was known as the 'Manila' galleon, a ship that started from the Philippines, but carried Chinese products.

Japan was the first country to exploit the situation. At the end of the 16th century, she was producing approximately 2,000 kg of silver per annum. This was only half the quantity being sent from America to Europe at the same date, but it was nonetheless considerable. The most interesting aspect is the extent to which Japan's main characteristics paralleled those of the west: internal development, a rush on precious metals, and utilisation of the disequilibrium in the price of silver with mainland Asia. As in the 19th and 20th centuries, Japan appeared more like Europe than like China. Was this coincidence, or a common reaction to a similar cause?

It has to be remembered that though these powerful Asian economies preserved a relative autonomy, they were, after the opening of Far

[8] A. Kobata, 'The Production and Uses of Gold and Silver in 16th and 17th century Japan', *Economic History Review*, XVIII, 1965, pp. 245–66.

East ports to the Portuguese and, via the Philippines, the Spanish, in direct contact with European traders. Moreover, there existed in contrast to the Middle Ages, a world market for cotton cloth, silk, porcelain, gold and silver, which made precious metals the medium of direct exchange with the three main export products of India and China. To understand this kind of trade it would be as well to bear in mind the complexity of the social realities and the attitudes to money, which could vary enormously within the large expanses of India and China.

Hindustan, or northern India, is a world in itself, and a world which changed considerably in the course of the 16th century. Within it there were various monetary systems. In Bengal there were two types of currency: the common currency was based on cowries, sea-shells used as money, while large scale transactions were conducted in a currency based on silver. In Delhi circulation was overwhelmingly in copper coin. Commercial and industrial activity on a wide scale was practised in Gujarat, the regions of the upper Indus, and this attracted gold and silver coin from Persia, the *pagodas* of the Deccan, and cruzados and zecchini from Europe. It was a land where in the countryside tribute was paid in gold and silver.

The establishment of the great Mughal Empire, under Akbar, introduced into northern India a monetary system based on the silver rupee; this coin contained between 10 and 11.5 grams of fine silver. The stability of the system was maintained uninterruptedly from 1556 to 1605, and political stability and monetary stability went hand in hand. But it is the balance of trade which dominates the monetary situation, and the rupee system relied on considerable quantities of imported Spanish silver. Rupees were made mainly from melted-down reals.

In the Deccan, the rich productive area of Vigayanagar, gold was predominant, in the form of *pagodas* which had a carat level approaching that of the Portuguese cruzados and saotomés. Common currency, however, was still much more primitive than the cowry system; stones, needles, and unmarked pieces of copper were all used. Everywhere there was a dual system with both a current coin, which was always more or less 'fiduciary' (i.e. with no guaranteed intrinsic value, and taking many forms), and a strong currency, accepted in large scale trading. In the latter, gold and silver coin were used, but they were often weighed, 'sounded', and tested like a precious commodity. The rate of exchange between the two types of currency (current, fiduciary money and precious, commodity money) could vary, and was an index of the stability of internal prices.

In the peripheral areas of Asia the most complex systems of primitive currency were to be found side by side, and were often inter-related. Indo-China had a 'homeric' kind of currency in which axes and textiles were the basis of estimating exchange prices. The most developed system was that of Bengal, where cowry shells were the basis of account-money: 80 cowries equalled 1 'pone', 16 'pones' equalled 1 'cahon', and so on. But in so far as these systems did meet real silver coin, the ratio varied: according to the state of the market, the Persian *larin*, a solid coin, was worth between 40 and 48 'pones', or 3,200–3,840 cowries. All the usual features of the relationship between an internal fiduciary money and an international metal currency, therefore, can be found within this system.

From the 12th to the 15th century, China replaced practically all circulation of gold and silver, and even of small copper coin, by a completely token circulation of paper money. But at the end of the 15th century, this system was overtaken by galloping inflation, as a result of an unlimited multiplication and, therefore, a total depreciation of the paper money. In the 16th century, a primitive kind of triple monetary system was adopted, involving: (a) a circulating currency consisting of small unmarked copper coins which had a hole in the middle, so that they could be threaded together on a silk thread; (b) exchange by barter, in which rice served as a unit of measure; and (c) the settlement of large payments in gold and silver, in the form of ingots. Silver ingots were the main monetary commodity, and were valued very highly (as already noted) in relation to gold. There was a certain amount of gold coin, but it was used only occasionally, for ceremonies, presents or rewards; for example, gold coins were thrown to professors at the end of lectures.

To conclude this brief excursion into the monetary system of Asia, we should note that, as a result of the Portuguese navigators, the variations in value of the three monetary metals – gold, silver and copper – on the Far East markets, played an important role in forming the flow of trade and currency circulation. The enormous quantity of copper necessary to produce certain Asian current coin turned European copper into one of the main components of maritime trade in the early 16th century; it was shipped by the Portuguese from Hamburg to Lisbon and the Far East, at the rate of over 500,000 kilos a year. The copper was exchanged for Mina gold, and to it the Fuggers owed part of their fortune. But in the middle of the 16th century, the industrial price of copper tended to rise above the monetary price offered in the East, and the trade therefore declined. Later it was the western countries, especially Spain, which, from the early 17th century onwards, minted massive quantities of copper coin. The process was then reversed, and Japanese copper was imported into Europe by the Dutch East India Company.

Monetary circulation can be based on anything from the most primitive system (barter or cowry shells) to the apparently most modern forms (paper money). A monetary metal is something which is used to pay for international and distant transactions, has its own trading value and costs of production, and enters international trade circuits as an actual commodity. Metaphors about chasms or cyclones have been used to express the attraction exerted by China or India for gold and silver, and to explain the influence of such distant economies as those of the Far East on the economies and currencies of Europe. It is essential to be clear about what this means. What establishes the different pressures is the disequilibrium between the relative values of commodities on the one hand and precious metals on the other, depending on whether one is in America, Europe or Asia.

We can divide the world into three general categories: (a) two very productive and dynamic areas: Western Europe and monsoon Asia; (b) two very backward areas where Europe conquered and then began by exploiting their mineral deposits: Africa and America; and (c) Portugal, a country which was both a conquering and a trading nation, and which tried to control the points of contact in order to take advantage of the price differences between such distant places. According to Godinho: '. . . from the Cape of Good Hope to the Pacific, two great anti-cyclonic areas supplied the whole of the Eastern world with the yellow metal: the Kafir and Ethiopian areas of Africa, and South East Asia, the latter being much more important, since it produced twice as much. In between, there was a low pressure area, India, which attracted most if not all of both flows of gold.'[9] João de Barros, the great Portuguese expert, pointed out that the Malabar coast was marked by an absence of gold, and was therefore hungry for it. But this was true of the whole of the Deccan and of Hindustan. They were all part of the attraction area.

The next point to examine is how the Portuguese, who had mastered the Far Eastern routes from their positions on the African coast, attempted to control the intermediary routes through the Middle East, and how in part they achieved it.

[9] Magalhães-Godinho, op. cit. p. 285; cf. also the maps at the end of the volume.

(4) The Portuguese and the disputed area of the Indian Ocean

As we have seen, Jean Bodin thought that the greatest economic development of modern times was the establishment of the Portuguese, at the
expense of the Venetians, in the key positions of the Middle East.
We must now see whether he was right.

There are two problems. The first is whether the Portuguese dealt a
mortal blow to Venetian participation in the Eastern trade, and whether
Venice was ruined by it; this view is no longer accepted. The second is
whether, as is often suggested, Europe was 'drained' of gold and silver
through importing commodities from the East, and, to answer this,
one has to distinguish between different periods.

At the beginning of the 15th century, the Middle East trade was still
very important and the Portuguese attempted to capture it. A million
ducats a year were minted in Venice, and half of them were sent via Cairo
and Aden to India, in order to import precious commodities. Nubian
and Ethiopian gold caravans were still travelling to Egypt, and gold
sherafim were being coined in Cairo. Gold coin was also being minted
in Aden, at the mouth of the Red Sea, and in Hormuz, the key to the
Persian Gulf. A considerable quantity of coin was leaving Mecca via
the Red Sea to be exchanged for spices in India.

Albuquerque, who had learned about this trade from Jewish merchants
in Cairo, wanted to conquer the port of Massawa, in order to control
the flow of Ethiopian gold into Mecca through the Red Sea. The traffic
through the Red Sea consisted mainly of gold, especially of Egyptian
sherafim and Venetian coin; in the Persian Gulf it was mainly in the form
of silver, in *larin*, that were minted especially in Hormuz. These coins
were of a special shape, little bars of silver, which were flattened in the
middle and folded over, were very easily camouflaged and of very high
value. They sold in India at a 20% premium, and they bought Asian
textiles and spices. The *larin* continued throughout the 16th century.
Despite Portuguese intervention, India went on using Portuguese
cruzados, Venetian zecchini, and Egyptian *sherafim*, (all three containing
around 3.43 grams of fine gold). Rather than one replacing the other,
the trade was shared among them.

Precious metals were not always being 'drained' away to Asia: in the
late 15th and early 16th centuries, commodities were often exchanged
for commodities. In the early 15th century Venice had been sending
50% of the ducats she minted eastwards, but by the end of the century,
she sent only 20–30%. This was natural, because in this period gold
was very expensive, and bought a larger quantity of commodities in

Europe than in the East; it was, therefore, better to send commodities and not gold to the East. In 1503, the Venetian galleons sent to Beirut and Alexandria exported only 100,000 ducats as opposed to 500,000 in 1423; this was in part a result of Genoese and Portuguese competition, but also because of exports to Malabar in India and to the Far East. These included copper, vermillion, mercury, steel, arms, saffron, scarlet cloth, silks, taffeta, camlets, tapestries, glass beads, mirrors and rose water, which were exchanged for spices, precious gems, and Indian cotton cloth. In other words, during the period of low commodity prices in the last years of the 15th century, it was more profitable to export these goods than to export gold.

In the first half of the 16th century, the Portuguese also exported more commodities than coin to the East, and more silver than gold. The 'drain' of precious metals attributed to Portugal is also extremely relative. Here are some figures for total export via the Cape route:

1504 :	30,000 cruzados	1528 :	200,000 cruzados
1505 :	80,000	1531 :	28,000
1506 :	40,000	1533 :	135,000
1521 :	32,441	1535 :	80,000
1524 :	100,000	1546 :	30,000
1525 :	27,000	1551 :	40,000

This is obviously irregular and weak in comparison to Venice.

Portugal also exported copper, cinnabar, mercury, coral and lead; in the years 1552–1557, the annual average value of exports was 350,000 cruzados, of which only 100,000 were in gold or silver. Moreover, the East attracted more silver than gold: in Melinde, in Africa, it was worth twice what it was in Portugal, and in Cochin in India, as many as 16,000 marks in silver were received from Portugal, in the period 1510–1518, as opposed to only 33 marks of gold. As for copper, hundreds of thousands of marks were sent. The balance of payments was definitely favourable to Portugal. In Goa, commodities were partly paid for in bills of exchange, and partly in gold sent to Lisbon. This gold might in turn go to Hamburg, to be exchanged for copper and silver. The overall situation was that during the first half of the 16th century, the biggest profits in trade with the East came from exporting, in the following order: coral, vermillion, mercury, copper, silver and only after that, gold.

In the second half and especially the last years of the 16th century, silver, which was abundant and cheaper in Europe, was transferred in massive quantities to the East, where it was much more highly valued and paid for more products. This was Spanish silver from America, although the Portuguese were able to intercept part of it. The flow of silver from West to East to pay for the Oriental trade increased between the beginning and the end of the 16th century from 20,500 kg to 64,300 kg; at the end of the century Europe was producing scarcely 20,000 kg. Almost all of it, therefore, came from America in the form of Spanish crowns or 'reals'; these were known as 'pieces of eight' because they were worth eight ordinary 'reals' – they were a 'hard' currency. Marseilles was one point of departure for this trade, with the Turkish empire as an intermediary. But the English East India Company also paid for its purchases in silver. In Italy, in 1575, there was reported to be an export trade to the East in wine, oil, some cloth, books, glass, and reals. Spanish 'reals' were considered to be a genuine commodity. Many of these reals in the Mediterranean trade, however, came from Portugal. In 1580, a five-ship fleet left Lisbon with 1,300,000 cruzados worth of reals, or pieces of eight.

In Europe there was an enormous and increasing demand for three Oriental products: silk, porcelain and tea. All were paid for in reals. Used as they were to Oriental trade, the Portuguese tried therefore to obtain reals. They managed to do so by circumventing the controls, and the Spanish often turned a blind eye to this (Portugal was at this time united with Spain, though she kept her own monetary and customs system). These fraudulent operations took place in the Azores, in Madeira and in Lisbon, where ships from the Americas were diverted; even Brazil got hold of some silver from Peru. Oriental trade therefore involved the Portuguese directly in the American traffic, and recent research in the Lima archives by Gonzalo de Reparaz confirms the dominant role played by the Portuguese in Peru after 1580.[10]

---

[10] Gonzalo de Reparaz, 'Der Welthandel der Portuguesen im Vizekönigreich Peru im 16 und 17 Jahrhundert', *Kölner Vorträge zur Sozial und Wirtschaftsgeschichte*, Cologne 1969, vol. 4.

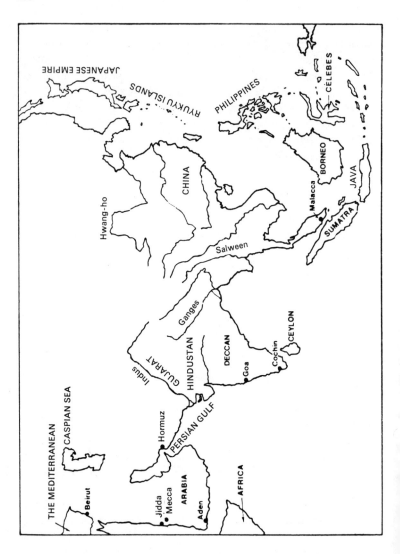

Figure 4. Asia.

12

The Gold and Silver of the Americas

(1) The growth of shipments

I shall now simplify and re-examine Hamilton's figures on the shipments of gold and silver from America.[1] The value is expressed in millions of pesos, the peso being a Spanish accounting money equivalent to 450 maravedis; it was stable throughout the century and until 1600 it expressed a silver value as well as a nominal value.

These are the figures for the first three decades of the 16th century:

1503–1510	1.18 millions of pesos
1511–1520	2.18
1521–1530	1.17

The fall in the last decade is possibly due to corruption.

The three following decades show a rapid expansion:

1531–1540	5.58 millions of pesos
1541–1550	10.46
1551–1560	17.86

This amounts to six times the total of the previous thirty years; the decade 1531–1540 alone brought in more than the previous three.

The two decades 1561–1580 show a continued increase, with a tendency for the rate to fall:

1561–1570	25.34 millions of pesos
1571–1580	29.15

[1] Hamilton, op. cit. pp. 42, 180.

In the last two decades of the century, by contrast, there was a leap to twice the previous level; a deluge of silver poured in, and more was shipped during these twenty years than throughout the previous eighty.

1581–1590	53.20 millions of pesos
1591–1600	69.60

By giving figures for weight instead of value, and giving the figures for each metal separately, it can be seen that whereas at the end of the 15th century figures of a few hundred kilos appear exceptional, they are now running into thousands.

	Kilos of gold	*Kilos of silver*
1503–1510	4,965	0
1511–1520	9.153	0
1521–1530	4,889	148

This was almost exclusively the age of gold.

1531–1540	14,466	86,193
1541–1550	24,957	177,573
1551–1560	42,620	303,121

It was at this period that silver supplies increased very rapidly, though gold still had an important role (the increases for gold were respectively 72% and 70%; for silver, they were 102% and 70%).

1561–1570	11,530	942,858
1571–1580	9,429	1,118,592

Over these twenty years, gold supplies fell rapidly; silver again shows a great leap ahead.

1581–1590	12,101	2,103,027
1591–1600	19,451	2,707,626

Gold now became strong again, while silver was running at two and a half times the figures of the previous two decades. A comparison of these weights all too often leads to the conclusion that gold, since it fell to a tiny percentage of the silver weight, was unimportant in the last years of the century; but gold was worth 10 to 12 times as much as silver, and once silver became more abundant, gold increased in value.

Until 1536, gold was worth 10.11 times as much as silver

From 1537 to 1565 gold was worth 10.61 times as much as silver

From 1566 to 1608 gold was worth 12.12 times as much as silver

The result was that, until 1560, gold represented more than half of the value imported, and never made up less than 8% even later on. Contrary to what Hamilton appears to suggest, and to what has sometimes been repeated on the basis of comparison by weight alone, the real transition from the influx of gold to the avalanche of silver took place not around 1540, but around 1560. This has important implications for the European monetary system, as Spooner clearly shows.[2]

A study of gold in the world cannot be restricted to Europe and to the other places of gold's destination. The conditions of production are also important, both because they formed a part of American history, and involved the enormous problems of colonisation and the exploitation of man; and because the cost of production has monetary effects that are as important as the quantities produced.

(2) The origins of gold: the different sources and conditions of production

We have already looked at the first period, involving the Caribbean Islands, and seen that, after 1525, Santo Domingo, Cuba, Puerto Rico and Jamaica were, one after the other, drained, depopulated and then abandoned. The search for gold continued on the mainland, in Central America and what is now Venezuela. The continent became known as *Tierra Firme*, but this was not common usage in 1525–1530, because it was for a long time believed that the entire area was an archipelago. Since Magellan's voyage, it had been known that it was possible to sail round it, and it was thought that the south-east passage lay a few hundred leagues from the *Tierra Firme* of the North. In fact, it was thousands of miles away, and it was a long time before the great size of the continent was recognised.

It was in the search for gold that, in 1513, Nuño Vázquez de Balboa

[2] Frank Spooner, *L'économie mondiale et les frappes monetaires*.

reached the Pacific coast for the first time. The isthmus became the first mainland Spanish colony, preceding Mexico. This colony was called *Castilla del oro* (Golden Castille); although the name was perhaps illusory, the illusion of gold forms a large part of this story. Places like 'Villa Rica' and 'Costa Rica' were not as rich as those who so named them thought; for example, the writer Velasco said of the Veragua region: 'There is gold running through the earth in many places, and it can be found wherever you dig to the depth of five feet. Every negro extracts at least one peso a day, there are good deposits in all the rivers and streams, and the gold is of good quality.'[3]

A peso was equivalent to 4.18 grams of gold; this would be almost a kilo of gold for every 200 days worked. There was obviously a feverish search for slaves, because as we know, the Indian population was soon wiped out by the work. Historians of the Indies are agreed on this point: some, like Father Bartolomé de las Casas, denounced the greed of the white men; and others, like Fernández de Oviedo, placed the blame on the aggressive nature of the Indians. Forced labour gave rise to revolt, and this in turn led to depopulation.

It is a curious paradox that the search for gold depopulated the Panamanian isthmus, but required that it be re-populated after the 1530s, when it became the link between the Pacific and the Atlantic, between the silver mines of Peru, and Nombre de Dios, later known as Porto Belo, the Atlantic port from which silver was sent to Europe. According to Pierre Chaunu, the two ports, Panama on the Pacific and Nombre de Dios on the Atlantic, handled 45% of all shipping between Seville and America for almost a century; the two ports were linked by a system of bearers. By the middle of the century *Castilla del oro*, drained of gold and men, had become the route through which silver was transported. The conditions for this traffic were extremely harsh: paths had to be hacked through the tropical forests with *machetes*, there were clouds of mosquitoes, dangerous crossings over roaring torrents, and the risk of ambush by runaway slaves.

The islands of the West Indies form an arc and contain an 'American Mediterranean', the Caribbean, with the northern coast of South America as its southern boundary. In the 16th century, the coast of Venezuela stretched between the mouths of two great rivers, the Magdalena (now in Colombia) in the West, and the Orinoco (the frontier with the Guyanas) in the East. Here too the Spanish *conquistadores* soon

[3] J. López de Velasco, *Geografiá y descripción de las Indias*, Madrid 1894, pp. 348–349, quoted in Chaunu, op. cit. vol. 8, p. 893, n. 3.

landed in search of gold, but they had to break up into isolated nuclei because of the mountains and marshes, and the area became known as the 'islands of Tierra Firme'.

Eastern Venezuela, bound by the savannahs of the Orinoco – the *llanos* – was for a long time impenetrable. It was pearls rather than gold that were found there; they were especially common on two islands near the coast, Cubagua and La Margarita, and as they were valuable and very light, they played a role similar to that of gold, and were sometimes used as money. They were obtained through barter or the exploitation of forced labour, and pearl-fishing therefore destroyed the labour force in a manner similar to that which was induced by the search for gold. The fall in population led to man-hunts into the interior, in order to transfer labour for the pearl industry to the coast and to the islands.

Western Venezuela was the first part of the country to be discovered and it was the lagoon of Maracaibo which gave rise to the name 'Venezuela', little Venice. Between 1528 and 1541, the whole country was given over to a German trading company based in Ulm and Augsburg, the Welsers; they were involved in the business of the Portuguese colonies in Hamburg, had founded a bank in Seville and another in Santo Domingo, and were creditors of the Emperor.[4]

The nature of the company is significant: the 'concessions' signed by Charles V and the Welsers accorded to the latter a mission of military, political and economic conquest. They or their representatives were at once 'Governors', 'Commanders-in-Chief', and expedition organisers, and there was confusion about the distances involved, their rights stretched all the way to the Straits of Magellan. At the same time, however, they were merchants; and there was no clear distinction between their economic and political powers. Though this confusion was usual in the 16th century, the Spanish, who formed the majority of colonists, were reluctant to accept it. The Welsers were accused of organising the whole project solely for their own material interest. Matters took a dramatic turn: Spanish and German agents were murdered, and lawsuits were instituted by the Welsers; but they had to abandon them around 1550, after retreating back to Germany.

Gold played the major role in the founding of the Welser company, but more as an intention – or illusion – than a reality. Their original aim of organising systematic mining is evident from the fact that German miners were brought to America from Joachimstal, and a company of

---

[4] cf. the work of a Colombian historian of German origin, Juan Friede, *Los Welser en la conquista de Venezuela*, Caracas and Madrid 1961.

them marched through Seville to the sound of fifes before embarking. The plan was a total failure: in the period around 1530, Venezuelan gold was being extracted from alluvial beds rather than mines. No silver was discovered, and the miners could not bear the climate. Most of them died, and those who came back were disappointed and angry. Gold was, nonetheless, found. The Welser concessions included the right to mint the gold produced, and they had the lease of production. Thousands of small producers brought them granules or nuggets of gold, which they paid for in cash; these had then to be refined and minted, and a fifth paid to the king. These rights were farmed out to the Spanish and seem to have brought little return. Gold produced in this way left for Spain via Santo Domingo.

Despite these drawbacks, the very existence of this system and the fact that gold was discovered, even if in small quantities, encouraged men to dream of a country where everything was made of gold. This was the origin of the El Dorado myth. Born from the mediaeval legend of a kind of earthly paradise, and from the belief that gold was produced by the high temperatures of the Equator, the myth of El Dorado was confirmed by objects which the Indians brought for barter, and exacerbated by natural difficulties and the hostility of the Indians. It provoked gold-fever and gold rushes similar to those of California and Klondike in the 19th century. No gold was found, but vast areas were discovered and occupied.

The legend of El Dorado took many forms, and gave rise to adventurous expeditions. The German Alfinger, thought he would find El Dorado on the plateaux of what is now Colombia, among the Chibcha tribes. He made his way up the Magdalena river, and although he lost his life in the expedition, he had opened the way for a major colonisation of the interior. In Santo Domingo, still the seat of the longest-established Spanish administrative authorities, apparently well-founded reports were put about that the gold country had recently been discovered on the continent, directly south of the island, and half-way between the Atlantic and Peru. Others thought that El Dorado lay beyond the rapids of the Orinoco, up towards the high plateaux.

No one had an accurate idea of the distances between the places that were already known, and this is what led to the famous encounter in 1539 between three expeditions of different origin: the meeting of the German Federman, coming from Coro, the Spanish Quesada expedition from Santa Marta, and Belalcazar, Pizarro's lieutenant from Quito (now Ecuador, but then administratively dependent on Peru), on the plateau of Bogotà (now in Columbia). As a result, the Andes region was better known, and it was more securely controlled.

In general, real gold and non-existent gold were equally important in the Discovery, the Conquest and the Colonisation of the Americas. From an economic point of view, the results were apparently poor. In the course of their law-suit, the Welsers claimed that they had lost 100,000 ducats, and around 1540 they withdrew from the American operation voluntarily. Their accounts show that they paid the king, as a fifth part of their income, 17,000 pesos, 2 tomins[5] and 8 granules of gold; this would give a total of 90,000 pesos of gold produced, exchanged with the Indians, or looted, i.e. 380 kilos in 10 years. Deducting costs, the emperor could have gained no more than 135 pesos a year from the company. How accurate the accounts are is not known, but they give some idea of the distance separating the illusion of gold and the real costs involved. A really important discovery could not have been concealed.

After 1533–1534, the successes of Pizarro in Peru and the seizure of the Inca treasures (which, curiously, were not associated with El Dorado) led to the separation of Venezuela from the colonial economy as a whole; colonists and labour were inevitably drawn towards the recently discovered countries or towards the Panama trading posts. Just as Cortes's discovery of Mexico had depopulated the West Indian Islands, so the discovery of Peru reduced the population of Venezuela for a long time to come.

Peru was most important after 1545 and particularly after 1570, when the silver mines of Potosí began production. But Peru began to be significant with the discovery and pillage of the Inca treasures, i.e. with a period of gold. Alvaro Jara[6] gives an account of the exact figures for the royal *quinto*, or fifth, levied on Peruvian gold. This tells us nothing about the way it was produced, but at least it gives the amount accurately. The series begins on 16th April 1531, with Pizarro's landing at Coaque, a village on the Pacific coast exactly at the Equator. As it covers all gold on which a fifth was paid to the king, it obviously includes the famous Inca treasures, which had been accumulated over centuries for ornamental and ritual purposes. Initially at least, what it refers to is not so much 'production' as violent looting (as described in the earlier chapters of this book).

[5] 1 tomin=9.26 grains of silver.
[6] Alvaro Jara, 'La producción de metales preciosos en el Peru del siglo XVI', *Boletin de la Universidad de Santiago de Chile*, 1963.

The precise total value of the famous Atahualpa treasure in Cajamarca is given: 2,475,302 gold pesos, of variable quality (from 4 to 22 carats). Its value was finally calculated to be 600,655,410 maravedis, which corresponds to the 1,320,000 gold bezants mentioned by Bodin. Obviously, there could have been some embezzlement and fraud, but the figures for gold and silver production in Peru for 1531–1535 are as follows:

	Kilos of gold	Kilos of silver
1531	489	183
1532	489	67
1533	5,639	11,537
1534	3,470	56,534
1535	1,649	27,183

Considerable quantities were involved, and it is understandable why Peru so excited contemporary imaginations. In the following years, however, the figures fell: in 1536–1540, only 2,891 kgs of gold and 34,900 kgs of silver; in 1541–1545, a total increase of 12% for gold and silver together, though gold was still dominant. In other words, the first phase of the Peruvian discoveries, before the great period of the silver mines, was mainly one of gold treasure.

A comparison of the gold produced in Peru in the period 1531–1540 to the gold imported through Seville for the same period, shows that the quantities were almost the same. While this does not mean that all the gold reaching Seville came from Peru, it does show that the production of the rest of America did not exceed what was kept in Peru, plus what was lost or embezzled. Peru was already the leading producer.

In coming to gold in Chile, it is necessary to refer once again to the work of Alvaro Jara: he has studied the Conquest as a business 'operation', its private character and feudal style, as well as its effects on an Indian society which finally revolted.[7] The interest of his work for a study of gold is that it gives figures for production: according to one account, 7,000,000 pesos were produced between 1540 and 1560; but recent studies give an annual average, for 1545–1560, of 2,000 kg, with a sharp fall to 500 kg after 1560. War became the great obstacle to production. There was a new gold rush in 1595–1599, abruptly halted by the great revolt of 1599 which stopped production.

The second interesting point in Jara's work on Chile, as far as gold is concerned, is the information it gives about the labour force: the words of the Indian chants and songs prove that they felt the obligation to extract gold to be a terrible burden. This is how they referred to their spears: 'This is my lord: this lord does not make me dig gold, nor carry crops, nor wood, nor keep his sheep, nor sow nor reap; and as this lord keeps me in freedom, it is with him I wish to go.'

It was very difficult to find labour both for agricultural production and labour to work in the mines, especially at a time when the development of the nearby Peruvian silver mines was attracting labour from every quarter. This led to the development of *maloca*, the practice of man-hunting, which was carried out mainly by 'friendly' Indians; they were paid 20 pesos for every captive (brought in collar and chain), and these were then bought and re-sold in the markets of Peru for 100 pesos. Alvaro Jara does point out, in another article, that attempts were made to protect the Indians.[8] Under the governorship of Hurtado de Mendoza, in 1557–1561, the lawyer Hernando de Santillán had the law of the 'gold sixth' passed, under which one sixth of production was reserved for the benefit of the Indians. It was not given to them directly, but was converted into capital; in principle, it was to be used to increase the community's flocks and means of cultivation, but in practice, the 'protectors of the Indians', the officials who administered the levy, used it as a means of speculation and patronage. Even in the 17th century, Indian communities were already taking the matter to the courts, and the suits themselves show that the law was applied.

There were two other countries where gold was mined in the 16th century: the Buritica area of what is now Colombia, and certain areas of Mexico. They will be dealt with in the next chapter.

---

[7] Alvaro Jara, *Guerre et société au Chili. Essai de sociologie coloniale*, Paris 1961; cf. the review of this in *Annales E.S.C.* November–December 1963.

[8] Alvaro Jara, 'La estructura económica de Chile durante el siglo XVI', *América indígena*, XX, no. 1, 1960; and 'El salario de los Indios y los sesmos del oro en la tasa de Santillan', *Universidad de Chile: Centro de investigaciones de historia americana*, Santiago de Chile 1960.

13

Innovations in the New World

So far we have been discussing American gold. In all cases – in the West Indian Islands, the very minor discoveries made in pursuit of El Dorado, in the gold beds of the Panamanian isthmus, the treasures of Peru and the Chilean gold rushes, i.e. everywhere until the 1550s – gold was always obtained either by plunder and looting, or by barter in the absence of a market economy, or by searching for gold nuggets in gold-bearing sands.

The search for nuggets, in which a kind of sieve was used to riddle the sand, was more tedious than it was exhausting, but the population was displaced as the gold beds were used up one after another. The labourers were uprooted from their traditional agricultural occupations; crops on which their subsistence depended disappeared; and their organisms, used to slow and discontinuous work, offered no resistance. Female labour, in particular, was moved around, and customary methods of childbirth and breastfeeding were interrupted. All of this facilitated the outbreak of epidemics. The population almost disappeared on the Islands; on the plateaux and in the valleys of the continent it was reduced rather less savagely, though falls of 80–90% were recorded in some places.

Chaunu has stressed the destructive nature of the first phase of mineral production.[1] This production was, he says, carried on 'outside the laws of economics'. By this he means that in conditions of free competition and free trade the price of a commodity basically depends, in the long term, on its cost of production, and that wages tend at least to ensure the subsistence and reproduction of labour. However, this is precisely the opposite of what happened in the first stage of gold extraction in America; Indian labour did not have a normal subsistence level which permitted its reproduction. This is not to say that American gold and

[1] Pierre Chaunu, *L'Espagne au temps de Philippe II*, Paris 1965.

silver 'cost more than they were worth' or that 'they did not cover their costs of production'. On the contrary, they earned incomparably more in Europe than their average costs of production in the Indies (plunder being a factor in this).

What does have to be taken into consideration is the expense of loans, the daring and effort, the losses, the risks and the time wasted in the conquest and in shipment: only the hope of enormous gain could spur men on through the discovery and the conquest. Labour, however, was scarcely counted in the calculation of costs. The Spaniards, according to Chaunu, regarded this labour as freely given to them, like air or water.

The problem was that while it was free, it could not last for ever. This marked the beginning of the process of the destruction of profit by means of profit itself; Sartre has tried to describe this in his *Critique of Dialectical Reason*,[2] with specific reference to American gold and silver, although he failed to relate it adequately to the actual conditions of production. The colonist exploiting labour without thinking about its reproduction, laid the grounds for the disappearance of the labour force, and therefore his own ruin. Moreover, the mineral seemed to be so cheaply produced that he would exchange it for any product coming from Europe; he therefore began the process whereby the exchange value of the gold or silver, that is, of the commodity he produced, was reduced. In this way too, he prepared the ground for his own destruction.

This was basically the way in which the precious metals – especially gold, which was more important – were produced in the first half of the 16th century. It is not clear that the same was true for the second half. Opportunities for plunder disappeared, and the gold beds were used up; however, mines, including some gold mines, were discovered. These, especially the deep-lying silver mines, required excavation, drainage, and therefore capital; and they also required stable and almost exclusively male labour. Exploitation now tended to take place under increasingly more normal economic conditions, and the cost which this began to involve encouraged (or perhaps required) the introduction of technical innovations.

In Spain and the rest of Europe there were financial crises especially in the middle of the century and in 1557; Braudel suggests, very plausibly, that these were related to what he calls a 'change of fuel', that is, the replacement of gold by silver as the main stimulant of economic activity. The change, however, was not only in the leading mineral, but also in

---

[2] Jean-Paul Sartre, *Critique de la Raison Dialectique*, Paris 1960, pp. 234–247.

Figure 5. Latin America in the 16th century.

the nature of exploitation: from the gold bed to the mine, and from one type of labour to another; from scattered, badly-used village labour to the large, permanent labour force of the great mining centres of Mexico and Peru. These crises of falling production was not really overcome until around 1560 in Mexico and 1570 in Peru when new techniques were used to bring minerals which had a low silver or gold content into production.

It is, then, possible to relate, on the one side, the periodicity of gold and silver imports into Europe, the rate of 'general' price increases (which show a fall in the value of monetary metals), and certain financial difficulties of the Spanish state which affected the whole European economy to, on the other, changes in the conditions of the production of precious metals in America.

(1) The replacement of alluvial extraction by gold mining around 1550

The Buritica gold mines were opened around the middle of the century.[3] Lying in the kingdom of New Granada, in the hinterland of Cartagena de Indias, through which their production was exported, they fast became the most important mines in the continent. They were the cause of the changes in gold imports into Seville which we have already noted in Hamilton's figures, i.e. for the peak imports of gold by weight (42,620 kg between 1551 and 1560) and for the increase in gold imports at the end of the century, from 9,429 kgs in 1571–1580 to 19,541 kgs in 1591–1600. Between these dates, the exploitation of the mines fell off, because of the success of the silver mines. However, once the consequent abundance of silver led to a relative revaluation of gold, the gold mines became profitable once more. Activity in the port of Cartagena (which has been calculated by Chaunu) depended on these turns in the fortunes of the Buritica mines.

In 1582, there were only 12 Spanish 'citizens', i.e. long-established residents in the Buritica complex; but there were 200 'ordinary' Spaniards, i.e. recent immigrants, 300 negro slaves, and 1,500 vassal Indians, made over to the colonists who owned the mines under the *encomienda* system. At about this time (1580) other deposits were discovered nearby, and new towns such as Zaragoza and Remedios mushroomed. In 1588, however, a terrible epidemic almost wiped out the Indian population. Thousands of black slaves were then brought in for

---

[3] J. Parsons, *Antioqueño colonization in Western Colombia*, Berkeley 1949.

work in the mines.

In Mexico there had always been gold production. From 1519 Hernan Cortés's conquest had led to the looting of treasure, about which he always boasts in his writings. Later on, there was also some exploitation of alluvial gold, as there was everywhere in the southern tropical region. In the years 1540–1547, more systematic exploitation began in which the mines played their parts.[4] Hernan Cortés was a great businessman: he owned large agricultural property, shipyards, and gold beds where he employed slaves to gather gold for his own profit. Between 1540 and 1547 there is evidence that slaves were also employed along the Nuestra Señora de la Merced river, and in the Macuiltepec 'mines', both of which were Cortés's dominions: a total of 395 slaves were divided up into 'gangs' (*cuadriuas*) of 28 to 100 labourers. The price for an Indian slave in this kind of work rose from between three and seven pesos in 1525–1529 to 50 pesos in 1536 – an indication both of the increase in prices, and of the scarcity of labour. Each *cuadriua* was under the orders of a Spanish official, who kept a twentieth of the gold produced by way of wages, and the whole operation was under the direction of an 'overseer', who kept between a tenth and a seventh of the gang's product for himself.

This mine was based on slavery, but it also used the *encomienda* system to a considerable extent; in this case, this involved the services due to 'the Marquis' (who was originally Hernan Cortés) from the village of Tehuantepec. The *encomienda* was a kind of feudal estate and this one had been granted to him. The village had to supply the mineworkers with their subsistence, clothing (especially blankets), and transport, and to move equipment when the mines were exhausted. They were responsible for cutting timber and for building. They also had to pay an annual tribute of 1,650 pesos of 16 carat gold (two-thirds pure gold). This sum, together with the production of the mines, was sent in leather sacks to the Marquis's representative in Mexico City.

Figures for the years 1540–1547 show that production fell rapidly, from around 8,200 pesos in 1540 to 3,300 in 1544, 1,960 in 1546 and no more than 764 in 1547. Taking the average over eight years, it took a slave a month to gather the equivalent of one peso, or a little over 4 grams of gold. It should be remembered that at the beginning of the century, the rate of a peso a day was mentioned for Panama. The fall in later years was also due to a terrible epidemic, and in the end, gold mining

[4] cf. J. P. Berthe, 'Las minas de oro del Marques del Valle en Tehuantepec', *Historia Mexicana*, VIII, 1958, n. 29.

produced so little that the surviving labour force was transferred to the silver mines.

Silver now began to eclipse gold; in 1546 exploitation at the famous Zacatecas mine began and in 1548 the equally renowned Guanajuato mine was opened. The volume of gold extracted fell; the rise of the silver mines had begun. The two phenomena were related, not only to each other, but also to a tendency towards technical innovation; a document of 1545, concerning the Tehuantepec goldmine, mentions that a small quantity of gold ore had been sent to Mexico City, because there was no mercury to transform it. It seems then that by this date the mercury amalgam process for separating metal from the ore, common in Germany for a long time, was also known in Mexico. The most important conclusion is that towards 1545 the era of easy extraction came to an end, and a new kind of mining had to be organised.

(2) The Mexican silver mines and the mercury amalgam

The gold-fields of Mexico lay in the tropical south. The silver mines, however, lay to the north, on a line roughly following that of 500 mm annual rainfall; a certain level of dryness was necessary to avoid the constant risk of the mine being flooded, as there was little knowledge of how to remove the water. This same line separated the areas with a stable and relatively dense population of peaceful Indians, from the areas populated by Indian braves, nomadic peoples who were few in number and unconquered by the Europeans. It was what would in the United States be called a frontier. The mines often lay along this frontier. They were sometimes whole towns but there were also many ranches, isolated deposits, and camps. Most of these mines began to be worked between 1546 and 1556; some remained famous until the 18th century, when they achieved their highest output: these included Zacarecas, Guanajuato, Pachiuca, Real del Monte and Sombrerete. Some which produced the most in the 18th century lay far to the north, and were not completely opened until the end of the 16th century, when truces were signed with the wild Chichimeca Indians. This was the case with San Luis de Potosí (not to be confused with Potosí in Peru).

The introduction of the mercury amalgam process was a crucial episode in the exploitation of the silver mines. The stages of this process are important. The process was known by the 15th century in mines that were producing for Venice (though it is not mentioned in the famous treatise on metallurgy by the German Agricola). The rather unimportant dispute about whether the process was first introduced into

Mexico by the Germans or by the Spaniard Bartolomé de Medina, has apparently been resolved: a German, Lomann, was granted the right to use it in 1556, and Medina was granted it a year later. The most important point to note is the speed with which it took root. It is often just said that the change occurred in 1559. In fact, its use can be measured by the import of mercury, from Almadén, in Spain. The upsurge in this trade dates from 1562: in 1556–1550 the amount was 890 cwt and in 1561–1565, 3,000 cwt.

What did the technical transformation known as the 'mercury amalgam' consist of? The ancient Indian process consisted of successive meltings of crushed ore, in little pierced kilns; the final operation separated the silver from the lead by oxydising the latter. It was a long process, which used a lot of fuel. The new process was known as the 'patio' process, because it was carried out in walled-in patios; the ore had to be crushed under a mule's hoofs (or in a kind of mill), then mixed with mercury, with another product called 'magistral' (a kind of sulphate of impure copper), with salt and with a great deal of water; Humboldt, after visiting the mines in the 18th century, was to observe with surprise that the tank water in the 'patios' did not go bad, because of the chemical products mixed with it. The silver amalgamated with the mercury and gave an easily separable substance from which the mercury was subsequently eliminated by evaporisation. The superiority of this process lay in its economic use of both time and fuel, and even more, in the possibility of using lower grade ore; it made it possible to exploit veins which had previously been unprofitable. The old process was kept up for high grade veins, or when there was no mercury available, but, in the latter case, production was not very profitable.

The Mexican mines normally had a higher proportion of white workers and a smaller number of blacks. In Zacatecas in 1570, there were 300 Spaniards and 500 slaves, most of them Indians. Many animals were used for haulage (horses and mules), and many free *mestizos* were attracted by relatively high wages. The blacks, who were expensive and ill-suited to the climate, made up only 7–8% of the labour force.

The details of the structure of ownership and exploitation are not well known. The Mexican mines, though they were very different from European mines, were also quite distinct from the gold bed extraction of the 1520s, and even from the Peruvian mines. In the great period of silver production, the late 16th century, Mexico produced scarcely half of what Peru produced. In the 18th century, however, these mines, which were not so worn out, were to have a much higher production.

14

Potosí

We have now gone from gold to silver. From the 1560s silver in effect took the lead from gold, but did not exclude it altogether. This was because gold, although now an insignificant proportion of production in terms of weight, still made up a considerable share of the value; and because given the abundance of silver, gold rose in value relative to it and the demand for it rose once more. As a result, some payments within Europe were stipulated as having to be paid in gold. This notwithstanding, after the simultaneous discovery in 1545–1546 of the Mexican and Peruvian mines, and the application of the mercury amalgam in Mexican mines in 1559–1562 and in Peru in 1570–1572, what Pierre Chaunu has called the 'great silver cycle' began, reaching its peak, as we know, with the imports into Seville in the years 1580–1585 and 1590–1600. In the eyes of the world, silver became the symbol of quickly-made fortunes: for the French the word 'Peru' was synonymous with wealth, for the English the word 'Potosí'. This chapter looks at what is known about Potosí.

The word Peru was applied in the 16th century to the whole of South America, not just to the territories which bear this name today. The name, was, however, soon restricted to the high plateaux of the Andes, which lie between the two great mountain ranges, the coastal range overlooking the Pacific and the range of the interior. The southern part, 'Alto Peru' has now become Bolivia, and the region long known as the 'silver' land lay here, its main cities being La Paz, Chuquisaca (now Sucre) and Potosí. Whereas the French used 'Peru' as a synonym for fabulous wealth, the Spanish and the English used the name Potosí itself; the veins of silver varied greatly in quality and accessibility, but it was easy to imagine that Potosí was a mountain made of pure silver, and it deserves a chapter to itself.

(1) The information available

There is accurate and extensive documentation on Potosí, in both Seville and Peru; but it is scattered and has, so far, been very inadequately used. The American historian Lewis Hanke has begun research into the subject, but so far he has been overwhelmingly an historian of ideas. Maria Helmer has also announced a major work on the *mita*, the forced labour of the Indians, but so far only fragments of this have been published.[1] Pending the appearance of these works, it is best to consult a document of the period when the mines were at their height, the *Relación general de la Villa Imperial de Potosí*, written in 1585 by Luis Capoche, the owner of two hydraulic ore-crushing machines.[2] It was intended as a report to the new Viceroy and brings the reader directly into contact with the problems of Potosí. It is very fully documented, with names, figures and lively anecdotes; and if somewhat naively expressed, it is an intelligent account. It reflects the mentality of a property owner and technician, but it looks at the problems without violent prejudice. Finally, it does, if in a confused way, encompass the geography, history, technology, and the economic, social and moral aspects of Potosí mining. I shall base this chapter on it.

(2) Location and technical conditions

Potosí lies at an altitude of approximately 4,000 metres, on a cold, desolate, windy, dusty plateau, totally devoid of agricultural resources, except for a few fields of potatoes. Everything, and everybody, had to be brought to this city whose population rose in a few decades to as high as 160,000.

Mercury had also to be brought in while the silver had to be exported. The journey to Lima, the capital of Peru, took two and a half months, the journey from Huancavelica, the mercury mine, took two months. The nearest port, Arica, a barren and isolated place, was 500 km away, and Buenos Aires, on the Atlantic, was 2,400 km away. In the 18th century Buenos Aires became the main destination; at this time it was already regarded as a possible port, but it was not yet used by much

---

[1] Marie Helmer, 'Un tipo social, el minero de Potosí', *Revista de las Indias* XVI, 1953, pp. 85–92, and 'Notas sobre la encomienda peruana en el siglo XVI', *Revista del Instituto de Historia del derecho*, Buenos Aires, no. 10, 1959.

[2] Luis Capoche, *Relacion general de la Villa Imperial de Potosi*, Biblioteca de autores españoles, vol. CXII, Madrid 1959. Introduction by Lewis Hanke.

shipping. The trade with Huancavelica meant that the normal route lay across the plateaux towards Lima.[3]

The silver mountain itself, the *cerro*, was isolated; it measured about six miles around the base, with a much smaller hill next to it. Although its slopes were steep, they were accessible to mules and horses. Some of the veins were rich, but there were poor ones too. There were vast quantities of waste extracted, and these had to be dumped in the old shafts as they were abandoned. The veins could be between two and six feet wide. At the end, though, some tailed off to only two hands breadth (less than eight inches). Conditions were far from ideal.

(3) Discovery and stages of development

The silver was discovered in 1545, and this was no accident. As in Mexico, it was at this time that the highly profitable but destructive old methods stopped producing. Genuine deposits were looked for, and they were found. The first mining phase was from 1545 to 1564, when the richest veins were used, following the old Indian system. The ore was smelted in kilns (*guairas*) which were fanned by bellows. Some technical progress was, even at this stage, made in this system: during the 1550s a man from Seville improved the furnaces by including a kind of chimney inserted in the base. In so doing he earned himself a fortune and a title. He had a *guaira* designed on his coat of arms, which is still to be seen in Seville over the gate of his palace. Capoche tells us that he had nightmares about this image as a child, and he also recalls the time when the whole mountain would be lit up like an amphitheatre by *guairas* glimmering like tiny stars. This indicates how dispersed the mining activity was, and how many people were involved in it in this first phase.

The 1560s were years of depression: the system produced less and less, as the four main rich veins were worked out. Gradually, the mines were abandoned, the labour force dispersed, and the population of the city declined. But a new phase began in 1570–1572, with the visit of the Viceroy Francisco de Toledo, one of the great organisers of the Spanish colonies. De Toledo introduced the mercury amalgam process, which made it possible to use poorer ore, and organised the mercury mining in Huancavelica. He also established the *mita* system under which a certain percentage of the Indians of each village were mobilised for forced labour.

[3] See the map on p. 114.

The decline in production was then gradually reversed. From 1570 to 1573 production went on falling:

	pesos
1570	177,000
1571	167,000
1572	129,000
1573	105,000

From 1574, production rose, and, by 1582, had increased eight times over:

	pesos
1574	193,000
1575	256,000
1576	336,000
1577	475,000
1578	530,000
1579	688,000
1580	749,000
1581	803,000
1582	860,000

There was a certain amount of stagnation in the 1580s because water to drive the crushing machines was scarce, and because of a shortage of mercury. The very fact that Capoche could present the Viceroy with this list of figures in 1585 does, however, show how far the question of production was already uppermost in the minds of the colonists. Capoche appends an interminable list of mines under prospection, which shows the possibility of expanding production for many years to come. The downturn did not, in fact, come until the 17th century.

These facts show that studies of the conjuncture which assume the predominant role of precious metals, have underestimated the importance of the problems involved in their production. Imports to Seville, European prices, the tonnage of Atlantic shipping, and mercury consumption have all been studied. What has not been examined is the problem of the costs of production in the different mines (in Mexico and in Peru), the different phases of mining, technical innovations and the rate of profit. The value of a product, whether of metals or of anything else, depends on its cost of production. Capoche's report is not specific enough to enable us to calculate these, although it suggests the existence of documents which would provide the basis for such work. What it does do is to give an account of the organisation, or rather the successive kinds of organisation, of Potosí mining.

(4) The Potosí mining system

In principle the subsoil belonged to the king. There were, therefore, in theory no mine-owners, only holders of permanent concessions, who were formally responsible for mining operations. These are the people referred to by the word *mineros*; they were numerous and of different kinds and Capoche gives long lists of them. On the mountain alone, there were 577 concessionaries for 94 veins; the veins were granted out in stretches several yards long and the average concession for rich veins was 12 *varas*, and for other veins about 30.5 *varas*.[4] The concessionaries themselves, ranged from the king and the highest officials down to the widows of colonists, low-ranking priests and small companies, even sometimes to Indians – and to Portuguese, Florentines and Englishmen. It does not seem to have been a homogeneous system, and hence there was a conglomeration of various disparate, unrationalised mining enterprises. Most mining was done indirectly, under a lease or farmed out to a small company, and was sometimes handed over to a foreman.

The first phase (1545–1564), that of the *guaira* technique, was left almost entirely to the Indians. The Indians who embarked on the adventure of mining were allegedly 'venturing of their own will', *ventureros de su voluntad*. They made an agreement with the owner of a concession to be allowed to exploit so many *varas* of his vein. They were therefore called *indios-varas*, or 'yard-Indians'. They were supplied with excavation tools, but had to bring their own candles. At the entrance to the mine the owner sold them the ore they had extracted from the vein, which he evaluated by sight, and they turned it into metal, selling it back at a profit. If they gained nothing from the operation they had to be content with the fragments of ore which remained. For the Spanish and the Indians to be able to agree on this, the veins had to be rich. The concessionaries who had only poor veins tried to mine

---

[4] 1 *vara* = 0.836 metres.

them directly with hired Indian labour or *encomienda* labour and they then sold the poor ore directly at a small profit.

In the second stage of mining (after 1570–1572), a larger labour force was supplied by the *mita* or forced labour system. Technology made it impossible for the immiserated Indians to go on treating the ore: the Indians now played a smaller role and gained less from it. Nonetheless, some agreement still subsisted between owners and Indians on the following basis: the Indian extracted all the ore he could in one day, and himself took away all he could carry. This the owner permitted; and he then used serf labour to remove the rest of the ore. It was the tenants of concessions rather than the *mineros* themselves who followed this practice. But, as the *mitayos*, the conscript Indians, were never enough for the growing volume of mining, free labour was hired, at the rate of 4 reals a day, and these labourers were less subdued: (the *mitayos* earned $3\frac{1}{2}$ reals). As everything now depended on the number of Indians the administration allotted under the *mita*, many small or poorer quality concessions were abandoned; their owners continued to demand a certain number of *mitayo* Indians, whom they made over at a profit to more important miners.

A concession was more important because it gave the right to have Indians than because of the ore itself. For every concession, Capoche gives the length and depth of the vein, but also the number of *mitayos* theoretically allotted to it, and the number actually supplied. Since there was a considerable gap between the two figures, it is possible that free labour – paid on a time or piece work basis – played an important part in spite of the *mita*. This shows that the social relations of production around the Potosí mines not only changed a great deal; they also remained complex.

The need for a technical transformation had become apparent once the richest veins had begun to run out, and the introduction of the amalgam process required a volume of investment unknown in the initial phase. The first problem was to excavate the mine-shafts. The *mineros* were accustomed to pay a fifth of their production to the excavators. Each vein had its own shafts and there was no communication between them; they were generally dug horizontally from a point on the mountain-side. Although it was thought that the best ore might be found further down, there was considerable fear of floods. Capoche openly discusses the different aspects of the problem: excavation, security and production. 'Although the shafts to the "Chilean" metal which lies in the deepest parts of the mine, may give silver of higher value than what is obtained now, it must be seen if this is worth more than the extra that would be spent in going down and coming up, for this is important for security and economising on the labour of the Indians. There are other questions too: many shafts have led only to waste or poor metal, whose quality is not equal to its cost, and their owners do not have the means to take out the good and remove the earth and worthless ore, which is costly and gives no profit.'[5] These are the views of a genuine commercial undertaking.

From the start, experiments were made. On 11 April 1585 success was finally achieved in an excavation begun twenty-nine years and two months before by 'an Englishman from London' who had been suffocated along with a number of Indians while trying to open a shaft with coal fire. The survivors of his company, a Florentine and a man named Toribio de Alcazar, had just obtained the right to use 16 Indians from the provincial authorities (*Audiencia*) at Chuquisaca, and 'the town is very happy with this great success, for many say that it will bring new prosperity and wealth to Potosí for many years.'[6]

The amalgam treatment, however, required costly, complex equipment. The ore-crushing mills developed from the manual type to the horse-drawn mill and the water-mill, but better machines gradually eliminated the primitive kind. In 1585 there were 25 in Potosí itself, 23 in the surrounding area, and many more expected. As hydraulic power depended on streams that flowed irregularly, attempts were made by using reservoirs to overcome at least the problem of seasonal droughts.

Iron cost 70 pesos a hundredweight; a wooden axle, 7 metres long, for a hydraulic machine, cost 1,500 pesos and at the outset a riddle for the crushed ore could cost as much as 150 pesos. As iron was scarce, riddles were even made with silver wire. Added to all this was the tremendous problem of transporting men, provisions, and ore over a short distance, and mercury and the mined silver over thousands of miles. It is clear, therefore, that the cost of silver was far from negligible, and that, whatever the price of labour, including the *mita*, the costs of equipment and investment were considerable. To understand how these distant mines could prove capable of eliminating the German silver mines from the European market, comparative figures would have to be calculated, as Humboldt did for the Mexican mines in the 18th century. It was the vast quantity of silver available which was to ensure American supremacy.

---

5 Capoche, op. cit. p. 105.
6 ibid. p. 104.

Though it was less fatal to the population than work in the gold beds, it is labour in the silver mines which has remained the historical symbol of Spanish colonial oppression of the Indians. Why should this be? The work was certainly very hard. It is unlikely that greed, insecurity, the availability of servile labour, and recent memories of the exploitation of the gold beds had given rise to much more humane concepts in mining; some mine-owners, and even more, the overseers, known as *pongos*, were undoubtedly quite brutal towards the labour force. The form of forced labour known as the *mita* was in some respects horrifying. As evidence of this, and of protest against it, there were cries of indignation and despair from the disciples of Bartolomé de las Casas. Brother Domingo de Santo Tomás wrote: 'What is being sent to Spain is not silver, but the blood and sweat of the Indians.' Although Brother Domingo had obviously not read Karl Marx, the latter produces almost exactly the same formula at the end of the chapter on primitive accumulation in *Capital*.[7] The outcry by these witnesses is more convincing than the 'black legend' spread in the 17th century by the enemies of Spain, especially the Dutch, who were carrying out acts of colonial violence at the same time with far less scruple than the Spanish.

However much it is accepted today, the critique of the 'black legend', should not lead us into blindly accepting the rose-coloured view of some modern historians, who claim, on the basis of the enacted laws, that an 8-hour law, paid holidays and social security, existed in the mines of Potosí in the 16th century. The picture sketched by Luis Capoche is neither exaggeratedly black nor naive and idyllic, and the following points are especially worth recording.

First, the work was harsh. The Indians spend eight hours down the mine, but the length of the shafts meant that each men spent only four hours working. They went down by ladders with wooden rungs and leather handrails, one going up and the other down. There were *barbacuas*, places for necessary rests. The workers went down in threes, the first carrying a candle; but candles gave little light and were often blown out by the draught. When he came up, each man had to bring two *arrobas* (23 kg) of ore in a kind of sack tied to his chest. The average distance down the shaft was 150 *estados* (250 metres), but there were

---

[7] Karl Marx, *Capital*, vol. 1, Moscow 1961, p. 760. 'If money according to Augier "comes into the world with a congenital blood-stain on one cheek" capital comes dripping from head to foot, from every pore, with blood and dirt'. Had Marx known of Brother Domingo's letter he might have quoted it in preference to Augier. Capoche also says 'es mas sangre que metal' ('It is more blood than metal'), op. cit. p. 158.

also: 'mines 400 *estados* deep (about 670 metres), a distance sufficient to tire a man carrying a heavy load on the flat, let alone the Indians climbing up and down with such difficulty and danger, and they are to be seen arriving breathless, drenched in sweat and drained of colour.'

Owners and overseers were also harsh: 'The only relief they have from their labours is to be told they are dogs, and be beaten on the pretext of having brought up too little metal, or taken too long, or that what they have brought is earth, or that they have stolen some metal. And less than four months ago, a mine-owner tried to chastise an Indian in this fashion, and the leader, fearful of the club with which the man wished to beat him, fled to hide in the mine, and so frightened was he that he fell and broke into a hundred thousand pieces.'[8] It is this kind of eye-witness account that makes Luis Capoche's document so interesting.

Working conditions were unhealthy. The immediate danger to the Indians working down the mines was that they would catch pneumonia, as they came out of the warmth of the mine and went down the mountain-side at a height of 4,000 metres, without protection from the wind. In the long term the main danger was silicosis of the lung, which was contracted in the dust and candle fumes of the mine-shafts.

Pay was extremely low, but even though forced labour was not free, it was not the same as slavery. The *mitayo* Indian had the right to be paid a daily wage in silver which was to provide his subsistence: the sum fixed was 3½ reals, but in fact the owner would only pay according to a certain scale, i.e. the Indian who did not reach the target set would receive only a part of his wage. The freely hired Indian or *mingado* was paid 4 reals and had the right to negotiate over his pay, but many disputes arose as a result of this practice. *Mingado* labour was very unreliable and it led to many complaints. Consequently, there was a continuous search for *mitayos* or straightforward slaves and those were obtained by all manner of means.

The *mita* was the system established by the Viceroy Francisco de Toledo as the only means of making the Potosí mines produce as much as possible, and it was in theory related to Inca practices of individual duties which were owed to the State. In fact, the *mita* was not a personal service but a collective levy on whole villages and communities. Each community had to allocate young men for work in the mines. The practice was begun in 1559 when Indians were conscripted under the pretext of making them pay in labour the tributes in kind owed by the com-

[8] Capoche, p. 109.

munity. Transformed into a new system by 1570, the *mita* was the subject of much debate in both America and Spain. Some theologians opposed it, and others justified it. In the end it was made law and generalised throughout the Spanish Empire.

In principle, there should have been conscription only on a rotating basis, once every thirty years. In fact, as with taxes, the calculations were defined by what was needed, and the numbers of men required were allocated among the different Indian communities who then had to choose the men. This gave enormous powers to the Spanish judicial authorities (*corregidores*) in the provinces and to the Indian *caciques* in the villages. Villagers preferred to be ruined economically rather than to be chosen: they gave everything they owned, as much as 15 or 20 head of cattle, in order to be exempted. The ones who had to leave were the poorest; they went with their families, and abandoned their parcels of land, thereby ruining the fields. The requirements of the mines, 13,000–17,000 *mitayos* a year, set over 40,000 people moving along the roads to the mines.

The *mitayo*, uprooted from his traditional surroundings, and reduced to working 280 days a year in the mines, for a wage which in theory was not to be scorned, but which was cut down in practice by the scales and rising prices, was in an ambiguous position; he was part serf, and part proletarian. The debate about the *mita* is indeed far from over, and some aspects of it have yet to be investigated. Capoche, who knew the place well and was not given to expressing strong feelings, concluded that for the Indians the *mita* was a *riguroso verdugo*, a harsh scourge.

Capoche was even more indignant about the fact that Indians could be sold into slavery even though the Laws of the Indies formally forbade it. Most of them had been captured in the Chilean wars, and were bought illegally for 80 or more pesos. A real market in men was created, especially as the climate was unsuited to the introduction of negro slaves. Capoche's indignation makes it clear that he did not confuse *mita* with slavery: the *mitayo* was theoretically free; he was brought into the mines for a certain length of time; he was owned by no one and was paid a wage. On the other hand, he did have to feed himself, while the slaves were fed.

Having said this, it is strange to find that these harsh conditions were continually contradicted, although not greatly improved, by laws, administrative actions and moral precepts concerned with the fate of the Indians. The impassioned, indignant sermons of some churchmen show that injustice and brutality unfortunately never disappeared, that theological discussions about natural right never resolved the debate in favour of actual equality, and that laws such as the 'New Laws of the Indies' in 1545 were never effectively applied, however admirable in theory. The formula of the colonists was 'Obey and do not carry out'.[9] Their argument was, of course, that the economic future of the whole system would be comprised by the liberal application of laws protecting the Indians, and that it was necessary to protect the work of colonisation (and especially missionary work) against the unrealistic views of the metropolis.

There were many theologians and preachers who supported this point of view, but the existence of this legislation and of the whole debate did have some results. Special officials, known as 'protectors of the Indians' were appointed, and although many of them used their positions to engage in various kinds of speculation, Capoche quotes examples of 'protectors' who took their work seriously and were scrupulously honest. There were some genuine social security institutions: hospitals, clinics and security inspections in the mines. There was even a workers' contribution to help finance the hospitals. This modern element is what has made it possible to glorify the social conscience of Spanish colonial institutions. With reference to security, Capoche cites the case of a catastrophe which killed 22 Indians. The inspectors had already warned the mine-owner about careless procedures, and after the disaster he was arrested and fined 8,000 pesos. This was very little for 22 deaths, but it is a clear indication that there were limits to the exploitation of the Indians, at least in theory.

Capoche held the very modern belief that the king and the Viceroy decided to impose duties on the Indians not with a view to the special interests of the mine-owners, but with a view to overall economic development, from which the Indians too would benefit. In connection with the *mitayos*, he states that 'Your Majesty would not be able to keep them a single day in Potosí against their will' and he almost accused the Indians of lacking a class consciousness: 'if these people thought and were political', he wrote, 'they could force their masters to treat them better.'

It need scarcely be pointed out that the *mitayos* did not go to Potosí willingly: this is proved by the revolts, the buying of exemption, and the tendency to run away. Many were 'denaturalised', i.e. they abandoned their villages to escape the *mita*. It is a fact, however, that once Indians

---

[9] *Se obedece y no se cumple.*

were uprooted and taken into the Potosí complex, many tended to stay even after they were freed from the *mita*, to earn their living by hiring out their labour as free *mingados*. This seems to have been related to the original practice of Indian participation in the feverish search for silver and gain. This activity, which never disappeared, was always nourished by the existence of a free market in labour and silver ore.

The silver extracted from the ore by the amalgam method was assayed in administrative centres which also deducted the king's fifth. This fixed its value in 'assayed pesos', the Potosí currency. But in between leaving the mine and being assayed, the ore was sold several times over. The Indians participated in this circulation process. From the time when they processed the ore in *guairas* themselves, the right to trade in ore had never been taken from them. They obtained ore first by a custom which allowed them to work in the mine from Saturday night until Monday morning, on their own account; not a lot is known about this custom, called *caxchas*, but it seems that while it was resisted it was not eliminated. Ore was also obtained by the kind of labour contracts mentioned above, with wages being paid as a share of the product, or in pieces of mercury-silver alloy, by an agreement between the workers and the overseer.

The Indians who owned ore or alloy put it up for sale in a special public market with a place and time for each particular kind of ore; that is, silver was sold 'for silver'; ore or alloy was sold for current coin. The price was determined by the experience of the salesmen and the customer. Mine-owners protested strongly against this system in the latter part of the century. They realised that the free market in silver liberated some of the Indians from their proletarian existence, and this reduced the possibility of pressurising the labour force. In order to press for the prohibition of the market, they claimed that its trade was in stolen ore, and that any profit was made dishonestly. A prohibition was then enacted by the Potosí council, and confirmation of the decision was extracted from a new *corregidor*. But this caused unrest among the Indians, and the decision was annulled after consultation with the Protector. Capoche relates the episode at length, especially the controveries among lawyers and theologians; while some Jesuits had preached very strongly in favour of prohibition, other priests maintained that the free market was the Indian's only defence. This problem of the free market in silver was related to the whole problem of the free market in commodities, and to the atmosphere of speculation reigning in the city of Potosí.

(5) The Potosí markets and silver madness

Capoche described the city of Potosí as consisting of all kinds of markets: 'There is the square with the Palace of Justice and the Royal Palace, where the House of Trade and the Mint are. There is the *coca* market, and three markets where maize and flour are sold; there is one for cattle, one for wood and coal, and one for silver, which is worth seeing, for the metal the Indians take from the mountain is sold there; in other words, silver is traded for silver. Apart from these there are many other public places where great crowds gather and the Indians hold their fairs and markets, and they are so thronged that it is scarcely possible to get in.'[10]

The produce on sale was Indian, and this suggests that the agriculture of the country was doing well. Note, too, the market in the stimulant *coca*, which is harmful to the body, but which the Indians could scarcely do without, given the high degree of suffering endured while working in the mines. European products were also on sale, and the scarcer they were the higher the price. This contrast between commodities and silver in the very place where silver was produced, makes Potosí one of the great historical birthplaces of capitalism. The increase in the value of commodities through the devaluation of silver was a great incentive to merchants, and in the open marketplaces, even genuine aristocrats demeaned themselves in order to sell what they had received from Europe.

Potosí was not a city of the nobility. Capoche observed that there were few *encomenderos*; elsewhere it was this class which gave cities a noble air. Even traders only passed through. As there was no nobility, there were no grand houses; the overwhelming majority of the population was Indian. There was, however, extravagance in dress. Money madness attracted Spanish families whose women dressed as if they were at court. After the introduction of the amalgam process and the *mita*, there were now velvets, silk stockings, brocade and gold tissue, where before there was only dark cloth and leather hides. Even workers and mulattos had fine clothes. At the same time the city mushroomed in size: though it did not exist before 1545, there was a population of 45,000 by 1555, 120,000 by 1585 and 160,000 by 1610.

Despite the enormous difficulties of transport, the market was well supplied not only with fruit from Chuquisaca, but with excellent Castile wines. Under these conditions, money madness seized the whole population, and Capoche reveals the corrupting effects of such madness:

[10] Capoche, op. cit. p. 76.

'In Potosí there is no money other than silver, with which the mine-owners and *pongos* pay for the food and fruit and other refreshments that are brought to them; the young Indian women give themselves to them in exchange for silver, and their mothers take them up to the mountain for this very purpose.'[11]

The city developed under the double sign of the scales (for trade) and Venus (venal love) and the *Histories of Potosí*[12] describe more sophisticated forms of corruption. There were 700–800 criminals, 120 white prostitutes – which is astonishing given the small number of Spanish women emigrants to America – 14 gambling houses, and 14 dancing halls. A theatre seat cost 50 pesos. Extravagance was not just an individual trait, it was often practised collectively; in 1556, which was far from being the most prosperous year, the city spent 8,000,000 pesos to celebrate the accession of Philip II. In contrast, it should be noted that investment in hydraulic works, which, as mentioned above, was considerable, reached only 3,000,000 pesos in the following period.

There was a great deal of unrest in the city: numerous disputes and even riots took place, but they were not of a social nature. They were often about corporate privilege – the tailors took up arms over a question of privilege; the Augustinian monks resisted the forces of law and order with the sword; and the question of the free silver markets gave rise to epic disputes among preachers. These, Capoche says, were 'habitual in the New World, but particularly so in Potosí.' Priests disagreed violently about the place of honour in religious processions. Such was the vanity displayed at funerals that restrictions had to be introduced. The ban on Indian funeral rites had a deeper significance, as did the fact that they were obliged to buy things they did not want when certain commodities had not been sold. Such forced sales resulted in a longlasting hatred of the *corregidores*; under the mask of silver madness there lay profound racial and class conflicts.

Different authors give contradictory pictures of Potosí; it was an exalted and glorious place, 'the crucible of the Americas', 'the nerve centre of the State', 'the jewel of the Empire'; or on the other hand, something diabolical, an 'accursed mountain', 'the scourge of the Indian nation', or 'the abyss of iniquity'. It was the very symbol of the money-metal: it evoked dreams; gave immediate and overwhelming gratification, and brought wealth to individuals and power to the State.

[11] ibid. p. 154.
[12] On the many anecdotal histories about Potosí known as *The Histories*, see Lewis Hanke, introduction to the *Relación*.

But moralists were alarmed by the corruption carried in its wake, and economists wondered what the eventual effects of this silver fever would be.

15

Huancavelica and the Distribution of American Silver

(1) Huancavelica

The Huancavelica mercury mines were not just complementary to those of Potosí; they were the very condition of the latter's existence. Although Spain had mercury – in the Fugger concession at Almadén – it was very risky to send this mercury all the way to Peru, across two oceans and the Central American isthmus. Huancavelica was also a long way from Potosí, but Lima was relatively near, a fact which resolved the problem. Although the mountain route was over a thousand miles long – that is, a journey of two to three months – the mercury cargoes constituted a sort of exchange for the silver sent from Potosí to the capital. Trains of llamas – *recuas* – laden with mercury or silver became a familiar sight on the plateaux of the Andes.[1]

Huancavelica, known to the Indians for its vermillion production, was discovered to be a mercury mine in 1563–1564. The Viceroy Francisco de Toledo saw that the Potosí-Huancavelica 'axis' could become the 'axis of the Empire', and he therefore organised the mercury monopoly, the *mita* labour system, contracts for mining (*asientos*) and a transport system. The Huancavelica *mita* was even more dreadful than that of Potosí. The mercury mines were more unhealthy: it was reckoned that three years down the mine would destroy a worker's strength. The work was organised on a continuous basis, night and day; the Indians, however, preferred to work at night. In theory they stayed down the mine eight hours, but in fact conditions underground were such that a man could work only four hours at a stretch, and even this was enough to exhaust someone completely. Documents describe the

---

[1] There is an almost exhaustive study of available material on Huancavelica, but it does not pose the general questions: Guillermo Lohmann Villena, *Las minas de Huancavelica en los siglos XVI y XVII*, Seville 1949. cf. also Chaunu, *Seville* . . . vol. 8. 1, pp. 1111–22. For the distances see map on p. 114.

mine-shafts, the *socavon*, as lethal. Efforts were made to extract mercury without digging tunnels, but without success. The Indians feared *mita* labour at Huancavelica even more than at Potosí, and in the villages requiem masses were said when *mitayos* were leaving for the mercury mines. This did not prevent the work from attracting people, and many *mitayos*, once freed, continued working as free miners, a development which reinforced the belief that people never returned from Huanca-velica. The authorities tried to remedy this by returning those *mitayos* whom they had originally contracted for, but men still disappeared, and the villagers were still afraid.

With the introduction of the *mita*, mercury output reached impressive proportions: production increased from 2,000 cwt in 1570–1575 to 8,000 in 1581 and 13,600 in 1582. This represented the highest output ever reached, because as soon as Carlos and Juan Andrès Corso de Leca invented a process in Potosí for economising on mercury in the amalgam process, Huancavelica experienced over-production and surplus stocks. Clearly, neither the monopoly nor those to whom mining rights were granted were spared the classic worries of business.

Despite stagnation in production, which lasted with slight fluctuations from 1590 to 1610–1620, between 1560 and 1660 Huancavelica still supplied an annual average of 215 out of the total of 363 tons of mercury used in the Americas. (The other 148 were imported from Europe.) If one remembers that the annual average of silver exported from America over the same 100 years was only 163 tons, then one can see that mercury was produced on a massive scale, and that its transportation posed major difficulties.

The struggle to humanise conditions was even harder at Huancavelica than at Potosí, and the mines were described by priests and by the Protector of the Indians as 'human slaughter'. In 1603–1604, some *juntas*, municipal authorities, closed mines with deep shafts – thenceforward only those open to the sky were to be exploited. Chaunu has asked whether this humanitarian measure should not be related to the change in the conjuncture which occurred in 1604–1605; it was then that the increase in silver production began to falter and that general prices began to fall relative to it (i.e. silver became dearer). Humanitarianism was certainly not the only reason behind the measure; there was com-petition between the silver and mercury mines for labour, both for *mitayos* and for free workers; in Spain the influence of the Almadén concessionaries, rivals of Huancavelica, presented a problem; and lastly, stocks were accumulating and there was less demand for mercury after the technical innovations in Potosí. The measure taken in 1604 was therefore less a restriction on the work of miners, than a restriction on production: it fell to 12,700 cwt a year from a previous peak of 13,600 cwt.

As for profits on the concessions, an average production of 250 cwt per annum, a good average for a concession, would give a profit of approximately 2,000 pesos; this would have been modest enough. What we do not know is how much capital was invested to obtain this profit; moreover, it is estimated that at least 40% of real production was sold illicitly to the Potosí mine-owners, at unofficial, even more advantageous rates.

(2) The distribution of American silver

The questions now to be posed are how much silver remained in the Americas, how much was lost in transit between America and Spain, what happened to the silver reaching Spain, and how silver was distributed in Europe after leaving Spain.

It should not be forgotten that the precious metals which were discovered helped to finance the discoveries themselves, the conquest, and the building of cities and churches. Soetbeer has calculated that on average, 300 tons of silver a year were produced in America between 1560 and 1640, and Hamilton has estimated that 185 tons were exported to Spain. The first figure is by no means certain, but whatever the exact amount, there was a considerable difference between the volume produced and that which reached Spain. In the case of Potosí, for example, there was certainly intensive trading in silver among the Indians, salesmen and overseers, and some of it must have been kept by them. The greatest spending occurred in cities such as Potosí or Lima. Where it was exchanged for European goods, silver did go to Europe, but it was also spent on local produce (fruit and vegetables), and on keeping servants, and building; it was saved in the form of luxury objects, and was donated to the Church. This meant that at least some of the treasure remained in America.

Silver was also used to pay for the costs of the colonisation process. In Lima the Viceroy had to establish a war treasury; at the end of the 16th century, for example, Chile obtained quite considerable sums of money from Peru to crush the Araucan Indian revolt. The great silver centres – Mexico City and Lima – distributed treasure among the colonies. Lima in particular was obliged to cope with its own problems, since in terms of time it was five times further from Seville than Havana.

Finally, one should ask whether, as America became more and more able to live on her own resources, she sent less to Europe, and whether this led to the change in the monetary conjuncture. This is an hypothesis, and the reality is bound to be more complex; but it is surprising that the production of mercury did not fall to the same extent as the export of silver, and this would lead one to suppose (techniques having changed very little) that exports fell faster than production. Nevertheless, in the 16th century particularly, precious metals tended to drain away from the Americas, above all because their value was quite simply higher elsewhere. They purchased more in Europe or in Asia than in America. Therefore, to explain the massive transfer of gold and silver to Europe, it is not necessary to resort to the constraints and to the Spanish administration's desire to control the greatest amount possible. Mercado said that the high prices for European products common in the Americas 'destroyed both Republics, Spain and the Indies', in that these high prices attracted commodities from outside and led to a flight of gold and silver. This will be discussed later.

It is true that circulating coin was scarce in the Indies, but here it is necessary to distinguish between the situation in producing areas, where the problem was one of minting, and the situation in areas of America far removed from the mining districts, where both the metal itself and money were scarce. When America was first colonised, there was no money there, or very little. Exchange with the Indians was by barter, and European merchants compensated each other 'as in the Castile fairs', that is, by balancing debits and credits in account books or with bills of exchange. The balance was paid in precious metals, not in coin, but in nuggets, ingots, and bars of gold or silver. These 'changed in value like cloth', as Mercado put it, in stressing the commodity character of monetary metals at the point of production. These bars and ingots were marked simply with a stamp indicating that they had passed through the controls for the king's fifth; they were used almost as money because their weight was known and their standard guaranteed theoretically, although in fact much less so. In the first half of the 16th century, the great majority of purchases and exports were based on this system, and it was still being quite widely used at the end of the century.

The unit of measurement was the 'assayed peso', a gold peso worth 450 maravedis, which corresponded in theory to a coin of 4.31 grams of fine gold (cut at 50 to the mark and 22.5 carats). This currency was also known as the 'mine peso'. But up to 1550 the effective currency came from Castile; and under the pretext of 'transport costs', the Castilian silver real, worth 34 maravedis in Spain, was valued at 44 in America. This was absurd because the abundance of silver in mining areas made this coin more common and lower in value. While it was very acceptable because of its scarcity and usefulness, it sent nominal prices up even more. As this could not go on indefinitely, arrangements had to be made for minting on the spot. The Mexican Mint was established in 1535 and began producing coin in 1537. Similar plans were made for Lima and Bogota, but minting began at Lima only in 1565 and at Potosí in 1572. This obviously bears some relation to the phases of the greatest production of silver.

The mints produced not just the basic currency of the Spanish dominions, but, by the late 16th and early 17th century, a world currency: the 'piece of eight', a silver coin worth eight reals, or 272 maravedis. It was also known as the hard or strong peso, and later as the piastre, which became the precursor of the dollar – weighing 23.36 grams of fine silver, a bit more silver than in 6 Germinal francs (see p. 307). Once the system was established – leaving aside the adjustments that followed in the 17th and 18th century – these coins, produced in Mexico as well as in Spain (Madrid, Seville, and Segovia) invaded the whole world (including Africa and Asia).

Away from the mining centres, the problem was often not simply a scarcity of money, but the fact that there was none at all. The continent was vast, and populated by nuclei of Europeans, frequently very isolated from each other. Traders encountered the most unexpected difficulty with money. Around 1540 and until 1598–1599, there was no gold or silver circulating in the area known, ironically as it turned out, as the 'plata' (silver) area, later Buenos Aires. The same was true even during the 17th century for Asunción, the capital of the Paraguayan interior. When the authorities, collecting taxes in kind, wished to change them for money, no one had enough metal coin: exchange took place by barter or payment in kind. People used the words 'peso' and 'maravedis', but the difficulty was to give them substance. It was then decided that iron nails, metal casts and spoons, rare objects from Europe, were worth so many maravedis and would be accepted as payment. But precisely because they came from Europe, these objects varied in value according to the infrequent and irregular arrivals of ships. The price of the products therefore varied according to the abundance or scarcity of this object, money. Another attempt was made, this time with textiles, with the same results. As with any commodity money, people saved the money-object if it appeared that general prices were falling (i.e. that money was increasing in value) and the money commodity was made liquid on a massive scale, buying all kinds of products, if it appeared that prices were going up and money would be worth less. Any attempt to reintroduce silver as the circulating coin posed difficult problems of adjustment.

Thus, in the Americas, renowned for their gold and silver, there were areas which had no money. This was perhaps also due to pre-Columbian Indian customs, which had a completely different conception of money; but, in turn, the absence favoured the organisation of societies without money. The Jesuits' theocratic-communal Indian reserves in Paraguay (and their equivalents in all frontier areas) were based on an exchange of labour for products without the intervention of money. This shows that the effect of money and the reactions of societies to it, are dependent on both economic and social conditions and on mental habits.

Two additional problems: embezzlement and piracy. Embezzlement could occur during transfers from America to Spain, from Spain to other parts of Europe, and from the King to individuals, the latter being important because the King's silver had a greater economic influence than private silver and went to different people. As we have seen, the silver subject to the 'fifth' was transported by special officials from the mines to the control centres where the 'fifth' was deducted; from there it went to the mints or the ports. These operations were risky but profitable and embezzlement was a great temptation. There was undoubtedly very large scale embezzlement in the ports of America early in the century, in the period when isolated ships carried the cargo, and before the systematic organisation of money fleets. In theory, the risk of embezzlement should have been reduced when the fleets were organised. Hamilton has stressed how many precautions were taken: ships' cargoes were registered in great detail, oaths were taken, and a large number of officials were made responsible. Officials were particularly vigilant at the Panama isthmus where the governor and the Panama *Audiencia* were responsible. Nonetheless, Pierre Chaunu has shown how easily embezzlement was practised: many ships were unchecked or scheduled for checking only where they arrived; the very organisation of the fleets facilitated embezzlement, in that war ships in the convoys could take on silver (in particular the silver for the crews' wages), and so illegal cargoes were often taken on, as the Captains-General of the fleets were all powerful. It was profitable to carry precious metals which had avoided registration, either in order to evade the many taxes, or to by-pass Seville and to send silver directly to European markets where it was worth more.

At sea, it was sometimes necessary to put into port, not always voluntarily; there might be shipwrecks, both faked and genuine, or encounters with ships in difficulty; fishermen might come to offer their services, or it might be necessary to take on provisions when supplies ran out; and there were 100 other opportunities for making contact with smugglers. The oaths which sailors were required to take covered all these points; but the extent to which they were kept or ignored should not be exaggerated.

Among the Atlantic Islands and harbours other than Seville, the ports of call of the Azores and Lisbon were the main breaches in the security system: 70% of the ships which did not land first in Seville went to Lisbon for one reason or another. The importance of this for the Portuguese oriental trade has already been noticed. In the late 16th century, when Portugal was politically (though not altogether economically) united with Spain, it distributed a large quantity of piastres in the Mediterranean and around Africa. However, measures taken to have the treasure which had been accidentally unloaded in Portugal taken by land from Lisbon to Seville, reveal the extent of official concern about this possible source of embezzlement.

In Seville itself the House of Trade acted as both judge and protagonist in the organisation and control of the Seville monopoly. It did not, of course, exercise a *state* monopoly either over commodities or over silver; it acted as a simple control over all colonial trade, which was still entirely in private hands. The trading community of Seville (the 'university of merchants' as it was called) had considerable influence, and it was closely related to the House of Trade, the control body. This body organised trade and shipping extremely well, but it was concerned with private interests as much as with the interests of the State. The House of Trade in the end adopted the system: they insisted that the State recognise the existence of embezzlement, in order to force it to amnesty smugglers in return for payment of a forfeit (*composición*), rather than to halt trade altogether. This type of settlement first occurred in 1561, and was repeated several times at the end of the century (1593, 1595, 1597).

In this period, when massive quantities of silver were coming in, a special official was appointed to organise the imports. He was called the 'Master of Silver' and he was entirely in charge of it. In theory, he earned a large salary, as he took 1% of the silver under his control, but he had to pay all the employees out of this sum and to accept all the risks. A merchant such as Tomás de Cardona who became 'Master of Silver', acquired a kind of obsession with the silver problem from the job, and gave expression to it in numerous memoranda on the question of money. This was a typical instance of what was called *arbitrismo*, the contemporary mania for offering solutions to the ills of Spain.

Silver was imported in the form of ingots; it was weighed immediately and then locked up in the coffers of the House of Trade, under the control of the three highest officials. But it was not transferred directly to the Mint. The ingots were bought by individuals, known as 'buyers of gold and silver', and they finally took them to the mint. There were considerable profits here too, but it was also very risky, since it was not easy to give a sure estimate of the carat level of ingots. Although the profit per unit handled by these intermediaries would have been small, taken en masse, it must have been quite considerable. There were nonetheless many bankruptcies among the 'buyers of gold and silver'; in the mid-16th century there were 50 or 60 individual operators, but by 1615 there were only 8 'companies' (of which 4 went bankrupt) and in 1620 only 3 of these were left. The whole history of the change in the conjuncture early in the 17th century could perhaps be reconstructed by examining the development of the 'buyers' and 'masters of silver'.

Hamilton has emphasised the measures taken to minimise the extent of embezzlement, but this enables him to defend the accuracy of the figures compiled by him as typical of the overall imports of silver into Europe which first circulated in Spain. In order to establish the proportions of embezzlement, not only should the fraud itself be examined, but also the characteristics of when, where and at whose expense it took place. Despite everything, it is unlikely that fraud could completely falsify our knowledge of the import trends of American gold and silver, even if it obscures the absolute quantities. Certainly it should not be ignored.

American gold and silver was also diverted onto routes opened by warfare and by the actions of official or private pirates. There was an old tradition of piracy in the Mediterranean and the Atlantic: from the 14th and 15th centuries onwards Catalans, Genoese, Castilians and French had all engaged in it, especially against the Portuguese. In the 16th century it was the English who were most active. Hamilton maintains that piracy subtracted relatively little from the amount of American treasures which reached Europe, always for the same reasons. He estimates that between 80% and 85% of what left America reached Spain.

This is not impossible, and it is certainly true that popular imagination and a love of good stories have greatly exaggerated the effectiveness and relative importance of piracy, of 'trade at the point of a sword' and of all forms of violence and illegality practised against the Spanish Empire. All the same, in the 17th century Spain lost some very important naval positions to the English, Dutch and French, especially in the Caribbean. At first, pirates were mainly encountered near the coast. Seville had been chosen as the monopoly port precisely in order to prevent ships going too near to Portugal or to the French and English parts of the Atlantic. Already in 1523, however, the French had sacked Cortes' treasure ships; and in 1531 Francis I officially declared that the sea was common to everyone, and that the Pope's concession of the Americas to Spain was invalid. Throughout the first half of the century, it was the Portuguese rather than the Spanish against whom attacks were directed, since their ships carried much more precious cargoes. Even in 1555 the pirate Jacques de Sores, who had already raided Cartagena de Indias and Havana, was primarily aiming at Brazil. So too was the English pirate Hawkins, who generally sailed the route between Guinea and Brazil, seeking cargoes of slaves, which when captured, were as lucrative as cargoes of gold.

The real naval war began in 1566, under the stimulus both of the fighting in Flanders and of the growing flow of silver. Hawkins and his nephew Drake raided Havana, landed on 'Tierrafirma' and took enough plunder back to England to pay their creditors interest of 70%. These expeditions were privately financed, and before giving them a political veneer, Queen Elizabeth was personally involved in them like any other private speculator.

In 1568 there was a raid on the port of San Juan de Ulua, now Veracruz, where Mexican silver was loaded, and between 1575 and 1583 in particular the Spanish empire became the target both of the Dutch and of the English. Spain had just been victorious in the Mediterranean, defeating the Turks in the battle of Lepanto, but she fared otherwise in the fight for the Atlantic. With the cry 'Down with the Papists and on to Eldorado', Drake initiated a systematic struggle against the American treasure ships and raided Nombre de Dios and the Panama isthmus, through which Peruvian silver was transported on mules. In 1577 he excelled himself, passing through the straits of Magellan, sacking Lima, sailing up the American coast as far as California, and returning via the Far East and the Cape of Good Hope. He spent three years on the expedition; but he repaid Elizabeth 47 times the value of her initial investment, and the Queen knighted him on his flagship.

From 1583 to 1585, Drake and Frobisher attacked the Spanish coast at Vigo, as well as Florida, Santo Domingo, and Cartagena. It was then that the Captain-General of the Spanish fleet, Alvaro de Bazán, proposed that the English threat must be eliminated; England had to be attacked on her own ground and her fleets destroyed. 1588 was the year of the Invincible Armada. This episode did not destroy Spanish maritime power completely; the American empire was not lost, and in 1589 the English failed in their attacks on Corunna and the Azores, which they had hoped would be decisive. As the English were still at the stage of lightning attacks and raids, they were unable to advance and destroy their enemy. However, by raiding gold shipments from Venezuela in 1595, and seizing 20 million ducats in the raid on Cadiz in 1596, Raleigh did deal serious blows to Spanish 'treasure'. For Spain both the century and the reign of Philip II (1598) ended uneasily. Although the amounts lost through piracy were relatively slight, the 'defence' of the treasure involved enormous expenses, and this too is a factor which should be borne in mind.

16

Gold and Silver in Castile

We have followed gold and silver from the mines to Spain, and have seen what remained in America and what was lost through embezzlement or piracy. This chapter will attempt to show what happened when the supplies reached Spain: the impact they had there, why they left and what replaced them, as well as the psychological effects on the Spanish and the manner in which Spaniards were conscious of economic and monetary problems. Later on we shall examine the movements and the effects of the metal outside Spain (in France, Italy, England. . . .).

Once the cargoes of gold and silver had reached Seville, they had to be divided up into what belonged to the King, i.e. to the State, and what belonged to individuals or companies. Under pressure, the State sometimes took possession of individuals' shares, although this was not the norm. There was never any straightforward requisitioning, only forced loans in the form of bonds issued to the value of whatever the King had seized.

The proportion of gold and silver belonging to the King and to individuals must also be measured. According to Hamilton's lists, 447 million pesos were imported between 1503 and 1660, 117 million for the King and 330 million for private owners.[1] Rather over a quarter was therefore the King's. But although it was a smaller share the King's treasure had greater international influence, since it spread rapidly throughout Europe to pay the Crown debts. In comparison, the proportion belonging to private interests was especially important within Spain. The two types were linked, however, since the great international speculators, particularly the Germans and Genoese, had a really dominant influence, in the modern sense of the word, over Spanish private capital, in addition to control over royal silver. This capital was not

[1] Hamilton, op. cit. pp. 34–5.

negligible, but was of modest proportions and not accustomed to the ways of large-scale international finance.

The starting point for clarifying this is an examination of the relationship linking Sevillian imports of gold and silver to the public treasury, and that between the public treasury and international financiers. The latter were mainly Germans under Charles V and Genoese under Philip II, though the Genoese were operating under Charles V and German influences remained quite strong until the end of the century.

(1) The King's gold and silver: debts and asientos

From the reign of Charles I, who came to the throne of Spain in 1516, and ruled as Emperor Charles V from 1519 (abdicating all titles in 1556), the public treasury was accustomed to take loans from every source and from every corner of Europe too, as Charles had come to rule over the Low Countries, Austria, Italy and Germany as well as Spain. In Spain such loans took different forms: the issue of consolidated fixed-interest bonds, known as *juros*; forced loans of treasure from the Americas imported at Seville, in exchange for which the same kind of *juros* were given 'voluntary' loans, which were 'suggested' to the great lords and bishops – the Spanish historian Carande has said that Charles V was so affable he could make any man his banker; and, lastly, very short term debts contracted by the public administration in the form of bills of exchange which were redeemable at the next fair of Medina, Lyons or 'Besançon'.[2] The Besançon fairs were established by Charles V in the Franche-Comté to compete with Lyons, but they were never held in Besançon itself. Gradually they were shifted to Italy, in particular to Piacenza, even though they were still known as the 'Besançon fairs', and were eventually held at the gates of Genoa, where they were entirely dependent on the financiers of the city.

Such a system of short and long term debts required extremely good credit and the circulation of values through paper transactions. This point must be stressed, because it is very commonly said (and even sometimes written in serious books) that the only money known in the 16th century was metal coin. It is, of course, impossible simply to equate the fair payments, the issue of bills of exchange and credit, in other words the public and private credit arrangements of the 16th century, with modern 'book money', by which the circulation of gold is almost

---

[2] Carande. op. cit. vol. 3, Introduction, especially p. 15.

eliminated. In the 16th century, on the contrary, gold and silver circulated in long mule trains and convoys of carts, in the King's service as well as in the course of business. But it would be equally absurd, to think that every purchase in the 16th century was paid for in good coin from the Americas. This coin did not always reach down into the everyday channels of circulation, and, on the other hand, at the top a lot of large-scale payment was carried out without any transfer of gold or silver. Tomás de Mercado said that the fairs of Medina del Campo were a 'factory for contracts'; only paper was to be seen there, and not a single silver coin.

There were certain payments which did require metal coin (balances between countries, international debt repayment, the wages of mercenaries etc.). The problem was precisely how to pay quickly in metal where it was necessary, and how to recover the equivalent at the place of origin, that is, from the state coffers, where the gold and silver of the Americas and taxes were, however irregularly, collected. The only people capable of effecting such movements of metal to a given place and of waiting for repayment – with interest – by the state, were the great bankers. Their methods were well tried, and they were able to raise credit, from the public for fixed interest loans, or commercially.

These bankers were involved with the Spanish crown through the *asiento* system. This is a general word for contract, but it is also the specific name for a kind of contract giving a detailed account of the mutual rights and obligations between a financier (or finance company) on the one hand, and the King, on the other, for a particular undertaking. It covered all kinds of public business transacted by private concession holders, such as those that were found in France in the 16th century under the name *partis* (the financiers were called *partisans*) later known as *traités* and *traitants* and also as *fermés* and *fermiers*. In Spain all these were known as *asientos* and *asientistas*. The state signed such contracts for the collection of some taxes, the exploitation of certain Crown property, such as the Almadén mines or the income of the military-religious orders which were taken over by the Fuggers, sometimes for exploitation of whole colonial areas, as in the case of the Welsers in Venezuela, or more simply and more commonly, for granting a monopoly to supply the army or equip a fleet for the Indies. Any operation of this type was in fact a credit operation, since the financier always advanced the Crown considerable sums which were to be recovered later. There were big risks, and many spectacular crashes occurred, but it was precisely this element of risk which justified the high rates of

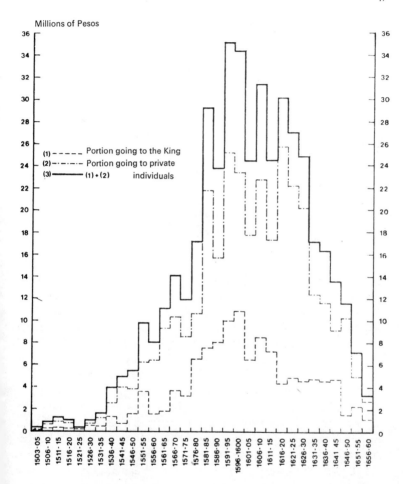

Figure 6. Total imports of precious metals into Spain, 1503–1660.

interest, and the opportunity for profit.

What guarantee was there for such operations? The influence of gold and silver from the Indies is often exaggerated, because in the early 16th century enormous credit operations were carried out on a quite different basis, such as Spanish mines, wool stocks, or public loans in Hamburg. Spanish and European wealth *preceded* the influx of American gold. The surprising fact about the 16th century, however, is the growing role of Castile in guarantees to financiers. Around 1515, loans to the King from Hamburg ran at around 50,000 Flemish pounds; around 1556 they had reached 7,000,000 pounds; but though they therefore multiplied by 140 times in 40 years, in 1556 they amounted to only a quarter of the monies loaned to the King by Castile. The only explanation for this is the influx of American gold and silver.

There does at least appear to have been one other guarantee. Spanish resources placed in the hands of the bankers included taxes collected by the Spanish treasury, which came largely from the peasantry of Castile. It seems unlikely, however, that such taxes, in particular taxes on consumption, could have increased as they did, without a certain basis of prosperity resulting from the penetration of precious metals in exchange for the agricultural and industrial produce of Spain. Price rises, stemming from the attraction of the American market, first benefited those whose products were in demand on the American market. Although Castile's efforts to meet the demands of royal taxation were, in the end, self-destructive, they could only have been sustained for so long on the basis of a major increase in the production of taxable matter; this in turn was a consequence of the colonisation process. The way in which the Spanish crown used American treasure shows that its direct share of the treasure was in reality inadequate. Had it been enough to cover its debts, Spain could have been relieved of the burden of taxes which in the end was her undoing, and prices would have risen less. In fact, the King's share hardly affected Spain, as it was already committed elsewhere.

In the third volume of his book on Charles V and his bankers, Carande puts forward the following calculations for the reign:[3]

> *1520–1532*: 'the years of apprenticeship'. In only 13 years, the Emperor borrowed 5,379,053 ducats, which, with interest, came to 6,327,371 ducats.

[3] ibid, vol. 3.

1533–1542: 'the years of success'. In these 10 years 5,437,699 ducats were borrowed, and the total debt this represented came to 6,594,365.

1543–1551: 'the years of uncertainty'. In these nine years Charles V borrowed 8,397,616 ducats, costing him 10,737,843.

1552–1556: 'the years of affliction'. In these five years borrowing reached 9,643,869 ducats, and repayments 14,351,591.

There was an astonishingly rapid rise in the yearly average: from 413,000 ducats per year in the first period to 1,929,000 in the last. A comparison of the rise in the sums contracted and the sums paid out shows that the cost of loans (accumulated interest, exchange, etc.) rose from 17.6% in the first period to 48.8% in the last. Total payments finally rose to 38,011,170 ducats, of which 33,102,305 was to foreigners (German, Flemish and Italian). The Crown itself began to export currency, and authorised other individuals to do the same by special export licences.

To sum up, the external debt contracted for the needs of imperial policy rose to 37,059,239 ducats, roughly two million more than the amount of precious metals reaching Seville and belonging to the Crown. This explains why the King was more than once obliged to requisition gold and silver belonging to individuals, to resort to forced public loans, and to demand much heavier taxation. Meanwhile fiscal revenue and financial speculation alike injected privately-owned American treasure into international channels; only the paths they took were different.

(2) Privately-owned gold and silver

It is necessary to distinguish between private gold and silver owned by *conquistadores*, colonists, emigrants and administrators, who sent silver back from the Indies on the one hand; and on the other hand, that owned by merchants, whether it remained in Spain or was exported. In the early period of colonisation, the remittances of *conquistadores* and colonists might be for those who had financed the expeditions; as already mentioned, the conquests were often financed by private interests. When the financiers were Genoese bankers or German companies, such as the Welsers, the gold and silver would of course be exported once more and used for further speculation. When the patrons held high positions within Spain, however, whether as laymen or churchmen, or as people close to the King, Spanish society gained directly, from above. The wealth obtained was predominantly spent on luxury consumption.

At a lower level, the *conquistadores* themselves and their soldiers, the emigrants and the mine-contractors (they are known to have been numerous and varied) did not retain all the precious metals they earned or seized in America. Many still thought of eventually returning to their families and their native land. Even the colonial administrators, who earned fortunes, came back. All this repatriated gold and silver was invested directly in Spain. The houses of the lesser nobility of Estremadura grew rich from the Indies, and even today, despite a certain rustic flavour, they give an air of grandeur to small towns such as Caceres, Badajoz, Trujillo and Mérida. Some of the ornamentation in fact records the Indian origin of the buildings, as with the inventor from Seville who had a *guaira* depicted on his coat of arms, or the houses in Salamanca which have figures of natives carved in the door lintels and window frames. The most famous *conquistador* house in Trujillo is Francisco Pizarro's, and in 1580 a Flemish traveller Philippe de Caverel, said that this house gave the town 'an air of the greatest beauty and civility, so that it is easy to guess it was built with Peruvian gold.'[4]

Seville, of course, also bears the traces of a wealthy past, such as Venice does. In particular, many churches, as in the Americas, benefited directly from the influx of gold, partly because members of the church had also enriched themselves and partly because of a large number of gifts from the faithful. Where precious metals and jewels were used for the decoration of churches, they were simply a form of saving (and here as in the Middle Ages, this phenomenon could restrict the circulation of money). The building, decoration and furnishing of these houses and churches also required a large number, as well as an elite group, of architects, builders, carpenters and sculptors, who were highly paid, creating great traditional artisan strata such as the Valladolid polychrome sculptors, the *tallistas*.

The increase in prices, which as we know began in Seville with the purchase of cargoes for the caravels, spread throughout the Spanish interior as a result of the sharply increased expenditure of those who benefited from the wave of gold and silver. Quite large sections of the population were made relatively better off by the tendency to employ more artisans and servants at higher wages. This chain effect was

4 Philippe de Caverel, *Ambassade en Espagne et en Portugal en 1582 du R.P. en Dieux dom Jean Sarrazin, abbé de Saint Vaast*, Arras 1860, p. 360.

reconstructed by the great economist Cantillon in the 18th century, on the basis of a simple theoretical argument.[5]

Remittances by merchants were rather different from those of emigrants and explorers, as they represented the return on commodities sent to the Indies. Of course, if merchants gained a profit, they did spend it on consumption, building, and good living, and this reinforced the effects already mentioned. They also had a preoccupation of their own: the need to buy cargoes for caravel voyages. The internal market was expanding as well as the external market. Ingots imported from the Americas by a particular merchant were bought up by the 'buyers of gold and silver', who gave them the equivalent in currency or in promissory notes for a certain fair, or in repayment on the sum advanced (as credit was more and more common). Remittances by merchants were therefore rapidly put into circulation.

There is still, however, a need to distinguish between Spanish and foreign trade. A Spanish merchant buying Spanish products for the caravels certainly did contribute to price increases, but in a way which favoured the Spanish producer, and which in turn encouraged the productive activity of the Spanish economy. The only problem is to establish whether the increase in wages and other costs did not remove too rapidly the margin so gained. Some sections of the population could gain, while social categories on fixed incomes would be very adversely affected: the aristocrat in debt and the squire reduced to near-beggary, both trying to keep their social standing without the wherewithal, were common figures in literature, from *Lazarillo de Tormes* to *Don Quijote*; and the concern of some theologians (such as Domingo de Soto in his *Deliberación sobre la causa de los pobres*) confirms that they had a basis in reality. These were times of inflation: the old landowner was mocked by the nouveau riche, and his only vengeance was scorn or fantasy. This fantasy transferred the experience of the Indies into literature, once it had ceased to be a common reality.

The case of a foreign merchant or one working for foreign companies was quite different. When a merchant paid for foreign supplies or exported profits, gold and silver left Spain. Merchants had no right to do this, because it violated the laws against exporting metals, which stemmed from mediaeval times and often are still in force today. While the legislation was very clear, the problem was rather whether such a prohibition could be maintained when the balance of trade was running

[5] Richard Cantillon, *Essaie sur la nature du Commerce en général*, Paris 1952, pp. 91–92.

into increasing deficit, and when any export of silver was profitable, since its value outside Spain was greater.

The prosperity of international financiers, especially those specialising in exchange, was made of course from the export of currency. As they had already done so with the King's silver, so now they proceeded to do the same in a commercial context as well. Felipe Ruíz Martin has established a chronology of this process, taking into account both the import trends and the problem of war expenditure.[6] Until 1551 and after the Peace of Cateau-Cambrésis, from 1560 to 1566, individuals were definitely forbidden to export gold or silver. The registered figures for official exports were very small: 15,000 ducats in 1528, 40,000 in 1529, 108,000 in 1532 and 30,000 in 1536. How, then, did silver get out of Spain? There was always smuggling, and Spanish currency was found in many boats which should never have carried it. Even the most honourable merchants, such as the House of Ruíz from Medina, were prosecuted for smuggling, and Azpilcueta said that ducats left Spain 'in olive-barrels and wine-casks'. It is impossible to give a figure, but it could not have been of decisive proportions because large-scale smuggling was extremely risky.

Bills of exchange, though not a means of exporting silver, were good for payment outside Spain as long as the equivalent was available in Spain. In principle, it should have been possible to balance all trade by this type of payment, but this was only so if the balance of payments was in equilibrium. This was not the case, since Spain bought more than she sold, and the only surplus she had was in silver. There was normally an abundance of silver in Spain and scarcity on the Flemish, Italian and French markets. So it was possible to make a profit through exchange, and the people best placed to do this were international speculators connected with the Crown by *asientos*, because this enabled them to place their silver on the most profitable market.

Purchasing in Spain was another means of using Spanish silver which could not be exported. In the first two-thirds of the 16th century, except for times of war, speculators bought many things in Spain in order to take advantage of the accumulation of silver – the Genoese in particular. It might be thought that this would encourage Spanish production, but the main purchases of the other Europeans were of food and raw materials, rather than manufactures. These included wools,

[6] Felipe Ruiz Martin, *Lettres marchandes échangées entre Florence et Medina del Campo*, Paris 1965. There is a good introduction which Ruiz Martin later expanded into a book, *El siglo de los genoveses en Castilla, 1528–1627: capitalismo cosmopolita y capitalismos nacionales.*

Granada silk, honey, oil, fruit, oranges, wax, iron, alum, mercury, salt and products from the Indies for re-export – cochineal, sugar, and dye-woods. Manufactured products covered some kinds of cloth, leather, soap and gloves. The overall effect was to increase the cost prices of Spanish products and labour; Spain's advantage was temporary, and it could not last.

In fact foreigners and their agents wished, as soon as they could, to export from Spain the commodity which would buy most abroad, that is, silver, and they therefore tried to obtain licences to export currency. Such licences were granted by the state when it could not do otherwise, but it gradually became a normal practice, as a premium of up to 8–10% could be obtained for these licences. Many were granted during the French war (1552–1557) and suspended after the Treaty of Cateau-Cambrésis; they were granted again after 1566, during the war in Flanders.

In the first stage, that of the French war, the massive exports of money were transported by the Atlantic fleets, plying between Basque and Cantabrian ports (especially Laredo) and Flemish ports. The silver was taken across Castile from South to North, from Seville to Laredo, via Madrid. During the war in Flanders, however, ocean-going shipping was blockaded by England and the Dutch, and American gold and silver had to take either the land route across France – until this too soon became impossible because of the Wars of Religion. Alternatively, whole caravans of silver were sent from Seville and Madrid to the Mediterreanean ports – to Barcelona, Cartagena, Vinaroz and Valencia – to be shipped to Genoa and from there redistributed through Europe. After 1576–1577, this practice became the rule.

The demand for Spanish products should then have fallen, and circulation should have been slowed down. Normally this would have reduced price increases (which were already less intense than at the beginning of the century) but for this to be possible the Spanish would have had to give up the levels of consumption to which they had become accustomed. Instead, the Genoese were able to make enormous gains from the Spanish situation. After the bankruptcies of 1557, which in particular affected loans made in the times of Charles V, and forced the Fuggers, for example, to fall back on their positions inside Germany, the Genoese saw that the 'campaign funds' required by Spanish ambitions would always have to be supplied by international financiers. The problem was how to raise the money. The Genoese were able to bring the large savings accumulated in Spain in the previous period of prosperity into use; they gave a new flexibility to the system of *juros* or royal bonds, accepting them in payment of contracts. These were immediately resold at a profit to the Spanish public, with whom the bonds were very popular, since everyone wished to live on interest. Churchmen, widows, well-off peasants, burghers and aristocrats all wanted to buy bonds, and so widespread was the demand that the interest rate fell from 10% to 7% in a few years.

The Crown and its advisers became aware of the danger, and there was a campaign against the Genoese. The King first tried to incorporate Spanish capitalists into the *juros* system: he wanted to make the House of Trade the main agent of trade with the Indies, on condition that the profits were made into 5% bonds and offered to the public; but the House of Trade did not pay the interest on them, and when the state gave way to the temptation to use its funds, these bonds lost 50% of their value. The Genoese bought them up and turned them into guaranteed bonds in their usual way.

After long debates in the Madrid Cortes in 1575, Philip II, who did not like the Genoese, and mistrusted them in the same way as some of his councillors, ordered that all *asientos* granted since 1566 be revised, and the balance liquidated at a rate which was disastrous for the *asientistas*. But there were no Spanish capitalists capable of replacing the Genoese in their role of raising credit and transferring necessary funds to the North of Europe; and complaints and threats from the Genoese (who were secretly aiding the Netherlands revolt) were in the end successful. Moreover, after 1580, the sudden influx of American silver led to a temporary illusion that there was an inexhaustible supply of wealth. Most of it, however, went to Italy. Then the difficult problem arose of devaluing silver in relation to gold, the latter being scarcer and in growing demand; in particular, the troops in North Europe insisted on being paid in gold. Once more, only the Genoese could help.

As a result of these various different phases, Spain was engulfed in a wave of silver and credit, while she went constantly further into debt and her foreign deficit grew. Productive activity was gradually reduced, and Spain became a country living on interest at just the time when prices again leapt upwards, in the last ten years of the century. It is possible to trace the evolution of this awareness, as the Spanish gradually became more aware of the dangers of the situation.

17

The Spanish Debate on Precious Metals

This chapter is concerned with how the Spanish realised the consequences of the massive influx of precious metals and rising commodity prices, how they became aware of the gains and risks involved, and how they came to understand the nature of this two-sided phenomenon. The Spanish contribution to early thinking about the price revolution deserves particular attention because little is known about it, and it is sometimes misrepresented. In French history, Jean Bodin's work of 1568 is taken to be the first analysis of price rises. The traditional assumption of French economic studies is that the Spanish experienced the price revolution without understanding it, and were concerned only to take draconian measures against the export of gold and silver, believing them to be the only source of wealth. This view is presented as a primitive form of mercantilism, and given cumbrously pedantic names such as 'bullionism' or 'chrysohedonism' (the belief that all happiness lies in gold).[1]

No investigation of the problem of the world's gold can neglect its subjective aspect. Was gold the supreme and only end, the 'sinew of war', the sole index of individual wealth and national grandeur? Or was it the symbol of corruption (*auri sacra fames*), the seed of the destruction of true wealth, which is to be found only in the production of necessities? It was Sully who said that the real treasures and gold-mines of Peru were her cornfields and pastures.

Moralists, theologians and writers, who were content to elaborate on classical and biblical maxims and familiar teachings, dominated the conflict between these two viewpoints. But there were also those who tried to understand the economic, sociological and historical effects of the imports of gold and silver, and it was naturally the Spanish who felt

[1] cf. Pierre Vilar, 'Les primitifs espagnols de la pensée économique: "quantitativisme" et "bullionisme"' in *Hommage à Marcel Bataillon*, special issue of the *Bulletin Hispanique*, 1962.

Fig. 11. Spain in the 16th century.

the first, most direct, impact of what was happening, since they were confronted with the phenomenon as it occurred. This meant that they thought about it and understood it better than anyone, a fact which is too often forgotten. 16th and early 17th century Spanish thought has a major place in the long history of man's economic and moral analysis of the problems of gold and precious metals.

The Spanish acted and reacted at different levels towards mining in the colonies and the rise of commerce in which monetary metals then played the leading role. In the Indies, as we have seen, the Potosí silver market set off a chain of economic growth, fortune-making, corruption, social struggles, disputes between authorities, and heart-searching by administrators and priests, all reflected in some very modern types of investigation, and in streams of invective coming from the pulpit. When the metal reached Seville, it set off a similar chain of reactions, though they were less marked. At the individual level, everyone tried to take advantage of the situation: fortunes were quickly made and lost, classes living on fixed incomes were slowly impoverished. Some people went on the attack, some on the defensive, and still others fell victims. Everyone had an individual strategy, with no guarantee that taken altogether they would prove harmonious. Generally, prices rose so much that in the end they threatened to destroy the very sources of income they had fostered, by destroying internal purchasing power and making Spanish production uncompetitive. At the State level, wealth produced the same effects as on individuals: the illusion of wealth led to indebtedness and in the end an inability to sustain day-to-day expenditure and the practices and ambitions which had been built up.

There were two lines of thinking about these developments: an economic analysis and moral critique of individual attitudes towards gold, fortune-making and impoverishment; and a social analysis and political critique of the attitude of the state. We must distinguish the different kinds of critique and analysis, according to where they were expressed and what moments in time produced them. Such is history: the explanation of the interaction of material events and the minds of men, by locating them in time and space.

(1) The different varieties of critique
There were three main types of criticism:

(a) The critique of the various Cortes: these were representative assemblies, which, in Castile, were essentially expressions of the towns (in actual fact of *some* towns only). They expressed the important, if narrow, views and interests of consumers, tax-payers and the artisan and trading classes.

(b) The analyses of theologians are particularly interesting because they represent the meeting of mediaeval Christian thought, scholastic reasoning and the Thomist morality based on 'natural law', with modern developments following the great discoveries, the flow of precious metals, commerce, and profit-making. Thomism and the Church were of course opposed to usury in principle, that is, to any interest-bearing loan exploiting poverty, need and scarcity; but the Thomist position, deriving from 'natural law', admitted of any rationally justifiable profit. For example, the 'just price' was not the 'morally' just price, but the 'common price' of the market-place, which was therefore considered 'natural' and 'reasonable'. Consequently a theologian charged with deciding the legitimacy of gain, had to go into subtleties of analysis to discover whether or not it was 'reasonable' to profit on a given exchange, a given fair-time payment or a certain maritime loan, and the confessor's handbook became a veritable economics textbook. The most intelligent theologians in fact tried to develop economic theory. Starting, by definition, from the level of the individual, their theories were, like 'modern' theories, individualistic, subjective and psychological.

(c) The reflections of counsellors of state, whether expressed spontaneously or on request, were the fruits of observing overall financial developments (the balance of trade and other accounts, domestic and foreign prices, etc.). This introduced the modern concept of national accounts, which today forms the legacy of mercantilism. The views of counsellors of state, rarely expressed in the early 16th century, were put forward during the mid-century crisis and again around 1600, and later appeared frequently in the writings of the 17th century *arbitristas*. Some of these were quite mad and others were extremely lucid.

(2) Where the critiques were made

These critiques are often illuminated by examining where they came from: the great commercial towns of Seville and Medina del Campo produced analyses of the effects of trade. The theologian Tomás de Mercado came from Seville, but he spent his life in Mexico and had been taught in Salamanca. His *Summa de tratos y contratos* is an account of trading operations seen through the eyes of a theologian. Around 1600, 'memorials' were drawn up by Medina del Campo to analyse the basis of the city's prosperity in the years of success, the reasons for its decline and the regrets of the merchants.

Industrial and manufacturing towns like Toledo and Segovia expressed the opinion of industrial producers who welcomed gradual price increases but were opposed to exporting raw materials and importing industrial products which competed with their own. Finally, areas with an agricultural or pastoral economy, such as Burgos, North Castile and Navarre were, by the end of the century, deploring the decline of agriculture, in a tone suggestive of Sully (and even of the physiocrats). They argued that land, as opposed to the chimerical yellow metal, was the only real source of wealth.

(3) The periodisation of critiques

Three main periods can be distinguished. The first, between 1500 and 1550 was one of good times for merchants, when only consumers were worried. The optimism of the first half of the century is evoked by the names Chaunu has given to the different conjunctural cycles: 1500–1510, the 'take-off cycle'; 1510–1522, the cycle of the 'greatness and monopoly of the Islands'; 1522–1532, the 'New Spain cycle', which was dominated by the conquest of Mexico; 1532–1544, 'Peru's entry onto the scene', and 1544–1550, 'the record years ending the period of easy prosperity'.

In Spain this period produced few critiques, but it did stimulate some theologians in the fair towns to begin writing, and there were complaints about rising prices and state expenditure from some Cortes. Theological tracts tended to come from the experience of the fair towns, from Medina del Campo and from Villalón, near Valladolid, in the years 1540–1545. There were, for example, the *Beneficial Treatise on Exchange and Business* by Cristobal de Villalón (Valladolid 1542) and the *Instructions for Merchants* by Saravia de la Calle (Medina del Campo 1544). These tracts describe and discuss the merchants' business at the fairs, the determination of prices and the legitimacy of exchange. They do not, however, oppose speculative price rises or currency depreciation, and are indicative of a period of rising prosperity; they remain unaware of the risks of the acceleration taking place.

Protests by the Cortes against the high cost of living, and measures against it, occurred in 1515, 1525, 1532, 1534, 1542, 1544 and 1548. The towns clearly stated that the source of price increases was exports, but they criticised only the export of foodstuffs and raw materials, especially wool and leather. As already mentioned, the Genoese often exported profits made in Seville by buying quantities of untreated wool and leather, and this increased the price of raw materials at the expense of Spanish industry. The Cortes however did not dare to demand that exports to the Indies be banned, though these took the heaviest responsibility for rising prices, because the increase in manufactured products favoured producers.

Nonetheless, by the end of this period (1545–1548) they had begun to criticise imports of foreign manufactures competing with Spanish products, and imports of useless objects 'only for diversion', and 'puerilities', such as baubles, bangles, cheap glassware, and playing cards. They pointed out that Castile also produced glassware and cards, and they finally proposed to solve the matter by making 'all foreigners selling goods to these Kingdoms promise to take payment in goods and not in money'. This amounted to proposing exchange agreements as a way of resisting the export of good currency. They had a good understanding of the problem: they saw that when a foreigner bought raw materials and sold manufactured goods, the balance of trade was left in deficit and good currency left the country.

Around 1548–1500 this increased awareness began to be expressed in a curious way. It became customary to say that 'Spain is the foreigner's Indies', and that 'they treat us like Indians'. The first, rather facile, explanation for this, is that the Spanish were astonished to see French and Milanese peddlers selling imitation jewellery, beads and trinkets to peasants in Spanish villages in exchange for good coin; hence the expression 'they treat us like Indians'. Contemporary accounts had spread stories about the American Indians who from Columbus onwards handed over gold and silver in exchange for glass beads.

The expression, however, had a deeper significance: after exploiting the Indies, which paid a high price for Spanish goods, Spain was in turn being exploited; she in turn paid a high price, in precious metals, for foreign goods. Theoretically, this process should have begun once prices rose faster in Spain than elsewhere, but as long as sales of Spanish goods to the Indies exceeded imports to Spain, certain classes at least could share in a general growth of incomes and capital formation. When, however, rising prices made it necessary to import more and more, to the point where imports exceeded exports, the tendency led towards a collective impoverishment, and this gave a sharper meaning to the phrase, 'the foreigner's Indies'.

The second major phase of criticism came in the years of commercial paralysis, 1550–1562. This is Chaunu's 'great mid-century recession'.

when there was a growing awareness of the dangers. In the years 1550–1562, the supply of gold dried up, and new mining techniques were established. Chaunu's figures show a sharp decline in the Spanish-American trade: the tonnage of shipping in both directions fell from around 12,000 in 1550 to 6,900 in 1556. Though prices were slowed down they did not fall, and wages rose, partly because there was a war going on until the Peace of Cateau-Cambrésis in 1559. In 1557, the greatest financial crisis of the century left the state virtually bankrupt; this benefited the Genoese and ruined the position of the Fuggers, and by selling royal bonds to the public, the Genoese helped to turn Spain from an entrepreneurial nation into a nation of *rentiers*.

The dangers were recognised and a remedy proposed by Luis Ortiz, a royal councillor, Treasurer of Castile and citizen of Burgos. His work remained unpublished until 1958, and has been more often quoted than read. On the grounds that six chapters are entitled 'How to stop silver leaving Spain', it has been commonly said that Ortiz was interested only in measures of coercion to keep it in the country. But after a detailed reading of the manuscript, E. J. Hamilton concluded that it contained a theory of the balance of payments which, for its time, was very perceptive and was so even by later standards.

Luis Ortiz argued the following. Spain should be rich and thrifty, and had to maintain a gap between production and consumption to allow for saving. 'Work is wealth', and the idle gentry, soldiers, servants, beggars, students, lawyers and men of letters had to be sent back to productive work and 'mechanical' employment. The real reason for rising prices was that the Spanish acquired everything through the work of others. The Spanish took gold and silver from the Indians for next to nothing; but foreigners in turn paid next to nothing for the same gold and silver, obtained not only by Indian labour but by Spanish courage and daring.

Ortiz proposed putting less silver in Spanish coin so that foreigners would be less tempted by it (in other words, devaluation to discourage imports); and forming a war treasury (so restricting circulation of the metal). He was therefore well aware that prices depended on circulation. He wanted women to use spinning wheels instead of spindles, so that they would produce four times as fast; he wanted canals and irrigation works built, and the flow of rivers to be altered. In other words, productivity should be increased and investments made in productive equipment. Ortiz recognised that this could not be done without silver, but he saw this not as wealth in itself, but as potentially productive capital.

Ortiz in fact proposed a modern type of 'stabilisation' programme. He wrote a good analysis of the 'national accounts', especially the balance of payments, listing all the parts of the 'balance of trade' which were in deficit (i.e. where imports exceeded exports), including interest to the King's creditors, and foreign monopolies, payments to Rome for indulgences, profits, savings sent or taken back home by immigrant labourers, and all the various components of 'invisible' trade.

Ortiz was not of course modern in every respect. He invoked the names of the Virgin and St. James and the seven choirs of angels and he wanted to ban the import of books not just to rectify the balance of trade but also to protect orthodoxy. Nonetheless he had a clear picture of the possible remedies. He did not, however, see all the causes of the dangers he denounced; he omitted to mention that idleness was often enforced by, or that an excess of servants and unproductive employ-ment was due to, the wealth Spain had previously gained from the exploitation of the Indies.

In his indignation at Spain being 'the foreigner's Indies', Ortiz did not pause to ask if this was not simply because she herself had exploited the Indies. He had no conception of the dialectic of exploiter and exploited, of coloniser and colonised. He was, however, right to think that if Spain had spent her wealth on productive equipment instead of on conspicuous consumption and on 'going to Salamanca', she would have become the world's first modern nation. It is doubtful whether this was historically possible, as the mass of metal was still far greater than would then have been necessary to buy machinery. We should remember the example of Potosí, where eight million pesos were spent on the coronation celebrations, as against three million for hydraulic works. Ortiz understood the dangers of such sumptuary expenditure.

The third period is that between 1562 and 1598, which experienced the late 16th century wave of silver. With Mexican and then Potosí silver, the volume of metal imports rose again, successive technical innovations making it cheaper and cheaper. There was, therefore, a new upturn in Spanish prices. But the appearance of wealth again obscured the overall problems: there were no more critical analyses like Ortiz's, but there were frequent protests from the various Cortes against alarming price rises. The large number of business crashes, and the rapid decline of the Castile fairs, produced numerous 'memorials' on the fragility of the mercantile economy in such towns as Toledo and Medina del Campo.

The most interesting theoretical development of this period is the elaboration of the theological explanation of rising prices. The existence of this school makes it necessary to modify the common assumption that Jean Bodin was the first to relate rising prices to the imports of precious metals. In particular two other men must be included with Jean Bodin as being the originators of the quantitative theory of money: Martin de Azpilcueta, the Basque theologian from Navarre, known as the 'Doctor of Navarre', and Tomás de Mercado, who has already been quoted frequently.

(4) Theories of theologians

Azpilcueta was a confessor and author of various Manuals 'for confessors and penitents' which dealt with cases of conscience in every aspect of morality: in their many editions they were very widely read in Spain, Italy and France. These manuals include a chapter specially devoted to usury, commenting on the commandment 'thou shalt not steal', and one of 'Resolutory Commentaries' on exchange; these present the cases in which it is legitimate or forbidden to lend, give security, form a company or make profits on bills of exchange. One or two quotations from these passages are worth noting, as they show an awareness of the relationship between an abundance of coin and rising prices.

This relationship was apparently familiar to all the scholastic theologians who attempted to discover why a currency did not retain the same value at all times and in all places. Azpilcueta gives eight reasons and quotes six authorities to support his point that 'The seventh reason why money falls or rises is the lack or abundance of it. . . .' It was, then, well established that money obeyed the law of supply and demand.

He is even more specific in the passage where, like Bodin, he discusses the relation between price increases and the discovery of the Indies: 'All goods grow dearer for the great need and small quantity of them; and in that money can be sold or changed in any other way, it is merchandise, as said above, and so it too becomes dearer for the great need and small quantity of it. Similarly, in the countries where there is a great want of money, everything, even men's labour, is given for less money, than where there is abundance of it, as experience shows that in France, where there is less money than in Spain, bread wine, cloth and men's labour are worth much less, and even in Spain, when there was less money goods and labour were given for much less than after the discovery of the Indies flooded it with gold and silver.'[2] This was written in

[2] Martin de Azpilcueta, *Manuel de confesores*, Estalla 1566, 'Comentario resolutorio de Cambios', p. 84.

1556, twelve years before Bodin, as part of the *Resolutory commentary on exchange*, which because of its theoretical importance, has recently been re-published in Spain and France.

Mercado's *Summa de tratos y contratos* was published in Salamanca in 1569, with a second edition in Seville in 1572. The first edition appeared at the same time as Bodin's *Response to Malestroict*, but according to the *imprimatur* date on Mercado's book the one could not have influenced the other: they were coincidental. Mercado attaches great importance to what is now called the 'purchasing power' of money. He calls it 'the esteem of money', meaning that at different times and places money is differently 'esteemed'; i.e. the quantity of other products it buys varies. He states that 'the difference in quantity equals the unequal reputation of the money', and provides an almost mathematical expression for the equilibrium between the effects of availability and the effects of demand.

Together with this logical, abstract investigation, Mercado's book describes all the transactions of Seville and the Indies, with concrete examples: for example, the way a speculator put up the price of velvet in Granada to load a caravel in Seville. Mercado, like Bodin, gives a list of countries in order of the cost of living, the reverse of the order for the 'esteem' of money. Money was valued least of all in the Indies since 'as that is where it is born and gathered, it is held in small esteem. . . .' He then lists Spain, which received most of this metal, and this is followed by Flanders, Italy and France. He even notes the regional variation of prices within Spain, depending on the distance from Andalusia, and the periodisation of price rises: '. . . we can see that a thousand ducats are esteemed much higher in Castile than in Andalusia, and even in the same town at different times we find the same discrimination. Thirty years ago it was a great thing to have a thousand maravedis, which are now counted as nothing, though the price of maravedis is the same.'[3]

The last phrase anticipates a possible objection of the kind made by Malestroict: 'the price of maravedis is the same' means that there had been no official devaluation or change in the legal ratio between silver coin and accounting money. What had changed was the general psychological view of silver. Mercado concludes: 'The difference in esteem for money in the same town determined by time in the same town is brought about by various means which, as I have said, cause this to occur in different towns at the same time.'

Mercado was well aware that money, being valued more highly abroad

---

[3] Tomás de Mercado, op. cit. fo 90 ro.

than in Spain, would tend to flee the country, since it brought more products elsewhere. The flows of money were counter-balanced by flows of trade, and foreign goods therefore invaded both Spain and the Indies. He realised both the causes of high prices, the abundance of silver, and the way price rises developed: merchandise was exported to the Indies at higher and higher prices and there was a tendency to go on spending more as long as more silver was available. Lastly he saw what the results of high prices were: there was no possibility of producing cheaply and everything was bought abroad.

Although the decline of Spain – even the economic decline – was still far off, this is why Mercado was disturbed and pessimistic: 'Hence the disorder: for rich and poor alike load the ships, and in so doing destroy both commonweals, Spain and the Indies, in Spain making prices rise with their great demand, and the great number of merchants approaching foreigners as well as Spanish for ridiculously high prices.' Such a situation could not go on: it would lead to the decline of Spain.

There was a fourth period, which came after the half-century between 1500 and 1550 when prices crept imperceptibly upwards, after the mid-century mining crisis of 1550–1562, and after the years of the silver imports, 1562–1598, when everyone began to denounce price rises and warn of the dangers. This was a period when everyone became aware of the dangers of inflation, which was strangling the Spanish economy in the face of foreign competition. It became clear that precious metals had made prices rise; that they had not remained in Spain, but had been replaced by vast credits, promissory notes, bonds and bad currency (common copper and low-grade foreign coin); that there was no work and that people were living without producing; and that taxes were very heavy because the state was massively indebted and had to carry out a policy for which it now had only a semblance of means.

(5) The decline becomes apparent: the 'curse of gold'

There now appeared an abundance – if not a super-abundance – of economic and political literature on the dangers facing Spain; it began with the death of Philip II in 1598 and continued until the dramatic crisis of 1640 when Catalonia and Portugal broke away. This literature necessitates a re-examination of two views which are still widely held: first, that the Spanish identified gold and silver with real wealth; and secondly, that moral opposition to the damage done by gold came late, in the 18th century, and was not based on an economic analysis.

In fact, the Spanish of the 1600s understood perfectly well that because they had too much gold, and later silver, these metals had been drained from the country; that despite this loss the metals had had a major influence on the domestic economy through the credits, guarantees, and interest payments to which the precious metals were committed; and that the 'inflation' in monetary circulation had compromised domestic and foreign expenditure, driven up prices and encouraged idleness and unproductive occupations. Moreover, they saw that rising prices had been fatal to Spanish production, which could not compete with foreign goods.

Authors varied in their reactions: some favoured a return, in almost physiocratic terms, to agriculture, others to industry (some even made a mystique of protectionism), and still others advocated an increase in population. Writers hostile to emigration, to gold and to silver, denounced the parasitism of living off the colonies altogether. Some moralists even introduced the idea that Spain was going through the cycle followed by the Roman Empire, that of prosperity, corruption and decline.

Strictly economic ideas were much clearer, and there were three characteristic versions of these. On the flight of gold and silver, the first such topic, the 1586 Cortes declared: 'It is evident to you from experience that scarcely has it come in than it disappears, and that the more of it that comes in, the less the Kingdom has.'[4] The 1588–1593 Cortes states: 'Though our kingdoms could be the richest in the world for the gold and silver they have got and still get from the Indies, they are the poorest, for they are only a bridge for these to go into the Kingdoms of our enemies and the enemies of the Holy Catholic Faith.'[5] And the 1566 Cortes said: 'Experience shows that when a fleet comes in from the Indies with much money, within a month or two there is no good money to be found for it is all exported at once in indirect ways.'[6]

On the mechanism and the contradiction of price rises, there is, to take one example, an admirable *Memorial* of 1600 by Gonzales de Cellorigo, which begins with a description of the plague of 1599–1600 in Valladolid, and goes on to examine the diseased state of the kingdom. There is one chapter entitled: 'That much money is of no substance to States, nor is their wealth in it.' In it Cellorigo demonstrates that rising prices and taxes impoverished a country in receipt of an abundance of gold and

[4] *Cortes de los antiguos reinos de León y Castilla*, Actas vol. 8, p. 52.
[5] ibid, vol. 11, 1588–93, p. 535.
[6] ibid, vol. 2, 1566, pp. 421–22.

silver, though 'things necessary to human life are lacking, such as when Kingdoms lack them, they have no true wealth'; that monetary wealth was 'made of air', 'in the form of papers, contracts, annuities, bills of exchange', here rightly equated with the gold and silver they replaced; finally, that 'If Spain has neither silver money nor gold money, it is because it has it, and if it is poor, it is because it is rich'. Five years before the publication of *Don Quijote*, and in the very same town, Valladolid, Cellorigo was expressing the profound contradiction between illusion and reality.

The idea of the primacy of production, especially agricultural production, was a third common topic and was being repeatedly and clearly expressed, at almost the same time as the French writer Sully declared that the real treasures and gold-mines of Peru were her cornfields and pastures. The view was held by Spaniards as well as Frenchmen as, for example, by Pedro de Valencia, who said in 1608: 'The harm came from having so much silver and money, which is, and, as I shall show in another paper, always has been, fatal poison to republics and cities. They believe money will keep them and it is not true: ploughed fields, pastures and fisheries are what give sustenance. Everyone should do his share of tilling: those who live on money from interest and are useless and lazy, are eating what others sow and reap.'[7]

There is a host of similar quotations from Arrieta, Lope de Deza, Navarrete and Caxa de Leruela. According to the latter: 'Since the Spanish came to place all earthly happiness in the obtaining of these metals, despising, as Columela says, the best and most blameless way of increasing and preserving their patrimony, that is, keeping beasts and ploughing the fields, they have stupidly lost both kinds of wealth.'[8]

In 1650 Saavedra Fajardo gave a literary account of the ruin brought about by inflation, correctly giving a place to psychological factors. In *The Idea of a Christian Prince* he wrote: 'The people on the banks of the Guadalquivir marvelled at the precious particles of earth brought to the surface by the labour of the Indians and transported thence by our courage and industry: but the possession and abundance of such wealth altered everything. Agriculture laid down the plough, clothed herself in silk and softened her work-calloused hands. Trade put on a noble air, and exchanging the work-bench for the saddle, went out to parade up and down the streets. The arts disdained mechanical tools.

---

[7] Pedro de Valencia, *Escritos sociales*, pp. 36–37.
[8] Caxa de Leruela, quoted in José Larraz, *La Epoca del mercantilismo en Castilla*, Madrid 1943, pp. 138–139.

Coins of silver and gold spurned kinship with base alloy, and refusing all other metals kept themselves pure and noble, and the nations sought after them by all manner of means. Goods became proud, and when silver and gold fell in esteem, they raised their prices. . . . As men promised more from their incomes than in reality they had, ostentation and royal pomp grew, pensions, pay and other items of Crown payments rose on the basis of this foreign wealth, which was too badly administered and kept to meet so much expense, and this gave rise to debt.'[9]

This literary account gave a foretaste of the economic analysis later supplied by Richard Cantillon.

[9] Saavedra Fajardo, *Obras*, Madrid 1946, vol. 1. pp. 527–29.

18

The Price Revolution in France

It is essential to examine the phenomena intervening between the arrival of precious metals in a country and the increase in prices: metal was imported in exchange for commodities, and analysis of the domestic currency of each country is as important as that of the internationally valid metal currency. To take the example of Germany: in the late 15th century, and perhaps up until the middle of the 16th century, central and southern Germany, where the silver mines were situated, were able to go on developing economically. As long as gold was the main element in imports from the colonies, the value of silver rose in relation to gold, and the mines were still profitable.

With the massive influx of what, for the sake of simplicity, can be called Potosí silver, the very basis of the prosperity of Fugger Germany was undermined and, from 1570 the country stagnated. The precise conditions of the competition between German and American silver have yet to be established, but the fact that German silver lost the battle is indisputable. By the end of the century the mines had been shut down; where there were any still open, the rate of accidents was increasing, and the German miners could not – or through the force of their traditions, would not – work at the wages they were being offered. They therefore emigrated, and found their way all over the world to Ireland, England, France, the Guadalcanal mines in Spain, and finally America. In 1576 according to a Swiss document, German silver was being 'sold at vastly too high a price'. Augsburg and Ulm in Germany, and Salzkammergut in Austria, gave up the place of honour they had held until the mid-16th century, and made way for the rise of the Baltic ports, the Netherlands, and finally Sweden. The latter gained from the rise in the price of commercial copper, which was produced there in considerable quantities, and which poured into Spain in particular, when, after 1605, she made up for the slackening in American silver shipments, with rash local issues of base metal.

In this chapter I shall, however, dwell in greater detail on the case of France. Here at the beginning of the 16th century, there were isolated regions of the country where the level of economic activity was low; silver or gold currency in any quantity were very rarely used in the normal course of business here, and external stimuli were strongly resisted. Some of these regions maintained their isolation into the 18th and even into the 19th century, but the 16th century was nonetheless the time when circulation – of men as well as money – became general, affecting all areas, if in differing degrees. The hard currency of Spain reached into poor areas like the southern Auvergne through the emigration of labourers and through the petty commercial dealings of wandering traders. Large-scale trade brought it into the great maritime areas of Brittany and Marseilles. Caught between German silver and Spanish gold in the first half of the century, and between Spanish silver and northern production in the second half, France was invaded by Spanish silver, especially after 1559–1560. This stimulated production, although by the end of the century inflation had reached alarming proportions.

Despite all this disturbance France remained highly regionalised. There was a multitude of *Hôtels des Monnaies*, mints, some of them very small, employing only a few people; they were always private, operating under licence from the State, and rarely permanent. The duration and relative size of the mint is a measure of its contact with economic activity in general: after Paris the most continuous producer of coin was Bayonne, followed by Rennes, and this is a sign of the 'westernising' or 'Atlanticising' of the French economy in the 16th century, while the regions in contact with Germany were in economic decline. The routes to the Mediterranean, from Bayonne and from Perpignan via Toulouse and Montpellier to Marseilles, were still important as a way of reaching Spain and the Levant, but the Wars of Religion caused considerable interruptions.

The organisation of the French currency took final shape in the 16th century, with the almost total suppression of baronial mints, some of which were still working at the beginning of the century. This was a major indication of the consolidation of the State and national unity. Above the scattered, discontinuous mints a 'Monetary Tribunal' was established, the *Cour des Monnaies*, which kept a check on coin by examining samples chosen at random and sent to it by the various *Hôtels*. Associated with this Tribunal there were royal officials, competent specialists who wrote numerous memoranda that were just as important as the famous works of Bodin, about which there has been considerable discussion above.

Bodin himself was, to some extent, an official. The Estates General played a similar role in France, in relation to money, to that of the Cortes in Spain, the difference being that they were not convened at regular intervals and there was therefore less continuity in their criticisms. The 1576 Estates established a monetary commission of which Bodin, as the deputy for Vermandois, became the guiding spirit. The merchants for their part wanted to make their voice heard 'on the issue of money', and though Malestroict maintained that monetary affairs were the concern of 'a small cabal', they were discussed by a lot of people, then as now.

(1) The various aspects of the problem of precious metals

France had few mines, and even fewer that were profitable; but there were some profitable ones (in Ariège, Béarn and the Massif Central), and sometimes there were *Hôtels des Monnaies* based on local production. This was, however, on a very small scale. For currency to circulate it was necessary either for foreign trade to bring in hard currency from abroad, or for substitutes to be created (small circulating coin for every-day use, or credit and bills of exchange). Alternatively, it had to be done without.

In periods of low economic activity currency was used as little as possible. When, however, trade brought in hard currency, this gave a stimulus to the circulation of commodities and money, and silver prices tended to rise; and when in turn trade brought in less money or no longer brought it in at all, it was tempting to sustain production and prices by issuing substitute currency. The relationship between hard currency and this current coin then depended both on the size of the issue and on the transactions it had to cover. The abuse of what was called 'black coin' led to price increases, and the livre tournois, in which these prices were expressed, fell in value relative to hard currency, the latter being able to buy more than current coin. On the other hand, if the circulation of good currency prevailed, prices might rise (in the sense that the value of silver itself fell), but the ratio of the livre tournois to hard currency would not change too drastically.

In the first part of the 16th century, as in all parts of Europe, the main commercial circulation was based on gold, and in the second half, the base was silver. At the beginning of the 17th century, silver was scarcer, and as elsewhere, more copper was minted. These developments were general to Europe, but the question is how they affected France. To determine whether it made a difference if gold or silver was dominant, we must separate the technical, economic and social elements of the problem.

On the technical side, the cost of producing gold and silver varied (according to the mine and to where it arrived in Europe), and supply varied from place to place. There was an open market in gold and silver, on which one metal rose or fell relative to the other; this depended in the short term on its abundance or scarcity, and in the long term on its costs of production and transport. The effects of the difference between America, Europe and the East in the value of the metal have already been mentioned several times, and similar variations occurred over shorter distances. At the beginning of the century, there was more gold in Spain than in France, and more silver in France than in Spain. Gold flowed into France, where its purchasing power was greater, and silver into Spain, for the same reason. But the only people who had a stake in this were first, a small number of speculators, and second, the officials of the French Mint.

The important point technically is that when gold and silver coins had a given content of fine metal, and there was an official accounting currency, (equivalent to so many pounds, etc.), it was necessary to maintain a constant official ratio between gold and silver values. On the market, however, the ratio was not constant. It was, therefore, always profitable to accumulate either gold or silver coin, depending on which was officially undervalued or overvalued by comparison with the free market rate. Governments periodically had to readjust official rates to correspond with the going rates, and they sometimes manipulated this procedure to establish a value above or below that of the market, depending on whether they wanted to attract or disperse a particular metal.

There were objective limits to this kind of operation, but they came into effect only when the disparity between the official and the market rate was such that one or other type of coin became quite scarce. Therefore, a continuous black market existed in whichever currency it was profitable to hoard or to spend. This caused concern, and it made many officials believe that the basic problem was the need for a fixed ratio between gold and silver. To the men of the 16th century, the ratio should have been constant. At the very least there should have been an optimal ratio. As it revolved in practice around the figure 12, many people thought that 12 was the ideal ratio, especially since men like Bodin had a strong belief in the harmony of numbers.

In the 16th century men were fully aware that relative availability at the fairs and markets favoured gold one day and silver the next, depending on what most people wanted; but they believed, not altogether wrongly, that these short-term variations were around a 'natural' gold–silver price, which remained a constant ratio. What disturbed them was that when there were abrupt changes in the conditions of production in the mines, the 'natural' price of gold and silver also varied in the long-term. I, for one, do not attach a great deal of importance to the gold–silver ratio, as not only contemporaries, but some modern authors do. Temporary speculation in whichever metal is rising in price, and the establishment of either gold or silver as the main circulating metal, tell us less about the society and the economy than the inter-action of an abundant money supply (in gold or silver) with trade, prices and production.

Nevertheless, the gold–silver problem had a significant social dimension. Silver, which was of less value per unit of weight, could be used for relatively small payments. It therefore increased retail as well as wholesale prices, the latter being more particularly affected by gold, by which large-scale transactions were governed. It need scarcely be added that what was true of silver applied even more to copper coin. If such coin multiplied (especially low value 'black coin'), retail prices would be especially affected. This black money, which was really token, was dangerous only if the issues of it exceeded the needs of the real growth of production and circulation. But although this often happened, it was a problem of a very different order to the gold–silver ratio.

The economic importance of a relative or alternating abundance of gold and silver was also significant. Silver (the same value of which weighed twelve times as much) circulated less easily than gold, and even more than gold it created a demand for replacing actual circulation with bills and credits. But gold and silver alike were monetary materials with the properties of a commodity, and came into circulation only at their own value, in exchange for products whose price depended on the comparison between the costs of production of the money-metal and their own production costs.

(2) Francis I's ransom: an example of the non-economic transfer of precious metals

Political operations – 'political monies' – were of basic importance in the 16th century. One example was Charles V's election to the Empire in 1519, which cost Francis I so much gold and involved Charles V himself in such enormous debts. After this came the battle of Pavia (1525), the capture of Francis I, and then the Treaty of Madrid (1526); these freed the king on condition that his children were handed over as hostages to guarantee agreements which the king had no intention of enforcing. In 1529 the treaty of Madrid was revoked by the 'Ladies' Peace': this promised Charles V 2,000,000 *escudos*, plus 290,000 to pay his debts to England and another 1,200,000 in cash, to be sent (as in fact it was) in a boat which crossed the Bidassoa river between France and Spain at the same time as the boat brought the princes back to France. The operation was carried out only after four months spent checking the *escudos* one by one as a result of which 40,000 more were demanded because some of the coins were imperfect.

This enormous transfer of gold had some very marked repercussions among the French nobility, clergy and tax-payers in general; but its economic consequences have yet to be researched. Direct transfers of money, as we know, are not always prejudicial to the party which makes them. Bismarck is said to have regretted demanding 5,000 million gold francs of France in 1871, since such transfers should require an equivalent export of products, thereby providing a stimulus to the economy. The gold transfusion of 1531 left French prices below those in Spain and the monies transferred began to return through trading by 1535, once Charles V had reduced the gold content of Spanish *escudos* in the hope of containing the spontaneous flight of gold which obviously resulted from price disequilibrium. France, having no mines, had to live on her own production. She could not have done so but for the marked progress in population and production of the years 1480–1525. As we have observed, Bodin realised that this initiated the process and that the sale of French products to Spain sustained it.

The exports have never been quantified, but a mid-century memorandum on the balance of trade shows that they were the products of French agriculture and industry, rather than luxury goods; the list includes wheat, wine, brandy, salt, canvas, cloth, garments, worsted, camlets, candles, hardware, hammocks, saffron, wool, honey, caryons, dried fruits, hemp, glazes, and even rye and chestnuts.

It should be noted that the simplicity of these products suggests that they did not provide big profits to the producers, but were supplementary sales made by people who produced their own subsistence and raised their standard of living a little through such sales. In France as in Spain there were small capitalists who acted as retailers; but this trade was only profitable if the agent was close to a navigable river, as land transport was too dear, except for light goods sold by peddlars.

In the first half of the century, therefore, France exported and was paid in gold; in the second half of the century, as Spain became less and less able to produce, she exported still more in exchange for silver. In the first half of the century incoming gold led to only modest price increases, at least until 1540, but after 1560 and especially towards the end of the century, there were steep rises.

(3) Price rises

The French price revolution is not as well known as the Spanish. Although Hauser published a study of it in 1936,[1] it is still not fully documented, and in this section I shall simply examine a recently published graph.[2] It is a graph of grain prices, taking wheat as a reflection of the average. There are some problems with such a choice, since grain prices are jerked upwards by temporary scarcity, and these appear to produce rises disproportionately larger than the overall trend. Furthermore, the circumstances of Paris were exceptional in the second half of the 16th century, which included the years of the Wars of Religion and of the Holy League. However, as this[4] the best graph yet produced it deserves some study.[3]

The graph begins in 1520, and in the early years of the century shortages distorted the overall movement. In 1520–1521 (all figures being for harvest years, i.e. from the 1520 harvest to the 1521 harvest), wheat rose to 2.68 livres tournois a *setier*[4] and in 1521–1522 it went up to 4.53 livres. The increase was high but short-lived. Between 1520–1521 and 1545–1546, the price of £4.53 was only once exceeded and then only slightly, at £4.61; a *setier* of wheat fell to as low as £1.60 several times before 1530. It should at once be noted that in the last years of the century, after 1585, it scarcely fell below 10 livres except for one year when it dropped to £8.25.

Extreme scarcity, or famine, was never a long-term feature, and is unrelated to monetary history. There is such a relation, though, in the

[1] Henri Hauser, *Recherches et documents sur l'historie des prix en France*, Paris 1936.
[2] M. Baulant and Jean Meuvret, *Prix des céréales extraits de la mercuriale de Paris 1520–1698*, Paris 1960.
[3] cf. the graph on p. 176.
[4] The *setier* was a unit which varied depending on the region and commodity involved; a *setier* of wheat in Paris equalled 156 litres.

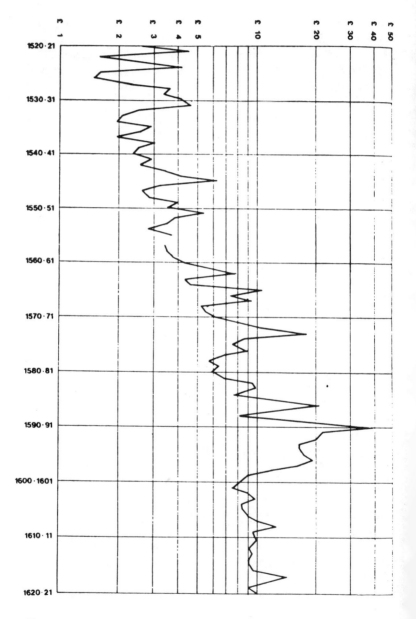

Figure 8. Nominal prices (in livres tournois) of a *setier* of grain in Paris (1520–1620). In harvest-years, i e. August–July. Logarithmic series.

case of an abrupt but steep rise in prices, which is not followed by a return to the previous low levels. This happened in 1545–1546:

1542–1543	£2.55 per *setier* (less than in 1520–1521)
1543–1544	£3.39
1544–1545	£4.04
1545–1546	£6.38

This broke all records, and set the lawyer Du Moulin writing down his first observations on rising prices. The interesting point is that wheat never again fell below 3 livres a *setier*. Nonetheless, the period in which gold was dominant was a time of relative price stability (although this does not mean that the economy failed to develop).

Following on the 1545–1546 increase, there was a second upturn, which gave rise to the debate between Malestroict and Bodin, and this showed, moreover, that though everyone in the 16th century could distinguish between an exceptional increase due to a bad harvest, and the constant rise in the cost of living (noted by both Malestroict and Bodin), it was when there were exceptional increases that prices were most discussed, as everyone was worried by them.

1563–1563	£ 4.53
1564–1565	£ 4.69
1565–1566	£10.70
1566–1567	£ 7.35
1567–1568	£ 9.37

After the exceptional price in 1565–1566 there was a slight falling off. At the time of the highest prices (1566) Malestroict thought that the rise was an exception. In 1568 Bodin replied 'Do you really think so? then why are prices still so high?', and he then began to look for the causes of secular increases.

The third great upward leap produced the discussion in the Estates General and the crisis leading to 1576–1577. The figures for this period are as follows:

1568–1569	£ 5.35 a *setier*
1569–1570	£ 5.49
1570–1571	£ 6.08
1571–1572	£ 8.06
1572–1573	£10.38
1573–1574	£18.06

These increases were unprecedented. After this the lowest prices were around £8 (1575–1578), falling again to £6 (1578–1582), but then there was a further upturn:

1581–1582	£ 6.67 a *setier*
1582–1583	£ 9.61
1583–1584	£ 9.93
1584–1585	£ 7.89
1585–1586	£11.65
1586–1587	£20.06

From now until 1600, the price of a *setier* never fell below 10 livres.

Leaving aside the price of wheat during the siege of Paris (£39.91 in 1590), prices in the last years of the century were around £16–20. After Henry IV captured Paris, prices fell, and remained stable at between £8.5 and £10 in the early years of the 17th century. Comparing the 25 years 1520–1545 with the 25 years 1575–1600, the average price rose from £2.88 to £13.33, i.e. it quadrupled. These figures are for Paris, where circumstances were exceptional. Emmanuel Le Roy-Ladurie has written a thesis on 16th and 17th century Languedoc, in which he gives prices for bread in Montpellier in the 16th century.[5] Though the price was controlled, it rose from £1.15 in 1520–1545 to £4.25 in 1575–1600, i.e. it increased by 3.48 times, just as prices in Paris did. In general, one can say that prices increased approximately fourfold between the periods mentioned.

(4) Depreciation of the livre tournois
The livre tournois was the accounting currency used to measure prices. When prices rose, the livre tournois can be said to have depreciated.

[5] cf. Emmanuel Le Roy-Ladurie, *Les Paysans de Languedoc*, Paris 1966. See the graph of wheat bread prices in Montpellier in the 16th century, vol. 2, pp. 944–45.

After a certain time, the authorities would acknowledge this depreciation and they then established a new ratio between the livre tournois and the actual metal currency. Malestroict, however, thought that he would prove the contrary – that price increases were the result of having, on several occasions, set a new ratio with silver coin; he thought this is what had devalued the livre tournois.

The records of this kind of official change show that, in fact:

In 1513 the livre tournois was worth 17.96 grams of silver
In 1521 the livre tournois was worth 17.19 grams of silver
In 1533 the livre tournois was worth 16.38 grams of silver
In 1541 the livre tournois was worth 16.07 grams of silver
In 1543 the livre tournois was worth 15.62 grams of silver

This represented a loss of 15% in 30 years: scarcely a major monetary crisis, especially in view of all the events mentioned (the wars and the ransom). At the most, prices as a whole increased in proportion with this slight depreciation.

In the middle of the century, the ratio of the livre tournois to silver began to change more quickly. In 1549–1550 the silver–pound ratio was:

1549   15.57 grams of silver
1550   15.12

And by

1561   14.27

As the next depreciation did not take place until 1573, one can say that in the 60 years after 1513, the livre lost only 25% of its silver content; while, during the same period, the average price of wheat had at least doubled, and the highest price of 1573–1574 was four times higher than the highest prices of 1521–1522. Bodin was then right when he opposed Malestroict with the argument that it was silver prices, and not just official prices, which had risen.

In the years 1572–1577 there were such violent changes that price rises were readily attributed to the disorder of the monetary system. The Wars of Religion, famines and consequent epidemics, and repercussions of the revolt in the Netherlands, which disturbed the flow of silver between Spain and Northern Europe, all contributed to the multiplication of 'black coin' (copper coins of doubtful standards) throughout France. In Lyons, the Spanish gold pistole, officially worth 58 French shillings, was selling on the black market at 100 shillings, and the Spanish silver real, valued at 5 shillings, for 12. These de facto 'devaluations' of the livre tournois were followed by legal 'devaluations', which, although much smaller, now came in rapid succession.

Whereas in 1561 the livre had been worth 14.7 grams of silver, in 1573 it corresponded officially to 13.19 grams of silver, in 1575 it corresponded officially to 11.79 grams of silver, in 1577 it corresponded officially to 10.71 grams of silver. This represented a loss of 33% in fifteen years.

It was at this time that, as a result of repeated petitions from the merchants of Paris and Lyons and the Estates General, the famous Ordinance of September 1577 was issued, in an attempt to alter the oldest-established French monetary practices. It forbade further accounting in livres tournois, and made a real gold coin, the *écu-soleil*, the unit in relation to which all other currencies were fixed and in which accounts were kept. This put an end to adjustments of the ratio of official and actual currencies, as solid coin was now the official accounting currency. At the time of the reform the *écu-soleil* was worth 66 French shillings, and it was altered to 60 shillings on the day when the reform took effect (1 January 1578). It was both an attempt at stabilisation and a slightly deflationary measure, as under the new system the silver equivalent of the livre tournois rose to the 1575 figure of 11.79 grams.

The question of whether the reform was successful revolves around two sides of the money problem as reflected in the monetary discussions of the period: on the one hand, domestic prices, with all the disorder of 'black coin', and high grain prices; and on the other, great international developments – the massive influx of American silver, the fall in its value, and the consequent general international price rises. The monetary theories current in France at this time form the subject-matter of the following chapter.

19

French Monetary Theory

In the first half of the century, economic activity in France was, as we have seen, in a state of equilibrium. Despite the non-economic losses of precious metals (the imperial election and the princes' ransom), money, especially gold, flowed back into the country through a variety of exports, and as a consequence of the expansion in population and production in the years 1475–1525. At the same time there were slight increases in prices roughly proportionate to the devaluation of the livre amounting to about 15% between 1513 and 1543. Abrupt, irreversible rises (due to shortages, and not followed by falls of an equal extent) began in 1545–1546, when they provoked Du Moulin's commentaries, and went still further in 1566–1568, (the Malestroict-Bodin debate) and in 1570–1574 (when they caused profound disturbances in the currency and in society in general). In all these cases, it is evident that monetary developments were the result of general political and economic conditions rather than their cause; they could only relieve or aggravate these conditions.

We must also look at the views of the people of the period. Merchants took a particular interest in monetary dealings and were very adept in them; but all those whose views are known were concerned with international trading, and dealt in internationally valid hard currency. Richet has published the opinions of some representatives of Parisian commerce, two hundred and twenty-four of whom met on 30 July 1572 in the 'Maison des merciers' in the rue Quincampoix. As they had no wish to be forced either to break their oaths or give up trade, they refused to take the king's oath to accept foreign currency at only the official French rate. They said that: 'Several merchants of this kingdom, including many of this your good city of Paris, especially the above-mentioned body of wholesalers of jewellery and merchandise, normally trade with foreign countries of every nationality, with different customs, laws and interests, and most of them ignorant of the customs, edicts, laws and decrees of France.'[1] So that it would kill such trade to impose Franch rates of exchange. This meant that they could now engage in international trade only by using money with a universally acknowledged trading value.

In 1576, François Grimaudet wrote: 'The value of money should be understood to be that at which it passes between merchants and in commerce by common usage and observance, and, as we have before said, the value of money depends upon public usage. It is the value at which it passes between merchants and other people that should be understood in such cases, rather than the value imposed by the Prince. The law that puts a value upon money retains its vitality so long as it is actually observed by the public. Its non-observance practically abolishes it.'[2] By this he meant that among merchants, especially merchants dealing in international currency, the value of official currency as proclaimed by royal edict should be the same as that of the free market.

The idea was then emerging of a 'natural' movement of money, resulting from 'common use' or 'the use of the people', i.e. market movements. This was to determine legal stipulations, and not vice versa. It was with this aim that Jean Bodin, Vermandois deputy in the 1576–1577 Estates General, argued that money should be coined by a single mint serving the whole country. It should have very accurate moulds to produce identical coins, with its standard metal content or 'intrinsic' value (on the precious metals market) being exactly equal to the 'nominal' value of the royal edicts. It was not possible to stabilise the currency so completely; but the September 1577 edict making the use of *écus soleil* compulsory, was a step in this direction. It was an attempt to bring circulation into line with the practices of large-scale trade, counting in hard currency and taking international variations into account.

The reform does not appear to have changed the habit of counting in livres; but 25 years later, in 1602, when the former system was brought back, the *écu-soleil* stood at a level of 65 shillings instead of 60; this represented a depreciation of 8 in 25 years. It can therefore be said that domestic currency was virtually stable throughout this period. Nonetheless, there were regional monetary disturbances as a result of the Wars of Religion and the circulation of 'black coin'. In 1592, in the lower Rhone area, gold escudos were fetching 90 shillings in current

[1] Denis Richet, 'Le cours official des monnaies circulant en France au XVIe siècle', *Revue Historique*, April–June 1961, p. 373.

[2] quoted in Richet, op. cit. p. 374.

coin instead of 60, and 72 shillings in Montpellier in the same year. There were therefore irregularities over time and space. But the years of the Holy League had been years of easy money in Paris, as Philip II promised the League 600,000 escudos a year (more 'political money'), and there were massive issues of coin. This, however, did not stop prices from rising rapidly as we have seen. But it was the circulation of silver coin, not an over-supply of copper, which led to general price rises, and this was itself the result of a fall in the value of silver emanating from America. Gold, which was worth more in reality than officially, had to be hoarded; otherwise it fled the country.

How did contemporaries view these events? Jean Bodin commented on them in the first, 1568, edition of the *Response to Malestroict*, the *Six Books of the Commonwealth*, and the second edition of the *Response* in 1578. Although he concluded that the 'main and almost the sole' cause of rising prices was 'the abundance of gold and silver', Bodin's 'quantitavism' was not in the least mechanical or schematic. He believed that France needed trade and production to attract an abundance of gold and silver. The components of this were: the 'foreign' trade of North Africa, Spain and the Levant (he stressed the need for exports, and especially those of salt); 'the multitude of people' who worked, emigrated and consumed (the demographic factor); the Bank of Lyons, which was used by emigrant Italians (people known as the *fuorisciti* from such towns as Genoa and Florence); monopolies – not in the modern meaning but in the old usage of a *coalition* of sellers to maintain prices, including associations of *gagne-deniers*, artisans, to increase retail prices and of *compagnons*, 'officials' to bargain over wages; there were protracted strikes in the 16th century, especially by printers; lastly, 'waste' or 'princely pleasure', and the imitative effect which generalised certain kinds of luxury spending (extravagant spending quickly put coin into circulation). He also included famines, but Bodin was wrong to think that what was an ever present element in old economies had contributed to the secular price rises of the 16th century. He believed that famine was artificial in France because, he said, it was due to grain exports, and he justified this by pointing out that grain prices were lower during the war with Spain because exports were held back. It is possible that he was right on this point; it would mean that in some regions of France, Spanish demand for grain made it scarcer in times of scarcity, and less abundant in times of abundance. This would also explain why price increases were irreversible.

Bodin was well aware that the ratio of 'current coin' to hard currency had been adjusted on several occasions, but he knew that such 'devaluations' bore no relation to actual price rises; they reflected the rise in nominal prices, and did not cause it. Being less of a theorist than the Spanish, Bodin tends to describe what happened and then try to see what the possible causes are. He is quite subtle and produces some good analyses, but it would be wrong to accept his claim that he is the first to point to American silver as the cause ('the cause no-one has touched on until now'). In Spain, this was already a common view, and Mercado and Azpilcueta had almost produced a theory of it.

After Bodin, this explanation became common in France too. Montaigne, for example,[3] alludes to it in his comments on Gomara's *History of the Indies*; this was abridged by Benzoni, translated by the Protestant Chauveton, and in every version it waxed more violent against the crimes of the Spanish. Apart from relating the cruel deeds perpetrated against those who possessed gold in Peru and in Mexico, Montaigne also reproduces the very important conception of the encounter between a civilisation without money and European monetary customs, and the harsh effects of the seizure of the treasure. He believed this to be the source of Spanish disappointments: 'With regard to the fact that the revenue, even in the hands of a thrifty and prudent king (Philip II), answers so little to the expectations given of it to his predecessors, and to that abounding wealth which they originally came across on landing, in the new world . . . the reason is that the use of money was quite unknown, and that their gold was consequently all collected together since it was of no use except for show and ostentation, as if it were a piece of furniture preserved from father to son by many powerful kings, who were ever draining their mines for creating that vast heap of vessels and statues to adorn their palaces and temples. Whereas our gold is all in circulation and trade. We cut it up small and adulterate it in a thousand ways, then we scatter and disperse it.

Imagine our Kings accumulating in that way all the gold they could lay hands on during several centuries, and keeping it idle.'[4]

Montaigne was surprised at how quickly the treasure came into circulation, but he did not know much about the mines (the writers he studied stopped short of the Potosí experience), and he gives the impression that from 1580–1585, Philip II benefited little from his mineral wealth. At about the same time, according to Philippe de Caverel, many of Philip II's enemies were hoping that in spite of America

[3] cf. Marcel Batallion, 'Montaigne et les conquérants de l'or', *Studi francesi*, Turin 1959.
[4] *The Essays of Montaigne* (trans. E. J. Trechmann), London 1927, vol. 2, pp. 375–6.

the king's power represented only 'smoke without fire'.

This gave rise to the impression repeated by 17th century Spanish authors, by Sully, Laffemas and Montchrestien in France, and by Antonio Serra in Italy, that gold and silver, while they were not themselves wealth, were the objects, or rather the indication, of profitable economic activity. To attract them one had to produce, either through agriculture and the keeping of livestock (Sully) or through industry (Laffemas and Serra). It was necessary to import a little, export a lot, and attract foreign silver in exchange for merchandise. While each country therefore had its own view of the matter, the overall situation, and the economic conjuncture, also influenced the evolution of ideas. The result was that around 1600–1610 there was widespread distrust of monetary inflation, which had then reached a new peak.

20

The Price Revolution in Italy

(1) The price revolution

Italian prices have been quite thoroughly studied, by Parenti for Florence, Fanfani for San Sepolcro, Cipolla and Aleati for Milan and Delumeau for Rome. In general there was no really strong rise in these towns before the mid-16th century. Rome, however, was an exception, for in the most brilliant period of the Renaissance, from 1500 to 1530, when the population of the city was expanding rapidly, prices did rise. Taking the decade of the 1570s as 100, the index for current prices in Rome, so far as it is known, reads as follows:

1500–1509	44.20
1530–1539	70.20
1540–1549	77.50
1550–1559	91.90
1560–1569	92.90
1570–1579	100.00
1580–1589	113.40
1590–1599	127.50
1600–1609	132.70

After reaching this peak prices stagnated or fell. But certain other points must be noted. The lists are incomplete and not very clear, and prices varied enormously as between different products: e.g. wheat reached a high point of 200.8 in 1590–1599, whereas meat rose to 133 only in 1600–1609 and the upper limit of wood and artisan production was 111. As in France, moreover, price increases after 1566 were due solely to the rise in silver prices, as there was no further devaluation of current coin. Increases over the whole century were, as in France, in the order of 1 to 3, while wheat prices as in Paris, went up four times.

Cipolla has observed that for Florence, Umbria and North Italy, it is perhaps a misleading exaggeration to speak of a 'price revolution', as the only very marked increases were between 1552 and 1560 (when there were very strong rises, especially in Florence, running at 5.2 a year).[1] The rises at the end of the century reached only 3.3% a year. In some years prices fell: they did so by 1.2% a year between 1560 and 1565, and by 0.4% between 1573 and 1590. Cipolla nonetheless concludes that increases did occur since 'prices did not fall in the years when they were low', thereby expressing the same paradoxical secular trends we have observed in France.

Cipolla disputes whether the most marked increases should be attributed to American minerals, as they usually are, since he claims that the increases of 1552–1560 have more to do with post-war reconstruction and the rapid population increase. It was in fact in the period 1573–1590, when prices did not rise and even fell, that Spanish silver turned away from the Laredo-Hamburg route because of the Revolt of the Netherlands, and carved out new channels from Madrid and Seville, through the Mediterranean ports of Spain (Barcelona, Cartagena, Malaga and Vinarca) and into Italy, especially Genoa. The diversion of Spanish silver into the Mediterranean, documented by Braudel[2] may then have influenced prices in Italy.

One possibility is that the silver obtained by the Genoese through their *asientos* with the Spanish crown was destined mainly for Northern Europe, as political funds to pay the infantry and mercenaries fighting in the Revolt of the Netherlands, and for this reason they provided no real stimulus in Italy. Apart from the interest on their Spanish accounts, the Genoese made profits in two other ways: they paid on average 3% of the sum exported to take silver out of Spain, but made 7% on the silver in Italy, where its value was higher. They also had to exchange the silver for gold, which was more in demand for these purposes, especially by the troops, and for this transfer they demanded a large fee. These transactions were carried out at the so-called 'Besançon' fairs in Piacenza, where the Genoese controlled exchange and speculation.

It is still not necessarily the case that such business was confined to the great financiers. Around 1590, three million ducats were transferred from Spain to Italy on the king's account, but a further three million were transferred by individuals. This must have been payment for

---

[1] Carlo Cipolla, 'La prétendue "révolution des prix"' *Annales E.S.C.* 1955, no. 4.
[2] Fernand Braudel, *The Mediterranean and the Mediterranean World at the Time of Philip II*, vol. 1, London 1972, p. 487.

operations in Italy that were more widespread and productive than those of the speculators. In 1575–1577, when Philip II and his advisers were trying to get rid of the Genoese, the latter argued that any decline in trade between Spain and Italy would be a universal catastrophe. They pointed out that the ratio of Spanish imports from Italy and exports to Italy stood at 3 to 2; the Spanish exported wool, cochineal, sugar, leather, oil (and even wheat, though to some extent this was illicit). These were generally raw materials, foodstuffs or products of the colonies, and were exchanged for gold cloth, velvet, silks, candles, paper from Genoa and arms, in other words, expensive manufactured goods. As Ortiz had seen as early as 1558, Spain exported little in the way of manufactures while she imported a great deal, and this accounts for the export of three million ducats to Italy through private transactions.

In 1585 Florentine textile production was in fact at its height, running at 33,000 rolls as compared to 14,000–17,000 in 1572. It fell off to 13,000 in 1589–1600, and to below 10,000 after 1615, and was not therefore prosperous in the long term. Venetian cloth production lasted longer, rising from around 5,000 rolls in 1527 to 15,000 in 1570, 22,000 in 1586, and 28,000 in 1600, and reached a stagnation point of around 20,000 by 1620. Italy therefore experienced an expansion of production at the end of the 16th century, although the extent of this varied in different years.

According to descriptions of Italy in 16th century Spanish novels and diaries, the Spanish thought that Italian prices were very low, and that Italy was a paradise of the easy life, free manners and luxury. The Spanish also had a vague idea, supported by the spectacle of official silver convoys to the Mediterranean, that their country was being shamelessly exploited by the Genoese, speculators who made profits of one hundred per cent. The great poet and polemicist Quevedo expressed this idea in the famous verse which sums up better than anything else, the 'great silver cycle':

> Poderoso caballero es Don Dinero:
> Nace en las Indias honrado,
> Donde el mundo le acompaña,
> Viene a morir en España
> Y está en Génova enterrado.[3]

(2) Italian ideas about money

There must, as we have observed, have been very different reactions

---

[3] 'A powerful lord is Don Dinero (Lord Money) / Born in the Indies where the world pays him homage / He comes to Spain to die / And in Genoa lies buried'.

within Italy to the European price revolution, as Naples, Rome, Florence, Genoa and Venice had quite different relations to the flow of silver from Spain. Rome attracted silver for religious reasons. The Genoese earned silver through speculations. Some areas produced exports for Spain, and in Naples, a Spanish dependency, the situation was similar to that of Spanish provinces outside Castile – they had their own currency and customs, but were in every other way dependent on the Spanish system.

The most important Italian monetary theorists were Scaruffi and Davanzati, and from 1600 or 1610 there were Neapolitans among the Spanish *arbitristas*, who proposed mercantilist, but not chrysonhedonist, measures.

Scaruffi was most concerned with the ideal ratio of gold to silver, and like Bodin put it at 12 to 1. His plan was not, however, to create a new, perfect currency, but to use internationally valid currency, which would not be subject to devaluation by government decisions. Davanzati showed himself to be much more interesting as a theoretician, as when he delivered his *Discourse upon Coin* to the Florence Academy in 1588. As a 16th century academic dissertation, it combined useful economic analysis with countless literary allusions to gold and silver, as well as ancient fables in which gold was the key to everything. He did, however, advance the view that the division of labour was the origin of economic relationships among men: 'One man labours and toils not for himself alone, but also for others and they reciprocally for him; and one kingdom or city supplies another with their surplus, receiving what they need in return. So one City helps another and one Country parts with its superfluities to another in lieu whereof it is from thence again suppli'd with what it wants'.[4]

Davanzati naturally goes on to describe and account for the origins and appearance of money, but he also tries to give an historical account of precious metals as money, with all the strengths and weaknesses of 16th century scholarship. He then goes on to analyse the 'essence' of money, a term, which still has scholastic overtones, and meant looking behind appearances for the real nature of money. Davanzati, like the Paris merchants mentioned above, was concerned to distinguish between money created by the State and money whose value varied in the course of market transactions. He wanted to reconcile the two. He allowed that the sovereign might choose which kind of money he would guarantee, but not that he had the right to change its silver or gold content:

[4] Bernardo Davanzati, *A discourse upon coins*, London 1696, p. 9.

only silver and gold were accepted 'by all peoples'. He did add that copper was the metal used in most 'current' coin, but he excluded the use of 'token money' convertible into precious metals. 'Money therefore is Gold, Silver, or Copper coin'd by publick Authority at pleasure, and by the Consent of Nations made the Price and Measure of things, to contract them the more easily.'[5]

He goes on to explain: 'I said Gold, Silver or Copper, because People have chosen those three Mettals to make Money of. If the Prince (by which word is understood whoever governs and protects the State, be it one or many, few or all) I say, if the Prince makes Money of Iron, Lead, Wood, Cork, Leather, Paper, Salt, or the like (as it has sometimes happen'd) it will not be received out of his Dominions, as not being coin'd of the Matter generally agreed upon. It could not then be universal Money, but a particular Tally, Countermark, Note or Bill from the Prince, obliging him to pay so much good Money when he is able.'[6]

What Davanzati has defined here, before its time, is the convertible bank note. He goes on to explain that if he speaks of coining 'by publick Authority', it is because only the authorities have the power to guarantee that coin is of the right standard without being obliged to prove it each time. When he says that minting takes place 'at pleasure', it is because the authorities can give money any form – the form is unimportant, but the coin should not be given a false price, 'as it must needs happen, if, after trying of them, they should be found not to consist of fine Metal enough answerable to their Names'. Lastly, to say that coin is 'by the Consent of Nations made the Price and Measure of things' means that any price expresses a 'common' will (a 'common' price being the price achieved on the market by the balancing out of the will of all involved in the exchange).

This leads Davanzati to consider the nature of prices, to quote traditional arguments about how 'use values' vary according to circumstances. Water is essential, but too abundant to have a price; rats are unpleasant, but people paid 200 florins for them during the siege of Casilino so as not to die of hunger. He then asks how one commodity therefore came to be worth a certain amount of gold, and another to be worth something different? 'To be always acquainted with the Rule and Arithmetical Proportion which things bear among themselves and with Gold, it were necessary to looke down from Heaven, or some exalted Prospect upon all the things that exist, or are done upon the Earth; or

5 ibid. p. 12.
6 ibid. pp. 12–13.

rather to count their Images reflected in the Heavens as in a true Mirror. Then we might cast up the Sum and say, There is on Earth just so much Gold, so many Things, so many Men, so many Desires: As many of those Desires as any thing can satisfy, so much it is worth of another thing, so much Gold it is worth.'[7]

His concept of value is very static, but it is also statistical, and suggests a vision of world planning. Davanzati knew it was only a vision, that each man knew little of reality and gave things a price according to whether they saw them in more or less demand at a particular time and place. Merchants, who were aware of the potential of the market, knew prices best. Davanzati also knew that the market could be turned upside down by a sudden abundance, including an abundance of gold. He gives what has become the classic example, the treasures of king Atahualpa of Cuzco. He repeats Bodin's views, and quotes from him. Lastly, he describes the money as the blood running in the veins of the Commonwealth, and ends with a critique of currency devaluation. His arguments were not new, and had in fact been used by Oresme in the 14th century, but he gives them new life: '. . . does it not follow, that as Money was brought down from twelve to one, so the Prices of things would be rais'd from one to twelve? The old Country-woman that us'd to sell her dozen of Eggs for an Assis of twelve ounces, seeing it look now so deform'd, and reduc'd to one Ounce, would have said, Gentlemen, either give me an Assis of twelve ounces, or twelve of those paultry ones that weigh but one Ounce; or I'll give you an Egg apiece for your Asses; chuse which you will.'[8]

Davanzati's work is, however, quite abstract, with very little observation of the contemporary situation and the effects of metal inflation. By contrast, Giovanni Botero's *Ragion de stato* and later, in 1613, the work of the Neapolitan Antonio Serra, advance mercantilist economic arguments. Antonio Serra's treatise was written in prison; whether for conspiracy with the utopian communist Campanella, or for forging money, which would obviously give him a certain authority on the subject, is unknown. The main interest of Serra's *Short Treatise on the Causes of why the Reigns of Gold and Silver Abound where there are no Mines*, is in what it says about industry. Serra was well aware that an abundance of silver did not constitute wealth in itself, but that it indicated some economic activity which gave the country a positive balance in its transactions with other countries. This had often been said before (for

[7] ibid. pp. 15–16.
[8] ibid. p. 23.

example, by Ortiz). He also knew that exchange was not the cause but the result of the balance of payments and differing price levels. This again is interesting, if not new. He preferred industry to agriculture as a means of producing exports to aid the balance of trade, because he had already realised that income from industry grew the more it developed, while agricultural expansion involved poorer and poorer lands and lower yields. This law, although not absolutely correct, was to play an important role later on, and it is interesting to see its first formulation here.

Serra's industrialising mercantilism was, like Laffemas's, characteristic of the turning point of the early 17th century.

21

Bullion in the European and Colonial Economies, 1500–1800

I shall begin by giving some figures for the 16th, 17th and 18th centuries, in order to compare known price movements with the estimated production of gold and silver.

The fall in Spanish imports of gold and silver in the 17th century is reflected in the figures for Seville which are recorded up to 1660, and are once again taken from Hamilton. The fall is irregular, gradual up to 1630 and steep from 1630 to 1660. The volume of imports by decade, was as follows:

	Kilos of silver	Kilos of gold
1591–1600	2,707,626	19,451
1601–1610	2,213,631	11,764
1611–1620	2,192,255	8,855
1621–1630	2,145,339	3,889

So far imports of silver remained stable and did not fall. Gold, however, fell steeply; although at the time it was worth 12 times more than silver in Spain (to be precise, 12.12), it fell because it was such a small fraction even in terms of value of the total quantity of American precious metals.

From 1630, silver as well as gold imports fell steeply:

	Kilos of silver	Kilos of gold
1631–1640	1,396,759	1,240
1641–1650	1,056,430	1,549
1651–1660	443,256	469

The rate was now down to less than 50 kilos a year. Was this because the American sources were drying up, or was Spain too exhausted to produce anything to send to America in exchange for the metal? The sharpest fall was around 1640; this was a year of tragedy for Spain, when Portugal revolted and broke away, and when Catalonia revolted and tried to unite with France. Although the latter attempt failed, the province of Roussillon had to be given up to France in the Treaty of the Pyrenees, in 1659. There were terrible plagues, in Barcelona in 1651–1652, and in Seville in 1649–1650, after which, as Chaunu says, 'Seville was no longer Seville'. The fall in the import of precious metals therefore corresponded to a surprising extent with a fall in Spain's power and commercial attraction; it represented the nadir of Spain's fortunes. The problem was now where the recovery would begin.

America was nonetheless not the only producer of precious metals, and Spain was not the only supplier; nor were precious metals the only profitable object of trade. Moreover, existing mineral wealth could drain away in exchange for other precious goods of the time – sugar, dye-woods, drugs, spices, diamonds and pearls. Those who gained from the political, military and economic disasters befalling Spain – foreseeable from the beginning of the century, and confirmed by the middle of it – were of course the French, but they benefited more territorially and strategically than in trade and colonies.

In contrast there were two countries which tried to capture the colonial wealth of Spain and Portugal. The first to succeed was a recently formed state which had in fact arisen out of a revolt against its Spanish overlords. The Netherlands, a Protestant country, in arms against the Spanish Hapsburgs from 1565–1570, formed an independent republic under the name of the United Provinces, and was governed in effect by Dutch merchants. Fishermen, sailors and 'makers of the sea roads', organisers of commercial shipping throughout the world, they explored the Arctic regions, and the African coasts, and occupied many Far Eastern islands which were thus transformed into the 'Dutch Indies', today's Indonesia.

They tried in particular to exploit Portugal's difficulties when she united with Spain and later separated; they drove the Portuguese out of all their Chinese trading posts, except Macao, and raided their Indian and East Africa strongholds. They tried, and even for a while managed, to take over Brazil, and were able to detach from it Dutch Guyana and the island of Curaçao, which was a centre for tropical products and for smuggling. It was the Dutch who, in 1626, founded a 'New Amsterdam',

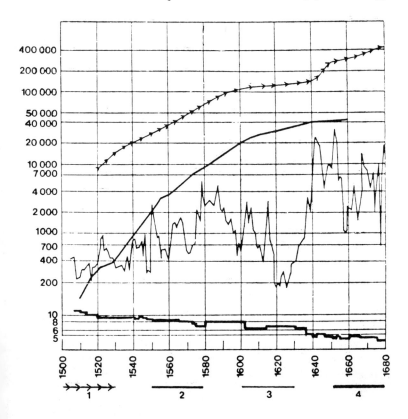

Figure 9. Increase in European stocks of precious metals and in the minting of coin in France (logarithmic series).

1. Cumulative mintings, in million livres (in France).

2. Cumulative imports of American precious metals at Seville (in million pesos).

3. Annual minting, in million livres (in France).

4. Value of the livre tournois in Germinal francs. (Graph taken from René Baehrel, *La Basse-Provence rurale*, Paris, 1961, graphs volume, graph no. VI.)

on the island of Manhattan in North America, the township which became New York after its surrender to the English. The great Spanish poet and pamphleteer Quevedo said of them: 'The Dutch, who because of the sea cover only a small stretch of land wrenched from it by what they call dikes, and who are rebels against God's faith and the overlordship of their king; having stolen their freedom and established a criminal government, increased their territory by treachery in arms, and by good luck gained the reputation of a warlike and wealthy nation, parading as the first-born children of the Ocean – these Dutch, I say, concentrate their hostility in the politics of commerce, and go for gold and silver to our fleets in the way our fleets go to the Indies for it.'[1]

As late as 1688, a publication appeared under the title of *Curious Dialogues of a learned Philosopher, a discreet Merchant and a well-informed Shareholder*, which contained an account of how Dutch seamen launched the 1604 campaign (after the founding of the East Indies Company), in the same year as Don Quijote launched his; instead of running into windmills, they came back laden with profits. The author, most probably a Spanish Jew taking refuge in Holland, is ironically appreciative of the contrast between the two kinds of undertaking.

The Dutch sometimes used methods derived from the Portuguese, for example when the officials of their companies were obliged, at least in principle, to repatriate their earnings. In the methods of violence and rapine employed against the natives of the countries they occupied, they had nothing to learn from the Spanish and Portuguese. The transfer of the inhabitants of Celebes to augment the Java labour force was similar to the slave trade, but the prisons where they were kept in Macassar before shipment were particularly unpleasant. In 1640, when the Portuguese rebelled against Spain and tried to sign agreements with the Dutch, as for example in Malacca, the Portuguese governor was assassinated by the very people to whom he had opened the door, and who did not wish to pay the promised fee. It was moreover from Dutch colonial history that Marx took the main illustration of his theory of violence as the principal agent of 'primitive accumulation'.

There is no doubt that by the middle of the 17th century, the Dutch Republic had as much capital as the rest of Europe together. The investment of this capital led to notable agricultural and industrial progress, in the tulip fields, in Amsterdam diamond cutting, and in Leyden textiles. But this concentration of trading capacity and productive activity

[1] F. de Quevedo, *La hora de todos y la fortuna con seso*, chapter 28.

possibly, and even probably, coincided with a period in which the rest of Europe was getting poorer, or was at any rate stagnating. The difficulty is to know whether the great tragedies and crises of the 17th century, the Thirty Years' War and the Fronde, reduced the distribution of gold and silver throughout the continent, or whether the fall in the imports of gold and silver itself lay at the roots of the general stagnation. The point at which different trends succeeded each other also requires analysis.

Approximate calculations of world production of gold and silver have been made by Soetbeer, and though these have been criticised, no alternatives have been offered. Production certainly fell less than imports from America to Seville, but in the 17th century output was at first clearly stationary for gold and falling for silver, while later gold production increased slightly and silver continued to fall. In the 18th century both gold and silver output increased fairly rapidly.

The figures given below are for the annual average production in kilos, over twenty years. The mid-16th century figures are:

Years	*Kilos of gold*	*Kilos of silver*
1541–1560	8,510	311,600

then came the peak of 1601–20:

1601–1620	8,520	422,900

Gold production was therefore stable, while silver was on the increase. After 1620 gold remained stable, but now the fall in silver production had begun:

1621–1640	8,300	393,000
1641–1660	8,770	366,300
1661–1680	9,960	337,000

The slight increase in gold production did not make up for the marked fall in silver, even in terms of value. But the fall was nowhere near the steep drop of imports into Seville. More of the silver produced in America may have remained there, and Japan was also producing silver: world silver and European silver were not the same thing. The quantity of precious metals produced in the world was probably greater in the 17th than in the 16th century, (29 million ounces of gold as compared to

24 million might be accurate); but world stocks, although larger in
1600 than in 1500, were increasing much more slowly, if not actually
falling. This is the most important point, and no doubt it was both a
symptom of, and a factor in, the relative economic depression which
affected the whole world, and particularly Europe.

From 1680, the fall in silver production was halted, and gold production began to increase at a faster rate:

Years	Kilos of gold	Kilos of silver
1661–1680	9,960	337,000
1681–1700	10,765	341,900

After 1700, output of both metals was increasing:

1701–1720	12,820	355,600
1721–1740	19,080	431,200

Thereafter 16th century records were broken, especially in silver:

1741–1760	24,610	533,145
1761–1780	20,705	652,740

Between 1760 and 1780, therefore, gold production fell below the
figures for the middle of the century, and, as in the 16th century, its
place was filled by silver, with a very high level of production at the
end of the century. In the first 20 years of the 19th century, however,
there was an almost complete stabilisation, and while gold fell only very
slightly, the increase in silver scarcely made up for it:

Years	Kilos of gold	Kilos of silver
1781–1800	17,790	879,000
1801–1820	17,778	894,150

In the 18th century gold stocks grew on average at three times the
16th century rate, and silver stock twice as fast. But European price
increases and all aspects of money matters do not seem to have brought
about a dramatic 'revolution' as they did in the 16th century. This may
have been because the initial stocks were greater; or because the supply

was regular (there was no great looting of treasure as in 16th century Peru and Mexico); or because European imports were less concentrated: the Spanish still largely monopolised American gold and silver (moving the monopoly port from Seville to Cadiz did not change this). Not only was there more smuggling but there were British, French and Dutch parts of the Americas which might not produce mineral wealth but did channel some of it away. Above all, it may have been because European production and trade was developing at a much faster rate than in the 16th century. All these factors help to explain why the European economy appeared to suffer less disturbance, though there was a much greater quantity of precious metals spread throughout Europe than in the 16th century.

We still need to examine geographical differences (not all countries experienced the dynamic growth of the period), movements over time, and the rate of increase, which varied at different times. Lastly, we must analyse what interrelation there may be between the movements of precious metals and economic developments (price increases, the development of the firm, rising production, etc.). This involves studying the origins of the turning point, how the European economy moved from the stagnation and difficulties of the 17th century to a new level of development.

Some of the information we have is fairly accurate, especially for food prices, and there are some other safe indices, such as for the circulation of trade, over large or small areas; but information on population and production from the mid-17th to the mid-18th century is much less reliable, and, above all, less continuous.

There is no doubt that internationally silver prices plunged downwards around 1660, reaching an initial low point at some time in the 1680s, and another around 1720–1721. The price of a *setier* of white wheat in Paris, for example, which had risen in 1590–1591 to as much as the equivalent of 475 grams of pure silver, and had often reached the equivalent of 200 grams in the 1630s, varied around 100 grams between 1660 and 1690, sometimes falling to less than 80 or even 70 in 1688–1691 (though there could still be steep rises in famine years). Goubert's study of the Beauvaisis shows wheat-silver prices falling by 30% between 1627–1630 and 1672–1679, and by as much as 45% in 1725–1741 (see p. 201). Outside France, however, there is no doubt that there was a period of rising prices, between 1683–1689 and 1701–1710, which was not entirely due to unusual weather conditions or to domestic monetary inflation. Prices again fell markedly between the high points of 1709–

1710 and the trough of the 1720s, especially for wheat.

It is tempting to think that low grain prices, which might mean lower profits and therefore 'stagnation' for producers and traders, worked in favour of the consumers and the propertyless; if mortality therefore fell, this would lead to population growth. It can sometimes be shown that this was so, and perhaps the Colbert era in France (1660–1683) was less damaging to the population in general than to external economic development. For this to be so, local currency had to be stable enough for the fall in silver prices to be reflected in nominal prices, and secondly, there had to be no climatic changes of the kind which brought scarcity and therefore temporary but dramatically high death rates. In France the famines of 1693–1694 and 1709–1710 were catastrophic, and in 1720–1721 only the inflation produced by the Law system concealed the fall in grain-silver prices.

It is therefore difficult to draw general conclusions from price movements; but there was a definite expansion of trade on a world scale between 1680 and 1715. A period of low prices for all products meant that precious metals had high purchasing power, and in such periods metals were therefore in demand. This explains why, in the late 17th century, Europeans were engaged in a furious search for gold and silver in Africa, America and the Far East.

Pierre Chaunu has provided a summary of his own researches on the 'Manila galleon', Frédéric Mauro's discoveries about Brazil and Louis Dermigny's about Canton.[2] His conclusion is that while between 1620 and 1650, the Far East trade showed all the symptoms of decline, and while it registered sharp falls on all indices between 1650 and 1680, there was, from 1680 to 1715, an exceptional recovery in the trade in precious metals and other precious goods. Such a recovery could not have immediately affected the whole of Europe; but from 1680 to 1715 the two Northwest European countries which had continued to advance economically in the 17th century – the United Provinces and England – went through a phase of enormous development. Paul Hazard has called this the period of 'the crisis of the European consciousness', of an intellectual stirring heralding the 'century of the Enlightenment'.[3] But there was an economic impetus behind this intellectual development. As Chaunu puts it, in England 'the 18th century began in the 17th'. The

[2] Pierre Chaunu, *La civilisation de l'Europe classique*, Paris 1966; Frédéric Mauro, *Le Portugal et l'Atlantique au XVIIe siecle (1570–1670)*, Paris 1960; Louis Dermigny, *La Chine et l'Occident: le commerce à Canton au XVIIIe siècle*, Paris 1965, 4 vols.

[3] Translated as Paul Hazard, *The European Mind, 1680–1715*, Harmondsworth 1964.

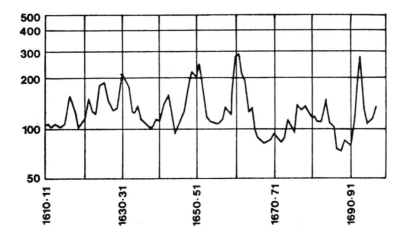

Figure 10. Silver prices in France in the 17th century. Silver prices of summer wheat in Paris (1610–1698). Nominal prices have been converted into grams of silver according to currency of coin. (From Baulant and Meuvret, *Prix des céréales extraits de la Mercuriale de Paris, 1520–1698*, Paris, 1960–1962.) Logarithmic series.

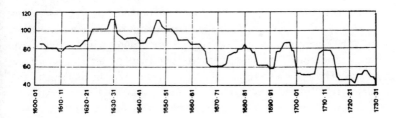

Long-term movement of silver prices for wheat in Beauvais, 1600–1730.

On indices drawn up taking 1601–1656 as 100, silver prices make it possible to establish an average span of 11 years. (From Pierre Goubert, *Beauvais et le Beauvaisis de 1600 à 1730*, Paris, 1960.) Arithmetic series.

same could be said of some areas in Spain, where, as my own work has shown, economic and commercial growth accelerated in the last years of the 17th century.[4]

The disasters which befell France towards the end of the reign of Louis XIV have perhaps detracted too much attention from this 25 year 'cross-cycle' of growth, in which Holland and England created or perfected great institutions like the Bank of Amsterdam and the Bank of England, and the ground was laid for the great phase of monetary stability which began in 1726. To understand the change from the stagnation and crises of the 17th century, to the long-term expansion of the 18th century, we must examine the situation in Holland, especially in Amsterdam, and then the situation in England.

[4] Pierre Vilar, *La Catalogne*, vol. 1, pp. 640–70.

*   *   *

Figure 11. Fluctuations in the Far East Trade in the 17th and 18th centuries: the Manila Galleon.

'These nine maps are chosen from the thirty-nine in the atlas which show the relative importance of trading sources for each five-year period. They illustrate a long period of commercial activity in the Pacific, in complete accord with the classic picture of the southern, Mediterranean and American directions of the period of European Atlantic development. The development of European trade in the Far East followed cycles of approximately thirty years: there was an increase from 1590–1620; high levels tending to fall from 1620–1650; a slump from 1650–1680; a magnificent recovery in 1680–1715; a long period of slack trade from 1715–1750; and an outstanding increase from 1750–1790. This period also saw the beginnings of Chinese population growth. Economists would say that we are dealing with a "long-term semi-Kondratieff", rather than what historians prefer to call secular phases. The maps also reveal a certain structure: in the dialectic of the three great land masses around Manila – America, China and India. Indonesia, being a constant but unimportant factor, can be left out, and so can America (Mexico), which although of greater weight was the other pole of the trade. The basic, dominant element was the rise of India, which paradoxically, despite the handicap of distance, was by 1787 of equal importance with China, even in Manila.' (Pierre Chaunu, *La Civilisation de l'Europe Classique*, Paris 1866, pp. 374–5.)

Figure 11.

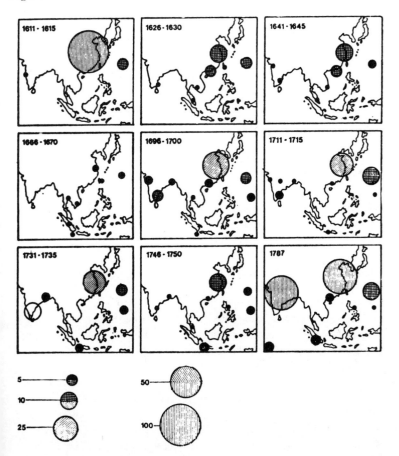

Millions of pesos

The Monetary Role of the Bank of Amsterdam

The United Provinces (often referred to as 'Holland' for simplicity's sake) were not, it must be repeated, simply a nation of traders and seafarers, but also had a highly developed agriculture, one that had dispensed with fallowing, and a textile industry which was at its most productive in the 1670s. It therefore, as the Spaniard Cellorigo said, attracted silver 'by virtue of its own wealth'.

Its wealth was in turn developed through the investment of capital which was constantly multiplied by direct or indirect exploitation of the colonies. The principal means by which the Dutch achieved this was their fleet, which employed 120,000 sailors and which, in the latter half of the 17th century, amounted to half of all world tonnage (excluding China). Dutch income from sea freight and insurance alone was enough to provide a surplus on the balance of payments. From the beginning of the 17th century, the most powerful of the great trading companies was a Dutch one: this was the *Oost Indische Kompagnie*: it was divided into local boards, the most important being Amsterdam, which had 23 out of the 73 directors. In some years the return on shares was as high as 75%. After the treaties of 1648 the Dutch also had an interest in the Spanish fleets to America, and this provided them with a further means of accumulating precious metals in Amsterdam.

The mineral wealth accumulated in Holland was used in the first place to pay for commodities from the East, which in some parts of Asia could be bought only for gold, and more often, silver; these metals were clearly necessary in order to establish a profitable market for Eastern goods in Europe. The United Provinces therefore used their superiority in production, trade, insurance and transport, to import precious metals in the form of ingots, bars and every type of coin, especially silver reals from Spanish America. Most of this was then minted as an internationally viable currency, the *negotie-penningen* (trade-coins).

It is very important to note that this internationally valid currency was not meant for domestic circulation. The Dutch were in fact pioneering a system applied in other ways in the 18th century, and this is examined below. The State had two currency systems. One was a domestic one, which had a flexible ratio to international currency, and which used coin containing slightly less silver than their official value, as a disincentive to exporting them. All foreign trade on the other hand used a high quality coin, which was a real international commodity money.

In the 17th century the United Provinces initially established 14 different mints for these purposes, and they were gradually concentrated until at the end of the century eight were left. They produced *leeuwend-aalders*, talers stamped with a lion, which were in great demand in the Levant and Asia Minor; *rijksdaalders* (State talers) which were used in the Baltic and Poland; gold ducats for Russia, and silver ducats which were used for most of the India and China trade. The English East India Company bought 7,000,000–8,000,000 florins' worth of silver ducats (internationally valid currency) for its Eastern trade each year. Nonetheless the Spanish piastre (the silver colonial coin) still had prestige, as its silver content remained unaltered; the Dutch exported most of the piastres they obtained. Just as however, the Florentine florin and the Venetian ducat are said to have been the dollars of the Middle Ages, it could be said that Dutch currency became the dollar of the 17th century. It was in any case basically a metallic commodity-money.

It might seem surprising, in a century which still thought largely in 'mercantilist' terms, that for Holland exporting precious metals was not only permitted, but was seen as an essential part of trade; no measures were taken against such exports, and from 1647 bullion was exported without protests from anyone, not even from the Mints, which made a profit by turning such metals into coin. These attitudes were not theorised nor did they represent a primitive form of 'anti-mercantilism'. Ideas result from events, and to the Dutch precious metals were a commodity like any other; so it was profitable to import and export them. If Dutch trade had regularly turned out to be in deficit at the end of the year, and the stock of precious metals and goods had been continuously whittled away, the attitude of the authorities might have changed. The free practices of the Dutch expressed the position of superiority which they had at that time.

Another expression of this was the solidity of the Bank of Amsterdam. It was founded in 1609 (that is, like the East Indies Company, early in the century). This was not a period of prosperity, but of monetary crisis: private banks were sprouting up everywhere, and speculating in the disparity in the silver content of different currencies, absorbing the strongest and putting the poorest coin back into circulation. Municipal banks were therefore established in a number of towns to act as cashiers for merchants. It was not only in Amsterdam that this kind of bank was established; in the very same year, for the same reasons, a similar bank was set up in Barcelona. While other banks remained highly localised, however, the importance of the Amsterdam trade was such that the Bank of Amsterdam became a great international institution. It should not be imagined, as many people do, that it was the bank which created prosperity and development; it answered a need, and though it may have been a necessary condition of development, it was never the only one.

The basic purpose of the bank was to facilitate deposit and exchange. It accepted deposits in any currency above a value of 300 florins, and registered it in the Great Ledger. It also had a monopoly of exchange. Any bill of exchange on Amsterdam had to be paid in at the bank, which guaranteed payment and was in turn guaranteed by the municipality. It carried out transfers between different parties, a function similar to that fulfilled by the 16th century fairs, but this time on a permanent basis.

It was not, however, a credit bank: it did not give advances, or discount bills and notes; in principle, deposits had to cover any transactions in which the party was concerned, and therefore no credit was given. There were two exceptions, the Indies Company, and the municipality of Amsterdam, but loans to these were, however, always of fairly modest proportions. The Bank did not make a large profit, and was not an instrument of accumulation. It made a very small profit on exchange, on the sale of bullion to the Mints and on the circulation of international currencies, but in the main this only covered its costs. It was on this basis that the Bank established its reputation in the first two-thirds of the 17th century, and consolidated it during the 'Dutch war' unleashed by Louis XIV, not without economic reasons, against the United Provinces. In 1672, faced with the threat of a French attack, the clients of Dutch banks were seized with panic, and some municipal banks, such as Rotterdam and Middelburg, put up the shutters. The Bank of Amsterdam went on paying out, and from then onwards confidence in it was complete.

The Bank stabilised the ratio between the internationally valid currency and the domestic currency of the Netherlands, but its existence did not prevent the usual monetary problems from recurring. There was a deterioration of the circulating currency, and poor currency came into use (especially the silver ducats and pesos of the southern Netherlands); but even if the bank did not make the circulating currency completely equivalent to international 'bank money', it did regulate the relation between them. A premium of 4 to 5% in favour of 'bank' money was always maintained and the margin scarcely ever rose above that. The bank therefore attracted foreign capital of every kind, especially towards the end of the century.

From 1683 the bank altered its practices to a certain extent. It began to levy a small charge for payments and transfers; it began to give advances to individuals at 0.25% interest a month on silver and 0.50% on gold; and receipts for bank deposits began to circulate and to be exchanged for current money. At the end of the century therefore credit operations and banknotes began to appear. The florin, which had simply been an accounting coin until 1691, then came into actual use; and this was because the increase in the circulation of money resulting from the movements of trade could be effected by means other than by precious metals.

These changes occurring towards the end of the century also reflected the growth in world trade which has already been mentioned. What is of interest to us is how the Bank of Amsterdam and the trade of the city resisted the dual impact on the United Provinces of the 'Dutch war', in which they were beaten by the French, and William of Orange's accession to the English throne in 1688, which in effect subordinated Dutch policies to English. It has long been thought that this marked the origin of the decline of the Netherlands and the rise of England.

In political terms this was so, but immediate economic decline was avoided, especially by Amsterdam. In 1699 the French ambassador could still report to the King that: 'Of all the towns of the United Provinces, Amsterdam is without any doubt the foremost in greatness, wealth and the extent of her trade. There are few cities even in Europe to equal her in the two latter respects; her commerce stretches over both halves of the globe, and her wealth is so great that during the war she supplied as much as fifty millions a year if not more.'[1]

At this period all French 'Northern' trade (trade with the Baltic, that is) was carried in Dutch ships, and the economy of the Netherlands did not begin to decline until around 1730. Its continued strength can be seen in the annual lists, published by Van Dillen, of the Bank of

[1] J. G. van Dillen, 'The Bank of Amsterdam', *History of the Principal Public Banks*, ed. by J. G. van Dillen, the Hague 1934.

Amsterdam's deposits (credit balances), holdings of precious metals, and loans to the Indies Company and the municipality of Amsterdam.[2]

1610–1616: deposits and holdings (nearly equal in quantity) varied at around 1,000,000 standard florins.

1619–1625: deposits and holdings of precious metals oscillated between 2,000,000 and 2,500,000, while credits to the East India Company rose from 300,000 to 900,000.

1626–1635: deposits reached about 4,000,000 florins while holdings were still about 3,000,000 to 3,500,000.

In 1640: deposits were at 8,000,000 and stocks of metals at 5,800,000 showing some disequilibrium; but in 1641 stocks rose to 8,300,000, exceeding credit on accounts.

In 1645 the figures reached heights rarely equalled subsequently: deposits of 11,288,000, and holdings of 11,841,000.

1646–1685: There was relative stagnation, reflecting the general depression of the European economy and the slump in silver imports from America. Deposits varied between roughly 5,000,000 florins (in 1673, during the war, they fell to 4,900,000) and 9,000,000.

1686–1691: rapid growth, bringing deposits up from 7,000,000 to 13,500,000, and stocks from 6,000,000 to 12,700,000.

1699–1700: record figures of 16,700,000 in deposits and only 13,700,000 in holdings (with commitments this time well above reserves of gold and silver).

1701–1709: a marked fall (to about 8,000,000 florins), but in *1721–1722*, the highest figures for two centuries were recorded, with deposits of 28,000,000 and 26,000,000 florins, and stocks not far behind. This was due above all to the flight of capital to Amsterdam after the crazed speculations of 1720, which was most intense in France under the Law system. It can therefore be said that up to this date Amsterdam was of the first importance in financial and monetary affairs.

In the 18th century, the deposits and holdings of the Bank fluctuated sometimes reaching 28,000,000–29,000,000 florins, as in 1772, but at others falling as low as 12,000,000. In these years the world stock of precious metals was increasing very quickly and prices were rising everywhere. The *relative* importance of Amsterdam therefore fell sharply. The real decline of Amsterdam, however, occurred only in the context of European consequences of the French Revolution and the Empire: deposits fell from 23,000,000 florins in 1792 to 140,000 in 1820. From

² ibid. pp. 117; see also his 'Amsterdam marché mondial des métaux précieux', *Revue historique*, CLII, 1926.

around 1780, moreover, there had been a marked change in the nature of the Bank, and holdings of precious metals tended to diverge further and further from the amount of the deposits (the former sometimes falling to 4,000,000 as against deposits of 20,000,000).

The main role of the Bank of Amsterdam, and of the Amsterdam market in general, was therefore to regulate and redistribute the stocks of precious metal used in international trade, especially in the 17th century and to a considerable extent in the first third of the 18th century. But the prestige of the Bank lasted long beyond this. In 1802, when it was losing its leading position, the French consul in Amsterdam explained that: 'Precious metals come to Europe from the New World, not in a constant stream, but at varying intervals, in the irregular bursts of a torrent rather than the smooth flow of a river. At the end of a maritime war which has kept the treasures of the mines pent up in the Spanish and Portuguese colonies, Europe is suddenly inundated with gold and silver in quantities far above what is needed, so that they would decline in value if they were put into circulation all at once. In such an eventuality, the people of Amsterdam deposited the metal in ingots in the Bank, where it was kept for them at a very low cost, and they took it out a little at a time to send to different countries as the increase in the rate warrants it. This money, then, which if allowed to flood in too rapidly would have driven up the prices of everything exceedingly, to the great loss of all who live on fixed and limited incomes, was gradually distributed through many channels, giving life to industry and encouraging trade. The Bank of Amsterdam, then, did not act only according to the special interests of the traders of this city; but the whole of Europe is in its debt for the greater stability of prices, equilibrium of exchange and a more constant ratio between the two metals of which coin is made; and if the bank is not re-established, it could be said that the great system of the trade and political economy of the civilised world will be without an essential part of its machinery.'[3] This was undoubtedly something of an exaggeration, a projection of the past into the present, since in 1802 there were all kinds of ways of replacing the Bank of Amsterdam as the regulator of the world system. Throughout most of the 18th century, however, it was true that the greater part of the precious metals used in European trade came from the American colonies of Spain and Portugal, and that a large part of this metal went to Amsterdam. Hence it was also true that one of the causes of sudden

[3] Van Dillen 'The Bank of Amsterdam', p. 105, n. 2.

changes in price movements was the irregularity of imports, due especially to war and the temporary stoppage of Atlantic shipping.

Dutch trade itself absorbed a lot of metal, because many European merchants were trading with America illicitly through Cadiz and took their earnings in precious metals to Amsterdam; alternatively, capital took refuge there to avoid the speculative crises on other markets (as with the Law system). Whatever the reason, the Bank of Amsterdam was for a long time an essential part of the monetary system of Europe and indeed of the world. The last occasion on which its primacy was undisputed was perhaps during the Seven Years' War (1756–1763). After this, English supremacy emerged.

23

The Establishment of the Bank of England

As in the case of the United Provinces, the technical side of monetary affairs in England cannot be considered in isolation from the complex dialectic of monetary affairs, commercial development, colonisation and political fortune. If late 17th century England laid the basis for what was to become the world monetary system (the gold standard and banknotes), this can only be understood in terms of the establishment of England's power, especially her international and maritime power, which was then taking place. In this chapter I cannot go into the history of England in the 17th century, a history that was so revolutionary and is still so much in dispute. There are some points, however, which must be mentioned.

The England of 1680–1715 was no longer the England of Good Queen Bess, of Gresham, Drake, Raleigh and John Hales's *Compendious Examination*. From being a nation of seafarers and pirates rather than merchants, England had become a great trading nation: between 1610 and 1640 her foreign trade doubled. Although the Cromwellian revolution and the disturbances of the middle of the century to some extent held back the rate of growth, the English merchant became conscious of being the natural pillar of the 'Commonwealth', with which he readily identified. This is evident in a work by Thomas Mun (1571–1641), a 'merchant of London' entitled *England's treasure by forraign trade*. Though it was probably written in the first third of the century (around 1629), it was published by Thomas Mun's son in 1667, and Adam Smith was later to say that it formed the basis of political economy, not only for England but for all trading nations. Mun speaks of money as the basic instrument for 'conserving' and 'increasing' the Commonwealth, and of the merchant as 'administering the patrimony of the realm', whose 'treasure' depended on foreign trade.[1]

[1] Thomas Mun, *England's treasure by forraign trade*, London 1664.

England's foreign trade was mainly with distant colonial areas. In 1621 Thomas Mun had also written two pamphlets in defence of the East India Company, of which he was a director, and which had come under attack from some sections of public opinion because of its enormous profits. In the second half of the century, another director of the Company, Sir Joshua Child, in his *Discourses on Commerce* (1688–1693) again developed the theory of commodities as the basis of the community's wealth. The theory known as 'mercantilism' was then closely related to the development of colonial trade. It was discussed in England more than in the United Provinces, because in England the merchants were not the only section of the ruling class, even though their influence was decisive in the last resort.

Industry leapt forward in the 17th century, even more than in the United Provinces. The American historian John U. Nef has even put forward a theory that this was the 'first industrial revolution', although on closer examination this seems rather too ambitious a claim. Around 1640, nonetheless, England displayed signs of industrial development to be found in no other European country. Coal was being mined for the first time for other than local purposes. Metalworks had advanced from being on a purely artisan basis to fairly large-scale production, there were paper mills employing several dozen workers, and these industries began to require considerable capital investment. This was true even in a consumption industry like brewing: whereas around 1450 the biggest London breweries had required capital of only £25 sterling, some were worth £10,000 by the second half of the 17th century, and there were few comparable establishments elsewhere in Europe. If there were signs of the future industrial revolution anywhere in Europe, they were to be found in England.

The agrarian structure of England had already begun to be disturbed by the impact of a monetary economy. The move to enclosures had begun in the 16th century, and more and more small peasant plots and communal lands were engulfed by great private estates. This made way for a change in the nature of agriculture, and an escape from a small-scale subsistence economy. In England the commercialisation of agricultural products had been going on since the Middle Ages.

These profound changes in the economy and society of England produced two political revolutions: the Cromwellian revolution and the 'Glorious Revolution' of 1688. I cannot here enter into the controversies which still surround them; but there is no doubt that by the end of the century, the views and interests of the 'moneyed men' of England, who had at first been despised, now held sway, even in affairs of state, and prevailed over those of the landed interests (a conflict later illustrated by Swift).

These considerations are important for the history of gold, because the monetary affairs of late 17th century England are inseparable from the world importance of the English economy. Two events in particular were of long-lasting importance: the formation of the Bank of England, and the monetary reform of 1694–1696, which indirectly heralded the future triumph of the gold standard.

(1) The Bank of England

As with the Rialto Bank in Venice, in the late 16th century, and the Municipal Banks of Amsterdam and Barcelona in 1609, the Bank of England was established in 1694 with the aim of ending a monetary disorder which had been brought about through the manipulation of private banks. Moreover it resembled the various banks founded at the beginning of the 17th century, in that it was not the instrument which produced economic upheaval, but economic developments which conditioned the future of the Bank. Though they were founded to resolve apparently similar problems and though the Bank of England was to become as important to world economic history as the Bank of Amsterdam a century earlier, it was to do so in a very different way.

In the late 17th century London there were no official moneychangers. Gold merchants bought and sold bullion and every kind of currency. Merchants were used to depositing their surpluses with the gold merchants, and they received in exchange receipts which, though of a private character, enjoyed a wide circulation as a means of payment. This was the origin of the 'bank note' covered by gold deposits, which was in theory redeemable at any moment. As the gold merchants were virtually certain that they would never have to pay out on all receipts at once, they soon began to make loans above the value of their holdings in precious metals. In contrast to the public system of Amsterdam, it was a private system which created credit and so gave a stimulus to the economy; but from 1683 the Bank of Amsterdam also turned to similar practices, though at first with some hesitation. These developments must be seen in the context of a marked upturn in commercial activity around this time.

In purely monetary terms, however, there were some risks in the role of the gold merchants; they were bound to speculate in precious metals, since these were their stock in trade. Like all financiers involved with precious metals, gold merchants kept, used or sold the best coin for international commerce, and put only the worst into circulation within England, in other words those containing less precious metal than their face value. Apart from foreign coins, which were often over-valued, they put out 'clipped' coin, those which had been eroded by use or had been cut down at the edges in order to re-use the metal clipped in this way. If necessary the gold merchants cut them down themselves. When under the Restoration (1660–1688), the edges of coins were embossed so that any filing down was plainly visible, gold merchants were quick to melt down money in order to speculate in silver bullion. They also played an important role in another respect, which was also a traditional part of the old monetary economy: speculation between gold and silver. The ratio between them was officially fixed by certain gold coins of a given weight with a particular face value, and silver coins of a given weight also with a fixed face value; but in the free bullion market, in England or abroad, the ratio of gold and silver did not necessarily correspond to the official values, and could change according to the supply and demand of one or other of the metals. It was therefore always profitable to transfer gold and silver to wherever they would fetch the highest price.

Around 1660, it was profitable to export gold, as in England the legal ratio of gold to silver was 13.3 to 1, while in Europe it was much higher. In 1663, an attempt was made to resolve the problem by minting a new gold coin containing less gold, but with the same face value: instead of making 41 coins from a pound of 11/12 gold, as previously, 44 were minted. The new gold coin, the guinea, was still worth 20 shillings of the circulating currency; this consisted basically of silver coins, many of them clipped. Although the official bimetallic ratio was therefore adjusted to the market rate, gold coin was still at a premium over circulating coin, and a guinea always cost 22 shillings instead of 20. Gold merchants therefore continued to find it profitable to supply guineas, which were needed in international trade, and to pay their own debts in current and if possible clipped coin.

The margin for gold was not very great in any case: in 1690, more than 25 years after 1663, it was still only 2 shillings in 20. There was therefore no alarming depreciation of the circulating currency relative to gold. In the Bank of Amsterdam there was also a considerable disparity between circulating money and fixed 'bank' money. To buy silver for export (i.e. good coin) cost 5s 3½d an ounce in London instead of the legal rate of 5s 2d. This meant a loss of less than 2.5%, and can scarcely be said to have constituted a monetary crisis. Relative currency stability was in fact a general feature in the period 1660–1690, (it was also to be found in France), and it was related to the general stagnation of prices.

However, the 1688 revolution then occurred, and this united England and Holland in the struggle against the hegemony of Louis XIV, and in 1689 there began a period of warfare. This lasted until 1697, and was followed by the Wars of the Spanish Succession between 1702 and 1714. All these wars caused upheaval in the financial system. Public finances, taxes and loans, were especially affected, but the long term monetary effects of this upheaval are what interest us here.[2]

Contrary to what had happened up to 1690, the London gold market system was no longer adequate in a war situation either for the State or for merchants. The State needed money and loans, while the gold merchants supported neither the new regime nor the war. In particular they were afraid that the king would refuse to pay the debts of his Stuart predecessors, and only a Restoration would have satisfied them on this point. The Crown and the great London merchants therefore united together in accusing the gold merchants of speculation, usury, clipping coin and even insolvency. In 1694, when the king had asked the merchants for a loan of £1,200,000 sterling, they used a new body to raise it. This was the Bank of England.

The merchants formed a share-holding association with a capital of £1,200,000, which was to be loaned to the King. The Bank issued the contributors with bank notes equal in value to their share of the capital; these could circulate and be used in payment, although it was not obligatory to accept them. In theory the Bank was provisional: its privileges were granted for only 12 years, and the king could even dissolve it before that time if he repaid the debt. The Bank for its part could pay out on commercial securities and give advances to individuals. It was therefore a credit institution which was in a position to replace the gold merchants. Though it was created later than the Bank of Amsterdam, the Bank of England immediately launched operations of a kind which the former had been dealing in for only a short time and unsystematically. From the start it was a more modern institution.

Its creation had immediate consequences: the king spent the entire

---

[2] See in this connection the extremely clear and well documented article by R. Mousnier, 'L'évolution des finances publiques en France et en Angleterre pendant les guerres de la Ligue d'Augsburg et de la Succession d'Espagne', *Revue Historique*, 1951, pp. 1–23.

loan on pursuing the war, and the merchants, who had confidence in the Bank, lent him more rather than keeping it among themselves. As a result, the circulation expanded rapidly by paper money of various descriptions. This development was not confined to England; it was also taking place in France, and it has in fact become a characteristic of wartime even in the present day. The important point to note is that though the increase in prices which resulted from this wartime inflation gave rise to some disquiet and provoked a famous debate about money, it did not create panic. On the contrary, despite speculation and disorderly issues of paper money which came to a head in 1720, the Bank of England was consolidated and the circulating currency was stabilised relative to international currency, thereby laying the ground for the gold standard.

(2) The monetary reforms of 1694–1696, and the debate between Lowndes and Locke

The Bank of England began operating in July 1694; the necessary capital was made available on 2nd July and its statutes were promulgated on the 24th. Within a few months, however, and very suddenly prices were rising steeply, in response to a sudden injection of credit in the form of the £1,200,000 loan to the King, in response to the use of notes made out by the Bank to its creditors, as well as to the food supply crisis of 1693–1694, which sparked off a rise in food prices almost everywhere.

This sharp increase in prices led to a loss of confidence in the circulating currency. It suddenly became apparent – though the process had been going on for a long time without disturbing anyone – that a large part of the money in circulation consisted of poor, filed-down coins, which could not be exchanged at the official rate on the international market. The gold guinea was officially worth 20s, but in fact it had for a long time been sold at not less than 22s, and had risen to $22\frac{1}{2}$s in December 1694. Although this was still not a problem, by June 1695 it could only be obtained for 30s. This represented a de facto devaluation of current coin by almost 50% in six months. This was as disturbing as if the ratio of paper money to gold increased by a half in the space of a few weeks today. In any case the premium of good currency over common currency was much greater for gold than for silver; the devaluation was only 25% in terms of silver. This is undoubtedly the best indicator, for the rate of English currency on the Amsterdam exchange fell by around 25%, not 50% (it varied between 22% and 27%). We can therefore talk about a devaluation of approximately one-quarter.

The fall was still too steep to avoid causing concern, and it became necessary to 'stabilise' the situation. Rising prices and popular lack of confidence in the currency were bound to lead to increases in the price of gold and silver, and to a further fall in the rate of exchange. English circulating currency had in effect long been token, in the sense that previously, because prices were stable, people had accepted coin readily without concern for its weight, even if it were cut down. From now on the public had to be supplied with coin of a silver content more closely equivalent to its official value. The classic solution in such a case was to withdraw all poor, 'depreciated' coin, refund it and circulate new coin with a face value closer to the market value of its silver content. The 'extrinsic' or face value had to be brought into line with its 'intrinsic' value, the market value of each coin as a commodity.

There were, however, two diametrically opposite ways of carrying this out. Coin could be put into circulation with a quarter less silver, and still be called pounds and shillings. This would be a way of acknowledging the depreciation of money in circulation by officially lowering the silver content of the accounting unit. Alternatively coins equal to the old value of pounds and shillings could be put into circulation, and this would involve maintaining the silver content of the official currency and circulating only good coins. The first type of operation is what is known today as devaluation (French *affaiblissement*), and it amounts to recognising what has in fact happened (rising prices and falling rate of exchange). The only cost to the state was the expense of 'debasement', the withdrawal of the old currency and the minting of new coins. This was expensive but not excessively so. It did however mean an official and irreversible devaluation of the currency, and would for example cut 25% (in this instance) off debts and fixed incomes expressed in terms of silver.

If, however, the state issued only coin of a silver content equivalent to its face value, it not only had to pay for the minting of the new coins, but for the difference between the theoretical silver weight of the coins, and the much lower real silver content of low quality coin, and this was a heavy burden. After the operation the same quantity of silver would be in circulation, but the number of coins would be smaller, and the total value would therefore be less (as each coin would still have its initial face value). The purchasing power of the mass of money in circulation would therefore, theoretically fall, and prices would also fall, in other words, there would be 'deflation'. It is, however, doubtful whether prices would fall as much as it was hoped. Those who gained from the operation would be creditors and people on fixed incomes: the loans of the former and the incomes of the latter would have the same value in terms of silver as before, and their confidence in the currency would be restored.

There was nothing new about the debate which went on in England over which solution was to be adopted: the arguments have been the same right from the time of Oresme in the 14th century, to the most recent discussions on devaluation. If the debate of 1694 is particularly well remembered, this is because it laid the basis for the long-term stability of the pound sterling and its relationship to the gold standard and because the protagonist of a fixed standard, in this case, was one of the most outstanding Englishmen of his time, the philosopher John Locke. Isaac Newton also participated in the debate.

Locke's arguments have been used on many subsequent occasions down to the present day. Doctor and famous philosopher though he was, Locke had been deeply involved in politics throughout the Restoration period and after the 1688 Revolution, of which he was both an influence and the leading theoretician. In his own business, he had already had frequent contact with the work of the Board of Trade, the governmental body most concerned with the English economy. In 1691, a year after his *Essay Concerning Human Understanding*, he wrote an initial treatise on money and rates of interest, and this was followed in 1695 by another on the monetary reforms then in progress, *Further Considerations Concerning the Raising of the Value of Money*, and by many speeches in Parliament and other writings.

His main opponent was Lowndes, the Secretary to the Treasury, who was responsible for formulating the government's monetary policy, and who advocated devaluation. Lowndes rejected various other solutions: for example, he did not want the content of circulating currency reduced, because he believed it was deceitful to circulate coin which had an identical weight and appearance, but contained less silver. His idea was that if silver bullion on the international market was rated at 77 pennies an ounce, when officially it was worth only 62, it would be correct and possible to bring the legal price into line with the market price. Instead of carrying out costly depreciations and recoinings, it would be sufficient to issue a decree proclaiming that from then on silver bullion or good currency would be worth 25% more at official rates. It was one way of carrying out a 'devaluation', what in France was called a 'raising' (*rehaussement*) of the currency – a misleading term, since it referred to a raising of the token value of good currency, and therefore a fall in the silver value of current coin and the accounting unit. This was the simplest and cheapest way of carrying out a 'devaluation' in the old kind of monetary systems where there was an accounting currency. Yet it was not so very different from the practices of today: in the French devaluation of 1958 it was decreed, from one day to the next, that the franc would be worth 20% less in terms of gold or foreign currencies.

Locke's objection to the proposal was that money had value only as an object; if a value was arbitrarily given, the proportions would be changed on paper, while the economic reality would remain unchanged. 'I confess myself not to see the least Reason why our present mill'd Money should be at all altered in Fineness, Weight or Value. I look upon it to be the best and safest from counterfeiting, adulterating or any ways being frudulently diminished, of any that ever was coined. It is adjusted to our legal Payment, Reckoning, and Accounts to which our Money must be reduced. The Raising of its Denomination will neither add to its worth, nor make the Stock we have more proportionate to our Occasions, nor bring one Grain of Silver the more into England, or one Farthing Advantage to the publick.'[3] Locke could only explain the increase from 62 to 77 pennies per ounce by the existence of clipped coin. He thought that 77 clipped pennies must weigh as much as 62 ordinary pennies and he was in fact right about there being clipped coin: an experiment or 'sample' was made to show that £57,200 sterling in silver coin, which should have contained 220,000 ounces of pure silver, contained only 141,000. It was calculated that at least 4,000,000 out of the 5,600,000 sovereigns in circulation had deteriorated in this way.

Locke won the dispute, the English State withdrew the silver in circulation and issued only coins with the full weight. The cost was £2,700,000, and this was recovered by collecting taxes in good coin and issuing paper money drawable on the Bank of England; creditors who had lent silver coin while it was losing value, were repaid in good money and they were also well satisfied. But for a long time afterwards the operation was a matter of debate. Sixty years later, Sir James Steuart was still scoffing at the English for having happily sacrificed £2,700,000 for the mere satisfaction of avoiding a lowering of their monetary standard. With the Napoleonic wars and the accompanying inflation, the controversy started up again.

The extent of the dispute stems from the fact that the possibility of

[3] John Locke, 'Further Considerations Concerning the Raising of the Value of Money', in *Several Papers Relating to Money, Interest and Trade, etc*, London 1696, pp. 108–9.

a devaluation depends both on the circumstances and on one's point of view (the interests of creditors and debtors, of exporters and importers being contradictory). It is difficult to take a position on the dispute between Lowndes and Locke because what was probably the real issue, why money had lost its purchasing power, was left unclear. Lowndes and Locke were in agreement in blaming this solely on the clipping of coins, but they do not seem to have asked either why the monetary crisis had not begun before 1695, since coins had been clipped for a very long time, or why the fall in the value of current coin in relation to precious metals and foreign currency was so much less than the extent of coin deterioration – 25% as opposed to 56%.

The circulation of clipped coin was in fact a case of a token money adapting to needs without causing excessive price rises, until the months after the founding of the Bank of England. It was the inflation of paper money, rather than clipped coin, which caused the steep increase. The proof of this is that once the monetary reform was accomplished, silver continued to leave England, and the flood of people trying to redeem bank notes for solid coin obliged the Bank of England to close for some time; simultaneously, its notes lost between 16% and 24% in Amsterdam, roughly the loss in value of current coin from before 1694.

When the silver content of the shilling was increased, gold, until then undervalued in England in relation to silver, rose to a higher value than in Europe: the ratio was 15.93 to 1 in England and only 15 to 1 on the continent. The yellow metal consequently flowed into England: from 1702 to 1717, 7,127,835 gold sovereigns were minted, and only 223,000 in silver. This surprising change made England, unwittingly and unintentionally, the home of the gold standard. But the small technical detail of a slight over-valuation of gold in terms of silver was not the only cause, and there are other aspects of this question which require discussion.

From 1696 to 1720, the over-valuation of gold at the official rate was gradually reduced, but it continued to hold the leading place. In 1698, Locke noted that the rate of 22 shillings for a guinea over-valued gold, and proposed that it should be reduced to $21\frac{1}{2}$s. In 1717, the great scholar Isaac Newton, in his capacity as Master of the Mint, wrote a report concluding that the guinea should be reduced to 21 shillings, and this was accepted. Even at this rate, which scarcely over-valued gold at all relative to silver, the yellow metal still came flowing into England: from 1727 to 1760 11,662,000 gold sovereigns were minted as opposed to 304,000 in silver.

The purely technical explanation is not in itself enough, and a second factor lies in the key episodes of the years 1694–1720. The revaluation of silver circulating coin and the influx of gold did not wipe out paper money inflation of various kinds: there were bank bills, issued in recognition of the Bank's debts to depositors, which gave interest and which were not therefore proper bank notes though they were used in circulation all the same; 'running cash-notes' redeemable by the bearer, which were guaranteed on metal deposits, and were precursors of the bank note; and even obligatory papers similar to modern bank notes. Credit of all kinds was encouraged, and John Argyll's proposals of 1695 were the first of several plans for paper money to be issued on the basis of securities in land as the French *assignats* were later. In other words, in the years 1688–1714, a period of successive wars, inflation reached new heights.

How was this inflation absorbed, and how did it in the end lead to an influx of gold and the stabilisation of English currency? Between the 'Glorious Revolution' and the treaties ending the Spanish Wars of Succession, the English economy developed and was consolidated by the conquest of the sea routes, through the South Sea voyages, the conquest of Gibraltar and Minorca in the Mediterranean, the Methuen Treaty with Portugal in 1703, and the gains from Spain made through the treaties of Utrecht (1713) and Rastadt (1714); in particular the English received the *asiento* to carry out the slave trade, and permission for 500 tons of shipping a year to trade with Spain's American colonies.

These political, economic, maritime and colonial victories took place as English production and trade were on the increase and as English intellectual horizons extended; economic thought was closely related to philosophy and science, as in the cases of Locke and Newton. It now becomes clear why it has been said that in England, the 18th century began in the 17th. The age of development, which appeared slowly and unevenly throughout the continent of Europe in the 18th century, entered its first glorious phase in England in the 1680s and 1710s. This phase was related to, and inter-acted with, the search for and discovery of new sources of gold, and these were destined to flow into England.

24

English Expansion and Brazilian Gold

The question to be answered here is how a century of low prices, that is, of a rise in the value of precious metals relative to commodities, and of monetary disorder aggravated by war, came to be followed by a century of rising prices and at least relative stability in European domestic currencies.

Preceding chapters have already examined the cases of England and Holland, the role of the Bank of Amsterdam and the creation of the Bank of England, together with the 1696 reform in England which, through a slight over-valuation of gold, turned it into the leading monetary metal in Britain. The conclusion must be that despite the complexities of monetary circulation in the years 1696–1714, when paper circulation played an important role, and despite the enormous tax burden of the wars and the fall of English paper money on the international exchanges, English currency began to be consolidated. This took place both through the expansion of domestic industry and commerce, and the maritime, colonial and commercial gains made from victories in the diplomatic and military fields. In America, the Caribbean, the South Seas and the Mediterranean, the way was prepared for gold and silver, especially gold, to flow into England.

To take one simple fact: in the twenty years from 1693 to 1713, English revenue from customs and excise trebled. It should also be remembered that in the intellectual turmoil of 1680–1715, described by Paul Hazard as 'the crisis of the European consciousness', discoveries in economics played an important part.

Since Paul Hazard's work, there has been a correct emphasis on the movement of ideas and of men, which in the period preparatory to the 18th century produced real changes in the mental structures of Europe. There was a great deal of travelling, especially by the English, not only to distant lands but within Europe itself. Intellectual prestige, formerly the preserve of Italy, Spain and later France, was rapidly acquired by the Northern European nations, Holland and England. The English Revolution of 1688, which took place at almost the same time as the revocation of the Edict of Nantes and the flight of French Protestants to Northern Europe, contributed to the spiritual revolution, which was extended by systematic propaganda. The spirit of 'reason' and the 'empirical' philosophy of Locke's *Essay Concerning Human Understanding,* prepared the way for ideas characteristic of the 18th century, while papers like the *Spectator* presented a new view of man.

This great intellectual movement, interestingly enough, belonged to a period of vigorous economic activity and international conflicts in which the main stakes were the great powers' share in the legacy of the Spanish Empire and world trade. More interestingly still, within the great sweep of intellectual discoveries, scientific economic thought was being born, and forging its main tools, hesitant and fragmentary though it still was. It was at this time that the first works of economic and mathematical calculation known as 'political arithmetic' appeared in England, with Gregory King's attempts to estimate the effects of variations in the harvest on fluctuations in grain prices. Early demographic and statistical studies were published: Graunt's figures on birth and mortality rates in England, King's essays on population and even on the national product (the figures from this are still used today) and William Petty's pioneering of the main ideas of classical economics.[1] In these early attempts at economic analysis, theory and practice were always related: the first application of probability calculations to human life was concerned with the problem of insurance, and as we have seen, men like Locke and Newton were well versed in monetary affairs.

At the same time, the last of the classical mercantilist works were being published in England, alongside the first expressions of economic liberalism in authors like Nicholas Barbon. In mercantilism, apart from the works of Joshua Child and Locke mentioned above, the conception of population and production as the basis of collective wealth was gaining ground in the writings of Dudley North (*Discourses upon Trade*) and Charles Davenant (*Essay on the East India Trade, Discourses on the Public Revenues, Essay on the probable method of making a people gainer in the balance of Trade,* 1697–1699). For these authors precious metals were merely symbols of wealth and a means of circulating it, while

[1] William Petty, *A Treatise of Taxes and Contributions,* London 1667; Gregory King, *Natural and Political observations and conclusions upon the state and conditions of England,* London 810.

real wealth lay in goods for consumption or exchange. Davenant, for example, wrote: 'Gold and Silver are indeed the Measure of Trade, but the Spring and Original of it, in all Nations, is the Natural, or Artificial Product of the Country, that is to say, what their Land, or what their Labour and Industry produces. And this is so true, that a Nation may be suppos'd by some accident, quite without the Species of Money, and yet, if the People are numerous, industrious, vers'd in Traffick, skill'd in Sea-Affairs, and if they have good Ports, and a Soil fertile in a variety of Commodities, such a people will have trade, and gather Wealth, and, they shall quickly get among 'em, a plenty of Gold and Silver: So that the real and effective Riches of a Country, is its Native Product. Gold and Silver are so far from being . . . the only Things that deserve the Name of Treasure, or the Riches of a Nation, that in truth, Money is at Bottom no more than the Counters with which Men in their dealings have been accustomed to reckon.'[2]

And again:

'We understand that to be Wealth, which maintains the Prince, and the general Body of his People, in Plenty, Ease, and Safety.

We esteem that to be Treasure which for the use of Man has been converted from Gold and Silver, into Buildings, and Improvements of the Country; As also other Things convertible into those Metals, as the Fruits of the Earth, Manufactures, or Foreign Commodities, and stock of Shipping.

We hold to be Riches what tends to make a People safe at Home, and considerable Abroad, as do Fleets and Naval Stores. We shall go yet farther, and say . . . that not only those Commodities, but even perishable Goods, may be held the Riches of a Nation, if they are convertible, tho' not converted into Gold and Silver; and this we believe does not only hold between Man and Man, . . . but between one Country and another.

Industry and Skill to improve the Advantages of Soil and Situation, are more truly Riches to a People, than even the possession of Gold and Silver Mines . . .! Tis not the taking in a great deal of Food, but 'tis good Digestion and Distribution that nourishes the Body, and keeps it healthy.'[3]

Davenant notes that in Spain, the common people, the 'Stomack of the Body Politick', were unable to 'digest' the surfeit of silver from the

[2] Charles Davenant, *Discourses on the Public Revenues and on the Trade of England*, London 1698, pp. 15–16.
[3] ibid. pp. 60–61.

mines. This had already been said clearly enough by early 17th century Spanish writers like Antonio Serra and Montchrestien. But rather than a pessimistic view of the abundance of gold and silver, we have here the optimistic outlook of a 'Commonwealth' which had been able to 'digest' money as well as attract it.

In England, then, during the War of the Hapsburg League and the Wars of the Spanish Succession (1689–1697; 1702–1714), monetary inflation went together with economic activity and an awakening – even the beginnings of a scientific attitude – towards this activity, which finally led to an influx of gold and an absorption of paper circulation. In the same period the 'gold cycle' of the Brazilian economy began; and as usual we must pose the question, without opting for either factor *a priori*, whether Brazilian gold was at the roots of the expansion of English production and trade (and their world-wide implications), or whether this expansion demanded or furthered the search for new minds, and thereby initiated the 'gold cycle'.

Again, it is not a matter of making either factor determinant; what interests us is the dialectic of their inter-action and their timing. The low world prices of the period of greatest recession (1660–1680) made gold, even more than silver, especially expensive in terms of commodities, and therefore increased demand for it: hence the frantic quest for gold. This search was not immediately successful, but it did produce results in the 1690s, and after 1703 there was a sudden expansion of mining output (and even more after 1708) which reached its height around 1720. It was in Brazil that these mines were found and this in itself was important to the metropolis, Portugal. During the late 17th and early 18th century, Portugal became if not totally dependent on England politically, at least strongly influenced by her economically, almost to the exclusion of other powers. Brazilian mining developments and monetary and economic changes in Portugal, therefore, can usefully be examined together in relation to the developments in England which we have just been discussing.

The Brazilian economy, and by implication the Portuguese economy, had not been in unmitigated decline during the 17th century. In the first half, the production of Brazilian wood, the exploitation of slaves, and latterly, sugar-planting, had bolstered up the Brazilian economy. Its most serious crisis began with the separation of Portugal from Spain in the 1640 war, and Dutch attempts to establish themselves in Brazil. After losing their conquest bid of 1657, the Dutch, together with a large number of converted Jews of Portuguese extraction, took over some

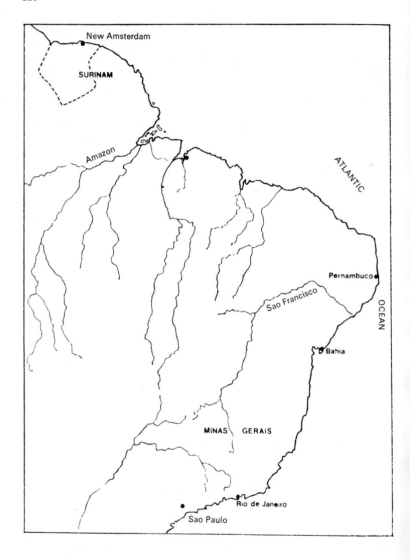

Figure 12. Brazil in the 18th century.

Caribbean islands (notably Curaçao) and organised sugar plantations on a scale which could compete with Brazil. The crisis came to a head in 1670, as shown in Frédéric Mauro's work which ends at this very date.[4]

There followed an attempt to revive Brazilian production by establishing manufacturing; but virtually free competition for English goods made this unprofitable. In the years 1670–1703, however, an equilibrium among three complementary kinds of production began to be established: Oporto wine was exported to England, English manufactures went to Brazil, and the products of the colonies were sent to Europe through Portugal. The slave trade from Africa to Brazil, which provided labour for the colonial economy, was also part of the triangle and in the last years of the 17th century, when Portuguese colonial trade required some 90 ships a year, the system was quite busy.

The Methuen Treaty of 1703 (named after the English negotiator) in a sense institutionalised the trade: it suppressed all tariffs on English cloth in the Portuguese colonies; secured preference for Portuguese wines on the English market (the sales and even the production of such wines were often in English hands); and gave the English complete freedom to trade with Brazil, thereby enormously increasing their chances of keeping stocks of goods to smuggle to the Spanish colonies. England's economic ties with Brazil were drawn even closer, and her activities in the Atlantic further increased, through the Anglo-Portuguese diplomatic and military alliance during the Wars of the Spanish Succession which was directed against Philip V, grandson of Louis XIV, and against France.

In the commercial triangle of Brazil, England and Portugal, the balance was always in England's favour. It was paid in Brazilian gold. In the crisis years of the 1670s, while English influence was steadily growing, the feverish search for gold began again in Brazil. As mentioned above, this must have been related to the increase in the value of gold relative to commodities in general. Exploration in the coastal areas produced little or nothing, but the interior, explored by Paulistas, men from São Paulo, a city famous for its intrepid pioneers, yielded an extraordinary wealth of gold and diamonds. In 1673 Fernão Dias País Lome, described as the richest of all 'Paulistas' and owner of the most slaves, organised a systematic exploration of the interior and assumed the title of 'Governor of the Emeralds'. He carried on his explorations for seven years and died without finding anything, though he had,

---

[4] For Frédéric Mauro, see chapter 21, note 2.

without knowing it, reached the very edge of the gold fields.

The government sent Don Rodrigo de Castelo Branco, a general administrator of mines who had worked in Potosí, in search of him: but the Paulista explorers did not welcome his presence, and he was killed by Fernão País's son-in-law. The latter won a pardon for the crime in exchange for revealing the whereabouts of the gold deposits of the Rio das Velhas and nearby mountains, and it was therefore he who opened up the mining area known ever since as Minas Gerais, or 'General Mines' (today a province of Brazil).

The strength of the exploration movement induced by hopes of great profit is apparent from the fact that at the same time, between 1698 and 1700, proper roads were built through the jungle, from Rio de Janeiro and the coast, deep into the interior of Brazil, under the supervision of the governor, Artur de Sá Meneses. This was the beginning of the real Brazilian 'gold cycle'. Some discoveries, such as that of Borba Gato, produced as much as 30 arrobas of gold at a time, or more than 300 kilos, creating the illusion that there was enough gold to last 'for centuries'. Some even said it would last 'for as long as the world shall endure'.

As well as mining deposits alluvial gold was found in the mountain sides. Nuggets of up to 3 or even 6 pounds in weight are recorded. The result was one of the first gold rushes of the Americas, similar to those which followed in the 19th century. From 1703 to 1720 a large number of Portuguese emigrated in response to the attraction: 'More Portuguese and foreigners are to be seen leaving for Brazil and the mines each year. . . . They include people of every station in life, men and women, young and old, rich and poor, nobles, plebeians, lay clergy and monks of every order, many of them leaving for Brazil without a monastery or a house to receive them.' The stampede of priests became a scandal. Attempts were made to forbid them from going near the mines; the Governor of São Paulo went so far as to ask for permission to apply excommunication as a sanction to maintain the ban. In 1720, Portugal had to impose a strict limitation on emigration.

In fact, large-scale mining began only in 1708. The 'Paulistas' launched a campaign of violence against the immigrants, whom they saw as intruders, and, in the manner of adventurers, they dealt with them quite unscrupulously. There were two brothers, Francisco and Benito de Amaral, who had been condemned as common criminals in Rio, but they were influential mine-owners and in the struggle over the mines they reportedly ordered men to be seized and slain on the slightest pretext. Under such conditions, the Portuguese were unable to channel gold exports and to ensure that royalties were being paid on production: people entered the mining areas secretly, and gold left by similar routes. Nuñez Viana, a Portuguese 'who attracted many people since he was rich, intrepid and quite unscrupulous', organised virtual revolts Confrontations between 'Paulistas' and immigrants sometimes involved forces of up to 2,000 or 3,000 men. Nuñez himself in effect declared his independence of the government, and though in the end he was beaten, he was treated leniently and finished up as a high-ranking colonial official. The episode of Brazilian gold, then, though it did not see a repeat of the extortion and pillage of the 16th century, was scarcely a model of economic organisation: it was more of a grand adventure. In addition, it also involved large numbers of negro slaves. According to the tax collections from the trade, the number of slaves shipped from Africa to the Brazilian mines between 1715 and 1727 fluctuated at around 2,200 or 2,300 per annum.

Brazilian gold did not end the monetary confusion characteristic of both Portugal and Brazil in the second half of the 17th century. In Portugal as in Spain, copper coin and worthless base coin multiplied wildly, and, as in England, the currency was plagued by the clipping of silver coin. In 1688 the Portuguese government had to acknowledge the fall in the value of its currency by a 20% devaluation, in which the gold coin previously worth 4,000 *reis* was revalued to 4,800 (the *rei* being a very low value accounting unit). This measure produced violent crises in the cities of Brazil by around 1690. In Rio, Pernambuco and Bahia, the increase in the price of gold meant that all ingots and good coin were bought up, and the search for gold, and the dispute over sources, became still more frenetic. The necessity for colonial currency to have a certain autonomy then became apparent: in 1694, a Mint, a *Casa da Moeda*, was established in Bahia, and another in Rio in 1702.

Trade was increasing under the impetus of relations with England, and under the wartime protection of the English fleet. From 1686 to 1700, revenue from the Rio anchorage levy, which gives a rough measure of traffic, rose from 16 million *reis* to 37 million, more than doubling in 15 years. Therefore the gold mines have been considered as independent of the expansion of trade, since this began before the discoveries; but the very hope of making discoveries was an attraction in itself, and when gold was found, the trend was confirmed and the economy consolidated. In a little under two years, from 15th October 1703 to 29th August 1705, the recently-created Rio Mint received 4,062 marks of coarse gold, or 3,655 marks of bullion, from which 77,760 gold pieces were coined to a value of 373,248,000 *reis*. The profit on the minting process was in the order of 54 million *reis*.

The increase in the amount of gold reaching Portugal in the early 18th century was as follows (the figures are Frédéric Mauro's):

	kilos
1699	725
1701	1,785
1704	9,000
1720	25,000
1725	20,000

The series is not continuous, and it does not give an accurate picture of the growth since in some years the amounts must have been much smaller; but the increase was nonetheless considerable, and it must have had a powerful psychological effect.

The first beneficiary of the sudden increase in gold production and gold imports into Europe was undoubtedly Portugal, but as with Spain in the 16th and 17th centuries, the final result depended on whether or not she kept possession of the metal. The constant surplus on England's trading balance with Portugal and Brazil drained away gold; and since this was in exchange for actual products it gave a greater stimulus to the English economy than if it had been obtained directly from mining. This is why England, which according to available calculations, minted approximately £15 million of gold coin in the 136 years from 1558 to 1694, was able to mint almost as much again, about £14 million in the 33 years from 1694 to 1727 according to available calculations. This influx of gold explains why, once the wars were over, the various forms of paper money could be fairly easily reabsorbed, and why the currency was stabilised.

This only happened, however, after a phase of wild speculation, similar to the French experience under what was known as the 'Law system'. In 1716–1717 Walpole drew up a plan for wiping out the National Debt, which stood at some £54,000,000, by buying up the annuities owed to the Bank of England and the South Sea Company: this involved decreasing the rate of interest on the debts, from 7–9 to 4% or 5%, and forming a sinking fund. But in 1717 Walpole's successor, Stanhope, handed the organisation of the project over to the Bank and the South Sea Company: bonds for the sinking fund were then offered for sale to the public, and the State became more and more in their debt.

Following the example of the Law system, adopted in France in 1719, the South Sea Company set out to buy up all public debts, with the State supporting the Company's monopolies (all English trade outside Europe, the Spanish contracts, etc.). As in France, the Company's shares then became the object of a frenzied wave of speculation, with all kinds of minor companies following suit and issuing shares (speculative issues, sometimes based entirely on fictitious firms, and known as 'bubbles'). The Company was rash enough to take on the bubbles and (on the international plane) the Law system at the same time. This resulted in a general panic, which also affected the Company's shares. From December 1720 to April 1721, amid an atmosphere of revolt, the situation had to be stabilised and measures taken against certain high-ranking people. The political crisis passed and the South Sea Company survived, thanks to the intervention of the Bank of England and that other great enterprise, the East India Company. Although some speculators were ruined, the three companies were able to maintain their shares at a reasonable level; they began to make profits again and the sinking of the national debt became part and parcel of their renewed prosperity.

The monetary crisis was therefore brought to an end. Despite the small quantities involved, rapid circulation of silver coin met the needs of everyday use, while the minting of gold met the needs of international trade. Until the next major change in the world ratio of gold and silver took place, in 1774, England was troubled neither by the export of good coin nor by the deterioration of current coin. The easy solution of this problem was clearly related to the development of other institutions and practices in banking and credit. From 1720–1721 until major world conflicts were resumed in 1792–1798, England experienced a monetary stability characterised by the import and minting of gold.

Monetary Stabilisation and Economic Change in Spain

In the study of the change in the conjuncture leading from the economic problems and monetary confusion of the 17th century to the general growth and financial stability of the 18th century, the case of Spain is important: here the period of bad currency in Castile came to a dramatic end. It was preceded by a regional recovery and followed by the alignment of Spanish currency. Stability was finally achieved, between 1725 and 1735.

(1) The situation in Spain up to 1680–86

After being the major colonial power, the owner of the American mines, and the epicentre of the price revolution in the 16th century, Spain underwent terrible monetary catastrophes in the 17th century. After the age of gold, which lasted until 1545, and the age of silver, which lasted until 1600–1610, Spain, in a manner of speaking, fell back into the Bronze Age: meaning in this case, coin made of an alloy containing an increasingly higher proportion of copper. The spread of base coin was the curse of the century: there was a Spanish saying to the effect that copper coin had done more damage to the Kingdom than the Revolt of the Netherlands. The minting of copper began to reach alarming proportions in 1605, and then rose so rapidly that it set off the increase in European copper prices: Swedish copper was shipped down to the Cantabrian coast of Spain to be sold at a high price in exchange for silver.

This multiplication of copper, amounting to a genuine inflation in low value coin, was a way of keeping a high level of monetary circulation in the country, in the hope of maintaining prices and incomes at the high rates they had reached when Potosí silver was flooding into the country. Silver was still coming in but more slowly, and the more that arrived the faster it was spent, especially for the wars in the Netherlands.

Around 1640, 92% of the money circulating in Castile was of copper and this rose to 95% in 1660–1680. What this meant at the current price levels can be imagined: 100 pounds' weight of cheese cost 400 pounds' weight of money.

The depreciation of current coin is clearly illustrated by the fact that good silver coin (the only currency valid for foreign trade) could only be had at a 50% premium in 1650; and this figure rose to 150% in 1664; then in 1670–1675, after the failure of drastic measures to reduce the premium, to 200%, climbing to a high point of 275% in February 1680. Inflation was not continuous, as there were attempts at deflation, in the form of massive withdrawals of base currency; but each crisis dealt a heavy blow to the interests of individuals and the working of the economy, without serving any useful purpose. The measures failed, since copper quickly came back into circulation and the premium on silver was re-established.

(2) Autonomous regional economies

In describing the inflation of 1605–1680 I have referred to Spain, when I should have said Castile. Despite the achievement of political unity under a common ruler, a long time before, the old autonomous kingdoms had retained their own fiscal, monetary and tariff systems. This applied not only to Portugal (which became independent again after the 1640 revolt) but to the smaller political units making up the 'Crown of Aragon': Valencia and Catalonia. Earl J. Hamilton's study of money and prices, to which I have so often referred, shows that this monetary autonomy could have surprising results: Valencia was completely untouched by the catastrophic inflation of copper coin, while Catalonia had a similar experience to Castile, though at a different time and for different reasons.

The currency of Valencia remained stable in relation to silver; there was no appreciable inflation of copper coin, and nominal prices therefore more or less followed the curve of silver prices, reflecting the international conjuncture of the 17th century very clearly. They fell rapidly from 1650 to 1670, less rapidly but still quite clearly from 1670 to 1688, and then turned, rising quite steeply between 1688 and 1710. The economy of Valencia thus went through a period of low and falling prices, scarcely favourable to a dynamic economy, but possibly quite beneficial to consumers. In any case there were no disasters or drastic swings, and eventually the tendency was towards an upturn in the economy.

This was in stark contrast to the economy of the rest of the country. But one should not deduce from this that each state's monetary policy was completely decisive: the stability of Valencia was as much the result as the cause of very special economic conditions. It was a small country with a population of only 250,000 to 300,000; very fertile for horticulture, which was increasingly developed after the expulsion of the *moriscos* in 1609; and a particularly sheltered corner of the peninsula. But it can be said that its monetary autonomy spared it the turmoil of Castile. Valencia simply witnessed a succession of sharper and more gradual recessions in the second half of the 17th century, and conditions improved after 1688. In Valencia the general movement seen throughout Europe prevailed, while Castile had an aberrant internal currency system.

Catalonia differed from both Valencia and Castile, but deserves careful study. Despite the monetary crises of Castile, Catalonian currency held out well until 1640: gold re-appeared in circulation when it was slightly over-valued and there was an adequate supply of silver after 1619, when excess copper coin was successfully withdrawn.

During the Catalan rising against Castile and the war which lasted until 1659 and which brought a terrible plague, the currency crises of Catalonia were worse than in Castile. The doubloon, worth 58 Catalan shillings in 1640, was worth 320 in 1654; in other words, the Catalan pound – the accounting currency – which was officially equivalent to 2.22 grams of pure gold in 1640, was worth only 0.38 grams in 1654. At the end of the war 'black' copper coin was withdrawn by the cartload. Though the withdrawal only began in 1654, by 1660 the doubloon had fallen from a high point of 320 shillings to 120 and later 110; a devaluation of almost a half relative to 1640. But in sharp contrast to Castile the crisis lasted only twenty years before stability was re-asserted.

The authorities in Barcelona took advantage of this situation to mint small coins, for circulation within Catalonia, with a silver content which was very carefully calculated in relation to the market value of silver. They were made in such a way that their 'intrinsic' value (the market value of their silver content) was approximately the same as their 'extrinsic' (official) value; but the official value was slightly greater so that there would be no temptation to export the coin and to buy more with it abroad. The system was successful and the currency was stabilized. From then on, as in Valencia, prices fell slightly until 1688 and then embarked on an uneven, irregular but definite increase, from 1688 to 1709–1710.

This was in line with international trends and with developments in England (Catalonia was by this time trading directly with England). Within the region, the period was a profitable one for merchants, and producers had surplusses to sell. The prices which increased most rapidly were export prices for wine and oil, the main local produce; while the price of wheat, which had to be imported into Barcelona from Northern Europe and the Mediterranean areas of the Middle East, rose less steeply, benefiting (or at least not harming) the mass of consumers. Small vineyard and olivegrove owners prospered, and as a host of small-scale industrial enterprises sprung up, great plans were made for Dutch-style trading and banking 'companies'. A book was written entitled, *The Phoenix of Catalonia*: it symbolised the hope of an economic renaissance. Here as in England, the 18th century began in the 17th.

These tendencies were strengthened by a new political development. At the time of the succession to the Spanish throne in 1700, when Louis XIV accepted the Spanish crown for his grandson, Catalonia pronounced against the French king and in favour of the Austrian pretender. In 1705 she found herself at war with both France and Castile, fighting on the side of the English and Portuguese. English and Portuguese money flowed into Catalonia, and prices tended to rise within a framework of monetary stability. Meanwhile Archduke Charles of Austria was proclaimed King of Spain in Barcelona, and he had 5 gram silver coins minted with his portrait. They were to be valid throughout Spain, and were modelled on Catalan domestic currency, which as described above had been stable and non-exportable since 1674.

This development was significant because it instituted the custom, adopted by Spain in the 18th century, of maintaining a domestic currency in standard silver coins of a low value, suitable for small transactions and at a value slightly above that of the market (to prevent exports by speculators), while the great colonial pieces of eight – also known as the hard peso or piastre, and the precursor of the dollar – were reserved for foreign trade. The system was similar to those which we have seen being established spontaneously in the Netherlands and England. It tended to standardize the ratio of current coin to international currency and prepared the ground for the great monetary stabilisation later in the century.

The Archduke's small coin was named after its Catalan model, the *peçeta* (Catalan) or *peseta* (Spanish), meaning little coin. It became the main unit of Spanish currency in the 19th century, with a silver content close to that of the livre tournois, after its stabilisation in 1726. It was therefore also close to the 'Germinal' franc, which took over from the livre and was the main monetary unit in France throughout the 19th century. It was, then, in 1700–1710 (and for Catalonia even from 1674) that the classical silver coin of modern Europe was established. After the terrors of the 17th century crises, Castile too began to stablise her currency automatically on the same basis.

(3) Final crises and the recovery of Castilian currency

In 1680 Castile made a final bid to end the inflation of copper coin, and withdrew it from circulation en masse. It was an act of drastic surgery and it ruined many people: but whereas all previous attempts had been followed by renewed inflation, this was for the first time successful. It is interesting to examine the reasons for this drastic crisis, and the subsequent relative success in stabilising the currency.

The first reason for the end of copper inflation was that industrial demand for copper raised its price above the monetary value. Iron-mongers and even gold merchants melted down copper coin to export the metal, as they had already done with silver: they thereby confirmed the theory that any metallic money, having a cost price, is a commodity, and becomes a commodity again when the monetary value ascribed to it enters into conflict with its metal value on the market.

Though the subject has not been fully researched, it is more than likely that the 1680s saw, if not a recovery in the population and economy of Castile, at least a halt to their decline. The great 17th century monetary crisis coincided with a fall in the population of Castile of 25% between 1651 and 1682, and this decline reached 50% in such formerly prosperous cities as Toledo, Segovia and Valladolid. Meanwhile, trade with the Indies and Toledo wool production fell by 75%. Copper inflation and the monetary crisis must have been as much the result as the cause of the economic crisis, though they would of course have aggravated the problems. Even before 1680, there was a flood of reports to the King which offered solutions to the crisis, especially by means of the 'reduction of copper' and an 'unburdening of the kingdom' (amortizing the national debt). Such reports disappear after the monetary stabilisation begun in 1686, a sign that the crisis was passing. The question is whether this corresponded to some expansion in population and production.

The 'deflation' process (the reabsorption of copper coin) was not uneventful: its effects were quite drastic. At the beginning of 1680, the maravedi, the small accounting unit, taking into account the premium of silver over copper, represented 28 milligrams of solid silver. It became equivalent to 62 mgs after copper was withdrawn on 22 May 1680: in other words, its value more than doubled. Between 1680 and 1682 there was therefore a fall in the nominal prices of goods in Castile which averaged out at 46%. This was in fact a sign of success, because if prices had stayed high it would have been necessary to find some new means of circulation. But the economy was still not responding. In theory, falling prices should have suited the consumer at least; but it is necessary to take into account all the losses and delays caused by such a massive operation as the withdrawal of millions of kilos of copper. Ordinary people lost their normal money without being able to replace it with good coin. Debtors who had taken out loans in times of bad currency had to make repayment in money worth twice as much, and most of them went bankrupt. For a time good coin was hoarded. Servants and workmen went without pay, and there was chronic unemployment everywhere. In the King's own stables horses were killed because there was no way of feeding them. The description of this crisis by his agents induced Louis XIV to invade the Spanish-held positions in the Low Countries. This was the supreme crisis of the reign of Charles II, the Bewitched King, and the monarch of Hugo's *Ruy Blas*. He was a sick man whom it was wrongly expected would die at any moment; in fact, his reign went on for another twenty years, and in rather better conditions, judging by the state of the currency.

The end of the crisis came in 1686, when the currency was reformed in line with Catalan currency (see above). On 14th October 1686, the silver real, the only coin unchanged since the times of Ferdinand and Isabella, was minted at 84 to the mark instead of 67, each real containing 20% less silver than before. This applied only to Spain, not to the colonies, and in America coin was still minted at the old values (especially the piastre or 8 real piece). A distinction was established between 'new silver' and 'old silver', the latter being worth 20% more, with satisfactory results: the international prestige of colonial coin did not suffer at all, while an acceptable domestic currency was established, one that was not over-valued and therefore did not tend to leave the country.

On the ratios established in 1686, gold was worth 16.48 times as much as silver in Spain, a much higher ratio than on the European market (14.80 in Hamburg) or even in England (15.39). Gold was of course particularly highly valued in Spain because it was much scarcer than silver: but such a high official over-valuation should have attracted a flood of gold to Spain. The Spanish economy, however, did not have the same attractive power as England did at the time: legal measures on their own are never powerful enough to exert an influence outside of real economic forces.

Nonetheless, the basis was laid for the stabilisation of Castilian currency: an effort was being made to attract gold, domestic silver money of a lower value replaced copper in daily use, and 'old' colonial silver was kept for international trade. All this was more or less in line with what was happening in the Netherlands and England. Fourteen years of monetary stability followed, with prices tending to rise gradually, in Castile as well as in Valencia and Catalonia. This suggests that the international upturn in the conjuncture from 1680–1688 had penetrated Spain and even Castile, though it was obscured by the 1680 monetary crisis. A confused awareness of this recovery may help to explain the halt in the writings of the *arbitristas*, and the loyalty to Charles II expressed by provinces such as Catalonia, which sided with the Hapsburgs against the French king Philip V.

After his accession in 1700, Philip V, the grandson of Louis XIV, installed himself in Castile surrounded by excellent advisers, including well-known Frenchmen like Orry and Amelot, and lesser known but highly specialised men such as Patino and Rodrigo Caballero. In the monetary field Caballero consolidated and stabilised the two-tier system of new coin with 20   less silver than old colonial coin.

This dual standard was confirmed in 1716 and given a new nomenclature: 'national silver' referred to colonial coin and 'provincial silver' to domestic currency. In the domestic sphere low value coin was minted for small-scale transactions: the large quantity of 'silver reals' minted in 1706 and 1707 by Philip V had precisely the same value as the pesetas produced in Catalonia from 1674 and by the Archduke in 1707. Philip V's coins contained 5.066 grams of silver, the Archduke's contained 5.096, while the city of Barcelona minted at 5.1 grams. This set a pattern for the future peseta, which corresponded closely to the 1726 livre tournois, and for the future franc, though the latter was slightly heavier than either.

These measures were all the more important because after the suppression of the privileges of the rebel provinces in 1716, current coin was the same throughout Spain. (Barcelona kept her own accounting currency, but no longer minted coin.) Spanish currency was unified and stabilised, with a distinction drawn between domestic ('provincial') currency and international currency: apart from some small adjustments (especially the reduction of the gold–silver ratio to 15.06) in the years before 1737, this made the early 18th century as Earl J. Hamilton has said, a period of stability and recovery for Spain. From 1739, Spain even won some points in defending the American colonies against England. Mexican silver was once more mined and flowed into Cadiz in massive quantities. The economic growth of the 18th century then began in earnest; but the ground for this expansion had been laid as early as 1680, through monetary stabilisation.

26

From Colbert to Law

In the period of transition from the difficulties of the 17th century to the growth of the 18th century, the case of France is perhaps the least easily definable and the most complicated. France's political hegemony was now under attack, and she had to try to defend herself, at the cost of economic sacrifice and expedients which were often ruinous. In the last years of Louis XIV France was reminiscent of Spain towards the end of the reign of Philip II and in the early 17th century, and monetary indicators again prove reliable: French currency went through terrible crises in the late 17th and early 18th century. It is therefore difficult to say whether France really took part in the early inter-cyclical recovery as England and Spain did, between 1680–1686 and 1705–1710. But international conditions in the end prevailed and by 1726 in France as elsewhere, monetary stability had been achieved. Since in analysing this difficult case, every period presents a series of problems, certain distinct phases will be considered.

(1) The Colbert period: 1661–1683

In this phase the state was struggling against economic depression and the 'deflationist' atmosphere prevailing in Europe, together with the economic hegemony of the Dutch, which cast a shadow over French political hegemony. It was a period of silver scarcity, low prices and a fairly low level of circulation: the main current coin for ordinary purposes was of copper (Madame de Sévigné complained of the weight of the bags of copper coin her tenants delivered to her). There was however no inflation of the kind experienced in Spain, and the livre tournois maintained a very stable rate on the Amsterdam exchange. Colbert's aim, at least initially, was to stimulate industrial production and exports, and to reduce public expenditure; but he was very rigid on the question of monetary stability. The existing values could not be maintained absolutely (in 1674, 4-sol coins were issued with a silver content below the official rate), but in essentials they were held, and this showed that the difficulties were not particularly acute (there was also stability in England at the same period). The problem is whether this stability was a good thing: it meant that old debts were a heavy burden (as Emmanuel Le Roy-Ladurie notes in the case of the Languedoc peasantry[1]), and it did little to attract silver and increase exports. French merchants in Cadiz asserted that Colbert's ban on paying for silver at more than the legal rate was prejudicial to their sales in Cadiz and to the repatriation of profits.

(2) The period of wars: 1689–1717

As always, the wars (the Hapsburg League Wars, 1689–1697, followed almost at once by the Wars of the Spanish Succession, 1702–1714) entailed new military and diplomatic expenditure, monetary inflation and public debts; they led to the circulation of all kinds of paper money and eventually to changes in the ratio of the domestic and international currencies.

Until 1700 there were no violent changes in exchange rates, and the nature of those which did occur is in doubt – sometimes fictitious changes were said to have taken place, in order to discourage saving and to put silver savings into circulation. But the most important development was that between 1683 and 1715, while the annual average minting of silver fell by a quarter, a circulation began, not of banknotes, for there was no French equivalent of the Bank of England, but of bills of exchange on the Treasury, the war fund and the lending banks. Dealers, tax farmers and tax collectors in turn put paper money into circulation. Finally, in 1701, proper 'money bills' were circulated as cash, in exchange for silver taken in to be melted down in preparation for monetary reforms. This was still not paper money, as in 1704 they were ascribed interest as if by way of recognising a debt; but in 1707 they were made obligatory. They nonetheless depreciated so much that in 1706 the famous financier Samuel Bernard had quantities redeemed at a 78% premium to compensate for the loss in value of the notes. By 1708 the notes in circulation had reached a total value of 371 million livres tournois.

[1] Emmanuel Le Roy-Ladurie, *Les Paysans de Languedoc*, Paris 1966.

(3) The liquidation of debts and the Law system: 1715-1726

In 1715, the public debt stood at over 3,500 million livres tournois: the first problem was how to liquidate it. Notes were devalued by 25 . Coin was melted, and the amounts due were revised by a Chamber of Justice. By the end of 1717 the debt was down to 2,160 million livres. This was not enough, however, and business was not recovering. Partly because of the prestige of the Dutch companies and of the Bank of England, the Regency government then allowed itself to be led into accepting the plans of the Scottish financier John Law. On 2nd May 1716 he was authorised to create a private bank on a 20 year concession, which soon encompassed the whole of public finances and attempted to monopolise foreign and colonial trade.

A detailed study of the Law system cannot be made in the context of this book, but it is necessary to look at its relation to the problem of money, and how its liquidation led to the 1726 stabilisation. The Law Bank, which was created as a purely private institution, agreed to have 75 of the shares making up its basic capital paid in State notes. The Bank in turn issued notes and the State accepted payment of taxes in Law banknotes. Law's main creation, however, was an enormous Trading Company to trade with the western hemisphere, especially Louisiana, for which he issued 200,000 shares at 500 livres tournois apiece. He then bought out the old Eastern and China Companies and acquired control of the Senegal slave trade. At the same time he took over the domestic monopolies of tobacco sales, minting, and tax collection. It was, in short, an attempt to replace the dealers, financiers and tax farmers of Louis XIV's time with a single great 'system', while all private individuals, share-holders and traders were invited to take part in speculating on foreign and colonial trade by becoming shareholders of the company. With the whole system based on these shares, an immense pile of credit was required. The public had to provide the money; but meanwhile, the Bank, which became the Royal Bank in 1718, had acquired the right to issue notes to circulate as money. From then on there was a danger in the credit operation: the public was so enthusiastic about the chance of profit that the shares, worth 500 livres initially, were being sold for 18,000 by the end of 1719. But it was unclear how they could be redeemed. On the other hand, paper money, which the State supported by all means possible, and which had at times been more acceptable to the public than metal coin (there was a premium on the latter), was still in theory redeemable. A spontaneous or deliberately instigated moment of panic was therefore enough to bring the whole edifice down, whether by massive sales of shares or by massive demand for repayment. And this was what actually happened. Law of course defended himself and was supported by the State, though confusedly: every means was used, from the forced circulation of notes and the prosecution of holders of metal coin, to currency changes and a new issue of shares, but each attempt failed.

The system was liquidated mainly through deflation and successive changes in the currency, which continued until the decree of 26th May 1726, which set 24 livres tournois as the official rate of the gold louis, the 'two *écusson*' coin, whose weight and gold content had already been fixed in January of that year. At the same time the silver *écusson*, fixed in January at 8.3 to the mark and at a silver level of 11, and henceforth known as the *laurier*, was set at 6 livres tournois. The ratio of silver to the livre tournois remained unchanged until the end of the Ancien Régime, and the gold ratio until 1785, when it was very slightly readjusted. This gave the livre tournois a silver value of 4.505 grams, almost the same as the content of the Germinal franc established under the Consulate at 5 grams of which 9/10 was pure silver, (or 4.5 grams of pure silver). 1726 was therefore the starting point for the monetary stability of the 18th and 19th centuries (the episode of the *assignats* apart), and this now enables us to consider the problems raised by the transition from the 17th to the 18th century.

(4) The fall in silver prices in France

There appear to be conflicting interpretations of price movements in France during this transitional period. Pierre Goubert, in his work on the Beauvaisis,[2] holds that silver prices were falling until 1730 or even 1735. By providing mobile averages (the central rather than the average value over 11 years, to eliminate the excessive influence of famine prices) he shows clearly that grain prices were falling between 1650 and 1730, and that each low point reached in the cyclical variations was lower than the last. This is completely in accordance with Beveridge's earlier findings about prices in Europe and with Labrousse's work on France as a whole: the price increases of the 18th century did not begin until 1733.

These were all silver prices, and the great revival of American silver production dates from the second third of the 18th century, not from

[2] Pierre Goubert, *Beauvais et le Beauvaisis, 1600–1730*, Paris 1960.

around 1680. It would be interesting to know if France felt any of the effects of the export of Brazilian gold, around 1700. But the long fall in silver prices in the 17th century lasted throughout Northern Europe until 1730–1735. According to Goubert, the Beauvaisis and Northern France in general followed the pattern of Northern Europe rather than that of Spain or Portugal, where the 17th century fall seems to have both begun (1600–1610) and ended (1680s) earlier; in Northern Europe it only began in the 1650s and lasted throughout much of the 18th century.

Jean Meuvret has published brief but useful studies of 17th century prices,[3] which show (mainly from examples in the region of Paris) that France did nonetheless share in the price increases of 1688/90–1715, although in the form of an inter-cycle, i.e. intercepting a fall which continued until 1733. In his thesis on Basse-Provence,[4] René Baehrel comes to rather different conclusions, by using original statistical methods and deliberately concentrating on nominal prices. According to him the 17th century price fall began in the 1600s, as in Spain, and ended around 1690. Given what we know about Spain, it seems reasonable to conclude that the South of France, which was part of the economy of Marseilles and the Mediterranean, was more likely to follow Spain than Beauvaisis, but the methods used are however so different that it is difficult to draw comparisons. For another part of the South, Languedoc, Le Roy-Ladurie has found that nominal prices tended to rise from 1690, but the lowest silver prices (for wheat) were not reached until 1720 and this was also the case in Spain.[5] The importance of the increases between 1680–1690 and 1710–1715, therefore, depends both on the fluctuations in domestic currency and on the region under consideration.

(5) French imports of precious metals

As will be discussed later, French imports of precious metals in the 18th century came through trade with Cadiz, via the Atlantic ports, especially Saint-Malo, as well as over the Pyrenees and through Bayonne. The highest level of imports was recorded at the time of the Spanish crisis of 1636–1640, which made it possible to carry out the great French monetary reform of 1640, in which gold played the leading role. Even

[3] cf. Jean Meuvret, 'Les mouvements des prix de 1661 à 1715 et leurs répercussions', *Journal de la société de statistique de Paris*, 1944, pp. 109–119; and 'Circulation monétaire et utilisation économique de la monnaie en France aux XVIe et XVIIe siecles', *Etudes d'Histoire moderne et contemporaine*, vol. 1, 1947, pp. 15–20.

[4] René Baehrel, *La Basse-Provence rurale (fin du XVIe siecle) 1789*, Paris 1961.

[5] Le Roy-Ladurie, op. cit. p. 599.

after 1650, it is erroneous to think that French trade with Spain, and therefore with America, was paralysed. It might have been growing more slowly, but it certainly did not stop.

Albert Girard's work[6] does not give a continuous series of figures for the transfer of precious metals to France each time the Atlantic fleets returned to the colonial monopoly ports of Spain, but it does give gross amounts for some individual years:

	pesos
1670	1,300,000
1671	3,446,000
1672	2,889,000
1673	5,648,000
1679–1681	4,490,000
1681–1682	2,700,000
1682–1683	3,020,000
1685	670,000
1686	1,940,000
1689	4,000,000
1698	1,517,000

These are obviously only rough estimates and are also discontinuous: but it does appear that the best period for French imports of precious metal preceded both the Spanish monetary reform of 1686 and the period of the great wars, even though the French merchants of Cadiz criticised Colbert on the grounds that a devaluation of the French currency (fixing a higher price in livres tournois for Spanish coin) would have attracted still more silver to France. It was also true that the largest profits on Spanish coin bought in Genoa were gained by exporting it directly to the Levant. The worst phase was the period of the great

[6] Albert Girard, *Le commerce français à Séville et Cadix au temps des Habsbourgs*, Paris 1932.

wars. Spanish currency was stabilised, England was resolved to cut off French overseas trade, and French silver stocks were no longer replenished regularly. Between 1688 and 1715, less and less silver was minted.

This explains the obsession of French businessmen, followed by French statesmen, with Atlantic trade which was still of great importance under Louis XIV. Research by the Faculty of Rennes into the Saint-Malo trade has shown that around 1680 the port had 120 ocean-going vessels and was visited each year by 2,000 trading ships with a combined tonnage of 100,000. This places a questionmark over Pierre Goubert's considerable pessimism about the French economy in the reign of Louis XIV.[7] Above all, it accounts for the fervour with which some of Louis XIV's advisers pressed on him the idea of accepting the Spanish succession for his grandson. Many of them imagined that this would result in a joint Franco–Spanish rule of America.

During the Wars of Succession there were moments when this seemed possible. Louis XIV had sent some of his best advisers to his grandson. Though England blockaded Atlantic communications as far as possible, the Spanish fleet did sometimes get through under the protection of the French navy, and some silver reached the French ports (30 million piastres of it in 1709). The end of the war, however, brought disappointment to many Frenchmen: it was the English who made maritime gains, in particular winning the *asiento* of the slave trade from the French, and Philip V and his Spanish advisers later proved well able to look after the interests of Spain. They carried out the successful monetary reforms and the first protectionist measures, which were taken to extremes on the pretext of health controls at the time of the Marseilles Plague of 1720. Trade in Cadiz between France and Spain reached its lowest point in 1720, and this may also have helped to produce the low point in French silver prices which was reached about this time.

(6) Silver prices and nominal prices

Wartime inflation, currency changes and the circulation of bad paper money meant that current prices could easily rise while silver prices were falling. Current prices were the ones that mattered to most people, and the dispute about reconstructing price series, whether silver or nominal, is not simply a technical question: it is important for economic

[7] Pierre Goubert, *Louis XIV et vingt millions de Français*, Paris 1966.

history. The consumer saw only current prices, and paid in current coin. If he had to 20% more of it for the same product from one week to the next, he 'felt it in his pocket', as Malestroict said. Current prices were therefore the most important in terms of social effects.

The economic effects are rather a different matter. Anyone who had accumulated current coin by means of the increase in nominal prices, and intended to spend it in foreign trade, knew that he would have to buy good money for bad at a rate which would wipe out his profits. He would therefore keep on raising prices, and this is how domestic inflation developed. The effects of falling silver prices thefore multiplied: they were bad for producers and merchants, and drove them to reduce the value of the currency by pushing up prices; they also set off a rush on the sources of gold and silver, which were constantly increasing in value. The sources they went to were the colonial trade, and to a lesser degree, the mines themselves. The Cadiz trade and Brazilian mining were, as we have seen, strongly affected.

Increases in grain prices due to bad harvests were in nominal prices, but they were disastrous for the mass of the population. In the period of the great wars at the end of the reign of Louis XIV, there were two years of peak prices, the result of bad harvests which were among the most notorious in French history, in 1693 and in 1709–1710. High prices were not confined to France: Spain too experienced dramatic increases. It would scarcely be reasonable to include these peak prices in calculations of long term price movements; the exceptional levels completely obscure the significance of the latter. Instead of stimulating production and commercialisation, such famines could reduce population and production, sometimes with long term consequences.

The distinction between long term and cyclical or short term price increases is essential; but disasters like 1693 were not decisive. They were followed by brisk population increases and good harvests. In the words of Pierre Goubert: 'The excellent harvests of 1694 and 1695 miraculously did away with scarcity and famine, and cereal prices fell back to their low pre-war levels. Throughout most of France there was a great flurry of spring-time weddings rapidly followed by a series of christenings. Freed from the burden of those who could not work – the old people were decimated in 1694 – and those who for the time being could not work – the children – many families nosily celebrated the easier conditions; bread at 6 pence a pound, plenty of work, and rather higher wages, as there was a shortage of weavers and even of labourers. In the cities and the textile towns workshops readily set to work, as low prices, lower taxes and the reopening of the sea routes multiplied demand.'[8] This occurred in the 'pause' of 1697–1701, but when the war was renewed and after the dreadful winter of 1709, the terrors of 1693 returned. The whole of France suffered: vines of the South froze and many vineyards went out of production for several years (it took at least three years to dig up the old vines and grow new ones). Under such conditions, the period 1689–1715 was a wretched one for France.

(7) Economic theory in France: from Vauban to Law

In England in the atmosphere of growth and prosperity of the 1670s various schools of thought grew up and gradually began to develop scientific economics, while France produced both bitter but often constructive critiques and ambitious reform projects such as Law's. In his *Project for a Royal Tythe* (1707), Vauban wrote that population and prices were falling, that at least one tenth of the population was reduced to beggary, another five tenths were scraping a bare living, and three tenths were burdened with debts and law suits; only a tenth, including all the upper classes, were living in ease.[9] It is his pessimism not the accuracy of his calculations which is important. Vauban believed that 'for the past thirty or forty years, the land has been producing a third less'. Like Davenant in England and Sully earlier in the century, he held that 'the greatness and true wealth of a nation does not lie in a great quantity of gold or silver', but in 'the abundance of its products, which are so necessary to sustain men that they cannot do without them'. He condemned luxury imports and came near to condemning foreign trade as such. Agricultural production to him was essential, and taxes were a plague, because the system was in such chaos. He therefore advocated a single land tax of one tenth, and drew up an accounting and statistical system for carrying it out. Money is scarcely mentioned, except to say that it should be made to circulate more easily; he draws the classic comparison with the blood of the human body. His work though not particularly original, does give the flavour of the times in its note of alarm.

Boisguilbert is more interesting in terms of economic thought. He published his *Détail de la France* in 1695, followed by the *Factum* of 1704–1707, a treatise on the grain trade with 'considerations' on wealth.[10]

---

[8] ibid. p. 172.
[9] *A Project for a Royal Tythe, or general tax*, London 1708.
[10] Boisguilbert, *Le détail de la France*, Paris 1966, vol. 2, chapter 3.

Like Vauban, Boisguilbert believed that agriculture was central to the wealth and the economy of a country, and he made a violent attack on Colbert, who gave preferential support to commerce and manufacturing. He thought that high grain prices favoured producers and therefore that there should be freedom to export. He also believed that 'silver is only the way and the means, whereas the necessities of life are the aim and the goal'.

More subtle than Vauban as far as money was concerned, he believed that the amount of silver in a country contributed nothing to its wealth, 'as long as there is enough for the prices of necessities not to be forced down'. The qualification is important, indicating that Boisguilbert, the advocate of high prices (who therefore shared the viewpoint of producers and traders) had understood that high prices were related to an abundance of coin. But he would undoubtedly have preferred a faster circulation with the same effects as an abundant supply, so that paper could even be used in place of money; in all cases, he wrote, 'what gives life to these notes or paper money is the known solvency of the issuer.' Like Vauban, Boisguilbert realised that the national revenue had failed considerably; but he did not attribute it entirely to the bad system of taxation. His aim would have been to increase agricultural production and prices, in order to make it possible for the state to demand more of its subjects.

John Law, the son of a Scottish gold merchant, had thought a great deal about banking and trading companies. His importance lies not only in the grandiose experiment he carried out, but in the ideas he put forward, first in Scotland and then from 1705 onwards in France. The scope and degree of originality of Law's ideas have often been debated; they were often contradictory. Initially, in Scotland, he supported the idea of paper money guaranteed by land values, and he proposed this, without success, in England. In 1706–1707, in a report to the director of the French Treasury, Desmaretz, he put forward the ideas of monetary stability and stressed the harmfulness of changing the face value of metal coin.

Nonetheless, in *Money and Trade Considered* (1705), he related the problem of money to economic problems in general. Like many people he thought that 'National Power and Wealth consists in numbers of People, and Magazines of Home and Foreign Goods', adding that 'these depend on Trade, and Trade depends on Money'. . . . 'By this Money, the People may be employed, the Country Improv'd, Manufacture Advanced, Trade Domestick and Forreign be carried on, and Wealth and Power attain'd.'[11] It was especially important that money should circulate like blood through the body, and the central bank could be conceived of as a heart, constantly putting money into circulation instead of letting it lie stagnant.

Although in some parts of his work Law admitted of the concept of commodity-money, he attacked precious metals on the grounds that they fluctuate in value, as they obviously had since the discovery of the Americas, and he believed that paper money sensibly issued by a Bank and guaranteed on land, would be more stable. Law had studied the dual circulation systems of Holland and England, and had noted that the metal holdings of the Banks were below the value of the notes in circulation. He believed that foreign trade could be reduced to simple exchange, and that if necessary, domestic currency could be made independent of metallic money. In Scotland he had also observed that if a domestic currency was revalued (by a decree increasing its equivalence in precious metal), metal coin would be attracted to the Bank-vaults in the days before the measure came into effect, because of the threat of depreciation. Law therefore thought that this solution could always be used to re-float a bank in danger, and he tried to put it into practice in 1720 during the downfall of his own 'System'.

All this gave him an excessive confidence in the idea of paper money. In the end he saw money as nothing more than a token: 'Money is the Measure by which Goods are Valued, the Value by which Goods are Exchanged, and in which Contracts are made payable.'[12] He also seems to have taken rather too seriously a saying about the Bank of Amsterdam which, because it inspired so much confidence and was not a credit bank, rarely had to repay its clients. 'A good bank', so the saying went, 'is one which does not pay out'. Law believed that by inspiring confidence he too would never have to pay out.

Law, as we have seen, ended up by confusing the concepts of credit, bank notes and paper money – hence his errors and failure. Inspired by the success of the Dutch and English, he prematurely questioned the old concept of money. He has often been referred to as a precursor of modern monetary systems, because of his monetary 'determinism' and his confidence in the creative function of credit; but his 'genius', which was put to the test by reality should not be exaggerated.

Another banker, Richard Cantillon, was enough of a realist to predict Law's downfall quite accurately, and make his own fortune out of it.

[11] John Law, *Money and Trade Considered*, Edinburgh 1705, p. 59–61.
[12] ibid. p. 61.

Cantillon wrote an *Essai sur la nature du commerce en général* which remained unpublished until 1755. In it he defined the likely effects of 'fictitious and imaginary' money, which he thought would 'have the same drawbacks as an increase in the real money in circulation, increasing the prices of land and labour and making goods and manufactures dearer . . . but this covert abundance vanishes at the first hint of discredit, and precipitates disorder.'[13]

Cantillon nevertheless grasped the advantages of banks of the English type: 'The banker can lend 90,000 ounces of silver out of the 100,000 he owes and not need to keep more than 10,000 for all he might be asked for: his business is with wealthy and thrifty persons and while one asks him for 1,000 ounces, another will be bringing him 1,000; it is enough for him to keep in the bank one tenth of what has been entrusted to him. In London they have had some experience in this matter, so that instead of people keeping most of these 100,000 ounces locked up all through the year, they are accustomed to deposit them with a banker, with the result that 90,000 out of their 100,000 are put into circulation. The image one may have of this kind of bank is that the bankers or gold merchants help to accelerate the circulation of money, they give it out at interest on their own account and at their own risk, and they must nonetheless be always prepared to pay on any of their notes however many are presented.'

Between the contrasting views of Law and Cantillon, in the first third of the 18th century, the earliest conceptions and critiques of an 'inflation' of credit and money appeared – an inflation which might be creative or destructive according to the different viewpoints – together with ideas about the role of banking in this economic process.

(8) The low point in silver prices and their stabilisation

1709–1710 marked a high point for grain prices throughout most of Europe, but it was followed by a particularly steep fall in both nominal and silver prices. Between 1714 and 1720, a cyclical price fall, following on a series of bad harvests in the previous decade, may be seen as a link with an inter-cyclical fall, running counter to the tendency for prices to rise between 1688 and 1710. At the same time, in 1720, the Law speculation in France and the South Sea Bubble in England led to a temporary increase in prices, which then fell sharply. The harvest of 1720–1721,

---

[13] Richard Cantillon, *Essai sur la nature du commerce*, p. 343.

which was a very good one throughout Europe, marked the low point on the curve of grain prices; it wiped out the remaining (and anyway highly localised) effects of currency speculation wherever it had really affected prices.

Finally, it is worth noting that the Law experiment, and its resolution, may have made and destroyed a few fortunes, but it also had a more general result worth mentioning: it liquidated a considerable number of what had become quite heavy debts, especially among the peasantry. 'In 1716–1720', wrote Emmanuel Le Roy-Ladurie, 'Law, the debtor's liberator, appeared: the abundance of Law notes rapidly enabled debtors and the heirs of debtors to make repayment, if necessary borrowing the money at very low rates of interest.'[14] A period of debt repayment – around 1720 – followed therefore on the period of heaviest indebtedness from 1660 to 1690. With low grain prices, debt repayment and the monetary stabilisation of 1726, even France undisputedly embarked on the 18th century, the age of economic development, long term price rises and, this time, monetary stability.

[14] Le Roy-Ladurie, op. cit. pp. 599–600.

27

The 18th Century Conjuncture

The events of the 1680s onwards heralded the creative and dynamic aspects of 18th century Western European economy: the change in the general price trend after the great 17th century depression, which had been particularly marked from 1650 to 1680; the revival of foreign trade, as for example with the Far East; and an intensification of economic rivalries between France and the Netherlands and then England, in particular in the Wars of the Spanish Succession, which compromised the future of the American colonies. (By 1713–1715 this competition had produced a wartime economy with all kinds of inflation, and its consequences were apparent as late as 1720–1721, with the Law system speculation in France and the South Sea Bubble in England.) Other aspects were the development of new attitudes in England introducing, side by side with strictly scientific discoveries like those of Newton, concepts of economic statistics and calculations. Lastly, the success of mine prospecting in Brazil, stimulated by the high price of gold, resulted in the production of greater and greater amounts of gold, and its export to Europe via England and Portugal.

This period of feverish activity and monetary somersaults still did not show the characteristics usually attributed to the 18th century; these, more strictly speaking, belong to the second half, since they did not affect all European countries, at least not in the same way. Price increases came to Northern Europe only later, and havoc could still be wreaked by the terrible French famines of 1693 and 1709. Population growth was therefore irregular, uncertain, and took place unevenly in different countries. Price increases, where they occurred, are still difficult to interpret; where they were due solely to artificial inflation as with the Law system, they could conceal localised low prices due to abundance (as with grain prices in 1720–1721), but they did not amount to a constant incentive to trade and industry.

Many historians and economists have therefore taken the view that the tendency for economic and demographic stagnation lasted at least into the second third of the 18th century. There are two dates within this period up to 1733 which I take to be of particular relevance: the first is 1720–1721, when the Law system liquidated numerous debts and when at the same time grain prices reached their lowest point in both silver and current money: an absolute low point, but one preceded and followed by several years of low prices; the second is 1726, when French currency was decisively stabilised, and when Europe as a whole, especially Spain, the owner of the silver mines, experienced a similar de facto stabilisation.

The end of monetary disturbances in Europe meant that a certain equilibrium had been achieved between the production and circulation of commodities, the domestic currency of various countries, and the production and import of enough precious metals to cover international exchange. As this equilibrium lasted for a long time – almost two centuries with the exception of the French Revolution and the Napoleonic Wars – the date at which it began marks an important stage in the economic history of Europe and the world.

As far as economic history is concerned, this monetary stability makes it easier to compare national price movements. The relation between prices, wages and incomes was undisturbed by confused monetary changes. The old debate between Maleistroict and Bodin, over whether price rises were or were not the result of governmental currency changes, was now redundant, and Ernest Labrousse has aptly described the situation introduced by the 1726 stabilisation as a period of 'economic visibility'. What this good visibility reveals is a long term increase in prices of a fairly general and regular kind, prevailing over periodic short term fluctuations (of about ten years) which were still largely conditioned by the irregularity of the harvest.

A thorough study has been made by Labrousse of the consequences of this dual movement in France:[1] how men made fortunes or were impoverished, according to the period and their social class, and what were the social and sometimes even the political effects. The most debatable point, of particular interest to economists, though historians cannot afford to neglect it, is the problem of what caused the long term price movement and its general nature. In so far as the monetary policy of separate states no longer had much effect on prices after 1726, and

---

[1] Ernest Labrousse, *Esquisse des Mouvements des Prix et des Revenues en France au XVIIIe Siècles*, 2 vols, Paris 1933.

there was a coincidence (with a few exceptions) between the movement of nominal prices and prices expressed in precious metals, it appears that any price movement involving commodities as a whole would express a change in the value of the metal, which measured other prices. This was how long term price movements were viewed in the 19th century.[2]

What then determined the market value of precious metals? Abundance and scarcity, the need for supplies and the difficulty of obtaining them, could be important everywhere in the short term. Over great distances the vast disparity in conditions of production and in the demand for precious metals and other commodities, came into play. For example, Brazil with her gold mines and Mexico with her silver mines sold their metal cheaply and had to pay for imported commodities at very high rates; while in Asia, precious metals, especially silver, bought a relatively large quantity of luxury or consumer goods which were later re-sold at higher prices in Europe. Lastly, in general and in the long run, what has to be taken into account is the cost of production of the metal relative to the cost of production of commodities in general, while giving full autonomy to each specific price which in the long term depends on the costs of production of the commodity in question.

There is then no doubt that the discovery of the mines, the technical and social conditions of mining and its profitability, played a part in the general rises and falls of gold and silver prices for commodities in general. Monetarist theories hold that these variations in the conditions of production of the precious metals determine major economic changes, with price increases stimulating economic activity, and falls discouraging it. Mining discoveries thereby become an 'exogenous' influence on the economy, and more or less 'contingent' on chance findings. The theory of the neutrality of money, on the other hand, holds that real economic factors – population, technical invention, advances in production, exchange, navigation, etc. – are what determine price movements and the demand for money: the latter automatically adapts to needs and does not therefore play a determinant role. In economics as in history, there is in fact no such thing as unilateral causation, only inter-action and dialectical movements which tend to suppress and then re-create the conditions of their own existence constantly. This accounts for the swings in price trends, although these are of doubtful 'periodicity' and pose other problems.

As we saw at the turn of the 15th and 16th centuries, periods of low

[2] cf. J. A. Helferich, *Von der periodischen Schwankungen im Werthe der edlen Metallen von der Entdeckung Amerikas bis zum Jahre 1830*, Nürnberg 1843.

prices in Europe gave precious metals outside Europe high prices, which were themselves a spur to exploration and discovery; once finds were made, the growing production and falling production and transport costs of the precious metal led to an upwards trend in 'general prices', i.e. those of commodities as a whole. Overall trends should not, however, lead to a neglect of the conditions which produce short term price variations, and the irregularities found even in long term increases.

The starting points in the 18th century were the same. The 17th century fall in metal prices was an incentive to American mining. At different dates, depending on the country, metal-prices rose as imports of gold and silver were increased. The 18th century, however, cannot be completely equated with the 16th; the latter was the age of the 'price revolution' because of the great discoveries which changed the dimensions of the world and brought a mass of precious metals flooding into a Europe, where production and the level of commerce were still very restricted. The 18th century evokes not the 'price revolution' but the population explosion, the agricultural revolution and the industrial revolution, although each of these concepts has to be very carefully defined and located in time and space. But in any case, while rising prices may have aided these developments, the rises were not sufficiently 'revolutionary' to be taken as their cause. In the 16th century the influx of precious metals and price movements might appear to be the motors (though not always a constructive force); but in the 18th century they appear rather as the regulators and the consequence of other aspects of growth.

A general increase in population is the first economic factor to be analysed. This growth was uneven, and the period of growth varied from country to country, but it was universal. England's population rose from 5 to 9 millions, an increase of 80%. Eversley has made more detailed studies of the rate of growth in certain areas, such as Worcester.[3] There is a surprising contrast between the 18th century and previous periods and between the first two thirds of the century and the last. From 1553 to 1665, there was an increase of 25%; from 1665 to 1776, 50%; but in the 25 years from 1776 to 1800, there was an increase of 30%. The take-off therefore occurred only after 1740, as the mortality rate rose commensurately with the birth rate from 1720. It is often said that this was caused by gin-drinking; my only comment would be that the fall in the death rate came after the 1750 laws against alcoholism.

[3] D. E. C. Eversley and D. V. Glass, *Population in History*, London 1965.

The birth rate then levelled out, but the 'natural' increase (the difference between births and deaths) went up. The end of the century saw a veritable medical revolution, with first inoculation, and then vaccination, against small-pox. Moreover, despite the horrors of the incipient industrial revolution, the concentration of workers in the cities, the development of wage labour and the increased demand for sales of foodstuffs, famine ceased to exist in Great Britain.

Between 1720 and 1800, the population of Sweden increased by 66.6%. Germany, which lost a sizeable percentage of her population in the 17th century, became more densely populated throughout most of the country in the 18th century, and experienced an overall growth of around 100%. In Russia, the population increased by 68% between 1724 and 1796 and by 50% after 1743. In particular there were big migrations, and a concentration in the 'black lands', where the population rose by 125% between the first two dates. The growth in the Voronez region was of the order of 380%. Similar developments occurred in the Mediterranean: the population of Spain as a whole rose between 60% and 80% (from 6 or 7 million to 11 million); but the figures for Catalonia doubled and those for Valencia trebled, these too being regions which had suffered depopulation and were now being resettled, especially in the irrigated regions of the periphery.

France is one of the countries about which least is known, despite the efforts of a few scholars from the 18th century onwards (Moheau, Messance and d'Expilly). On the eve of the French Revolution the population was 26 million and it rose to 28 million by 1800; but it is unknown whether the figure was nearer 17 or 20 million at the end of Louis XIV's reign, when the expansion began. Though the birth rate began to fall, the population certainly grew in the 18th century.

As this is not a demographic study, the details are unimportant. What is important is the fact that the growth was general if uneven. The repopulation and reclaiming of good land, and the concentration in towns and on the coasts, indicate that there was a growth in production and trade; scarcity, or at least famine, was rarer or even disappeared, and family incomes increased through the employment of women and children and through medical progress, which varied enormously from country to country. All this could scarcely be the result of monetary factors alone, though there may have been some connection. Many authors in fact suggest a relation between price increases and the growth of population, such as increased demand; but this is scarcely satisfactory, for in so far as the long term increase in nominal prices coincided with prices expressed in precious metals, the value of the precious metal is as relevant as the supply and demand mechanisms of each commodity. In any case it is impossible to explain a generalised increase in the population by an increase in the mining of gold and silver.

The economist Paul Bairoch, examining the problem of 'under-development' and economic 'take-off', has recently developed the theory that it is only agricultural progress which can ensure the necessary conditions for population growth and the beginnings of industrialisa-tion.[4] The argument is certainly a logical one: higher agricultural productivity is the first requisite for feeding more people and for more people not working in agriculture, and Bairoch has tried to support his hypothesis with statistics for England and France in the 18th century. His proof for England is relatively convincing in that we have fairly sound information on the subject of technical innovations in agriculture. We are also dealing with a rather small country in which the structure of rural life had been changing for a long time, and where modern industry appeared only in the 1760s. The main developments in agriculture were the enclosures, Tull's husbandry, Townshend's agronomy, the rise in crop yields and in agricultural productivity (as the increase in production was achieved with a smaller number of peasants). There was also an increase in the weight of cattle, observed by Mantoux, and important mainly because so little attention has been paid to it. These all occurred before 1760, and until the early 19th century England was still exporting her agricultural surplus, in contrast to the pattern established after the final triumph of the industrial revolution. The agricultural revolution came first.

Bairoch's attempt to do the same for France, using the work of Toutain, is less convincing. Toutain's calculations are for the growth in the value of agricultural production, including price increases which as we know were considerable; but he takes his figures for the volume of production from rather dubious sources. Now what is relevant is precisely this volume, and its relation to the acreage and to the number of workers. I have discovered however, that the situation in Catalonia supports Bairoch's theory fairly well. In the first half of the 18th century there was an extension of the area under cultivation, through reclaiming good land in previously depopulated areas, intensifying the cultivation of the best lands, especially through irrigation, and specializing in products particularly suitable to the climate and intended for export,

---

[4] Paul Bairoch, *L'évolution agricole et pays sous-developpés*.

while subsistence foodstuffs were imported.

The most important point is the last one: exporting wine and brandy, and importing cereals and salted fish involved contact with international, especially English commerce. It also enabled most people to eat fairly well, since peasant wine-growers and traders made considerable profits, and it was therefore possible for the population to increase considerably between 1716–1717 and 1734–1735, with a high birth rate and low death rate. The result was that by the middle of the century a cheap labour force was available for hire to the small and medium capital accumulated by trade and agricultural production. The ground was laid for new maritime and trading initiatives, and for the beginnings of industrialisation.

These localised developments then spread: regional concentrations of population attracted the agricultural products of the rest of the country and fostered local trade. There is therefore a complex, reciprocal relationship between agricultural progress, population growth and exchange between regions and nations. But there must be some doubt as to whether this expansion could have lasted without a powerful long-run external stimulus, such as the American trade was to Catalonia, and world trade obviously was to England.

The same regional example of Catalonia shows something of the impact of foreign trade on economic and social structures. The mountainous areas of Catalonia were scarcely affected by foreign trade and its consequences, and around 1760, people could still be seen paying for their purchases with small bags of grain. Feudal practices and attitudes persisted. The tithe was in part redistributed to the poor, but those who wanted more wheat also bought it from the tithe collector: it was a vicious circle. The young people left never to return, and the population stopped growing. Agricultural prices were still low relative to the increases occurring elsewhere in the course of the century: but in years of scarcity everything grew dearer and cereal prices reached tragic heights, forcing the poorest to emigrate.

In the coastal areas, by contrast, where local and foreign trade had developed, all payments were in money. Agricultural rents had to be paid in money, not in kind; more and more people were earning a daily wage and not living on subsistence production, and this meant a growing domestic market. People increasingly went over to commercial or industrial production of such things as wine, brandy, and dye-stuffs. Cereals had to be imported, and prices reached international levels, rising higher in relation to the quantity of trade with America. Industry was created to take advantage of the surplus of labour and the possibility of exporting; while wheat imports reduced the high prices of bad harvest years. A transition from the economy of the Ancien Régime to a modern economy was therefore in progress.

The problem is to determine how far these trends and changes had gone in each country. In France, in particular, it is far from clear what happened. The traditional theory was that there was great prosperity, to which the magnificent ports developed in the 18th century bore witness: Nantes, Bordeaux and Marseilles, the centres of colonial commerce and of the slave trade. More recent works by Ernest Labrousse and Herbert Lüthy[5] are of the opinion that this development of the ports was rather superficial in character. The ports were entrepôts rather than anything else, and the interior of France played little part in international trade. In other words there were two French nations, one still submerged in the economy of the Ancien Régime, and the other, which was far smaller but was progressing.

It would be interesting to be able to establish this geographically and in detail. Throughout the century most of France certainly suffered from violent short term increases in cereal prices, and economists of the latter half of the century, especially the physiocrats, wanted France as a whole to experience the more general, regular, long term price increases which could be generalised only through international trade. French foreign trade nonetheless made a great leap forward between 1715 and 1789. According to Arnould, the classic source published during the French Revolution, it increased fivefold in value and threefold in volume between 1715 and 1787.[6] More precise figures are given in a document published by Ruggiero Romano from the records of the *Bureau de la Balance du Commerce* established in 1713.[7] The total value of foreign trade rose from 87 million livres tournois in 1716 to 263 million in 1720, simply under the effect of the Law system; but after the 1726 monetary stabilisation, it rose again from 200 million to 300 million in 1739, 550 million in 1764 and 750 million in 1771. Every time there was a war the figure of course dropped, particularly during the American War of Independence. The French economy was therefore characterised by considerable, discontinuous but rapid growth, a permanent positive

---

[5] Herbert Lüthy, *La Banque protestante en France de la Révocation de l'Edit de Nantes à la Revolution*, Paris 1959, 2 vols.

[6] Ambroise-Marie Arnould, *De la Balance du commerce et des relations commerciales exterieures de la France dans toutes les parties du globe*, Paris 1791, 3 vols.

[7] Ruggiero Romano, 'Documenti e prime considerazioni intorno alla "Balance du commerce" della Francia del 1716 al 1781', *Studi in onore di Armando Sapori*, Milan 1957, vol. 2, pp. 1267-1298.

balance of trade (and therefore of imports of precious metals) and a particularly strong growth of colonial trade, which rose from around 35 million in 1726 to 210 million in 1777. More was imported from the Caribbean than was sent there, but the products of the colonies were re-exported at a great profit: the re-export trade increased eight times over between 1716 and 1787. It would obviously be impossible, therefore, to make an evaluation of the 18th century conjuncture and the relation between prices, the movement of precious metals and overall development, without giving some attention to the growth of international trade.

The same was true for England. Between 1702 and 1772 English foreign trade increased almost threefold. French foreign trade increased more rapidly than English between 1725–1730 and 1780, and caught up with it in terms of value, but its starting point was lower, and the per capita rate remained lower. Finally, while the last 20 years of the century were troubled times in France, England's foreign trade doubled in the last 35 years of the century. It is the structure of English foreign trade, and the changes in it, which are particularly interesting. In the 18th century, foreign trade is said to have been 'Americanised'; but in the case of England, it would be more correct to say that it had been 'globalised'.

	British exports to:		British imports from:	
	% 1701–1705	% 1796–1800	% 1701–1715	% 1796–1800
Europe	71.1	47.8	55.7	33.9
America	6.4	37.5	19.4	36.3
Asia	4.7	11.2	18.5	22.9
Africa	0.1	5.2	—	0.3

This shows that at the end of the 18th century, approximately two-thirds of Britain's foreign trade was outside Europe.

Taking into consideration the fact that in 1784 and 1785, when there was a revival in Spain's trade with the American colonies, some £8 million sterling in gold and silver were coming into Cadiz (or between a third and a quarter of all England's foreign trade), it has to be admitted that America, through her price levels and production of precious metals, had a very marked effect on the European economy.

In conclusion, however important the upward movement of prices was, monetary developments can scarcely account for the development of 18th century Europe in terms of population, agriculture, commerce, and even industry (the only place where a great industrial development had taken place by the end of the century was England). Equally obviously, however, European expansion was related, in a reciprocal manner, to the movements of precious metals: economic activity attracted gold and silver, and they in turn were an incentive to further activity. For every local or regional case the inter-connections have to be closely studied. In particular it must be recorded that in the first half of the century, England based her currency on her relations with Brazil and Portugal, and therefore on gold; while France developed her relations with Spain and the Caribbean in particular, and so opted for a silver currency.

It can now be asked whether gold imports, especially those into England in the second half of the century, would by themselves have been sufficient to finance such a major development of production and exchange, since banking and credit, although not unknown in the 16th century, had now become a permanent fact of everyday life. Once again, precious metals and money in general cannot be treated in isolation.

28

Bullion and the Ancien Regime

Documentation on the relationship between the development of trade and the circulation of silver in 18th century France is to be found in the work of Dermigny and in that of Rébuffat and Courdurié.[1] Though some of their terminology and conclusions are open to discussion, these provide some very interesting facts and accounts. For example, even if great political events all have some economic basis, it is incorrect to reduce the economic element to being only the attraction exerted by precious metals. There is an element of truth in saying that the great political battles of the 18th and early 19th centuries – the Wars of the Spanish Succession, the Bourbon Pact between France and Spain, the 1795 Treaty of Basle, and the Napoleonic rivalry between France and England, not to mention the measures instigated by the financier Ouvrard – were only part of the struggle between the two precious metals: gold, which was England's preserve, and silver, which France tried to hegemonise through the union with Spain. But this is too abstract a way of formulating the events. In reality a great battle for world power and for colonies was taking place and precious metals were only a part of this.

Mexican silver was indeed one reason for the special importance of trade with America and with Spain, the latter being theoretically a necessary intermediary, and often accepted as such, despite the existence of smuggling. But a lot more than monetary metals was at stake in Anglo-French rivalry over the East Indies, in the struggle for North America and even Canada, and the dominance of the Caribbean Islands in the trade of the great French ports. Dermigny himself, in his recent

[1] Louis Dermigny, 'Circuits de l'argent et milieux d'affaires au XVIIIe siècle', *Revue Historique*, 1954, vol. 212, pp. 239–278; and 'Une carte monétaire de la France au XVIIIe siècle', *Annales E.S.C.*, 1955, pp. 480–493; Ferréol Rébuffat and Marcel Courdurié, *Marseille et la negoce monetaire international (1785–1790)*, Marseilles 1966.

work on China and the West,[2] shows that the gold trade was less profitable than trade in tea; the average profit on gold was around 33%, while for some other commodities it could be as high as 150%. The directors of the English East India Company put the gold trade between India and England in the hands of their subordinates rather than keeping it for themselves, although in France the reverse was the case. The position therefore varied from place to place and between different periods.

A further example of this arises from the last years of the Ancien Régime in France, between 1774–1776 and 1789, when prices fell and monetary metal was dear. This was what Labrousse has called the 'low price inter-cycle' of the reign of Louis XVI, and he has established it as one of the fundamental troubles and tensions which led to the Revolution. Dermigny has suggested that there must be some connection between the French Revolution and the penetration of silver circulation into the depths of Africa and Asia: but one of the best-known aspects of the economic crisis of this period – the problem of wine production – is perfectly easily explained by heavy harvests and overproduction together with a crisis on foreign markets for wine. There is no indication that the high price of money was caused by anything other than a momentary fluctuation in the course of economic growth, and while it is possible to put forward hypotheses about the origins of short term movements being in the silver mines of America, this scarcely amounts to a worked out answer to the question.

It is equally interesting to see how American silver passed into the French monetary system and economy. But in so doing the following points must always be taken into account. In the first place, the monetary stability of the 18th century offers a clear illustration of the role of precious metals. There was no tampering with the currency, no playing about with sudden swings in the exchange rate; the flows of money-metal were clearly the result of the balance of payments. Gold and silver were no longer the driving force of personal fortunes, which were now counted as much in assets and credits as in money. But the influx of metal was still a sign of superiority in production. Spain nevertheless made progress during the century, and by becoming more independent reduced foreign profits at her expense. In this respect, it would be worthwhile to study the changes in the cost price of American gold and silver, especially towards the turn of the century.

[2] See p. 200, n.

It is also relevant to see whether the silver of Spanish America was more important than the market it provided, or vice versa. To say that Mexican silver was 'vital' to the French economy seems to imply that the main interest of the Spanish American trade was the silver it earned. If the return of the Spanish fleets to Cadiz was one of the main concerns of the traders in Bordeaux or at the fairs of Beaucaire and Pézenas, given that the fleets brought payment on their goods, it is also true to say that they were equally concerned with the departure of the fleets, and with loading them. If nothing was sent, there would be no returns to look forward to, and if the returns, instead of being in silver, were in products of the colonies which could be sold at a profit, so much the better.

Dermigny aptly quotes a document from 1729 in which some Languedoc businessmen complain of the scarcity of coin at the Pézenas fair as well as in the markets of Lyons and Marseilles, which is caused by the late arrival of the Spanish American fleet; they say that its return will re-establish confidence. But there are many more documents which indicate that the condition for a good fair was the departure of the fleet, and this applies especially to Beaucaire: 'The putting off of the departure of the Cadiz fleet to next year has been a great loss to this fair, both for the lack of confidence in trade which such an event creates, and for the notable fall in the sales of all goods normally loaded onto the fleet.'[3] The main items of this trade were fine linen and hardware produced in the towns of Languedoc, the Cevennes and Gévaudan. Other circumstances, such as a bad harvest in Spain, measures taken by the government in Madrid, or a war which held back the American fleets, could have the same effect. Precious metals therefore were not the only important factor in the trade; the market for the products which gold and silver bought was equally important.

The volume of pure silver imports, however, was still of great interest. The more trade developed, the more necessary it was to have the means of transferring investment funds, using either the liquidity of the currency or credit (the other possible solution). Moreover some forms of foreign trade required payment to be made in silver coin and often specified which coins. For example, in Africa and the Levant, drugs, cotton thread, wax and many other goods could only be bought for silver.

Some 16th century trade flows therefore remained very important.

[3] Vilar, op. cit. vol. 3, pp. 42–51; the original is in the *Archives departementales de l'Hérault*, C. 2309 (1740) et C. 2827–28 (1778).

As Dermigny puts it: 'There was a vast movement of silver from West to East, from the Americas to the Far East, through Europe and the Mediterranean, quite apart from the other route from Mexico to China via the Philippines. This movement covered a whole period of world history.'[4] This much was true, but there was nothing new in it, and many other products could be chosen to show the reverse flow. For example, one might say that Aleppo cotton was bought with American silver, and was taken from the East to France or Spain; there it was transformed into coloured cloth and sold in Lima or Mexico for silver which was then brought back to pay for the Aleppo cotton.

There was nothing inevitable about this pattern of exchange. Towards the end of the century, around 1780, the Spanish realised that it would be more profitable to spin their own American cotton than to buy cotton thread in Aleppo, and they therefore created companies which contracted to buy and spin cotton from the colonies: American cotton was exchanged via a closed circuit linking the producers and the Spanish cotton weavers who sold cloth back to America. The medium of silver therefore lost its importance.

If there was a silver liquidity problem it was because Spain owned the American mines and therefore aspired to maintain a monopoly on trade with her colonies and to control exports abroad of silver bullion and coin. It was not that Spain wished to set up a closed system: she could not hope to supply all the commodities her empire needed, and silver was an export product like any other; but what she wanted was to make the foreign producers and merchants who wanted silver pay for it. To a country like France, importing silver from the Spanish empire involved the problem of negotiating payment, while individual traders often faced the problem of smuggling. It was not that the trade was absolutely forbidden; the difficulty was to make a profit on it.

There were two possible ways of obtaining silver illicitly. One was known as *l'interlope*, direct and clandestine trade with America. Instead of going through Cadiz, which was compulsory until 1778, or through one of the other approved ports after this date, ships might try to land directly in South America. This was done both to avoid paying customs, sometimes to buy colonial products more cheaply, and lastly, to sell European goods on the American market at a greater profit. Another frequent practice was to evade Spanish export controls when the fleet returned to Cadiz, in other words to evade what are now called exchange

[4] Dermigny, 'Circuits', p. 241.

controls, by smuggling commodity silver past the customs. Instead of going through the *trocadero*, the place where exchange was carried out, chests of sacks of Mexican piastres were thrown up onto the quays or breakwaters, by men known as *metedores*, smugglers. Dermigny aptly says of the foreign merchants in Cadiz: 'Piastres figured in their normal trade alongside wine, cereals, silk, soda and cochineal, and were regarded as a commodity. The trade in commodity silver – in so many bars, ingots or piastres – often had nothing in common with the functions of a real Bank, but it reflected the popularisation of silver as an object of ordinary consumption, whose production increased the more its costs of production fell.'

The trade simply evaded paying customs duty, although this was not particularly high anyway. A French report on this trade of around 1750,[5] clearly lays out the points which concerned the authorities in their discussions with Spain. The Spanish government wanted to control all trade in gold and silver, and to increase the duty from 1%–2% to 3%. They therefore proposed to institute a kind of exchange control, requring merchants to pay by means of bills of exchange, and reserving the right to pay the balance in silver. This would ruin the Cadiz smugglers (middlemen in the shipment of precious metals). Not only the Indies trade was involved, but all trade with Spain, such as the sale of French cereals in the eventuality of famine in Spain. The memorandum stated that 2% but not 3% would be acceptable, and that this would have to be negotiated. Meanwhile, private interests might as well go on smuggling, even though morally the principle of it was to be condemned and one had to recognise the right of the Spanish State to levy a percentage on the export of silver. It was recommended that Spanish control agents should be humoured and if necessary bribed.

This was the position in the middle of the century; much later, in 1786, the financier Cabarrús, from Bayonne, created the *Banco de San Carlos*, the first attempt to form a national bank in Spain. It tried to impose a duty of 5% on all exports of piastres, and thereby created havoc in the trade with France. This is discussed at length in consular correspondence and in the papers of the Maison Roux of Marseilles (from the period 1786–1790) which have recently been published in the work of Rébuffat and Courdurié mentioned above.[6] This concern with what were in fact quite light customs duties draws attention both to the importance of the silver trade and to the small size of the profit margins; fairly

[5] Archives Nationales, Affaires étrangères, B 111/333.
[6] see p. 263, n. 1.

large-scale trading was necessary to make much of a profit.

The main sources from which France obtained silver were Cadiz, the Atlantic, direct imports and the cross-Pyreneen trade. In Cadiz the most important foreign concerns were the English companies, Gough and George Browne, and the French companies, Jolif, Magon & Lefer, Le Couteulx, Lenormand & Cie., Casaubon & Béhic, Gilly Frères, Fornier Frères, and others. Among the latter, the chief companies were from Nimes and Carcassonne in the South, and from Saint-Malo (the Magon company), together with branches of banking houses (e.g. Le Couteulx of Paris and Rouen).

Silver was certainly of great importance to such companies; but their main concern was the import-export trade, which exported European products to the Indies in exchange for colonial goods. In the correspondence between the Gough Company and the cotton manufacturers of Barcelona there is a constant stream of instructions about the tastes of the Lima clientele. The Cadiz trade was therefore governed by the American market, and piastres were only sent to cover the balance after the purchase of colonial sugar, cotton, cochineal and other goods.

The galleons' Atlantic ports-of-call, notably the French West Indies and in particular Saint Domingue, which was half-French and half-Spanish, were good places for smuggling. Dermigny gives two examples, one of them interesting for what it has to say about the American interests of a Protestant family from Nîmes which was to produce a famous politician: Guizot. The other indicates some significant connections. Millot, a Saint Domingue trader, sent piastres to the Roux company in Marseilles, which sold them on the Marseilles market and sent the proceeds to the Paris banker Waters; here they were paid into the account of the Gough company of Cadiz and this almost certainly means that the latter had sent goods of that value from England. The circuit was thereby completed and undoubtedly no duty was paid. In this context it should be noted that Saint Domingue was to France what Curaçao was to Holland.

Direct imports of piastres into French ports included French ships which had taken on cargoes of piastres in Cadiz or Santo Domingo, as already discussed. But there were also Spanish captains and ship's masters who would bring piastres to the ports of Brittany, to Sète and to Beaucaire, in exchange for French merchandise. They often did so illicitly, paying no duty, and loaded and unloaded on deserted beaches. Some indication of the importance of direct purchases by Spanish seamen is apparent in the difficulties created in Beaucaire by the slightest changes in the Spanish exchange rate (as in 1737 and 1772), or by any attempts to control the trade: in 1775, five Spanish customs officers were sent to Beaucaire to keep a watch on trade with Spain and this closed the fair down for two days: yet in these two days 40,000 piastres worth of illicit transactions were made, and this rose to 100,000 in half a day after the customs men had left.

The reverse could happen just as easily, and it has to be remembered that this was a trade in commodities. In Beaucaire in 1774, for example, the number of piastres available led to a considerable fall in the rate of exchange, and this was simply because the Catalan fishermen who normally sold sardines in Beaucaire had had a very bad year, and had been obliged to bring liquid silver instead of their usual merchandise to pay for the purchase of French goods. Silver, like any other commodity, therefore rose and fell in price. There were people who specialised in speculating on such fluctuations, the most expert being the Portuguese Jews of Bordeaux, London and Amsterdam. But the flow of silver into France was nonetheless only secured by production and by exports. As Boulainvilliers wrote of Brittany: 'Textiles attracted silver because they were shipped to its place of origin', i.e. to Spain.

Trade across the Pyrenees was a permanent feature of this process. It had become apparent in the 16th century that crossing the frontier was worthwhile as long as there was a possibility of making a profit out of transporting silver. It was largely a smallscale trade involving pedlars and emigrants, and is of no particular interest because it was continuous and involved small quantities. For particular places, however, it would be worthwhile studying imports across the Pyrenees. In the 16th century, it will be remembered, Bayonne was one of the most active markets in France because of contact with Spanish silver. In the 18th century also Bayonne prospered, producing famous financiers as it did in the 19th century, men like Zulueta and Cabarrús, and later Laffitte and Basterrechea.

It would also be useful to make a detailed chronological account of the transfer of silver across the Pyrenees. For example, there was a significant contrast between the two halves of the 18th century: in the first half, Spanish wages were as low as those in France, while in the second, with wages in Catalonia much higher, there was a constant flow of French emigrants to the Spanish factories, and a return flow of money sent by them. The wars also played a major role: during the War of the Austrian Succession, the expenses of the Spanish State and difficulties at sea (caused by English pirates) led to the traffic described in the chronicles of the monastery of Vilabertran in Ampurdán: 'On the 8th of November 1745 there passed through Figueras 7 carts laden with gold; on the 19th of December, 6 cartloads of money; on 21st January 1746 22 cartloads of money passed through Figueras and spent the night at La Junquera; on the 20th of April, through Figueras, 5 carts of gold; on the 20th of May, 9 cartloads of gold and 900 chests of silver, which they say are for the galleys; on 13th February 1747, 19 carts and a light carriage laden with money for the army of Provence, going to Montpellier; on the 31st of May, 22 cartloads of money: it was the eve of Corpus Christi and they stayed in Figueras; on the 8th of June a further 12 carts, each carrying 20 hundredweights of solid silver pesos; on 27th October, 18 carts of money, and on 13th December, 20; on the 25th May 1748, 18 carts and a light carriage; on 18th August, 20 carts of money and the troops coming back to Spain, and a detachment from Valones was billeted in Vilabertran; on the 22nd April 1749 13 cartloads of money passed through Figueras to pay for the damage done by the troops in a convent and elsewhere in Piedmont.'[7]

This gives some indication of the cost to Spain of waging a war in another part of Europe. It was the same as in the 16th century, although now on a smaller scale. Sometimes transfers were made for more normal, regular purposes. In connection with Cabarrús's restrictions on the export of piastres, it was shown that in 1786 the sale of French lamb to supply Barcelona with meat, alone required the export of 2,000,000 piastres a year.

We now know how American silver got into France, and sometimes into other regions of Europe such as England and the North. There were three main circulation channels, the first of which was France which acted as a bridge between the Mediterranean and the Atlantic. Piastres circulated too between the Atlantic and Mediterranean via the south of France; they were brought to Sète and Agde by the Spanish, and were then taken to Marseilles, the centre of demand. They also circulated officially in financial exchanges mainly through Montpellier, which was a great centre of public finance.

Was there really large-scale speculation in silver in the course of this circulation? There were regional fluctuations in exchange rates, so that it was possible to make small profits by transferring silver to wherever there was a greater balance of bills of exchange, or a greater demand for silver for the Levant trade. Both Dermigny's examples from Mont-

7 José Pella y Forgas, *Historia del Ampurdán*, Barcelona 1883, pp. 712–714.

pellier and the recent study of the Roux company in Marseilles make it clear that such transfers were only profitable in very large quantities.[8] Despite the extent of circulation between Bayonne, Toulouse, Montpellier, Marseilles and Lyon therefore, there was no real speculation in silver.

As far as international trade in gold and silver coin is concerned, the Amsterdam exchange often assumed responsibility for supplying silver coin to markets which required it, notably in the case of the Africa Company during the Anglo-Spanish war (1740–1744). The very fact of spreading the risk by loading only one money-chest onto each ship, illustrates clearly the commodity nature of silver. Geneva also had piastres to re-distribute; this was because Switzerland sold coloured cloth and bleached cloth to Spain for printing. The piastre, worth 78 tournois shillings and four pence in Geneva, was worth 87 shillings and four pence in Marseilles: this was because it was in great demand for Africa and the Levant. Even taking into account the risks and the cost of transport, it was profitable to send the coin down from Geneva to Marseilles.

War supplies, as we have seen, could involve massive transfers, and certain finance houses such as the Hogguers of Lyon and the Thellusson of Geneva specialised in transactions of this kind. Such businesses however were also involved in the grain trade, in coal, glassware, and brandy. In the first half of the century they even had interests in mining, when the Genevans took over all the mines in the lower Pyrenees; but in the second half of the century these concerns were destroyed by competition from Mexico. Certain currencies were attracted to Africa and the East and this also contributed to the circulation process. Curiously enough, Asia and East Africa had a preference for talers bearing portraits of the Empress Maria Teresa: many Austrian mints therefore specialised in producing these from melted down piastres and they were then profitably exchanged for gold or slaves.

To get an overall view it is worth quoting a document from 1786 which expresses satisfaction at the increase in the circulation of coin in France, at least until 1778: 'In this interval of 26 years – 1755–1781 – France annually received 60 to 80 millions from Spain, exported about a half, and converted the remaining 30 to 40 million, which constituted the balance of trade, into French currency. This was apparently exported to Germany to pay for the war, until the peace treaty of 1763. After this

[8] Rébuffat and Courdurié, op. cit; Charles Carrière, *Les negociants de Marseille*, Marseille 1973, vol. 2, Chapter 9.

period, the proceeds of the balance of trade seem to have stayed inside the kingdom, increasing the circulation by 600 million in 15 years of peace time.' There is no guarantee as to the accuracy of these figures, but they reinforce the impression gained from all known indices that the most prosperous period of the 18th century was from the end of the Seven Years' War (1763) to the beginning of the American War of Independence (1776).

1778 brought the American war and the concomitant increase in expenditure. Some markets were closed (especially those for wine), and most Spanish ports were opened to trade with America so that Spanish trade and industry revived. This was followed by Cabarrús's measures to prevent the export of piastres (by means of a slight devaluation and the raising of export duties), which contributed to the crisis in the French economy on the eve of 1789. But it should not be forgotten that general price level. Indirect finance, especially banking credit, has to height in 1780–1789.

Having said all this, there is still some confusion about the mechnisms connecting precious metals, circulating currency, trade and the general price level. Indirect finance, especially banking credit, has to be taken into account: even in France this acquired considerable importance during the 18th century, and in England it may have played the leading role, by reducing the circulation of actual metal coin. This problem forms the subject of the next two chapters.

29

Banking and Credit in France, 1726–1790

The following two chapters examine the relationship between circulation, production, precious metal imports and price movements during the long period of general development from the 1726 stabilisation to the galloping inflation of the revolutionary period. This was marked by the issue of French *assignats* from 1792 and by the forced currency of banknotes in England from 1797.

In the case of France we have only examined the means by which silver was obtained and was circulated, from Spain and the colonies, through the Atlantic ports and the passes in the Pyrenees to Paris, Lyon and Marseilles (especially the latter, where it could be exported in exchange for oriental imports). The conclusion we reached was that silver – which after all behaves like any other commodity – was a less important factor than the market for the products for which it was obtained, and less important than the profits to be made from the cash purchase of certain African and Asian goods. Of course there were possibilities for speculating on the value of currencies and of bills of exchange, since these varied from town to town and from country to country; but the profits per unit were small and the trade was only worthwhile if massive quantities of silver were involved. Commodity production and trade in general were considerably more important than the superficially attractive activities of silver speculators.

This does not mean that the problems of money and credit can be left out of any attempt to understand the general movement of the economy: on the contrary, it is very instructive in this respect to compare the two most advanced countries in 18th century Europe, France and England. The financing of economic activity in the two countries was at quite different levels of development. The Bank of England and private banks became the basic agents of monetary circulation and credit expansion in England; while the experience of the Law system and the practices of the inland revenue for a long time prevented modern finance and credit systems from triumphing in France.

Certain recent works on the history of French banking and public finances make a distinction between two different kinds of French *homme d'argent* or man of money: the *financier* and the *banquier*.[1] The financiers were the main agents of public finance and were involved with problems of taxation, State expenditure and loans, and with speculation on controlled dealings such as the grain trade and the Paris food supplies. Dealers (*traitants*), State contractors who had been the main financing agents under Louis XIV, were declining in importance in the 18th century; but they were replaced by *fermiers généraux*, tax farmers who advanced the king amounts due in the form of taxes and then collected them, thereby becoming the main financial force in the land. The *raison d'être* of these financiers, who were part of the machinery of the régime, and were generally Catholics, with a network of agents throughout the Provinces, disappeared with the reform of the whole taxation system carried out by the Revolution. Many were physically liquidated – Lavoisier for one.

'Bankers' (*banquiers*) were in a different category altogether. They were essentially concerned with private business and international trade, and it was not easy to identify the sources of their profits and dealings (with the result that they were less distrusted than the 'financiers'). Many of them were Protestants, and this has given rise to something of a myth about a 'Protestant International'. Their religion was not their most significant characteristic, however; far more important was the fact that as dissidents they were excluded from certain areas of French social life, and related by family ties and mutual trust to the exiles of the Protestant 'diaspora', which had followed the Revocation of the Edict of Nantes. They were especially active in the great economic centres of Europe, in Amsterdam and above all in Geneva. Geneva's situation made her a centre of European trade and finance, and, though this is sometimes forgotten, of advanced production: the clock industry, which involved considerable trade in precious metals for industrial use, and a highly developed textile industry producing cotton cloth and coloured fabrics, which was in continuous contact with oriental and colonial trade.

The Protestant bankers and their contacts in Geneva did not repre-

---

[1] Herbert Lüthy, *La Banque Protestante en France de la Révocation de l'Edit de Nantes à la Revolution*, Paris 1959, 2 vols; Jean Bouvier and Henri Germain-Martin, *Finances et Financiers de l'Ancien Regime*, Paris 1964.

sent the sum total of French banking: there were also great Catholic merchant bankers, such as the Magons of Saint-Malo, the Le Couteulx of Rouen and Paris, and the Labordes. In general they had closer relations with the authorities than the Protestants: the Labordes, for example, were bankers to the Court. Therefore they suffered in the Revolution in the same way as the financiers, whereas Protestant businessmen like the Perregaux, Mallets, Hottinguers and Vernes survived more easily, thanks to their international contacts. After the Revolution they played a major role in creating and administering the Bank of France.

(1) Banking in 18th-century France

Banking was the intermediary between trade and the system of deposits and credits which trade required at a certain level of development. The banks also handled exchange, that is, the paying of accounts in foreign currency. In the 18th century, however, these functions were never in any way separated from trade. As Samuel Ricard says: 'A businessman used the banks when he had nowhere else to keep his money, and a banker would speculate on merchandise when he could see how to make an honest profit.'[2] In cities like Paris, however, banks were more specialised and further separated from trade: 'Paris banking had reached incredible proportions: no other city in the Universe could be said to excel her in this respect.'

In 1703 there were 21 bankers in Paris, in 1721 there were 51, and in 1776 there were 66. According to Mirabeau they engaged in 'every aspect of trade'. They bought and re-sold private trading notes such as shares and (French) East India Company bonds, royal credits, leases, national lottery tickets, and stakes in public finances. This activity was far removed from that of a bank which aims to channel savings and to redistribute credit, or to issue banknotes based on gold deposits. Nonetheless, by increasing the mobility of trading notes and of values in general, 18th century French banks speeded up payment and therefore circulation.

Some aspects of the development of French banking repay more detailed consideration. The leading names were those of the royal and Court bankers, Pâris-Duverney and De Laborde. They depended directly on the prosperity of the royal exchequer and the favour of the Court: they had to solve problems of public credit and royal allowances,

---

[2] Samuel Ricard, *Traité général du commerce des principaux états de l'Europe*, Amsterdam 1700.

which often lay outside normal economic activity. They were quite different from the Le Couteulx, who are described in the following way by Berryer, their lawyer during the Revolution and the Terror: 'The Le Couteulx were a long-standing Paris banking family, one of the oldest established of the Paris bourgeois class. As the patriarchal family of Le Couteulx grew, instead of turning to other professions, they began founding branches of the bank in other cities, and even in other European countries. There was one very important agency in Rouen, to serve the factories and manufacturing establishments of this industrial town. There was another in Cadiz, where all the first-born sons of the family went for their training for several years, returning to take the directorship of one of the central establishments in Rouen or Paris. Every year, the two families of Paris and Rouen, with their wives, children and grandchildren, met on a given date in a great house which they jointly owned on the road halfway between Paris and Rouen, near Vernon (in the Department of Eure). The books of both houses were taken there for the annual inventory, which was signed by the heads of the families, after which they parted and each went his own way. In the Le Couteulx archives in the Place Vendome I have seen a bookcase full of the great collection of all the ledgers they kept for 150 years, complete with inventories. At the end of one of these ledgers, begun in 1720 after the fall of the Law system, there was a note in the handwriting of the then head of the family to the effect that he had not wanted to have anything to do with the operations of the Law bank; he had made his funds over to his own branches and so saved them . . . and that this must be a warning to his successors never to indulge in speculations on State paper money or credit of any kind connected with gigantic and risky enterprises.'[3]

The most illuminating points to come out of this are that the Le Coutelx were an old-established Parisian bourgeois family; that they were determined to establish themselves in what were then the most strategic places: Cadiz, the source of silver, where the young men were trained in international business, and Rouen, the meeting point of mercantile capitalism and early industrial capitalism; the annual meeting and the care with which the archives were kept show the patriarchal traditional attitudes of the old trading houses; and finally, their caution towards the Law system reveals that the company was built on constant, cautious calculation rather than on adventure.

---

[3] Berryer, *Souvenirs*, Paris 1839, pp. 142–143.

In contrast, we might take the example of the development of a Protestant concern employing a man who became a leading public figure on the eve of the Revolution, Jacques Necker; an employee of the House of Thellusson, he became one of the greatest Paris financiers and was for a time the hope of the realm. The Thellussons had originated in Lyons and emigrated to Geneva, and from the late 17th century on had been related to Protestant families engaged in many different activities: the Van Robais, who ran the royal textile factories at Abbeville; the Tronchins, who owned a variety of mines in the South of France, and were heavily involved in speculating on army supplies to the French troops in Italy around 1730; and the Vernets of Marseilles and Geneva. They were also united by marriage to the Labahard Bank of Paris. In 1756 a large share of this business passed to a young member of the Thellusson family, and he together with a still younger employee of the firm, Jacques Necker, founded Thellusson, Necker and Company in the rue Michel Le Comte in Paris.

The Seven Years' War (1756–1763) made the fortune of the Company, and especially Necker's. I have pointed to the dual economic effects of wartime several times: it makes trade in general more difficult, (especially overseas trade, normally so profitable), but it also allows for considerable profits to be made through speculation because of the scarcity of certain commodities and the increase in transport and insurance rates. Sensational crashes occur at the same time as great fortunes are made. Necker was accused of having profited from the war and from its dishonourable outcome for France. There are two contradictory legends about him a laudatory one spread by his family, and another violently hostile version put about by his enemies, especially the banker Panchaud. In 1762 Necker had allegedly bought Canada bonds depreciated by 80%, after receiving secret information that the treaty surrendering Canada to the English would guarantee full repayment of French debts to Canada; according to his enemies, he denied his informers a share in the profits of this speculative coup. Transactions of this kind do not explain everything, but this example does indicate the importance of the English business to the Thellusson Necker bank, and this was also evident from the bank's relations with the French East India Company.

The East Indies trade was, as we have mentioned, one-way: in general luxury goods were bought in the Indies and the Far East – cotton cloth, Chinese lacquers, porcelain, all of which were very fashionable in the 18th century – and they were paid for in silver. Credit was therefore necessary. During the Seven Years' War, when France got into debt, she used the Company's funds, and it was therefore necessary to rebuild from scratch afterwards. Moreover, in contrast to the English company, its French equivalent was always a 'company of contractors rather than businessmen' (Raynal). By the Treaty of Paris, France kept five trading agencies, and this left the door open to renewing the trade. But it remained a problem whether the Company could be re-floated. Necker was able to succeed in this in the name of his bank, by interventions with the Board of the Company, despite the fact that he was only an ordinary shareholder. He obtained credit for the Company from the English house of James Bourdieu and Samuel Chollet; the government supported him against the majority of the shareholders; and he managed to get the silver piastres from Cadiz needed for the Company's purchases. Naturally, he earned a very large commission for this. When its monopoly was revoked in 1769, Necker's enemies accused him of making a fortune out of the downfall of the Company. But his supporters (according to Morellet) described his actions in the following way: '(he) owed his fortune to the bank and to some profitable transactions with the India Company, before he became a director. Profits of this kind, though the rate of interest is low, are always considerable when large capital is employed and . . . only ignorance or pettiness, or most often both together, can make this out to be a crime.'[4] In any case it is perfectly evident what kind of operations were profitable for a *banquier*: and once Necker had made his fortune, he retired to take up a diplomatic post as the envoy of Geneva to the King of France. His wife opened a famous salon which laid the basis for Necker's political career. The Thellusson bank however continued to trade in Cadiz, dealing with the silver fleets. In 1776, Necker made a profit both from the fall of Turgot and from the bad start to an institution established by his old adversary, Panchaud. The letter was something much closer to a public credit bank: it was the *Caisse d'Escompte*, or Discount Bank.

(2) The 1776 Discount Bank
Necker had one fervent enemy, Isaac Panchaud, who was familiar with English institutions; he advocated the establishment of a public bank which could lower the rate of interest and so permit the formation of a sinking fund for the national debt. Panchaud was involved in many unsuccessful enterprises, but he was regarded as an expert on exchange

---

[4] Abbé Morelleter, *Mémoires*, vol. 1, p. 365, quoted in Lüthy, op. cit. vol. 2, p. 387.

and credit by men such as Mirabeau, Talleyrand and Calonne and by the financiers of future régimes, men like Mollien and Louis. Despite a series of failures, in 1776 he gained the ear of Turgot. The Discount Bank was created on 23 March 1776 to further the interests of trade by cashing bills of exchange and all commercial bills at a maximum interest rate of 4 . The Bank did not have the right to engage in commercial or colonial speculation (a sign that the Law experience had not been forgotten); but it could trade in precious metals and foreign currencies, though it did not have a monopoly of such trade. It could issue redeemable notes, which if the venture was successful might result in a circulation of bank notes. In effect it was an institution for lending cheaply to bankers and businessmen favoured by the management, who reserved the right to give or refuse the discount. It was a private bank and five out of the seven directors were Swiss – this 'precursor' of the Bank of France was in no way a national bank.

From the very outset what weakened the Bank most was the fall of Turgot and the opening of the American War of Independence, which brought chaos to trading conditions with Asia and America. At the end of 1777, the Bank had issued only 320,000 livres tournois of notes; and though it had cashed 30 million worth of trading bills, it would have languished if Necker, by now Director of the Royal Treasury, had not transformed it. It was taken over by a more traditiona. Paris banking consortium involving the Le Couteulx, the Cottin bank, and others. Dealing in bills then rose to 81 million in 1780, and notes in circulation to 11 or 12 million. Necker then forced the tax-farmers to accept bank notes in payment. In his famous *Compte-rendu* he defended his administration of the Bank; this had in fact been extremely correct, and was taken as the model for the future Bank of France. Necker was nonetheless accused of making it into no more than a 'bankers' bank', lending at 4% to businessmen who were well in with the directors, and who in turn lent out the money again at a much higher rate.

(3) The last ten years of the Ancien Régime
The Discount Bank in fact ensured the success of Necker's loans and by this means it financed the American war. The inflationary climate accepted and almost certainly deliberately stimulated by the Calonne administration makes the last years of the Ancien Régime a contradictory period of French history. On the one hand, as Labrousse has written, agricultural prices tended to fall, there was a major crisis in wine produc-

tion and the burden of taxation on the poor peasantry, the majority of the population, grew heavier.[5] On the other hand, a new East India Company was created, and the triangular trade between France, Senegal and Saint Domingue was at its busiest, while State expenditure reached dizzy heights, and all exclusively on the basis of loans. 'Today a million louis d'or are referred to as a hundred years ago you might speak of a thousand. People count in millions, and no business is ever spoken of in anything but millions: whether you wish to build a house, go on a voyage or buy land, millions dance before your eyes. These millions make everyone think they are poor, and no one dare speak of an income of 40,000 livres as a fortune.'[6] This quotation shows that speculation in trade, and the policy of loans, together with the beginnings of a credit policy still cautious and applied to a very restricted circle as it was, gave an artificial impression of prosperity in Paris, while the base of the fiscal system – the farmers and producers – were less and less able to pay up. The financial and banking system did not, in fact, contribute to the development of the economy. Moreover, during these years trade with Spain, which had supplied France with silver for so long, declined to the advantage of a Spanish economy which was experiencing a new expansion and growth (the growth of manufacturing and of direct trade with America, and the founding of the San Carlos Bank in 1782). Such were the monetary aspects of the crisis of the Ancient Régime.

[5] Ernest Labrousse, *La crise de l'économie française à la fin de l'Ancien Regime*, Paris 1943.
[6] Sébastien Mercier, *Tableau de Paris*, Paris 1788, vol. 10, p. 248.

30

Banking and Credit in England, 1726–1790

(1) The Bank of England

The Bank of England, whose origins have been described in a previous chapter, developed steadily during the 18th century. In 1772, a reserve fund was established to guarantee its solvency: in 1742, 1764 and 1781 its privileges were renewed, though on each occasion it had to pay heavily in interest-free loans to the Treasury. The Bank's capital rose from £9,800,000 sterling in 1742, to £10,780,000 in 1764 and £11,632,000 in 1781, a regular if not enormous increase.

The Bank's monopoly on issuing banknotes was not like that of a State Bank, as it was still quite free to take decisions and issue money as it wished; but it was the only bank which could issue notes redeemable on demand in under six months. The 'bank notes' were simply credit notes: though they were printed, the actual sum was not specified, and was written in by hand. Apart from this major difference from modern money, the notes were considered by merchants to be a means of payment equivalent to coin; this confidence of merchants was the most important determinant of the Bank's strength.

In 1745 a dynastic crisis of the English Crown – the threat of a Stuart restoration – started a panic and a run on the Bank. The Bank resorted to a measure which had already worked once, in 1721: it paid out, but in six pence pieces, which took so long to count that the rush of clients was stemmed. What saved the Bank, however, was a proclamation by the merchants of London, that they would accept and encourage payments in bank notes. In 1773, another obstacle to the acceptance of the bank note as currency was overcome when the death penalty was introduced for forging notes on the Bank of England, thereby putting them on a par with coin.

(2) The spread of provincial banks

Economic development stimulated the creation of banking institutions just as much as the latter stimulated the former; and this is illustrated by the fact that though Bank of England notes scarcely circulated outside London, and the Bank had no branches, banks nonetheless spread not only within England but in Wales and Scotland as well. In England itself, outside London, measures to protect the leading bank laid down that only associations of no more than six people could carry out banking operations; and this led to a proliferation of small banks formed by a few individuals and often based on ordinary shops. In 1750 there were 12 of these outside London, within England as such, and by 1793 there were 400. This was too many, and although there were many complaints about the resulting disorders, such a spontaneous development was typical of the England of the day.

Outside England, especially in those regions of Scotland most affected by the beginnings of the industrial revolution, contemporary observers were struck by the large number of banks – which were at a much higher level of development, since the English restrictions on numbers did not apply. This is discussed in Adam Smith's great work, *An Inquiry into the Nature and Causes of the Wealth of Nations*, the basis of 'classical' political economy, which was published in 1776. It appeared during the American Wars of Independence, a period of temporary difficulties, which nonetheless marked the culmination of a period of dynamic development. There were three main aspects of Adam Smith's writings on banking: the theoretical side of it, much disputed in monetary controversies; the descriptive aspect which gives an account of the contemporary growth of banking; and finally an economic analysis of the relationship of such growth to economic development.

Adam Smith held that the basic error of the mercantilists (whom he did not fully understand) was that they confused wealth and money; and it was therefore quite natural that he should find confirmation of his own views in the fact that it was possible to replace gold and silver coin by paper tokens. Money was a means, not wealth itself. 'The substitution of paper in the room of gold and silver money, replaces a very expensive instrument of commerce with one much less costly.'[1] How was this substitution effected? 'When the people of any particular country have such confidence in the fortune, probity, and prudence of a particular person, as to believe that he is always ready to pay upon demand such

[1] Adam Smith, *The Wealth of Nations*, London 1963 (Everyman Edition), p. 257.

of his promissory notes as are likely to be at any time presented to him; those notes come to have the same currency as gold and silver money, from the confidence that such money can at any time be had for them.'[2] For Smith the value of a bank note depended entirely on the possibility of redeeming it, in other words on its 'convertibility' into metal. He therefore fell into the mistake of constantly equating 'banking money' with 'paper money'. What he describes is simply a credit instrument which increases not the amount of money in circulation, but the velocity of circulation. 'A particular banker lends among his customers his own promissory notes, to the extent, we shall suppose, of a hundred thousand pounds. As those notes serve all the purposes of money, his debtors pay him the same interest as if he had lent them so much money. This interest is the source of his gain. Though some of those notes are continually coming back upon him for payment, part of them continue to circulate for months and years together. Though he has generally in circulation, therefore, notes to the extent of a hundred thousand pounds, twenty thousand pounds in gold and silver may frequently be a sufficient provision for answering occasional demands. By this operation, there-fore, twenty thousand pounds in gold and silver perform all the func-tions which a hundred thousand could otherwise have performed. . . . The whole circulation may thus be conducted with a fifth part only of the gold and silver which would otherwise have been requisite.'[3] The concept of the gold-coverage of banknotes always being less than the total value of notes is here applied to private bankers lending at interest to their customers: in other words, to a credit system. Smith does not confuse it with paper money, payment on which, he says, would depend anywhere on the good standing of the issuing authority. He constantly criticises Law for his grandiose, unrealistic schemes, while believing that Law's influence was at work in the 'banking fever' which was particu-larly marked in Scotland. Smith criticises excessive issues, holding that competition between banks would anyway force them to be cautious and not exceed their possibilities.

With these reservations, he describes with approval the proliferation of Scottish banks: 'An operation of this kind has, within these five-and-twenty or thirty years, been performed in Scotland, by the erection of new banking companies in almost every considerable town, and even in some country villages. The effects of it have been precisely those above described. The business of the country is almost entirely carried

[2] ibid. p. 257.
[3] ibid. pp. 257–8.

on by means of the paper of those different banking companies, with which purchases and payment of all kinds are commonly made. Silver very seldom appears except in the change of a twenty shilling bank note, and gold still seldomer.'[4]

Adam Smith establishes a relationship of cause and effect between the establishment of banks in Scotland and economic growth: '. . . though the conduct of all those different companies has not been unexceptionable, and has accordingly required an act of parliament to regulate it, the country, notwithstanding, has evidently derived great benefit from their trade. I have heard it asserted, that the trade of the city of Glasgow doubled in about fifteen years after the first erection of banks there; and that the trade of Scotland has more than quadrupled since the first erection of two public banks at Edinburgh.'[5] Smith is nonetheless cautious: 'Whether the trade, either of Scotland in general, or of the city of Glasgow in particular, has really increased in so great a proportion, during so short a period, I do not pretend to know. If either of them has increased in this proportion, it seems to be an effect too great to be accounted for by the sole operation of this cause.'[6] All the indications are, however, that the manifest progress in Scotland's 'agriculture, manufactures and trade, . . . the annual produce of its land and labour', could have been achieved without an increase in the supply of money, and especially of gold and silver; the increase was rather in the rapidity of payment effected by the banks, which were set up everywhere, even in the villages.

The important point is the modern element of inter-action between economic development and the increase in banking institutions, which had not reached such a level of development in France. A modern economy was developing in England. The 'wheel' of the firm rolled on with the aid of circulating credit (Smith's image). Gold and silver were turned into security stocks, and were used above all for payments abroad. This does not mean that paper circulation was the essence of the English monetary system of the 1770s. According to Sombart, the share of paper money in 1750 was barely £2 million out of a total of £100 million, and still less than £10 million out of £100 million by 1780. There had been considerable but limited progress, and the role of precious metals was far from over.

4 ibid. pp. 261–2.
5 ibid. p. 262.
6 ibid. p. 262.

(3) The circulation of gold and silver

After the stabilisation of 1721–1726, there was no major disparity, in England or on the continent, between the value of the currency in circulation and the market prices of precious monetary metals. There were still, however, enormous international transfers. Gold flowed into England (mainly from Brazil and Portugal), and silver flowed out to cover purchases in Asia and the Far East. Between 1733 and 1766, 65% of England's exports to Asia were in the form of silver bullion and, even more, of silver coin. The total value amounted to some £400 million sterling, as opposed to only £9 million spent by France on similar transactions. This gives an indication of the gap between the two economies. After 1765 and the British victory in India, during the very earliest period of the industrial revolution, in which textiles predominated, Britain sent an increasing volume of manufactures to India in exchange for the usual exotic products. This produced profit on both sides, and therefore limited silver exports.

The supply of Brazilian gold, however, was beginning to dry up, and then there was a tendency to export gold (which was rising in value), and re-import used silver. In 1773, Lord Liverpool, a minister of George III's, denounced the debasement of silver coin and even of gold coin in almost the same tones as those used by Locke in 1696. The gold coin was then melted down and re-cast, at the same face value, but with the intrinsic value restored. On the other hand silver was relegated to a secondary place, broadly speaking as a token currency, with no weight controls. Thus the law of 10 May 1774, apparently unimportant, in fact prepared the way for the gold standard. Firstly, it limited silver currency: for sums above £50 payment in silver might be refused and payment in gold could be demanded; this reduced silver to the role of small cash coin; and secondly, the law laid down that once gold was recast at full weight, coins would be allowed to deteriorate by only 1 38/39 grains a guinea, a tiny proportion.

Later, in 1802, when Lord Liverpool was 78, he published a justification of these measures, clearly stating his preference for the gold standard: 'The Money or Coin, which is to be the principal measure of property, ought to be made of one metal only.'[7] For the richest trading nations, he added, gold should become the universal monetary standard automatically and without any special legal measures. What he laid down here became the doctrine of 19th century England.

[7] Lord Liverpool, *Coins of the Realm*, London 1802, pp. 12–13.

This account shows that far from being in opposition to one another, the move towards gold coin as the universal standard, and the development of banking and credit, took place simultaneously.

(4) Trade crises and monetary policy

As international trade and credit developed, there was a change in the nature of crises. Under the old régime these were usually crises of high grain prices caused by poor harvests, but now trade crises were periodically unleashed by excess credit and by saturated markets. To describe the process in a simplified form: economic activity and prosperity meant that a constantly growing number of firms borrowed, bought and raised prices, until the possibilities of realising their assets and of selling were exhausted; the following sharp decline in profits led to generalised panic in certain sectors, and to business crashes. Such 'trade crises' occurred in England in 1763, 1772 and 1783 (roughly, one per decade).

On the last occasion, however, the Bank of England for the first time acted according to a systematic policy. When gold was observed to be leaving the country – the first sign of a crisis – credit was at once restricted and loans to the State were refused. When gold began to flow back into the country and the exchanges started moving in a favourable direction, the Bank began to issue notes again and to lend to the State. This was the first example of 'credit control', of deliberately holding back and then stepping up circulation, according to changes in the conjuncture revealed by movements in gold and on the exchanges. England, therefore had reached a precociously modern level of development, and 'modern' methods of containing crises though they may have been perfected since then, turn out not to be so very new after all.

(5) Banking in the rest of Europe

It should not be thought that France and England were the only countries to experience innovations in money and banking. Leaving aside Amsterdam, which until the 1760s, was still of relative if declining importance, and Geneva, the financial centre of Europe, it should not be forgotten that Sweden too had pioneered certain aspects of banking, while Hamburg was an essential part of the European exchange market. However, the development of banking should not be confused with the creation of national banks or similar institutions, or with the issuing of paper money in specific circumstances. The most obvious example of artificial inflation in the 18th century is that of the English colonies in America during the War of Independence, when the different States involved issued inconvertible paper money which rapidly depreciated.

In Europe itself paper money was issued in rather less exceptional circumstances, Spain being a case in point. In 1780, in order to finance the American war without imposing too great a burden on the Spanish tax-payer, the government obtained a loan of 9 million pesos from a banking consortium which included Necker and the Bayonne financier, Cabarrús. It was guaranteed against future silver imports from America which were held up by the war, and raised from the public by the issue of interest-bearing royal bonds of a high face value (600 and later 300 pesos). The bonds depreciated by up to 22% during the war because they were issued in such large quantities; but in 1782, Cabarrús founded a national bank, the Banco de San Carlos, which as I have already mentioned was intended to hold a monopoly on piastres imported through Cadiz, and to levy a constant percentage. The bank began by re-absorbing some of the bonds, and massive imports of Mexican silver did so much to restabilise the situation, that the bonds were soon circulating at a premium over metallic money. Charles III then took advantage of this to issue more bonds, this time for public works (the Aragon canals). When based on firm monetary foundations, the credit system could therefore take varied and very useful forms; but merchants never regarded the Spanish bonds as equivalent to paper money, and this saved them from total disaster during the period of depreciation which came later in 1794–1796, during the war with France.

Thus with the special exception of America there were between 1726 and 1792–1797 no real instances of inflation. What occurred was a development of credit.

Mexican Silver and the European Conjuncture

The question of the Mexican silver mines is basic to an account of the production of monetary metals in the second half of the 18th century, and there is an exceptionally good source for it in Alexander von Humboldt's *Political Essay on the Kingdom of New Spain*, a technical, economic, geographical and historical account by one of the most observant travellers of the early 19th century.[1]

The most important pieces of information he gives about the mines are the following. There was a strong geographical concentration of silver production: in the last years of the 18th century two-thirds of all American silver came from Mexico, and of the 2,500,000 marks of Mexican silver annually exported from Vera Cruz to Europe and from Acapulco to Asia, half came from only three mining districts, Guanajuato, Zacatecas and Catorce, a quarter of the total being from Guanajuato alone. Vera Cruz exported two-thirds of the silver brought up from the mines, and the most productive mining district was no more extensive than the Freiburg mines in Saxony. Silver production was therefore extremely concentrated geographically.

Mexico produced very little gold – 1,000,000 piastres worth a year, as opposed to 22,000,000 worth of silver; this came from a few isolated, insignificant mines, or as a by-product from the silver ore (which contained an average of 2.3 thousandths of gold). The mines did not, however, produce very high quality silver. Humboldt set out with the idea that Mexico was overflowing with mineral wealth and great nuggets of pure silver were to be had for the taking. What he found was that much of the ore contained only two or three ounces of pure silver a hundredweight, which was below the European average: for 3,000,000 marks of pure silver 10,000,000 hundredweight of ore had to be mined. In the

---

[1] Alexander von Humboldt, *Political Essay on the Kingdom of New Spain*, London 1811 reprinted New York 1966, (vol. 3), Book IV, Chapter 11.

best mines, such as Valenciana (near Guanajuato), the average rose to 4 ounces a hundredweight and the maximum to 9 ounces.

Nevertheless, Guanajuato appeared to be producing more in the 18th century than even Potosí had produced in the 16th. Humboldt's calculations, based on a thorough study of Spanish documents, show that the annual average production of Potosí had been:

2,227,782 piastres between 1556 and 1578;

3,994,258 piastres between 1579 and 1736; and

2,458,606 piastres between 1737 and 1789,

while in the latter period, Guanajuato was producing 4,500,000 piastres a year, much more than in the best years of the 16th century.

Humboldt's figures are given in detail in an appendix (see p. 349) but here is a simplified table:

Annual average	Piastres
1766–1775:	3,032,050
1776–1785:	4,669,286
1786–1795:	4,868,266
1796–1803:	4,913,265

The great leap in production was around 1775–1776, and is clearly related to price movements in Europe.

(1) The Valenciana mining company

If we compare Humboldt's impressions of the greatest mine of the period, which he visited and studied in detail, with Luis Capoche's *Relación* on Potosí,[2] it becomes clear that there are major differences both in the characteristics of the mines and in the preoccupations of the authors. Capoche, writing in the 16th century, stressed the number and the variety of the concessions, the relations between the mining contractors and the labour force, and the problem of the free silver market in which the Indians participated. Humboldt, in the 18th century, took visible pleasure in stressing the ideas of the 'enterprise' and the qualities of the

---

[2] See above p. 120.

'entrepreneur' (not actually using these words, though they are implicit in his description). The explorer filled with unswerving faith in his discovery, as described by Humboldt, was to become a familiar figure in 19th century American history.

Around 1760 Obregón, the future *conde*, count, of La Valenciana, was a modestly well-off colonial farmer. He gained support from men of a similar station who contributed small sums to his prospecting. By 1766 he had dug to a depth of 80 metres and his costs outstripped his income. Despite this he accepted all the hardship, being, according to Humboldt, as obsessed with mining fever as other men were with gambling fever. In 1767 he formed a company with Otero, a small

Figure 13. Mexico in the 18th century.

trader from Rayas, in 1768 came the first important discovery, a major vein, and in 1771 the mine definitely got under way. From 1771 to 1804, the average value of production was 14 million livres tournois, 6 million of this being clear profit for the mine-owners.

A town quickly grew up where formerly there had only been a few goats grazing on the hills, six years after the discovery it had acquired 8,000 inhabitants. But there was no growth comparable to that of Potosí two centuries previously. Obregón retained his original simple habits and straightforward manner. The company was divided up into 24 'shares', ten for the descendants of Obregón, 12 for the descendants of Otero and two for a third party, Santana. During his visit Humboldt met two of Otero's young sons, each of whom owned 6 million livres tournois in capital, and received 400,000 livres each year from the profits of the mine.

Such people were prosperous and successful businessmen; and far from taking a passive role, they had, by the time of Humboldt's visit, initiated large-scale developments, and had planned a great shaft, due to be finished in 1815, to economise on labour. Already, though, their expenditure was increasing. From 1787 to 1791 the costs of running the mine were 410,000 piastres; from 1794 to 1802 they came to 890,000 piastres. The gross profits shared out also declined drastically between 1797 and 1802:

	piastres
1797	1,249,000
1798	835,000
1799	668,000
1800	503,000
1801	401,000
1802	285,000

The question which arises is whether, by the turn of the century, the great mines were being worked out, and whether the history of La Valenciana was repeating that of Potosí. Whatever the answer, there had for a long time been a vast difference in the output of Mexican mines like La Valenciana, and that of the European silver mines.

(2) Comparative cost of Mexican and European silver

It was Humboldt who drew the comparison, and his calculations are one of the very few pieces of documentation on the subject we possess: the relationship between the problems of precious metals and the problem of their costs of production having all too often been dismissed as irrelevant. The differences in production costs have also frequently been wrongly interpreted: they have often been attributed to the discovery of particularly high-grade ore, or to the fall in Indian wages relative to European wages. According to Humboldt's figures neither of these is the explanation. The two great advantages of Mexican mining were firstly the thickness of the veins of ore, and secondly, the productivity of the labour obtained from the native population, rather than their low wages.

The version of Humboldt's table given below is re-organized to show the characteristics of the Mexican mine, La Valenciana, in one column, and in the other those of the Himmelsfürst mine in the Freiburg massif of Saxony.

	Mexican mine	*European mine*
I PHYSICAL CONDITIONS		
(a) Water	none	8 cubic feet a minute: 2 pump-wheels needed
(b) Depth	514 metres	330 metres
(c) Grade of ore	4 ounces per cwt.	6–7 ounces per cwt.
(d) Thickness of veins	3 branches of 40–60 metres	5 veins of 0.2 or 0.3 metres
(e) Ore extracted per year	720,000 cwt.	14,000 cwt.
(f) Gold dust used	1,600 cwt. at 250 livres tournois a cwt. = 400,000 livres tournois	270 cwt. at 100 livres tournois a cwt. = 27,000 livres tournois

	Mexican mine	*European mine*
II HUMAN CONDITIONS		
(a) Number of workers	3,100 mestizos 1,800 of them down the mine	700 miners, 550 of them down the mine
(b) Daily wage	5–6 livres, or 100–120 tournois shillings	18 tournois shillings
III ECONOMIC CONDITIONS		
(a) Silver produced	360,000 marks	10,000 marks
(b) Net expenditure	5,000,000 livres tournois	240,000 livres tournois
(c) Net profit	3,000,000 livres tournois	90,000 livres tournois

In other words, although wages were six times as high and costs 20 times greater, four to five times as many workers as in Europe shifted more than 50 times as much ore, extracted 36 times as much silver and generated 33 times as much profit. The exploitation of labour is not measured by the worker's wage but by the difference between productivity and pay.

Furthermore, the apparently high wages of the mestizos and Indians must in any case be judged according to the relative cost of living, which in the mining areas was very high. The labour force in the mines was burdened down by debt, and wages were always spent in advance. The work was undoubtedly exhausting, but nonetheless high nominal wages, as always, attracted labour, and it must not be forgotten that it was even harder to work as a *peón*, an agricultural worker, or as a common labourer in the workshops, especially those producing textiles.

The difference in the cost of producing an ounce of silver in Mexico and in Europe suffices as a measure of the attractive power exerted by Mexican silver. In the mining districts themselves, maize, the daily subsistence food of the country, worth 9 livres tournois a *boisseau* (12.5 litres) where it was produced, was as much as 22 livres. The attraction also operated over long distances, and all Europe wanted to produce for the Vera Cruz market, the point at which European goods were imported into Mexico.

The silver had to be taken over long distances; to reach Europe or Asia Mexican silver not only had to be shipped across the ocean (which became progressively easier) but it had to be got to the coast. Before going to Vera Cruz, the port for Europe, or Acapulco, the port for Asia, it had to pass through Mexico City to be minted (mainly into piastres) at the famous *Casa de la Moneda*. It was over 100 leagues from the mining districts to Mexico City, 69 from Mexico City to Vera Cruz, and 66 from Mexico City to Acapulco. Long mule trains carried the silver ingots and chests of coin one way, and tallow, flour, iron, wine, wool, mercury and luxury goods the other way.

Nor were the roads easy: Humboldt compared their contours to the St. Gothard Pass. The route to Acapulco and the Pacific involved crossing rivers in rafts held up by dried gourds, which did not help to calm the traveller's nerves; sometimes for more than a week the rivers were too swollen to cross. As with the old Panama route in the 16th century, the movements of silver encountered exceptionally great natural obstacles. But the flow between Acapulco, Mexico City and Vera Cruz was, by the end of the 18th century, worth 320 million livres tournois a year.

The road between Mexico City and Vera Cruz had been improved by large-scale public works, which had cost the *Consulados*, or chambers of trade, of the two cities some 15 million livres. The greatest difficulty the Europeans encountered was the climate: not in Mexico City, which was at a healthy altitude, but on the plains. Humboldt describes the relief of the traveller on reaching an altitude above the swamplands and the damp heat.

All these difficulties and dangers did not deter men greedy for profit. It is surprising to find this illustrated in the simple correspondence of low-ranking employees of a small Catalan company which exported brandy and cloth to Mexico, in the hope of making the greatest possible profit in silver in return. Here love of silver and fear of death are strangely balanced: 'As to what you write about my weariness of being in the Company, do not believe it so: though it is true that I tire of this city (Vera Cruz), I do not regret coming here, for thank God, only now I am here can I see how much better business is than I thought, and thanks be to God for it. If I am weary of the place it is because of the daily difficulties and sudden deaths which occur every day, to the extent that you may be speaking with a friend one day and two days later learn that he is dead; this is enough to frighten anyone, and you must not think it strange that I have become tremendously afraid in this country.

Everyone can die at any moment. We are all exposed to the same dangers, and who does not fear death?'[3] The letter is dated 9 December 1795, in a period when the death rate was high; but conditions of this kind were almost always the case.

The profits which made men face these dangers arose both from the slightly higher value of Mexican silver, and the periodic shortages which sent the prices of European goods shooting up. Humboldt wrote: 'From 25 to 30 millions of piastres are sometimes heaped up in Mexico, while the manufacturers and miners are suffering from the want of steel, iron and mercury. A few years before my arrival in New Spain, the price of iron rose from 20 francs the quintal to 240, and steel from 80 francs to 1300'.[4]

The prices of all imported goods could vary enormously according to the area or, locally, according to the arrival of individual ships. The agents of Spanish companies lived in a constant state of anxiety; the arrival of a ship could totally upset market conditions; if the consumption of local spirits was banned or re-authorised, this could sometimes double or halve the price of imported liquor. In the first two-thirds of the 18th century, goods arrived from Spain in fleets escorted by convoys, to be sold at a regular fair such as that of Jalapa, a town between Mexico City and Vera Cruz; but after the fleet system was given up and 'free trade' declared (1778), each ship sailed when it liked. In one sense this expanded sales and competition, but it also made it more difficult to realise sales on the market.

The Mexican market was certainly important for Europe: around 1800, the average value of Vera Cruz exports was 21.8 million piastres 17 million of them in silver, 2.4 in cochineal and 1.3 in sugar. The average value of imports at Vera Cruz was 9.2 million in textiles, 1 million of paper, 1 million of brandy, 1 million of cacao and 1.4 million of mercury, iron and steel. More than half of the export of piastres (9 million out of 17) therefore went to pay for the purchase of textiles from Europe. This gives a measure of the impulse the Mexican mines gave to European industry, and in particular to the cotton industry.

The rest of South America, which had previously been much more important than Mexico for precious metals, cannot be left out of account. Around 1771–1773, at the same time as the great phase of Mexican mining was beginning, new mines were being discovered or old ones

[3] Correspondence of the Alsina company of Calella, Catalonia; private archive material communicated to the author by H. Moreu.
[4] von Humboldt, op. cit. p. 105.

re-opened in Peru and the Andes (at Gualgayoc, Guamachuco, Conchuco). Such coincidences are always significant: and at the same time New Granada (in today's Colombia) also began to supply gold once again (4,714 kilos a year around 1800). But out of 795,000 kilos of silver supplied by Spanish America at this date, 537,000 were Mexican and only 250,000 came from the vice royalties of Buenos Aires and Peru. Chile and Peru had a joint foreign trade of 12,000,000 pesos, with imports and exports roughly balancing. As the Pacific sea route was a long way round, the silver from Peru was channelled overland, from northern Peru through modern Colombia (Bogota) and from southern Peru, now Bolivia, across the pampas to Buenos Aires. The two channels were also used for smuggling, in which the English were particularly expert.

A final point about the American market is that while it is true that the precious metals, and in particular silver, played by far the most important role in trade, metals were not the only source of profit for European merchants: profits were in fact doubled if in return for their exports to America they could import colonial products like sugar, cochineal and dye-woods. Ports like Havana carried out as much foreign trade as Vera Cruz. Havana exported an average of 13,000 cases of sugar a year between 1760 and 1763, 50,000 from 1770 to 1778, 103,000 in 1794 and 204,000 in 1802, a similar increase, and no less important, to that of Guanajuato silver, which after all was only one colonial commodity among many. However, the balance of America's trade with Europe was still covered by crude silver, and this was also needed for trade with the East.

(3) The repercussions of American silver and trade on European prices

In the long term, the exploitation of the great mines and the enormous difference in the costs of production of American and European mining led to the fall in the price of silver and to a general rise in silver prices throughout the world, though at different rates.

Even in the short term, the encounter between silver and commodities in Mexico, Cadiz and the ports of Europe, led to rapid price rises of the kind we have seen taking place in the Jalapa fairs and the Vera Cruz market. The goods most valued in the Indies – textiles, paper, books, hardware, iron and steel – could suddenly become extremely dear if the trade was interrupted; but to some extent the same thing happened with goods which were dear in Europe such as sugar, rum and cochineal.

In Europe, silver became dearer when Atlantic shipping was delayed, by war for example; but when the trade resumed waves of silver flooded into Cadiz, Barcelona or Nantes, and prices leapt upwards because of the sudden abundance of silver, so that all delayed purchases were now quickly carried out. Hamilton's studies of Spanish price movements show that the sharpest increases often correspond to massive imports of silver from the Americas.

The arrival of the fleets in 1784, after the American War of Independence, is a good instance of this. In Barcelona wages as well as prices were dramatically affected: from 1784 to 1785 wages in Barcelona rose from an index 118 to 145, a leap perhaps unparallelled in the history of wages. Apart from the local conditions which are part of the explanation, the reasons for this become clearer when it is discovered that in Barcelona in 1784 a shipwright's wages were 20 shillings (*sueldos*), while the rate in Cadiz was 28, on board ship for the Indies it was 37.5, and in Havana it was 112 shillings (3 hard pesos). The nearer to the source of silver, the higher were the wages (at least nominally, for prices also varied); and a sailor returning from Havana or Vera Cruz would demand more in his own country, and be the more likely to get it since the fleet had returned bringing an abundance of silver. There was a saying in Catalonia to the effect that a sailor built his house with the silver from his first trip and married on the silver from the second. This was how prices increased; in the short run they could rise very quickly, with the arrival of the fleets, but they did not subsequently fall back again. Hence the long term increases.

In the end, moreover, the long term increase was fairly homogeneous throughout Europe. When long term wheat price indices for Barcelona and France are compared, the average silver prices for the main cycles of the 18th century turn out to be very close:

	Barcelona	France
1726–1741	100	100
1742–1757	104.8	109
1758–1770	131	129
1771–1789	161.9	156

During the first half of the century, Barcelona had little contact with America: the increase was slightly less than in France. In the second half of the century Barcelona made progressively closer contact with America, and the increase was slightly higher.

(4) The shrinking margin between European and colonial prices

Little work has been done so far on a process which is clearly visible in any study of colonial trade in the late 18th century, viz. the shrinking margin between European and colonial prices, the margin on which the high profits from speculating in the Atlantic trade were based. Various developments contributed to this diminution: the improvement of sea communications, the multiplication of ships of all sizes and the greater security of voyages in times of peace; and the move towards the formation of a real 'world market': in wartime, in particular, when prices soared on the colonial market because of the scarcity of Spanish commodities and the proximity of the mines, the gap was filled by smuggling, and sometimes even by legal appeals to other non-metropolitan suppliers. There was, for example, a growth in trade among the colonies (they exchanged with, and produced for, each other); North European commodities were brought in (from Scandinavia, England and Germany); and finally, as the immediate effects of the War of Independence were overcome, the United States began to intervene: Spanish colonial trade went under the flag of the United States when hostilities between England and Spain made it difficult.

For example, the trade between the Catalan ports and the American colonies shows foreign products taking the place of local produce: Mexico and Cuba bought Russian instead of Catalan hemp. Whereas sails for colonial shipping had been made in Spain they were now being manufactured elsewhere in Europe. Salt beef and fish were bought in Scotland and Norway for mass consumption in Havana and Vera Cruz. Through the spread of international trade the prices of this class of common goods in Havana or Puerto Rico became lower than in Barcelona after the war between England and Spain began again in 1795. Even wages had stopped rising in the colonies: from 1795 to 1799 the average wages of a Havana worker fell from $3\frac{1}{2}$ pesos to $2\frac{1}{2}$, while in Spain the artificial inflation of paper money resulting from the war raised wages to their highest yet. It was at this period, too, that according to von Humboldt the Mexican mines began to require large-scale works and increased expenditure, and when their owners were threatened with falling profits. The margin between colonial and European prices, especially for silver, therefore shrank.

After 1805, when the French and Spanish navies were defeated at Trafalgar by the British, the Mexican trade was almost completely cut off, and vast stocks of silver accumulated in the Mint in Mexico City. Trade with Vera Cruz slumped. The English did allow the Spanish to import this silver when Spain rebelled against Napoleon in 1808: but from 1810–1812, the Mexican revolt against Spain threatened normal mining conditions there.

From 1795 onwards until after the Napoleonic Wars European prices began to increase because of the inflation of various kinds of paper money. The French *assignats*, Spanish bonds and obligatory English bank notes therefore opened a new period in monetary history.

32

Money in the French Revolution

The previous chapter has examined Mexican silver production and its costs, which fell at first but were by the end of the century definitely increasing. The diffusion of American precious metals and of colonial profits from Cadiz and France through the rest of Europe encouraged a clear, though irregular and limited, increase in prices, while periodic upswings were undoubtedly less extreme than in the 17th century and there was no violent divergence between the domestic prices of each country and international prices as expressed in gold and silver.

Even the many wars, which sometimes temporarily held up metal imports and forced governments to issue various kinds of token money, did not affect the monetary stability of the great European countries until 1789–1793. Spain easily re-absorbed the issue of bonds begun in 1780 by means of the silver imports of 1783 onwards. Prior to the Revolution, the enormous State deficit and national debt in France produced nothing worse than the minor conflicts over the 1776 Discount Bank. In England, economic development was already based on the Bank of England and banking credit; in 1774 a solidly guaranteed gold currency was established, and silver coin was legally restricted to a secondary role, a system which heralded the gold standard.

The relative harmony and equilibrium of the 18th century was to be disrupted by the French Revolution, the internal disturbances it entailed and the international conflicts which followed. The French Revolution should not however be viewed as a political event in some way external to economic reality, as an intrusion by an exogenous element. The Revolution, which caused such upheaval in the economy and the monetary system after 1789, was also a consequence of the economic developments of the 18th century, and of the resultant prosperity, as well as of the social imbalance they created. In so far, then, as it was related to the 'conjuncture' and therefore to the question of money and precious metals, the French Revolution forms part of our subject. I shall therefore summarize, and so far as possible simplify, the classic account given by Ernest Labrousse.[1]

(1) The 18th-century conjuncture and the origins of the French revolution

Prices rose in the 18th century. This means that prices in general, and foremost among them, agricultural prices, tended to rise irrespective of the cyclical variations of climatic origin. The increase was clear from at least 1733 and hardly slackened until the 1770s. The cyclical peaks of grain prices were however relatively less drastic than in the 17th century or early 18th century. There was no repeat of crises of the dimensions of 1693 or 1709, and since there were no cases of comparable mortality rates either, the population also grew.

The increase in prices and population produced certain results which can be divided in various ways: into the long-term and the short-term; into those effecting the privileged classes and those that affected the dependent social classes; and into those that affected producers and sellers (independent peasants, various kinds of artisan) and those that affected producers who were hardly self-sufficient or were genuinely dependent. Price increases impose suffering on those who buy, and profit those who sell.

The long-term eighteenth century price increases of 1726–1733 to 1776–1789 suggest that certain social classes were prospering; in the first place merchants in the great ports and the businessmen who serviced them (ship-builders and other suppliers). But also included were wider groups which are more characteristic of the society of that period: those living on land rents, whether rural property-owners in the modern sense or the holders of manorial rights collecting feudal dues. This kind of income was increasing faster than prices. It is possible that the increase was of the order of 80%, while prices rose between 53% and 63% between the 1726–1741 cycle and the cycle prior to the French Revolution. In terms of purchasing power landed income (going by rents) would then have risen by 25%, while daily wages fell by 25% in real terms. The peasant who did not sell anything on the market was therefore living on the edge of disaster. This meant that there was a long term contradiction between the two types of income.

[1] see p. 280, n. 5.

In the medium term, there was an inner-cycle of 12–15 years of stagnating or falling prices; this began around 1772 in viticulture, and in 1776 for agriculture as a whole. It lasted until 1787 and brought the difficulties of the *rentiers*, entrepreneurs, bourgeois and small proprietors (especially vineyard owners) combined with the misery of the mass of the population, who laboured under the double burden of taxes imposed by their feudal lords and by the Crown. The cycle became known as the 'Louis XVI sickness' since it began at about the same time as the king's reign (1774), and lasted until the very eve of 1789.

In the very short term, the bad harvest of 1788 drove grain prices up to astronomical heights unknown since 1709. In 27 Generalités (Provinces) out of 32, the peak was reached in July 1789: 34 livres tournois for a *setier* of wheat as opposed to an average of 20 to 22 in the preceding years. Economic and social contradictions were at their height and the investigations carried out at the beginning of the Revolution showed that eleven million French people were reduced to complete penury, many of whom were forced to go wandering through the land in search of the means of subsistence.

At this juncture, political opposition to the monarchy and the desire of the newly rich bourgeoisie to control the State – especially its finances – combined with a distinct kind of social agitation: May to July 1789 saw both looting of the grain convoys of a kind habitual in cases of famine, and riots by unemployed in the cities. In July 1789, the greatest peasant war in French history ('la Grande Peur'), merged with the great bourgeois revolution.[2]

(2) The French revolution and monetary problems

The monetary system was shaken to its very foundations, by the episode of the *assignats*; it is only of indirect interest to a study of precious metals, as it was an artificial and basically political monetary experiment. Nonetheless the episode suggests some useful considerations about the relationship between the currency, the home economy and the foreign relations of a country, and the role of metal money. Above all, the end of the experiment led to the establishment of the franc, which remained stable until the 1914 war; it is therefore worthy of some consideration.

The problem which gave rise to the *assignats* was the national debt, and the solution proposed was both political and social. Ecclesiastical

[2] Georges Lefebvre, *The Great Fear of 1789*, London 1973.

property, and later emigré property, were 'put at the disposal of the nation' in order to wipe out the national debt. Church lands were initially valued at 3,500 million livres tournois. This social measure was related to the conviction which had arisen in the 18th century that wealth had to be individual, circulating and constantly exchangeable according to the laws of competition, and not congealed in collective property which never changed hands (i.e. as mortmain).

The measure nonetheless posed an economic problem: who could buy such property, and with what money? Had the 18th century enriched certain categories of Frenchmen and impoverished others, and who was to benefit? There was also the moral, psychological and even religious problem of the condemnation by the Church authorities of the sale of ecclesiastical property, and the question of whether this would deter buyers. The measure was not therefore enacted under normal economic conditions; yet in the last analysis economic and monetary laws had to prevail.

As it was impossible to wait for the money expected from the sales until all the property had been sold, *assignats* were issued. In origin they were not a form of money, but an 'assignation' on the value of the expected sales, an interest-bearing acknowledgement of a debt. It is very important not to confuse the *assignat* (at least as it was originally conceived) with money guaranteed on the value of land in general such as was proposed in England in the late 17th century, and such as Law himself had for a time thought of it. Originally, that is, in December 1789, the *assignat* was in fact a bond in large 1,000 livre notes, bearing 5% interest. What is interesting is how it came to be used as money, as is evident in the decrease and then the suppression of the interest it bore, and the issuing of bonds for lower and lower quantities which could be used for smaller payments.

In April 1790, just as the scale of national property was being speeded up, 400 million livres' worth of *assignats* were issued at 3% interest (instead of 5%) and in sums between 200 and 500 livres. In September 1790 800 million *assignats* were issued without interest. The interest on previously issued bills was abolished. The bonds were for sums as low as 50 livres, but in May 1791 this was reduced to 5 livres. By April 1792, when war had begun, notes were appearing for 50, 25, 15 and even 10 sous.

At first it might have seemed that the main purpose of the *assignats* was to liquidate the national debt, and effect the purchase of national lands by the wealthiest creditors of the State: they would buy bonds for large sums, while the mass of the population would not suffer paper inflation. Less than three years after the first issue, the whole situation had changed. Everyone had *assignats*, which had become an obligatory currency and were depreciating so rapidly that all incomes, wages included, were threatened. The purchase of national property, meanwhile, was open to whoever could accumulate *assignats*. In the words of Georges Lefebvre: '. . . the new notes might be acquired by anyone. They were bought up rapidly, sometimes just to get rid of the paper, whose depreciation benefitted the poor as well as the speculators. One could say that the operation was to succeed in this respect the more it was to fail from the financial point of view'.[3] Price increases, the attempt to limit them by decreeing 'maximums', and the conflict between 'maximum' prices and 'maximum' wages dominated the relations between the Parisian masses and the revolutionary government. Such was the political and social importance of monetary affairs.

However special a case it was, and however closely related to political problems, the monetary phenomenon of the *assignat* was not independent of the prevailing economic situation and of international monetary developments. The problem is how the psychological aspect of public confidence in the system was related to the objective questions of the volume of money issued and the domestic and international price levels. The rapid devaluation of the *assignat*, for example, was not solely due to the excessive issues: Necker calculated that there was 2,200 million livres of precious metals in circulation in 1789, and an issue of 1,200 million guaranteed on national lands in September 1790 should not therefore have given silver a great premium over gold: but a 10% premium was nonetheless already being paid. This was because no-one believed in the promised restrictions, and everyone rightly thought that the State could continue to issue bonds above the figures specified.

In November 1791 the *assignat* had already fallen by 18% as measured by the premium for silver, and by August 1792 it had fallen by 43%, i.e. a given quantity of *assignats* was worth only 57% of its nominal paper value. It is a curious indication of the importance of the psychological factor that after 10 August, the September killings and the French victory at Valmy, the value of the *assignat* rose again from 57% to 72% of its value in metal money. This undoubtedly reflects an upsurge of confidence in the regime; as Hawtrey also observes in his work on money: the fall of summer 1792 had been excessive, the domestic

[3] Georges Lefebvre, *The French Revolution*, London 1961, p. 160.

monetary situation was still not desperate, and there was in fact an expansion of credit abroad.[4] Prices were also rising, indicating a fall in the value of precious metals. The depreciation of French paper was therefore held back for a while by the international depreciation of metal coin.

The *assignat* began to fall again in 1793. The purchase of gold and silver had not been banned in France (the Constituent Assembly remaining faithful to its liberal principles), and this makes it possible to measure their premium over paper money from day to day. Until April 1793 there was no ban on free trade in precious metals, and only in August 1793 was a ban placed on accepting *assignats* at a discount. It was therefore a long time before there was really a 'forced circulation', though from September 1793 this was given the sanction of the death penalty. There was however another way of showing a lack of confidence in the *assignat*; though it was impossible to give preference to precious metals or to give a discount on *assignats*, prices expressed in *assignats* could always be put up. Hence the famous 'maximum', the restriction of prices by the authorities which also began in September 1793.

This policy had a partial success. As long as prices were held down the *assignat* began to rise again, and it moved from 22% to 48% of its nominal value between August and December 1793. Coercion, energetic enforcement and foreign victories all played their part in this. Galloping inflation dates mainly from the Thermidorian Convention and the Directorate. From November 1794 the *assignat* fell to 24% of its nominal value, and by then 6,400 million livres in *assignats* were in circulation.

Once the 'maximum' was abolished an avalanche of speculation was let loose, and there was a flight from money: that is, people were buying anything at any price. Foreign trade could only be carried on with gold and silver, which became the objects of speculative buying. Metal coin was, however, scarce. As much as possible had been exported and most of the rest hidden. Nor did the economic situation allow of a renewal of stocks. From 1792 to 1797 the French Republic minted only 32 million livres of silver and none of gold. Meanwhile, 14,000 million *assignats* had been issued up to December 1795, and in February 1796 a maximum volume of 40,000 million was decreed.

It is not known whether this figure was reached (the highest level of circulation was perhaps 35,000 million). The workers who printed the *assignats* went on strike, and printing costs came close to the current value of the notes. The plates were then solemnly burnt in the Place Vendôme. The existing *assignats* however went on circulating, with abrupt swings in value and related speculation: in June 1796 the 24 livres gold *écu* was valued in *assignats* at 585 livres on the 7th, 1,000 livres on the 13th and 450 on the 16th. In October of the same year, it stood at 2,000 livres on the 26th, 3,450 on the 30th and 2,450 on the 31st.

In March 1796 an attempt was made to replace *assignats* by 'territorial payment orders' which would allow for the direct purchase of national lands at 22 times the rent they were yielding in 1790. The operation could have been profitable for the bearers of the Payment Orders. In fact, only promissory orders were issued, and they were at once confused with *assignats*: in 4 months they fell to 4% of their nominal value.

We now turn to how France emerged from this monetary crisis; it was the worst in her history, though not as disastrous as those of Germany or Hungary in the 20th century. In February 1797 obligatory acceptance was abolished, and it was forbidden even to pay taxes in *assignats*. Strangely enough, they remained in circulation for several months, and were even bought up by people who thought that the situation would eventually change. The most important developments were as follows: silver minting and circulation began again; national debts were liquidated by the 'two thirds bankruptcy': the 'consolidated third' gave some stability to income and the 'mobilised two thirds' formed an intermediary circulation between paper inflation and silver circulation. The State budget was restricted and a new fiscal system organised, which was simpler and more efficient. Finally 'deflation' was made possible by a series of good harvests, such as that of 1796 (there was, notably, a 30% fall in wine prices) and by a tightening of credit: loans to individuals were made at 2% per *month*, except for the major clients of certain banks. The result, apart from stagnation in domestic trade, was a large number of brutal crashes, brought on especially by a fall in colonial trade as a result of the slave revolt in Haiti.

International developments generally were not at all unfavourable to France: the Treaty of Basle secured the renewal or at least the hope of a renewal of overseas trade on a long term basis, through continued trading with Cadiz, the source of silver. At the same time the Italian campaign initiated the plundering of Europe by the French armies, a factor which should not be forgotten. Moreover, even apart from war, Northern Europe was opening up to French products. It was in this atmosphere that the Bank of France and the 'Germinal' franc, the stable monetary unit of the 19th century, were created.

The Bank of France was a continuation of the Mortmain Bank created by Gaudin and later administered by Mollien and of two private discount banks, the Current Account Bank of Perregaux, Récamier and Desprez and the Commercial Discount Bank. On 13th February 1800 the former was made into the Bank of France with a capital of 30,000,000 in 1,000 franc shares, with 15 directors and 3 auditors, who were elected by the majority of the share-holders. It was still basically a private institution with no monopoly for issuing bank notes. The Bank was at first very cautious; it gave little stimulus to business and little relief to the state, which was still dependent on individual financiers. In 1803 its capital was increased to 45,000,000, it was given the monopoly of issuing bank notes in Paris and it took over the Commercial Discount Bank. In 1806, after the financial crisis of 1805, the Bank was subjected to closer state control and a Governor was appointed; it was eventually given the complete monopoly of paper issues. But it was still a long way from acquiring the role being played by the Bank of England at the same time.

In 1793, out of a desire to adapt and standardise the metric system, the revolutionary government had laid down that there should be a 10 gram gold coin known as the gold franc and a silver coin of the same weight: but a law of 10 April 1795 provided for the maintenance of the old kind of coin, which was to be known not as the 'livre' but as the 'franc'. Only in 1799 were the terms franc, dixième and centime instead of livres, sous and deniers (pounds, shillings and pence) made obligatory in accounting; even so, the old customs lingered on for a long time, just as the metal coin of Louis XV's time (louis, écus and sous) went on circulating for thirty years, despite the fact that they were not in theory acceptable as money.

The new French monetary unit was finally fixed by law on 7 April 1803–17 Germinal, Year XI. It was to be a silver franc weighing 5 grams and of a grade of 900/1,000, therefore containing 4.5 grams of silver (the livre theoretically contained 4.505 but in practice it was 4.5). Coins of 2, 5, 0.5 and 0.25 francs were also minted. Gold coins were to be of 20 and 40 francs, and would be of the same grade, 900/1,000. 155 20-franc coins were minted from a kilo of 900/1,000 alloy, giving a 20 franc coin a weight of 5.806 grams, 322.5 grams per franc and a gold content of 290.33 mgs. The franc therefore had two legal equivalents: 4.5 grams of silver, or 0.29033 grams of gold, giving gold a value 15.5 times that of silver (the same ratio as in the times of Louis XV).

This was a bimetallic system, the assumption of it being that the ratio was constant: unlimited minting of the two metals was also allowed, and this gave the system enormous potential. Following the French example it was to be widely adopted in Europe.

33

Monetary Problems in England, 1797–1819

During the wars against the French Revolution and against Napoleon, there was monetary inflation in England in the form of foreign exchange crises and strong price rises. There was however nothing comparable to what happened in America during the War of Independence, or to the experience of the *assignats*. Undoubtedly, the interesting elements of the English experience are: the special conditions created in the monetary system by the existence of the Bank of England and its policies; the undramatic way in which the monetary problems were finally overcome; and the debate over monetary problems around 1810–1812 with its echoes of 1696–1697. This dispute, as famous as the previous one, is of course of more relevance today, since the issue was not what changes to make in the old system, but the nature and function of bank notes.

The controversy included intervention from the economist David Ricardo, the discussion of his theories by Fullarton and by the price historian, Tooke, and Marx's brilliant summary of it in *A Contribution to the Critique of Political Economy* and in *Capital*.[1] It provided the basis for the monetary theories of the 19th century. Then in the period between 1918 and 1939 monetary inflation on the continent, followed by the sterling crisis of 1931–1932, drew attention once more to the history of the English currency. This episode in particular was re-examined by the economists Silberling, Hawtrey and Viner. In France, Charles Rist turned to the analysis of the controversy about the nature of bank money and Francois Crouzet's thesis has illuminated the events and the general economic context of this very short but decisive period.[2]

I shall first examine the facts, and then the various interpretations.

---

[1] Karl Marx, *A Contribution*, pp. 56ff, 215ff. *Capital*, vol. 1, pp. 94ff.

[2] Charles Rist, *Histoire des doctrines relatives au credit et à la monnaie de John Law à nos jours*, Paris 1938; François Crouzet, *L'économie britannique et le blocus continental*, vol. 2, chapter 13. For Jacob Viner's work see *Studies in the Theory of International Trade*, New York 1937.

(1) Obligatory circulation and the gold standard

It is important to remember that the monetary situation in England was chronologically counter-posed to that in France. The episode of the French *assignats* took place during a period when English trade was developing; prices were rising but monetary stability was unshaken. English currency first ran into difficulties when the *assignat* was being abolished.

English foreign trade, like that of Spain, gained a lot from the eclipse of France during the years 1790–1793. This was also the period in which French gold and silver were being exported, mainly to England, through fear of what was happening in France, and because of manoeuvres by emigrés, and the relative economic freedom which merchants were allowed. In 1794–1796, however, a series of bad harvests, which occurred throughout Europe, forced England to import grain (to the value of £2.3 million in 1796); at the same time the end of the *assignats* in France marked the beginning of a return of precious metals to Paris. In 1795 and 1796, a crisis in the English exchange rate began to develop, especially in Hamburg, which governed the trade of Northern Europe.

In order to limit gold exports, the Bank of England introduced credit restrictions, but it is unlikely that the private banks followed suit. There was therefore a rapid increase in prices:

$$1790 = 100$$
$$1792 = 102$$
$$1793 = 109$$
$$1794 = 107$$
$$1795 = 126$$
$$1796 = 136$$

First third of 1797 = 143

The gold reserves of the Bank of England fell from £7 million to £1.2 million. Panic broke out: the bearers of Bank of England bank notes rushed to cash them. On 3 May 1797, the government issued the Bank Restriction Act, authorising the Bank of England not to pay out until 24 June, and the Act, introduced to last for a period of less than two months, remained in force until 1821.

Because the bank notes could not be redeemed they became a 'forced currency' but the notes were not, at first, legal tender, as in theory no one was obliged to accept them. In 1811, during a Parliamentary debate on money, Lord King announced that he would not accept any payment from his creditors unless it was in gold. It was only then (in 1812) that it was made obligatory to accept the notes in payment. The curious fact is that they were already fully accepted before this measure was enacted: before the 1810 crisis there had been a kind of tacit agreement among merchants to accept Bank of England notes, and, moreover, to accept them at their face value. How can this be explained?

As was apparent in the 18th century, the Bank was in fact an organ of the merchants, who placed their trust firmly in it. England now dominated the Atlantic and world trade; gold money was in common use, even for the payment of wages. Bank notes, by contrast, were not issued for less than £10 before 1797, and were therefore reserved for large-scale payment. Though the Bank made loans to the state, it was not identical with it. It had its own policies, and even in moments of crisis, as we shall see, it might lend more to private interests than to the state. For all these reasons, bank paper in England was far from being a simple token of money, and was much closer to being a form of credit-money. Contemporary observers tended not to make the distinction, and the question for us is whether it was important in practice.

It has to be emphasised that forced circulation, the non-convertibility of the notes, which was instituted in 1797, did not upset the economy, and did not degenerate into inflation. From 1798 the exchange rate on the Hamburg market rose; monetary depreciation did not begin before 1800 and only became serious in the years 1808–1810.

There are three indices of the depreciation of a currency: the price of the gold in circulating currency, the foreign exchange rate of the currency, and domestic prices. Such complex criteria present a problem, for monetary theoreticians stress one or the other according to their own views. I shall try to distinguish between an examination of the indices of depreciation, and an appreciation of them.

The first index of depreciation is the price of gold and silver in current coin. It is difficult to give continuous figures for this, as it was illegal to give a discount and the situation changed rapidly from place to place and from moment to moment. In England the gold market often does not figure in statistics, and silver prices were calculated on the basis of Hamburg quotations. Exchange is the second index: during the period under consideration, the usual exchange markets for sterling were often disturbed. Amsterdam was occupied by the French, Paris was the capital of the enemy country (though it provided regular quotations) and Lisbon was suffering from rampant inflation. The most regular market was Hamburg. In 1810, however, the insurance on shipping currency from London to Hamburg rose from 0.55% to 4%: and given that transport costs rose from 1% to 1.5%, cost margins exceeded 5%. Only when exchange variations rose above this did they have any significance – as long as they were less they remained below the 'gold point', the point at which it is better to transfer gold than to lose on the exchanges.

General commodity prices, the third index, are often the best symptom of currency depreciation. For England from 1790 to 1820 good series have now been established by Gayer and Rostow, and the series established by Silberling for the very episode we are studying may also be used. On these indices, taking 1790 as 100 and 1798 as 149, an initial rise takes place in 1801 (= 166) followed by a fall in 1802 (= 143) and the 1801 level returns only in 1808 (= 166). In the first decade of the 19th century there was therefore stability, with slight oscillations.

Strong evidence of depreciation begins to appear in 1808–1810: the exchange rate fell by 12% in Hamburg in the second half of 1808, falling to 19.5% below par in the first half of 1809 (the fall on Paris was 23.3%). Gold prices were 11.8% up on 1808, and 14.5% in 1809: the Spanish 'dollar' – the Mexican piastre – reached a premium of as much as 16.2%. In general we can say that English currency fell 10% relative to precious metals and 15% on the foreign exchange in two and a half years.

Current prices also rose appreciably:

$$1807 = 152$$
$$1808 = 166$$
$$1809 = 176$$
$$1810 = 176$$

Within this rise there were also shorter, more violent swings: from October 1807 to March 1809 prices rose by 25%, which was a considerable amount, and though the increase had not assumed dramatic proportions there was public concern. As in 1696, the increase in prices was what forced the question of the currency to the fore.

The factors behind the depreciation were of different kinds. (a) The Bank of England's gold stocks fell from £7,855,000 in March 1808 to less than £5,000,000 in 1810.

(b) The circulation of bank notes increased as follows:

$$1793 = 100$$
$$1807 = 137$$
$$1808 = 145$$
$$1809 = 148–166$$
$$1810 = 170–202$$

(c) Bank loans went mainly to the state in the first nine months of 1808, but from the end of 1808 to the end of 1810 they went mainly to private interests: the Bank's commercial account grew from £12,700,000 to £19,500,000. It was credit inflation rather than monetary inflation, and as such was a typical feature of a boom, of sudden and of widespread initiatives taken by private concerns.

(d) The balance of payments involves both the balance of trade and 'invisible' items (the transfer of funds for other than commercial reasons). Around 1808–1810 England's balance of trade shows both an export boom (though the blockade meant that many exports were held up and not paid for), and an even bigger boom in imports: the rise in English domestic prices encouraged buying abroad, and the trade deficit therefore rose from £8,600,000 in 1808 to £28,900,000 in 1810. Foreign payments also increased: a lot of transport costs had to be paid to neutral shipping, and when Spain was invaded after going to war with Napoleon she had to be given financial aid. English spending in Europe almost doubled on account of the war (rising from £6,600,000 to £12,400,000). The worst of it was that as Spain was now England's ally, this closed off Mexico to England just when the war practically opened the country up.

(e) There was an illicit drain of gold as a result of these developments which in its turn became a cause of the crisis: there was not a ship's captain in London who did not take golden guineas away with him, to sell at a premium of 22% or 23% in Europe. Crouzet has published documents about the London meat market in 1811 describing the intense trade in gold coin for melting down which went on there.[3] This was how the English monetary crisis developed in 1810–1811; but the crash was already overtaking the credit boom. The 1811 crisis was in fact universal, and it took much more violent forms in the continent than in England: the English monetary system was such that it experienced what was undoubtedly a fairly mild version of a generally sharp deflation. In 1812 prices fell to an index of 168, but rises and falls still alternated with each other: in 1813 and in 1814 wartime inflation and loans to the government pushed prices up to an index of 185 and 198 respectively, and the premium of gold and silver over current coin rose to 26% and 36%.

The 1814 peace made everyone believe that the pound would regain its parity and the convertibility of the bank note would be re-established. These hopes reduced the circulation of money and produced a business

[3] Crouzet, op. cit. vol. 2, p. 529.

crisis – as was to be expected. But political events again imposed themselves on the economic process: with Napoleon's return from Elba there was a new outbreak of distrust in the currency. After Waterloo there was more deflation and between the beginning of 1814, and the end of 1816, prices fell by 38%. In 1816–1818 there was yet another sudden upturn, with more inflation and rising prices, and this was followed by a fall in prices and a generalised crisis. Only in 1820 did gold return to its normal market price, of £3 17s. 10½d. per ounce, before it was officially pegged again in May 1821. The crisis was therefore a long one.

The establishment of the gold standard and of monometallism in England is a problem of a rather different kind. When payment in silver coin was restricted to £25, at least in 1774–1783, silver had simply become a small coin currency and gold was left as the only standard. Silver more or less fell into disuse until the 1797 exchange crisis, which created fears of a further devaluation of silver coin, and this therefore, as in 1774, led to measures in January 1798 to ban the minting of silver and to restrict the size of the coin. Although the establishment of a major paper circulation made the problem less pressing, Lord Liverpool, who had carried through the 1774 reform, wrote a memorandum in 1805, shortly before his death, recommending that systematic support should be given to a single standard: gold. A law of 22 June 1816 set out the rules of minting, criticised bimetallism and affirmed that only gold should be the standard measure of value and legal tender for payments, without any limitation of amount. Payment in silver coin was restricted to £2. There was still no absolute monometallism, however, for the Bank of England kept part of its stocks in silver (a fifth in the middle of the 19th century); moreover, silver could in theory be minted, though in practice the royal decree fixing the date on which this could begin was never announced. For all practical purposes the gold standard had been established.

(2) Ricardo and the 'Bullion Report' controversy

The monetary historian and economist Hawtrey has pointedly observed that in this controversy, and later comments on it, insufficient attention has been paid to the variety of factors which can enter into the explanation of the relationship between money, prices and business movements – and, I would add, the inter-action of these three. Before setting out the main ideas put forward in the course of the controversy, I should indicate the main characteristics of the forced circulation of English bank notes.

Despite the recent and disquieting examples of Law and the *assignats*, the English monetary developments of 1797 did not lead to panic: the Bank Restriction Act was applied and maintained for many years without excessive issues or public alarm, despite all the debates about it. Such stability evoked the admiration of Napoleon's financial adviser, Count Mollien.

This was perhaps because English paper money was not issued by the state, but remained 'bank notes'. But if the Bank did not issue money *through* the state it sometimes did so *for* the state. It nevertheless went on issuing to private interests, and the creation of private credit came to have a broad effect on monetary issues proper. In 1797, for example, the demands of the state were higher, as they were in 1808 and 1812–1814; but for a long time, in 1800–1808 and around 1810, credit to private interests was dominant and constituted a further factor in inflation, even though it was a stimulus to private business, and not solely to consumption. This dual aspect of banking money produced a confusion between 'credit money' and simple paper money, among both contemporary observers and later commentators.

The English were certainly provoked into thinking about the problem, which was basically whether gold was increasing in value, or paper money falling. The question was complicated by the fact that in the 17th and 18th centuries there had been a kind of inflation in the form of a down-grading of silver currency, and by the fact that it was only silver which was quoted on the Hamburg exchange market.

Like most protagonists in English debates over economics, Thornton was a businessman, a member of Parliament and an economist (though more of a practitioner than a theorist). In 1802 he published *An Enquiry into the nature and effects of the Paper Credit of Great Britain*, with the twofold purpose of justifying the forced currency of bank notes as it had been practised since 1797, and warning against an eventual abuse of such issues and an excessive swelling of the quantity of paper money. Thornton, although less well known than Ricardo, is in fact the best exponent of classical English monetary theory.

Despite the title of his book – with its evocation of 'Paper Credit' – Thornton does not really distinguish between the credit note and paper money: but nor does he equate English currency with the continental experiments (such as the *assignats*). He regards the institution of the Bank of England as of decisive importance. To him, it is the incarnation of English common sense. The English government would instinctively resist any attempts to issue paper currency wildly. Moreover, the Bank was independent and could resist the Government. There should therefore be no reason for an excessive premium of precious metals over paper currency.

In justification of all this Thornton cites the English spirit of stability (which begs the question) and, much more important, and with much more justification, the greater size of English wealth in production and commerce. The latter argument is clearly the crucial one. From the Napoleonic era England had acquired an economic advantage over other countries and this made it feasible to expect that when wartime conditions were over, the issues of paper money could quickly be re-absorbed.

David Ricardo (1772–1823) is mainly famous for his major work, *Principles of Political Economy and Taxation*, which appeared in 1817 and marks a decisive step in the construction of the science of economics. His earlier, much less detailed works, were specific polemics on the monetary question. Ricardo was born into the circle of the most competent dealers in currency and exchange, his father being a Portuguese Jew who had left Amsterdam for London, and had sent his son to be trained in Amsterdam. As a very young man David Ricardo had made a personal fortune, and he gave up business only in 1814. He bought property and entered Parliament.

In 1809 the *Morning Chronicle* published three articles by Ricardo on the relationship between the value of the circulating currency (Bank of England notes) and the value of gold bullion: and Ricardo's stand on the question dominated what were known as the debates on the 'Bullion Report', the Report of the Parliamentary Committee on Bullion. In 1811, after being contradicted by one of the best known economists and businessmen in the House, Ricardo issued his *Reply to Bosanquet*. In this famous exchange, Ricardo set out the principles of a theory of money which would be discussed throughout the 19th century under the name of the 'Currency Principle'.

His central idea was that of the unity of money. Any means of payment was money. Clipped coin and bank notes were similar phenomena, and the relationship between commodity prices and money was basically quantitative. The level of prices depended on the quantity of money in circulation, and internationally prices expressed the differing purchasing power of every national currency. Equilibrium was automatically established by the transfer of bullion or coin. With metal circulation, there was no danger of a multiplication of token money involving unpredictable price rises; but paper circulation always involved a risk of excessive multiplication (as the state might wish to issue as much money as would meet its needs). The excess of Bank of England notes was the cause of rising prices and of the premium of gold over the circulating currency; and the circulation of paper should therefore be reduced to the amount covered by gold in the Bank, in order to restore the parity of domestic currency and internationally valid metal currency. This was the Currency Principle.

Later, in his *Principles*, Ricardo was to adopt a more nuanced version of the quantitative theory of money; but he nonetheless always held that in the case of paper money, which represented a certain quantity of gold, each piece of paper would represent less gold and therefore less value if the quantity of paper rose while the quantity of gold did not. This does not mean that Ricardo condemned paper money or thought gold an ideal currency (its value could change and this in itself was a risk): in fact, Ricardo would have liked a currency exactly calculated to meet the needs of circulation.

In the light of the facts, Ricardo was both right, since English currency had been depreciating ever since it was made inconvertible, and wrong, in that the Bank had lent mainly to private individuals and only made modest loans in special circumstances to the state: it was the expansion of credit which gave the period its inflationary character, rather than the State's requests for issues of money. Nevertheless, the Currency Principle (with the bank note once more convertible and a proportion established between paper currency and metal holdings) continued to be the basis of English monetary policy; it underlay Peel's Statutes of the Bank of England, which were laid down in 1844 and which remained in force until 1928.

Ricardo's position could also be described as 'bullionism' (the obligation to back issues with gold bullion) and one of the main attacks on this position was made by Tooke, the author of one of the great English histories of prices. Tooke based his refutation of Ricardo on the detailed, empirical observation of price levels.[4] To him, money was not wealth, though gold was (it had a basic value); and price movements therefore depended essentially on public confidence in the currency. But the quantity of money depended on public demand and ultimately on the country's balance of payments, the quantity of bank notes being an effect and not a cause of the demand for them. The Bank therefore only issued what was required of it. This was the basis of the 'Banking Principle' the opposite of Ricardo's Currency Principle.

[4] Thomas Tooke, *A History of Prices*, 6 vols, London 1836–57.

It is not a question of 'choosing' whether monetary or non-monetary, political or economic, objective or psychological factors should come first in the analysis of inflation. For the England of 1808–1809, where the controversy arose, there is no doubt that the origin of the crisis lay in the balance of payments disequilibrium, in foreign subsidies (political factors, but of secondary importance) and above all in imports, which were favoured by the rise in domestic prices. Ricardo says: this is the reason, businessmen find it profitable to import, hence rising imports. Tooke says: imports were necessary, above all, because of the bad harvests. But the two explanations are obviously not contradictory.

In 1808, there existed a climate which favoured speculation: Spain, the owner of the Mexican mines, joined the English camp, thereby arousing wild hopes of profit; everyone wanted to buy, and asked the Bank for loans. Between October 1808 and October 1809, 755 banks were established in England and Wales and 123 in Scotland in an outbreak of 'bank mania', itself a sign of an inflationary climate. Ricardo laid the responsibility at the door of the government and the Bank, which had lent it too much. In effect his position was that of opposition to the government and to the policy of war to the death. It was similar to that of another Whig, Lord King, who had told Parliament in 1811 that he would demand debts be paid to him in gold. The Government, however, thought that the war effort and the threat of blockade made it necessary to live on inconvertible paper money and tried to persuade the 'commercial interest' that prosperity was inseparable from the bank note system.

Victory and the gradual stabilisation of the monetary situation, which had never been disastrous, justified the government's position. But the recovery was slow, as parity between the bank note and gold, demanded by Ricardo in 1809, did not automatically return, and it was not officially proclaimed until 1821. Then, with normal conditions restored, the theories of Ricardo and of the Bullion Report became generally accepted.

34

The 19th Century Conjuncture

The 19th century is taken here to mean the years between 1810–1821, the Napoleonic wars and their aftermath, and 1914–1921, the First World War and its aftermath. In terms of money and prices, the 18th century, marked by long term price increases and the development of American production of precious metals, ended with the experience of paper inflation and credit inflation in England and France; with severe trade crises such as that of 1811 and food crises such as those of 1812 and 1817; and with the slump in American precious metals production in the course of the emancipation of Latin America.

After 1817, once monetary stability had been restored, there was a general tendency for prices to fall, and this was not reversed until 1850. The 'conjunctural' problems of the 19th century revolve around the causes and effects of these changes: and for our purposes, they involve the relationship of the changes to the problem of precious metals, especially gold. I shall turn to the more difficult problems of interpretation after first establishing the facts and the more obvious correlations.

(1) Price movements

'General prices' are well known to change according to two different movements, one imposed on the other. The 'inner-decade' or 'short' cycles named after Juglar, the first economist to study them systematically, cover about ten years.[1] They encompass a phase of rising prices and growing trade ending in a 'crisis', with collapse on the stock exchanges, crashes, falling prices, and 'depression', followed by a recovery and renewed expansion. This cycle, now studied in great detail, is characteristic of the working of 19th century capitalism. Monetary

[1] See p. 41, n. 3.

developments have little to do with explaining it: it is more of a 'business cycle'. In the less developed countries, in the 19th century, it was still often combined with the normal climatic cycle of good and bad harvests.

There are long term movements above and beyond the shorter cycles: these push prices in a given direction up or down for 25 to 30 years, and then in the opposite direction for another 25 or 30 years. The dates of these cycles must be specified for the 19th century, but it has to be clear what we mean by this: they did not operate like clockwork everywhere at once, and the high and low points occurred in different years according to the product or the country at issue. I shall therefore put forward groups of years covering all the dates different authors have suggested for these changes, in order to find the limits within which these changes occurred.

The first high points in prices were reached between 1810 and 1821, more especially in 1815–1817, a period in which the end of the war coincided with the 1817 famine, and when there was a subsequent sharp drop in agricultural prices. The first low points in prices came between 1842 and 1850, depending on whether they are taken before or after the sudden upward movement in agricultural prices during the famine of 1847. The second high point was between 1870 and 1875, 1873 being the date usually given, specifically the eve of the generalised crash during the short-lived crisis of that year. The second low point was between 1890 and 1897, the dates usually given being 1895–1896. A third high point was reached between 1913 and 1920, because of the World War, and also, in this case, because of the widespread monetary inflation caused by the War; from 1920 onwards there was a tendency towards falling prices and towards a crisis, but many writers believe that the 1925 recovery makes it necessary to locate the end of the period of rising prices at 1929.

The two great cycles of falling and rising prices were therefore: 1817–1850–1873, and 1873–1895–1920. They are known as Kondratieff cycles after the Russian scholar who first studied them. Francois Simiand's terms can also be applied:

    1817–1850: phase B, falling prices and economic recession;
    1850–1873: phase A, rising prices and economic growth;
    1873–1896: phase B, as before;
    1896–1920: phase A, ditto (Simiand continued this phase to 1929).

These 'long term cycles' and changes in price tendencies are sufficiently well established for us to be able to take them as given. This is so at least for prices, because the precise rates of growth of production, are much more a matter of dispute: there was never a fall in output, though there may have been changes, swings or breaks in the rate of increase. It need scarcely be added that by 'price movements' we mean average price movements (the statistical establishment of which will always be disputable); all prices of all products do not follow precisely the same movement.[2]

(2) The production of precious metals

The 19th century saw a definite succession of developments in the production of precious metals which cannot be mathematically related to price movements, but were sufficiently closely connected for us to establish working hypotheses. From 1810–1821 to 1848, the silver mines of Mexico and Peru and the gold mines of Brazil were worked increasingly less because of the struggle for Latin American independence. Though the precise relationship has yet to be established, it was natural that precious metals should grow dearer relative to the constantly increasing production of a variety of commodities in Europe.

Between 1848 and 1851, however, the gold bearing rivers and then the mines of California were discovered, as was, shortly afterwards, the gold of Australia. We may at least advance the hypothesis that the discoveries were related to the fall in the relative value of gold, that is, the tendency for the general level of prices to rise. Nobody doubted the connection at the time. It is more difficult to say why the tendency was reversed soon after 1870; gold seems to have become dearer; perhaps the first, intensive, phase of mining had been worked through. In any case, the renewed rise in world prices after 1890–1896 corresponded with the discovery of gold deposits in the Far North of America and in South Africa. The period of this rise – 1896–1920 – ended with inflation comparable to that of the Napoleonic wars, though on a bigger scale, and the fall of 1920 may be compared to that of 1817.

(3) General monetary stability and the gold standard

Leaving aside the last period – the 1914 war – and with some reservations

[2] François Simiand's main writings on long term cycles are *Le salaire, l'évolution sociale et la monnaie*, Paris 1932, 3 vols; *Les fluctuations économiques àlongue periode et la crise mondiale*, Paris 1932; and *Recherches anciennes et nouvelles sur le mouvement general des prix au XVIe au XIXe siècles*, Paris 1932. For Kondratieff see N. D. Kondratieff, 'Die langen Wellen der Konjunktur' in *Archiv für Sozialwissenschaft und Sozialpolitik*, Bd. 56 3 Heft, Tübingen, December 1926.

about local or temporary phenomena such as the United States Civil War or the defeat of Spain in 1898, which were marked by atypical distortions, the period 1820–1920 was a period of overall stability in the ratio of domestic currencies and metal money. Bank notes did of course circulate, but they were convertible into gold at any moment. There was a development in credit, but credit is not money, and had long existed in some form as in the 16th century. Finally, silver, which retained its importance relative to gold in the first half of the century and posed technical monetary problems in the latter half, finally lost its monetary role. Gold became the standard par excellence, and in speaking of 'prices' we shall henceforward be thinking exclusively of 'gold prices'. From now on, whatever monetary theory one uses, it is quite possible to relate price movements to the problems of gold production. But having said this, we have to make a careful study of the facts and compare differing interpretations.

In the first place, although the economists and sociologists of the 20th century have given a great deal of attention to price 'fluctuations', to the 'conjuncture' and the relationship of these fluctuations to economic and social developments, the 19th century observers were equally impressed by the economic effects of the mining discoveries. A famous work by Emile Levasseur, for example, published in 1858, examines what he calls the fourteen 'revolutions' (changes in tendency) in the historical relationship between the value of gold and the value of commodities in general.[3] He holds that the last came with the discovery of the California mines, which he had examined together with those in Russia, Australia and elsewhere. He then analyses how trade distributed gold throughout the world and this affects prices and the income of different social classes. Lastly, he predicts new crises and examines possible ways of removing the worst effects of excessively rapid flows of gold, as well as those of silver, which at this time was still important.

Levasseur, who provides a lot of useful information and insights was not the only writer to live through the times of the Californian mining discoveries and to note their effects. In 1859, Marx pointed out in the preface to his *Contribution to the Critique of Political Economy* that his observations of capitalism were being made in the phase of development related to the gold discoveries: 'The enormous material on the history of political economy which is accumulated in the British

---

[3] Emile Levasseur, *La question de l'or*, Paris 1858.

Museum; the favourable view which London offers for the observation of bourgeois society; finally, the new stage of development upon which the latter seemed to have entered with the discovery of gold in California and Australia, led me to the decision to resume my studies from the very beginning and work up critically the new material.'[4] The ideas which gave rise to the *Critique of Political Economy*, and which Marx later made the basis of *Capital*, were provoked, as he himself declares, by economic changes due to this discovery of new gold mines.

(4) The production of precious metals in the period 1817–1848

The period of generally falling prices – of the revaluation of gold relative to commodities – between 1817 and 1848, corresponded to a fall in American production, especially of silver but only for the years 1817–1829. Mexico had produced 107 millions francs of silver in 1788 and up to 130 million in 1795, and had exported as much as 177 around 1800. But she produced merely an average of 65 million francs of silver between 1810 and 1825, a fall to approximately one-third of the previous level. In Peru, where 205 million in silver coins and 9 million of gold were minted between 1804 and 1808, only 202 million in both metals were minted in 1814–1819 falling to 45 million in 1820–1825. As a general tendency, however, prices continued to fall in Europe after the production of precious metals had begun to rise again in America and elsewhere.

From 1830 to 1840 Mexico minted 50 millions of silver a year and 300,000 francs of gold, which rose to 65 millions and 3 millions respectively in 1841, 71 million and 5 millions in 1844, and 132 and 8 million in 1848. A similar rise took place in Peru. In the other countries of the world, an effort was made to offset the problem of low production in the Americas. European silver production increased from 53,000 kg to 120,000 kg. Russia, which in 1810–1825 had an average annual production of 1,095 kg of gold and 12,612 of silver, increased this in 1825–1848 to 10,067 and 19,272 kg respectively. The conclusion must be that the fall in prices did not reflect a continuous decline in world production. It corresponded to a slump followed by a gradual re-opening of mines which were brought into operation because of the growing value of precious metals, but which still undoubtedly had a low level of productivity.

---

[4] Karl Marx, *A Contribution*, p. 14.

(5) Accident and adventure in the discoveries of 1848-1850

Californian gold was discovered on 24 January 1848, nine days before the signing of the Treaty making the provinces of California, New Mexico, Arizona, Nevada and Utah over to the United States in return for the payment of $15 million to Mexico. The gold alone brought in $45 million in two years; it was a good deal.

In January 1848 California had 15,000 inhabitants and San Francisco had 2,000. Attempts were being made to attract ranchers. A Swiss, named Sutter, until 1830 an officer in the French Royal Guards, had just set up a large rural estate near the River Sacramento, on a concession over sixty miles long. It had a saw-pit, the machinery for which had been brought from the East in ox-drawn carts, and the man who came to instal the saw-pit, James W. Marshall, found gold in the sands of the river. This was not kept a secret for long. The rush was under way. 'Property was invaded and the owners dispossessed. The fields and villages were soon abandoned: gold fever spread by word of mouth and seized on the inhabitants of San Francisco and Monterey, almost all of whom left for the mines. No workers or servants could be kept however much was promised them in wages. Masters, abandoned by their servants, decided to follow suit and go in search of their fortune. Employees left their posts, soldiers deserted, and the houses were emptied. By August the only people left in the whole of Monterey were the Governor and a few officers. As soon as a ship came into port, the sailors and ship's boys at once disappeared, and never came back: by the end of autumn more than ten ships lay stranded for want of a crew. The French government considered it advisable to contact their ships in all the Pacific ports, and make the captains swear not to put in there if they did not want to lose their crews.'[5]

There was allegedly a place where a small surface area (an *arpende*), has produced 500,000 francs worth of gold in two months, profits of 80,000 in two weeks or 800 to 1,200 in a day. As in Peru in the 16th century, the price of a bottle of wine rose to 43 francs, and a cook could earn 150 or 250 francs a day. There was a massive inflow of population: in August 1,700 people were working the original area, and in the spring of 1849, 17,000 emigrants left New York for California by sea. 80,000 tried to cross the Sierra Nevada, but only 30,000 succeeded.

In June 1850, the population of California had grown to 92,560 (six times the original figure) and by November 1852 the figure was 269,000.

[5] Levasseur, op. cit.

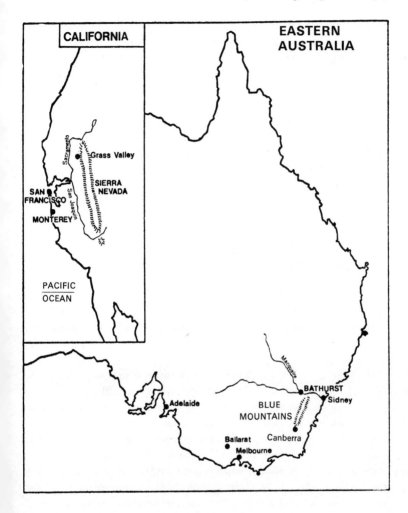

Figure 14. Gold deposits discovered in the mid-19th century.

Of these, only 7,000 in 1850 were women and in 1852 58,000. By 1856 the population had risen to over half a million, including many Chinese and immigrants from Europe. The gold-mining area was extended to cover a surface area of 750 miles by 70 in the Sierra and its neighbouring hills. For a long time extraction was alluvial and men went searching in the gold-bearing sands with knives, spades and *bateas*, the old kind of riddles used by the Caribbean Indians. Later a kind of hopper or filtering basket, a metre or a metre and a half wide was used; it was divided into tilted transversal surfaces, with a stream of water running through it, and some types used mercury. A longer hopper, the 'long tom' was then developed, and finally, the sluice; this followed the same principle, but had a very long channel along which the gold dust was caught, then amalgamated with mercury and extracted. A mercury mine, a new Almadén, was also discovered in California. This was still artisanal production of a kind not so very different from that of the 16th century; but between 1849 and 1851, proper mines were discovered in Grass Valley, Ophir City and Mariposa, where even though costs were high, good yields were obtained by crushing quartz. Although the first gold discoveries were virtually free, costs of production therefore increased rapidly. The impact on the ratio of the values of gold and commodities was instantaneous, while the more general effects made themselves felt gradually.

In the nine years from 1848 to 1856, California produced 752,400 kg of gold, which represented a value of about £100 millions in contemporary money. £80 millions of this went to three markets: New Orleans, New York and London. A flow of various commodities came back in return and San Francisco and Monterrey received 3,000–4,000 ships a year. Trade on this scale was reminiscent of 18th century Mexico: when there was plenty of gold or when communications with the mines were cut, or when there were plenty of commodities and only a little gold, selling prices fell and rose in a flash. Levasseur observed how necessary it was to distinguish between the price, which was subject to the laws of instant supply and demand, and the long term value: 'At first the miners exchanged "handfuls of gold" for basic subsistence requirements . . . Goods rushed in to the markets where they were at a great advantage, and competed to send down prices . . . They fell almost to the levels of the Old World, which at the same time were gradually rising because of the distribution of gold throughout Europe and America . . . An excess of gold increases the price of anything anywhere, and itself loses a part of its value each day. This is what is happening now, but it will still be some years before it spreads more uniformly among all trading countries and the same measure is given to goods everywhere.'

In Australia it was an emigrant who had already worked in California who prospected areas which geologists had pointed to in 1847 as likely to contain gold. Work first began in 1851 in the Northern Bathurst region. Gold was found in the Blue Mountains, at Sommer Hill, and then in the MacQuairie river. After August 1851, strikes were made in the South, and in 1852 near Adelaide. The low level of population, the scattered nature of the mines and the recent development of Australian sheep-farming made the impact of the discoveries less violent here than in California. The discoveries were nonetheless undeniably important: in the six years between 1851 and 1856, 500,000 kilos of gold were produced, almost all of which was exported through Melbourne.

Mine-shafts had to be dug and the gold was extracted by crushing quartz: but there were some periods of very high production, with a rate of up to 450 kg a year. Here too gold stimulated emigration: 372,000 immigrants arrived in 6 months, nearly as many as the population of Australia in 1851. The banks were very active, their credit rising five times over in a few years, before being restricted. Wages rose between five and seven times in the period 1851–1854, before falling again to half their peak by 1856.

Russia, which in 1826 had been producing 3,800 kg of gold, was producing 27,000 by 1847, an average maintained from 1848 to 1856: as a result it produced 718 million francs worth in 9 years, which was a considerable sum. Eastern Siberia produced more than half of it, but, although there was prospecting almost everywhere around 1851, no really important new discoveries were made. The rest of the world also increased production in this period despite the massive production of the three centres mentioned: in the nine years 1848–1856 these other countries produced 343,000 kg of gold to a value of 1,334 million francs (153,000 kg came from Africa, 138,000 from America excepting California, 108,000 from Asia, and 20,000 from Europe). But this was still less than a quarter of world production, and it was the Californian and Australian discoveries which profoundly altered the state of the gold market.

(6) Residual risk and technology in the simultaneous discoveries of the 1890s

Gold production rose from 650,000 ounces a year between 1831 and 1840 to 6,300,000 between 1851 and 1860, and then slowly fell back to 5,200,000 ounces between 1881 and 1890. The mines were not therefore being worked out, and though important new ones were found in Nevada (the Comstock Lode), no decisive new developments occurred until the 1890s. Production was fairly static, as is plain from the graph following Appendix II (see p. 352). A recovery took place in the 1890s. What has often been pointed out under very different historical conditions also holds true here: a fall in general prices expressed in terms of precious metals indicates a revaluation of the metal and an incentive to explore for it. After repeated attempts, success was finally achieved, and it is remarkable how the discoveries and the opening of the mines coincided in time over enormous distances, and took very different forms.

In the state of Colorado, gold was discovered in 1890 in Cripple Creek: the yield was up to 19 ounces a ton and this this earned the discoverer, William Stratton, $125 millions in 10 years. In Alaska, an almost unpopulated dependency of the United States, the famous gold rush was sparked off by a few Scandinavians; but the gold was alluvial and quickly exhausted, and the countryside was soon left as empty as it had been found: Alaskan gold, discovered in 1898, only acquired importance between 1900 and 1906, then fell off and finally dropped drastically.

In the Klondike area of Canada, along the river Yukon, which flowed down to the Pacific through Alaska, there had been talk of gold since 1886, but it was only in 1896 that gold bearing sands were discovered on the scale of the Californian discoveries of 1848–1850: a dishful of sand contained 12 dollars worth of gold. 30,000 prospectors arrived, after crossing the mountain range in Arctic conditions. Dawson City became legendary: absurdly primitive individual prospecting went on side by side with fairly modern establishments, and between 1896 and 1900 production rose to 1,350,000 ounces, or $28 million worth. There was a subsequent fall, and a turn to mining proper, a process repeated elsewhere in Canada, though on the opposite side of the country, in the Hudson Bay, then in the inland provinces and later still in the west again, in British Columbia. Canada became the world's third biggest gold producer, and by 1931 was the second largest (excluding the USSR). But this was in 1920–1940, whereas in the years 1911–1920 there was a fall of more than a half from the figure of 1,350,000 ounces. In the period under consideration, Canada experienced a gold rush and

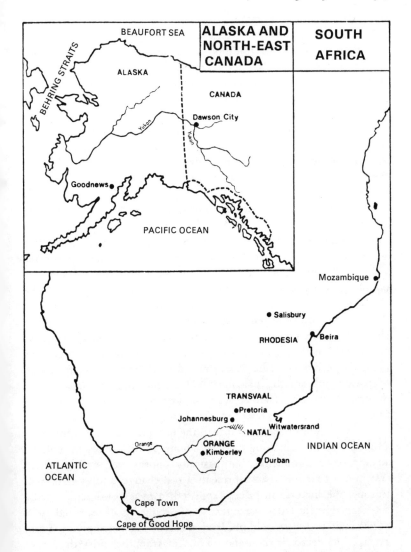

Figure 15. Gold deposits discovered at the end of the 19th century (1890–1900).

then a collapse in production.

In South Africa there had been a search for gold since the early 1880s. Here there was a historical tradition of mining, especially after the success of Kimberley diamonds. Finds were made which resulted in small rushes and then disappointment but finally in 1883 deposits were discovered in Witwatersrand on the plateau which marked the watershed between the Indian and the Atlantic Oceans. In 1885 the Struben brothers showed samples to the president, Kruger, in Pretoria, but the deposit on which Johannesburg was to be built was only discovered again by chance, in 1886. In 1890 only 440,000 ounces were produced, the real stimulus came later, with production rising to 3,638,000 ounces in 1899.

To repeat, the picture is one of simultaneous searches and prospecting and simultaneous discoveries. But there are also other points to take into consideration. First is the incidence of real speculation, (still of an adventuring kind, as when an ex-clown from London, Barnato, became a diamond king). There is also the role of combined economic and political calculation in the person of Cecil Rhodes, the creator of the De Beers Co., and a man who had the idea of uniting all Southern Africa under British hegemony; he had already created Rhodesia in the shape of a limited company, and his intervention eventually led to the so-called 'Boer War'. Important too was the deployment of genuine industrial techniques. Ore was extracted with dynamite, shafts 500 m deep were sunk, and above all, in 1890 MacArthur and Forrest developed the cyanide process which replaced mercury and which made it possible to extract all the gold present in ore.

A new era was opening, similar to the new era for silver from 1570: an industrial process using colonial labour (Indian or black) replaced an apparently productive but basically unorganised and primitive system of extraction. This represents a real change, and as in 1570 in Europe, the increase in prices expressed in metals was undoubtedly determined by the fall in the unit costs of production of the metal itself.

The main phases of gold production can be calculated giving world averages per decade in thousands of ounces, from the mid-18th century peak until 1910. The figures for silver have also been added to facilitate comparison. (These are also in thousands of ounces, not millions as in the Appendix.)

Period	Gold	Silver
1741–1760	791	17,100
1761–1780	665	21,000
1781–1800	572	28,300
1801–1810	572	28,700
1811–1820	368	17,400
1821–1830	457	14,800
1831–1840	652	19,200
1841–1850	1,762	25,000
1851–1860	6,313	26,500
1861–1870	6,108	39,000
1871–1880	5,472	66,800
1881–1890	5,200	97,200
1891–1900	10,165	161,400
1900–1910	18,279	182,600

35

The Relationship between Prices and the Output of Gold

(1) The purely quantitative explanation

This quantitative explanation derives from Ricardo and his Currency Principle; it has been upheld by the economist Cassel and perfected or modified by others.[1] It is based on a comparison of the actual quantity of gold in existence with the 'normal' quantity, by which is meant that amount strictly necessary and sufficient to keep price levels constant. This ratio between the actual and normal quantities is known as the 'relative quantity of gold': it has to be traced out in relation to general price movements.[2]

This comparison does not measure absolute rates but rates of growth. As price levels in 1910 were similar to those of 1850, the average rate of growth of gold available between those dates is held to be that which ensured price stability. The ideal and the real rate of increase in stocks is then compared year by year. In conditions such as these the curve indicating the 'relative quantity of gold' follows prices quite closely between 1850 and 1910. Cassel's conclusion is that between these dates, the basic cause of long term variations in general price levels was the change in the 'relative quantity of gold'. Equilibrium was achieved at about 3% growth in stocks a year. Below this there was insufficient gold and therefore falling prices; above it there was a surplus, and prices therefore rose.

Objections to this theory may simply be objections of detail: it is for example possible to distinguish between monetary gold and industrial gold, and take only the former into account; or to include silver, which Cassel does not do; or, like Warren and Pearson,[3] to compare the annual

[1] This chapter with the exception of the graphs is based on Gaston Imbert, *Des mouvements de longue durée Kondratieff*, Aix-en-Provence 1959, part 2, Chapter 1, pp. 213–266.

[2] See graph opposite.

[3] G. F. Warren and F. A. Pearson, *Gold and Prices*, New York 1935.

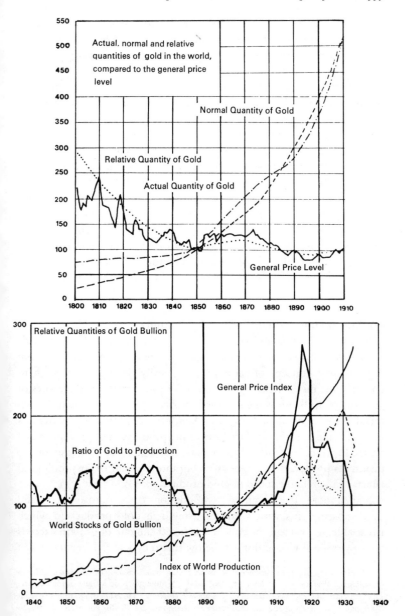

Figure 16. Quantitative interpretations of the relationship of gold prices and gold production. Above, Cassel; below, Warren and Pearson.

growth of stocks with the world production of commodities; this supposedly represents the total value to be covered (calculations are in fact made on the basis of the United States, France and England). The Warren Pearson graph is shown on the previous page.

In all these cases the simplest form of the quantitative theory is accepted: $PT = MV$ (where T is the volume of transactions, P the price level, M the mass of money and V the velocity of circulation). All forms of money can be identified with gold or assumed to be based on it; and in the last analysis gold is made responsible for the irregularity in long-term price movements and therefore in trade. This leads Ricardo to a desire to separate money from gold: one can therefore be a 'metallist' and condemn metal money. Nonetheless the main objection to Cassel's theory – even in the improved versions with their quite astonishing statistical proofs – is that they may hold fairly well for the years 1850–1910, but that the graphs they give for 1800–1850 and 1910–1920 are highly debatable. These theories therefore have no general value, or are in any case difficult to demonstrate by the methods proposed.

(2) Non-metallist quantitative explanations

It is possible, as Rist and Marjolin have done, for example, to provide explanations based on simpler statistical methods but with a more sophisticated concept of money.[4] Statistically, it may be enough to compare the movement of gold and silver production (or their rates of growth) with the movement of price indices. On the other hand, non-metallic forms of money may be taken into account. Lastly, attempts may be made to estimate the effects of the production of precious metal on credit, trade and price movements, not simply on the basis of the quantities produced, but also by taking into account the psychological effects of the relative speed of gold production.

Rist supposes that commodity production regularly rose by 4%, and by comparing this with a rate of growth in gold production which is variable, he reached the conclusion that if the rate of growth exceeds 2.3% prices will rise, and if it is below that they will fall (see the graph

[4] Robert Marjolin, *Prix, monnaie et production: essai sur les mouvements économiques de longue durée*, with a Preface by Charles Rist, Paris 1941; 'Mouvements de longue durée des prix et extraction des métaux precieux', *L'activité économique*, January 1937, pp. 119–144; 'Rationalité ou irrationalité des mouvements économiques de longue durée', *Annales sociologiques*, Series D. Fasc. 3, 1938. For Charles Rist see 'Quelques observations sur les relations entre la vitesse d'accroissement de la production de l'or et les mouvements des prix', *Revue d'économie politique*, 1938, pp. 1314–1324, and also p.9, n. 6.

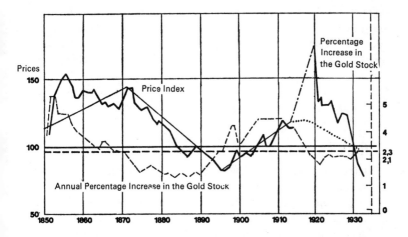

Figure 17. The increase in the stock of gold according to Rist. This graph indicates two series, on the left and right hand sides respectively. The gradation on the left indicates prices, and goes from 50 to 150; that on the right indicates the annual increase in the world's stock of gold. The line ------ running horizontally is that of a 2.3% annual average increase in the stock of gold, as estimated by Rist. This can be compared to the ------ curve which gives the yearly percentage increase in the gold stock. Prices are represented by a straight line ———; this price curve is intersected by a finer line ——— which outlines the 25-year periods (ie. semi-Kondratieff periods).

NB. In 1914 the price curves are interrupted and replaced by two discontinuous lines: ——— becomes ------ and ——— becomes ······ This is because from the beginning of the World War and until 1920 inflation replaced the monetary stability that had prevailed from 1850; this made the level of prices to a great extent dependent on monetary convulsions.

on page 335). For Rist, banknotes and bank deposits on which cheques
are drawn are not money because they return to the bank and only
affect the velocity of circulation. Only inconvertible notes, paper
money in the full sense of the term, issued without the backing of any
stock of gold, would be 'money' (though they would be dangerous
because their quantity would depend on quite arbitrary decisions).
Everything else would be credit. The movement of credit can of course
be determined by the movement of gold reserves: if the latter increase
rapidly credit will tend to increase, and the reverse will happen if gold
reserves fall or grow less quickly.

As the basis of this explanation, Rist and Aftalion take Cantillon's
arguments about the relation of price movements to the production of
precious metals.[5] They draw a distinction between gold-producing
countries and countries which procure gold by selling various products
to the gold-producers. In the former, a rapid increase in the production
of precious metals leads to a rapid rise in gold prices, and results in a
first wave of increases in the price of imported goods. This is then
transmitted to the countries which produce the commodities, where
the resulting increase in the income of certain sectors of the economy
leads to an increase in purchases from the other sectors. Price rises are
thereby generalised, and the spread of expectations and rising income
of shareholders in the gold mines (not all of whom live in the producing
countries) also play a role.

Nonetheless, this hypothesis of a new wave of investment corresponding to the initial phase of production of the new gold mines, does
not seem to be verified except in the years 1895–1914. The 1852–1855
episode was dominated by the rapid impact of the sensational new gold
mine discoveries on basic commodity prices. This contrast may reflect
different phases of development: in 1852–1856 the main factors were
surprise, and the law of supply and demand; after 1895 economic
calculations made it possible to discover how much industrial mining
would produce.

Marjolin, who has made as thorough an historical study as is possible
of the effects of gold production suggested by theory, has given a
complex explanation in which changes in the rate of interest (which
measure the ease with which credit can be obtained) are an important
mediation. He believes that when gold stocks are on the increase the
rate of interest tends to fall until these gold stocks have been incorporated

[5] Aftalion, *L'or et sa distribution mondiale*, Paris 1937.

into normal circulation.

In all the versions of the quantitative theory we have described – all of them 'monetarist' in the sense that they look to money for the explanation of economic movements – it is more difficult to find an explanation for falling prices than for rising prices. There may nonetheless be an obvious counter effect: any fall in gold production, any closures, must cut the income and expectations of certain categories of people and must therefore spread stagnation. Marjolin believes that this process begins with a tightening of banking credit, an increase in the rate of interest on loans, and that this then depresses business activity.

This last explanation is related to another, more generally applicable one: when the mass of manufactured commodities increases, there is a natural tendency for prices to fall, and this also affects the rate of interest. One always ends up by comparing two rates of growth, one for gold and the other for commodities in general; the intervention of other mechanisms in no way changes the quantitative nature of the explanation.

The objections to quantitative explanations have always rested on definitions of money and credit. Many economists have stressed that theories based on gold production (or, when applicable, silver production; whichever metal is in greatest use) can be applied to the old monetary systems dominated by precious metals. But they are less applicable in the 19th century, and not at all in the 20th, when token circulation, book money and credit have completely transformed the nature of money. In fact even in the old types of economy gold and silver were far from being the only means of payment, and in the modern system distinctions still have to be drawn between national currency systems and international payments, where gold may retain a determinant role. There is always some relation between price movements and monetary movements which can encompass all types of money, on a national or international scale.

(3) Monetary explanations taking all kinds of money into account
François Simiand draws a distinction between phase A in which metal coin increases; phase A', in which there is a slight increase in paper money as well as coin; and phase A'' in which paper money increases irregularly.[6]

The A phases differ depending on whether they occur in gold and

6 See p. 321, n. 2.

silver-producing countries or in countries which receive gold and silver in exchange for their own products. In the former case the increase in the supply of gold and silver produces a real if often irregular inflationary effect: an example is 16th century Spain, the example also taken by Cantillon. The producing or exporting countries which exchange for gold or silver, however, find that their trade is assisted by the increase in stocks and in prices.

A' phases can also vary in nature: inconvertible paper money, issued for example to finance a reconstruction programme, may result in a faster rate of increase of production, which works against excessive price increases. This would not happen where the purchasing power created is simply exchanged for services, or used for non-economic purposes. In such a case the increase in the monetary mass in circulation would not be accompanied by a corresponding increase in production, and prices would rise very rapidly.

In A" phases money is issued so unpredictably that any economic use of it is haphazard. The most difficult problem is how and why phase A' can turn into phase A". Simiand admits that in the 19th century there could be A' phases with a slight inflation of non-metallic money. It was however only during and after the 1914 war that inconvertible paper money issues impelled many countries into A" phases, where the psychological element of the flight from money makes it difficult to make any economic predictions at all. Complex explanations like Simiand's, which take into account every kind of money and the workings of the economy in general, are in principle monetarist but they leave room for the psychological element of precaution about the anticipated purchasing power of money. Dupriez has used the notion of an optimal reserve (*encaisse desirée*), which rises in the event of continuing low prices (when an increase in the purchasing power of the currency is to be expected), and falls in periods of increase (when it is possible to foresee a fall in purchasing power). He believed that the direct effects of an increase in gold production were undeniable, but that gold only set these affects in motion. The starting point for price increases was the development of credit in the non-gold producing countries.[7]

On the other hand, certain theories of long and short-term cycles in the economy can relate to other than strictly monetary mechanisms without giving up the idea that movements in gold production are central

[7] Leon H. Dupriez, *Des mouvements économiques généraux*, 2 vols, Louvain 1927,

to setting off these other mechanisms.[8] Such non-monetary factors include the relation between different types of interest, the marginal productivity of capital and variations in the rate of growth of capital goods and consumption goods.

(4) Non-monetarist explanations of the long-term 19th-century cycles

These non-monetarist explanations do not strictly speaking concern us here, as they do not consider gold and gold production to be basic. They involve looking for the origins of long-term price movements – and their relationship to the rate of growth of production – in sources internal to the economy as a whole such as technical progress, with the successive industrial revolutions of the steam engine, railways, petroleum, etc.; the exploitation of new areas of the world; or more simply, the rate of innovation, a general concept put forward by Schumpeter, for whom innovation and the putting into operation of innovations were the basic functions of the firm. These successive stimuli and temporary halts in innovation are invoked by such theorists to account for the origins of phases of relative growth and recession. For them prices are only an indication, not a factor in the process.

Other observers have stressed the importance of wars: those of 1793–1815, 1914 and 1939, clearly had an effect on production and on currency, which was comparable to that of a major mining discovery. Finally, despite its apparently secondary role after the industrial revolution, agriculture should not be left out of account. The development of competitive large-scale grain production in newly developed countries, pushed down world agricultural prices and forced the European countries to erect tariff barriers. This certainly played an important role in the economic depression that lasted from 1873 to 1896.

In all such attempts to explain the long-term phases of the 19th century, money becomes no more than a secondary factor, and prices a derived element. For a long time people even spoke of the 'neutral' character of money. In the light of the dominance of technology over our civilisation and the role of extra-economic events such as wars, it is undoubtedly very difficult to derive the secret of economic movements from variations in the mass of money which result from the quantity of gold available.

---

[8] cf. Ernst John, *Goldinflation und Wirtschaftsentwicklung. Gibt es lange Wellen der Konjunktur?* Berlin 1933.

It is equally difficult, however, to ignore the obvious historical importance of the monetary factor in the 16th century price revolution; in the economic disturbances of the 19th century during the mining discoveries of the 1850s and 1890s; and in the long periods of monetary disturbance, whether in the last years of Louis XIV's reign or in the 1920s and 1930s.

36

In Search of a Global but not
One-sided Explanation

I think it is important to make some modest attempt to sketch out, with the aid of everything that a long history has taught us, some guidelines for a better understanding of the problems of gold and money: not in order to take a position on complex economic theories, but to conceptualise money and precious metals as historical factors, and to conceptualise historical factors as elements of economies.

I shall arrange my remarks under three headings:

(1) Is the production of precious metals an autonomous phenomenon?

'Pure' metal monetarists, who look to the monetary metals for the cause of all economic movements, tend to say that everything depends on gold production, which in turn depends on chance discoveries. Some of what we have seen apparently supports their arguments, from the treasure of Atahualpa to the chance discovery of the Johannesburg mines.

'Pure' anti-monetarists, who concentrate on the observation of the economy in recent times, maintain on the contrary that gold production, like the production of any other commodity, follows laws of profit, and therefore increases when it is profitable, declines when it is less profitable, and ends when it is no longer at all profitable. Gold production is made out to be a consequence of other economic conditions, in particular the price movements of other commodities; it depends solely on their conditions of production, demand and supply.

Between these two positions are those who say: now that gold production has become one economic activity among all the rest, mining profits and production are clearly interdependent; but even in the 19th century, as the examples of California and the Klondike show, and far more so in previous centuries, discoveries and brute acquisition still depended on chance.

This was not completely the case, as we have seen. The search for gold, in Peru in the 16th century or Brazil in the 17th, was not based on precise economic calculations of comparative profitability. Nonetheless the more their prices rose relative to other commodities as a whole, the more fervently precious metals were sought. The great discoveries always took place in periods of generally low prices, in other words of very high relative prices for gold and silver. Christopher Columbus did not emerge by pure chance. The exact date of the discoveries was all the same a matter of chance, and the precise periodisation of the movements is therefore difficult, in a history which goes back so far. The discovery and sudden exploitation of undreamt-of wealth, at first often to be had for next to nothing, determined sudden change in the relative prices of gold or silver and commodities, initially on the spot (in Peru in 1534 and California in 1849), and then in the longer term, in the countries most closely connected with the gold-producing areas. We therefore have to look, not for some unilateral causation, for complete rationality or complete chance, but for reciprocal, historical causation which combines chance with necessary mechanisms of change.

These remarks are confirmed by comparing the production of precious metals with world prices. Gold production begins to increase, while prices continue to fall; the fall in general prices is an indication of the expense of the metal, and therefore of the potential profits from exploration and production. After the major discoveries, production rose and so did general prices (while the new mines were still highly profitable); but prices went on rising when the production of the mines and their profitability began to decline. Then prices too fell and after a time this made exploration and mining profitable again.

For the earlier periods of world history these developments cannot be precisely synchronised, but they can be more closely analysed for periods when there was a cohesive world market and normal competition, such as the years 1873–1914. What all periods have in common is the reciprocal nature of causation and of economic and historical inter-action: the 1914 war, which produced major changes in the monetary situation, in turn interrupted the workings of the pure economic model.

(2) Price movements and the value of precious metals

The price of a product on a given market at a given time, depends on its supply and demand and on local monetary conditions (i.e. the estimated present and future purchasing power of the circulating currency). Short-term price movements in a given country therefore depend on the specific economic conditions of that country and on its monetary situation – in particular, on the relation between the circulating currency and internationally accepted currency.

'General prices', however, i.e. movements involving all prices, and the long-term movements of 'world prices', i.e. prices on the world market presuming this is sufficiently unified, can only be measured in an internationally accepted currency; a currency which until very recently was always a commodity used to make comparisons among the others. For a long time this was gold and silver, then it was gold alone. In the long run the basic element in any variation in the ratio of gold and commodities as a whole, can only be a change in the ratio of their comparative costs of production. We have seen countless demonstrations of how the production costs of precious metal affect long-term price movements. This was seen with gold and silver in the 16th century, and with the comparative costs of Mexican and European silver studied by Humboldt. The 19th century was still dominated by abrupt changes in the conditions of gold production. The first rapacious prospectors sparked off local price rises and these gradually spread, but the discoveries of the South African Rand at the end of the century opened a new period in which, according to Dupriez, gold mining was less and less dependent on the whims of nature, and more and more firmly under the control of man.

Silver, after a very chequered history is no longer a monetary metal. Since the middle of the 19th century, it has not been mined independently but rather as a by-product of mining other kinds of metal such as lead, copper, zinc and antimony. The market price of silver no longer depended on its own conditions of production, and the quantities on sale no longer reflected a regulating mechanism. Despite the protests of the producing countries, and the interests most adversely affected, silver therefore ceased to be a monetary metal. Thus, the movement of prices expressed in metal depends on the value of the metal, that is on the variations in the productivity of the mines, provided this is seen in the long-term perspective and at the level of the world market. Unfortunately there are many theoreticians who forget this simple truth.

(3) Precious metals and money today
The last great problem relates to the concepts of gold on the one hand

and of money on the other. Historical reality is again and again carica-
tured by saying that gold is the currency of a former age; that it has
nothing to do with modern money. Historically speaking, nothing is
further from the truth, as neither gold or silver was ever the only form
of 'money'. If in the course of history there have been changes, devaluations, attempts at currency deflation and the like, this is because the
ratio of circulating currency to the internationally valid currency of
standard weight, has constantly been in flux. Most circulating currency
has been virtually 'fiduciary' (its stability vis-à-vis gold and commodities in general depending on the confidence the public had in it).
Such money, which depended on the domestic conditions of the country
where it circulated could never be confused with the international
currency. This often created problems similar to those of modern
inflation.

Credit and 'book money' are not recent developments either. In the
16th century more transactions were paid for in the account books of
the great fairs than were paid in gold and silver: only the balances were
paid in precious metal. It would therefore be quite wrong to counter-
pose some imagined age of metal currency, presumed to cover the whole
of previous history, to a period of modern currency which began at
some point in the 1920s.

The main novelties of the past thirty or forty years have been the
spread of payment on account, of 'book money', at the most everyday
and popular levels; the rise of systematic 'monetary policies', through
which the state intervenes into circulation and credit; and, since the
end of the Second World War, the acceptance of certain national
currencies, mainly the dollar, as the basis for international payments,
and the stability imposed in the ratio between this currency and gold,
whatever the variations in the conditions of production of the latter.
This only expresses the enormous pressure of the American economy
on the world economy, or at least on a part of that economy. As gold
has not stopped circulating and there is still a system of commodity
money for balancing trading operations between different world
systems, gold has not disappeared as a factor in the world economy. It
could only do so in a planned, united world economy and this does not
appear to be imminent. Moreover, the question of gold as a means of
international payment is not to be confused with the issue of everyday
money and of the currency in each national economy.

The question of why this did not occur in the 14th or the 17th century,
a question which leaves most economists indifferent, is of the greatest

importance to historians. In the past as in the present historians have been interested above all in discovering the social and sometimes even the political meaning of monetary problems. Perhaps in this way, by studying things more concretely and at the same time taking a broader historical view, they will be better able to discover the secrets, including the economic ones, of money and of the real function of gold.

Appendices

Appendix I – *Silver mined in Mexico, 1690–1800* (Humboldt, op. cit. pp. 242–3)

Years	Marks of Silver	Years	Marks of Silver
1690	621,883	1720	926,390
1691	731,024	1721	1,113,027
1692	629,732	1722	1,038,109
1693	329,691	1723	953,805
1694	687,121	1724	926,214
1695	470,740	1725	867,037
1696	375,366	1726	996,017
1697	524,699	1727	956,833
1698	390,560	1728	1,085,711
1699	412,327	1729	1,037,055
1700	397,543	1730	1,146,573
1701	472,834	1731	992,926
1702	590,900	1732	1,026,643
1703	715,206	1733	1,177,623
1704	685,532	1734	1,000,771
1705	558,491	1735	932,001
1706	726,122	1736	1,296,000
1707	674,709	1737	955,545
1708	675,012	1738	1,116,500
1709	613,428	1739	1,005,963
1710	789,480	1740	1,124,240
1711	666,598	1741	1,016,962
1712	783,932	1742	962,000
1713	763,279	1743	1,014,000
1714	731,861	1744	1,210,000
1715	749,284	1745	1,215,000
1716	767,969	1746	1,354,000
1717	794,204	1747	1,412,000
1718	843,951	1748	1,368,000
1719	853,965	1749	1,391,000

Years	Marks of Silver	Years	Marks of Silver
1750	1,554,000	1780	1,994,073
1751	1,486,000	1781	2,311,062
1752	1,603,000	1782	2,014,545
1753	1,364,000	1783	2,709,167
1754	1,364,000	1784	2,402,965
1755	1,469,000	1785	2,111,263
1756	1,447,000	1786	1,978,844
1757	1,474,000	1787	1,819,141
1758	1,500,893	1788	2,293,555
1759	1,532,000	1789	2,415,821
1760	1,408,000	1790	2,045,951
1761	1,386,000	1791	2,363,867
1762	1,189,940	1792	2,724,105
1763	1,385,298	1793	2,747,746
1764	1,152,063	1794	2,488,304
1765	1,365,275	1795	2,808,380
1766	1,318,829	1796	2,854,072
1767	1,225,307	1797	2,818,248
1768	1,444,583	1798	2,697,038
1769	1,404,564	1799	2,473,542
1770	1,638,391	1800	2,098,712
1771	1,506,255		
1772	1,996,689	Total	
1773	2,227,442	1690–1800	149,350,722
1774	1,516,714		
1775	1,675,916		
1776	1,936,856		
1777	2,248,613		
1778	2,334,765		
1779	2,199,548		

Appendix II – *Annual production of gold and silver and index of gold values* (*1493–1910*)

Period[1]	Gold[2]	Silver[3]	Value[4]	Period[1]	Gold[2]	Silver[3]	Value[4]
1493–1520	186	1.5		1866	6,540		81
1521–1544	230	2.9		1867	6,262		83
1545–1560	274	10		1868	6,238	43	83
1561–1580	220	9.6		1869	6,215		85
1581–1600	237	13.5		1870	6,050		86
1601–1620	274	13.6		1871	6,238		83
1621–1640	267	12.7		1872	6,650		76
1641–1660	282	11.8		1873	5,297	63	75
1661–1680	298	10.8		1874	4,967		81
1681–1700	346	11		1875	4,873		86
1701–1720	412	11.4		1876	5,016	68	87
1721–1740	613	13.9		1877	5,512	63	88
1741–1760	791	17.1		1878	5,761	73	95
1761–1780	665	21		1879	5,262	74	99
1781–1800	572	28.3		1880	5,149	75	93
1801–1810	572	28.7		1881	4,984	79	97
1811–1820	368	17.4		1882	4,934	86	99
1821–1830	457	14.8		1883	4,615	89	101
1831–1840	652	19.2		1884	4,921	82	109
1841–1850	1,761	25		1885	5,246	92	115
1851	4,049		110	1886	5,136	93	119
1852	6,709		106	1887	5,117	96	122
1853	7,227	28	87	1888	5,331	109	118
1854	6,309		81	1889	5,974	120	115
1855	6,639		82	1890	5,749	126	115
1856	6,827		82	1891	6,320	137	115
1857	6,662		79	1892	7,094	153	122
1858	6,309	29	91	1893	7,619	165	122
1859	6,674		88	1894	8,764	164	132
1860	5,932		83	1895	9,615	167	133
1861	5,885		85	1896	9,784	157	135
1862	5,815		82	1897	11,420	160	133
1863	5,932	35	81	1898	13,878	169	128
1864	5,862		79	1899	14,838	168	122
1865	6,380		82	1900	12,315	174	91

Period[1]	Gold[2]	Silver[3]	Value[4]
1901	12,626	173	85
1902	14,355	163	84
1903	15,853	168	84
1904	16,804	164	85
1905	18,396	172	87
1906	19,471	165	93
1907	19,977	184	97
1908	21,422	203	88
1909	21,965	212	90
1910	22,022	222	94

This graph represents the production figures in the above table.

NB. Both gold and silver production are shown in thousands of ounces.

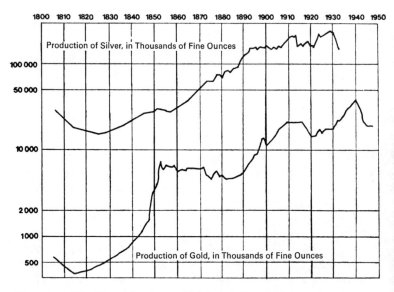

Figure 18. World production of gold and silver. (Appendix 2.)

[1] Up to 1850 for gold and 1875 for silver, the figure shown is the average of all years included in the column headed 'period'. After this point, the figure for production is simply for the year indicated.

[2] Gold production in *thousands* of ounces.

[3] Silver production in *millions* of ounces.

[4] Value of gold = index of the purchasing power of gold, taking 1900–1914 as 100.

Index of Names

Index of Authorities